TOTAL LANDSCAPE,
THEME PARKS,
PUBLIC SPACE

Miodrag Mitrašinović

TOTAL LANDSCAPE, THEME PARKS, PUBLIC SPACE

ASHGATE

This book is dedicated to my father Milan Mitrašinović (1928–2001) whose example and extraordinary humanism will nurture my being forever, and to Maja, Jilly, Dorotea, and Jasna who make my life worth living.

This book was generously supported by the Graham Foundation
for Advanced Studies in Fine Arts Publication Grant and by the
Publication Subvention Grant from the University of Texas at Austin
Cooperative Society.

Published by
Ashgate Publishing Limited
Gower House
Croft Road
Aldershot
Hampshire GU11 3HR
England

Ashgate Publishing Company
Suite 420
101 Cherry Street
Burlington, VT 05401-4405
U.S.A.

Ashgate website: http://www.ashgate.com

British Library Cataloguing in Publication Data

Mitrašinović, Miodrag
        Total landscape, theme parks, public space. - (Design and
        the built environment series)
        1.Public spaces – Design 2.Amusement parks – Design and
        construction
        I.Title
        711.5
ISBN-10: 0 7546 4333 6
ISBN-13: 978-0-7546-4333-3

Library of Congress Control Number: 2006927403

Design by HvADesign, New York

Cover image
Barrier Bench (Banc de Jardin), 2002. Philippe Million (French, Born 1967).
Galvanized steel, 95 x 184 x 60 cm, Courtesy Galerie Alain Gutharc, Paris.

www.thetotallandscape.net

Printed and bound in Great Britain by MPG Books Ltd, Bodmin, Cornwall

Acknowledgments

In many ways this book closes a fifteen year long period of my life, a period full of struggle, hard work, sacrifice, mistakes and very often bitterness and sorrow, but also full of joy, love and full of hope for what the future may bring. In that respect, first and most of all I wish to thank my family for the immense support I have enjoyed throughout this journey. My parents Dorotea and Milan, my sister Jasna, my grandmother Jelena, my wife Jilly and my daughter Maya were so giving and selfless that I cannot possibly express the magnitude of my gratefulness in words. The love, trust, sacrifice, support and help they all generously offered is simply unforgettable. They taught me that life without love, giving and trust is meaningless.

My formative years at the College of Architecture of the University of Belgrade, and then at the Berlage Institute in Amsterdam, were strongly marked by a few exceptional individuals whose influence cannot be forgotten: Ranko Radović, Bogdan Bogdanović, Mihajlo Živadinović, Miloš Bobić, Darko Marušić, and Herman Hertzberger. In ways both known and unknown to him, Elias Zenghelis was strongly influential and has been profoundly important in shaping my understanding of architecture: I am grateful for his mentorship, guidance and friendship. Much of my early thinking about public space and total landscape was formed through delightful discussions with my friends at the Berlage Institute: I am particularly grateful to Sarah Gansel for the unforgettable friendship and collaboration. In the initial phases of this research the University of Florida's College of Architecture was instrumental in facilitating my work. My academic advisors —William L. Tilson, Robert McCarter, Gregory L. Ulmer, Kenneth Frampton, and Richard H. Schneider— supported my work in many important ways. Many of the ideas that form the core of this work were formed through intense, passionate, and always inspiring discussions with Bill Tilson in different places across the world, from Barbados to Greece, over many years. As much as they are mine, they are also his ideas. I am forever indebted to him for his sincere friendship, unreserved commitment and invaluable support. I am also grateful to Greg Ulmer who was instrumental in making me understand why what I wanted to do made sense, and for generously opening entirely new worlds that my mind had not before seen, through personal conversations, his teaching as well as through his writings: CATTt, Mystory, Electracy and Imaging are only some of the intellectual treats I was generously exposed to in the Ulmerian universe and will forever remain indebted for. The very special acknowledgement and gratitude go to Kenneth Frampton, whose intellectual rigor, generosity, humanity, and dedicated friendship over the years have been exemplary and always inspiring. He has helped tremendously in numerous ways through all these years: if it was not for his generous support, my life would have taken a different course. Jo Hassell, Diana Bitz and Kim Tanzer of the University of Florida also helped with important comments and suggestions in the early stages of this work.

I am very grateful to Professor Takeyama Kiyoshi Sey of Kyoto University's School of Architecture, who graciously made my research in Japan possible. I am also grateful to researchers and students in Professor Takeyama's Laboratory who helped me with translating Japanese sources into English, with collecting important material, and by sharing with me valuable insights that would have been hidden to my eye if it was not for their friendship and commitment. I am particularly thankful to Suzuki Kenichiro and Hirao Kazuhiro. Nihon Sekkei staff, especially Okamura Kazunori, Motokazu Tashiro and Ikeda Takekuni, helped tremendously in my research on Huis Ten Bosch. Huis Ten Bosch Co.'s Henk Boer, Ben Steenkist, Fujita Yoji, Hanako Imamura, and especially Matsuda Yuji had shared with me precious thoughts and information. My friends Suehiro Kaoru and Noriko, Tai Mikio and Ozawa Takeo had helped me on my journey through Japan, its theme parks, public space and architecture in different but all very valuable and memorable ways. I would also like to thank Sato Yumi and Arai

Hiroko who translated, through long hours in our apartment in Kyoto, most of the Japanese material on Huis Ten Bosch into English. In respect to my research in Japan, my wife, Jilly Traganou, deserves special recognition and thankfulness for sharing with me her knowledge of Japanese culture and architecture: much of my research on Japanese case studies would have been impossible without her. Her immensely insightful and penetrating criticism at various stages of this work has tremendously contributed to the overall structure of the book.

University of Texas at Austin, particularly the College of Fine Arts and its Department of Art and Art History, as well as the Office of the Vice President for Research, have generously supported my work through numerous research grants, too numerous to be listed here. The actual writing of this book was made directly possible by Dean's Fellowship, as well as by the Walter and Gina Ducloux Fellowship, both from the College of Fine Arts. My sincere thankfulness also goes to my students at the University of Texas, both graduate and undergraduate, who (through a number of seminars, studios and labs) have brought to my attention valuable information and insights on American public space, and the attitude of the contemporary American society towards the notion of public good. The intellectual climate at the University of Texas at Austin has in many ways been outstanding, and my contacts with numerous extraordinarily talented and wonderful colleagues has also helped shape the content of this book, many times in ways not directly related to its subject matter. I am thankful to Sanford Levinson, Dana Cloud, David Huff, Christopher Long, Kate Catterall, Gloria Lee, Daniel Olsen and Christopher Taylor who offered advice and assistance when it was needed. Among many good friends, I would like to express a very special gratitude to Thomas Darwin whose advice and sincere friendship, especially in the closing weeks of the process of writing, were superb. Many of the ideas in this book emerged out of countless and enjoyable chats at JP Java's, through which Tommy and I had consumed enough caffeine to make the whole University of Texas sleepless for a week. I would also like to thank my graduate research assistant Jaladhi Pujara, who scanned most of my own slides used in this book. I am grateful to Deborah Sayre and Jed Lawnsby of DESL who always readily helped with many technical questions, and have gone out of their ways to generously provide valuable advice and accommodate my work. Joe Barroso was always kind and helpful in processing numerous grants that helped this book become reality.

I will forever be indebted to Predrag Dojčinović and Janneke Hazelhoff, as well as to the entire Hazelhoff family, for their dedicated friendship and tremendous help when it was truly needed. I am also grateful to Katie Salen for her committed friendship and manifold help: it is through the studio we co-taught at Parsons School of Design in spring 2004 that much of the ideas on public spaces in New York City evolved. Aviad Raz, John Findlay, Brian Lonsway, Joy Hendry, Susan and Justin Willis, David Lowenthal, Nick Stanley, Michel Conan, and Jennifer Robertson helped in kind ways in different stages of this work. This kind of work could not have been possible without advice and help of many dedicated librarians and archivists. I wish to thank the staff of the University of Texas Libraries (particularly Laura M. Schwartz), Avery Library at Columbia University in New York (especially Kitty Chibnik), Kyoto University Libraries, University of Florida Libraries, the British Library in London, the Anaheim History Room of the Anaheim Public Library (above all Jane K. Newell), the Benson Ford Research Center—The Henry Ford (Jim Orr), The Victoria & Albert Museum in London (Martin Durrant), Albertina Wien (Ingrid Kastel), Musee Mairie de Paris, and Disney Publishing Worldwide, Walt Disney Company (Margaret Adamic).

Many scholarly books could not have been published without grants. This book is no exception in that: generous grants by the Graham Foundation for Advanced Studies in Fine Arts and the University of Texas Cooperative Society Subvention Grant received in 2004 were used towards publishing expenses, and helped keep a great variety of images in the final version of the book.

I would like to express my most sincere gratitude to the team that put this book together: first of all my editors at Ashgate, Valerie Rose and Eleanor Rivers. Valerie was extraordinarily open minded, helpful, optimistic, generous and resourceful through the entire process, raising the professional editorial bar to entirely new heights. Her contribution to the making of this book is simply remarkable. Henk Van Assen and I have been talking about this book since August 1998. At the time, we did not know if the book will ever happen, and at times it truly seemed it would not. Henk's generous and friendly advice on all aspects of scanning, printing, color separation, hues and many other issues was how we started talking about it, as colleagues at the University of Texas at Austin. As many other things in life, this book became possible by a series of tiny miracles, and Henk ended up really designing it. I am very grateful for his outstanding dedication to this book and his generous friendship. I believe that best books are those in which one cannot tell where the writing stops and the design begins, where the two are equally important and simultaneous practices, and are experienced by readers as such. The writer is a designer as much as the designer is a writer. I think that this book, in many ways, does move in such an idealistic direction. In that respect I am also very grateful to Gloria Lee and Matthew Lynaugh, of Buds Design Kitchen in Austin, who designed all maps, diagrams and charts in the book. Their friendship, professionalism and talent have significantly contributed to the overall quality of the book. Additionally, I would like to thank Sarah Gifford and Amanda Bowers of HvADesign for their dedication to this project. I would also like to thank Karen Dodds for her contribution to the image selection.

The happiest living soul, when this is all over, will be our daughter Maya who patiently waited for dad to start playing with her. Much of this book was written with Maya sitting in my lap and writing her own 'books'. I am grateful to you, my love, for helping me on this journey by reminding me of what is truly essential, by sharing your view and insight on Disney's characters with me, and by rushing me to begin playing.

Finally, a note on the image copyrights: I took great care in identifying copyright holders and obtaining adequate permissions. When that has not been done it was either because I could not identify copyright holders or did not receive a response from them.

What, do you imagine that I would take so much trouble and so much pleasure in writing, do you think I would keep so persistently to my task, if I were not preparing—with a rather shaky hand—a labyrinth into which I can venture, in which I can move my discourse, opening up underground passages, forcing it to go far from itself, finding overhangs that reduce and deform its itinerary, in which I can lose myself and appear at least to eyes that I will never have to meet again. I am no doubt not the only one who writes in order to have no face. Do not ask who am I and do not ask me to remain the same: leave it to our bureaucrats and our police to see that our papers are in order. At least spare us their morality when we write.

(FOUCAULT 1972: 17)

Foreword

The idea of 'Total Landscape' first emerged to me in 1993 while working on the Global City project with my friends and fellow students Sarah Gansel and Antonella Vitale at the Berlage Institute Amsterdam (BiA). The project was supposed to rationalize an idea that essentially came from our professor Elias Zenghelis, who gently coaxed us into believing that that differences between what we call 'natural' and 'artificial' are no longer the differences of kind but of degree. The Global City project was about identifying a universal set of conditions characteristic for each point of a global network of artificial 'landscapes' that would allow intensified compactness and congestion in particular segments we called 'environments'. Typology and theme of environments depended on the percentage of density occurring in the particular landscape, in relation to the balance between 'natural' and 'artificial'. In that sense, the Global City project was an attempt to rationalize and articulate the idea of a globally emerging system that I cynically called The Straight Society. I had no doubt that most people experienced 'the logic of the inconceivable' of such a system because it runs as an undercurrent stream beneath what we daily experience in the world of appearances and the world as sensed. It occurred to me that what I was truly interested in was finding out how that system actually works through what seemed to be a totalizing system of forces, and just how such a complex artificial universe systematically links every artifice—whether a social relationship, an artificial rain, or an economic order—into a universal densely woven fabric. It was also clear that this man made, artificial system was in desperate need of a holistic, comprehensive, anticipatory, and sustainable understanding. I was not only interested in the question of form, place, and aesthetic, but much more in the set of conditions out of which it arises and the totalizing condition of convergence it successfully fabricates. The work of Superstudio, Archizoom, Archigram, the Situationists International, and the entire architectural avant-garde of the 1960s and early 1970s was instrumental in initially

formulating the question of condition. The key question guiding this quest at the time was the effect to which total landscape was influencing the practice and theory of architecture, because to most of us the early 1990s brought an obvious conflict that began emerging between architects and Architecture.

In many ways, retrospectively, the point of no return was a casual round-table discussion with French architect Henry Ciriani at the BiA, in spring of 1994, when Ciriani recounted his 'Schiphol airport experience': 'It's all there, everything you may ever want [...] it's clean, the music is discrete, everybody is kind and helpful, if you fall there is a medical crew to assist you in a second—it cannot be, it just cannot be, this is not life!' The subject of the discourse quickly changed and moved to the kind of architecture commonly spelled and pronounced with a capital 'A,' where apparently life is still possible and everything is just fine. It seemed to me that paradoxically, locations where 'life just cannot be' form an increasingly large part of our experience of the world; locations such as theme parks, airports, large shopping malls, all-inclusive tourist facilities, and increasingly also urban public spaces. At the same time I was involved in co-editing a volume of student writings and projects made at the Berlage Institute in 1992–93 titled *The New Public Realm.* Most of student projects at the time focused on the emerging, hybrid forms of public realm and public space. Through a series of competition projects (often co-designed with Sarah Gansel) I attempted to theorize a shift from forms of public space based on face-to-face interactions and collective programs, to public environments that are increasingly privatized, individualized, aestheticized and mediated by entertainment technology, and it seemed that the only force that kept remaining traditional public spaces together was their attachment to infrastructural systems: in short, they became a function of motion.

Total landscape was further elaborated in 1994 on the occasion of an exhibition of my projects titled, not surprisingly, 'Total Landscape'. I then embarked on a long search and study of 'the cases' that would enable me to unearth, document and interpret the hidden dimension of total landscape. Initially I merely offered criticism of the logic of enclosure and exclusion, as well as an enthusiasm for the potentially desirable role that digital technology can play in total landscape, but that did not take me far: what was *de facto* needed was a deeper understanding, a fundamental change in the way these issues are understood, a change that transforms perceptions of public space, a development of a specific vocabulary and the analytic tools for understanding total landscape, and a deep and thorough understanding of the processes of its production. The only way to get there was to identify 'cases' that would more precisely lead me to the ensemble of techniques, procedures, methods and practices that bring such controlled environments into being. In 1994, I had identified a number of possible cases and initially hoped to conduct a comparative analysis of theme parks, cruise ships, all-inclusive tourist resorts, extra large shopping malls, festival marketplaces, and airports in order to begin tracing the logic of total landscape. It did not take long to realize that theme parks, especially places like Walt Disney World Resort (WDW) or Huis Ten Bosch (HTB), would be ideal case studies due to their complexity, transparency, size, popularity, and also due to the so-called 'theme park model' that seemed to be an ideal entry into the discourse and problematique of the transformation of urban public space by total landscape.

The research was initially conducted during a two-year period (May 1996–June 1998), at the University of Florida at Gainesville (only two hours away from Walt Disney World Resort), and was divided into two major parts: research into relevant theoretical material, and the fieldwork and collection of the primary material related to case studies. The fieldwork in Walt Disney World Resort and other theme parks in Florida was conducted on several occasions from January to July 1996, when an extensive video and photo documentation was created, and a field-study was conducted with a group of students from the University of Florida. I carried out the study of the Japanese material at the School of Architecture, Kyoto University, where relevant documents were painstakingly translated to me by fellow students and researchers in Professor Takeyama's Laboratory, from August 1996 to September 1997. During the same period, the fieldwork on Huis Ten Bosch and other Japanese case studies was performed. Interviews with the design team at Nihon Sekkei, employees and top executives at Huis Ten Bosch Corporation, and guests at Huis Ten Bosch theme park were carried out in April 1997. The second, five-year-long phase of the research started in 1998 to be supported by numerous research grants at the University of Texas at Austin and extensive travels. My second visit to Japan in 1999 enabled me to perform additional research and update previous research findings. Finally, the Dean's Fellowship in 2003–04 helped to bring everything together in the book format.

When I started writing the *Total Landscape* and decided to keep the focus on theme parks, I hoped that this book could be written as a diary of an archeological excavation. In that sense I was hoping that the book would be similar to Paul Virilio's *Bunker Archeology,* in which Virilio documents concrete bunkers built on the cost of Normandy by German forces during the World War II (Virilio 1994). Virilio rightly understood bunkers and fortifications as clear expressions of Hitler's military understanding of territory, time, and subsequently of the concept of 'military space'. But Virilio's good fortune was in the fact that Hitler and his military commanders were long gone by the time he visited the coast of Normandy, back in 1960s. My problem was that I had to work with what art historians and curators customarily call 'a living artist'. Namely, despite an overall decline in attendance and the fact that the age of extra-large theme parks is gone, theme parks have been very much alive. Just as I enjoyed Virilio's discovery of the half-buried German bunkers and his interpretation, my reader, I hoped, would one day open these pages and would be able to understand the rationale of a strange civilization that had built such monstrous structures in order to produce 'the most transient, yet lasting of products: human experience'. My belief has been that exposing minute details and facts of the production of theme parks would in fact expose the historical and human condition of the present, hence the total landscape not as a theoretical framework but as a condition. In that sense, theme park is the ur-form of total landscape. I was coached by Walter Benjamin's attempt to create an 'Ur-history of the 19th Century' with his unfinished Arcade project through which Benjamin collected 'images' of 19th Century Paris that captured 'small, particular moments' and then attempted to present them in a form of montage. Such images, whether pictorially or verbally represented, were supposed to reveal the 'total historical event', the perceptible ur-phenomenon in which the origins of the present would be found (Buck-Morss 1991: 71–77). As Buck-Morss writes, Benjamin transferred Goethe's concept of the *urphänomen* that emerged in Goethe's writing on the morphology of nature, to his own work on history. The concept of ur-phenomenon suggests that there are ideal forms that can reveal, through an act of 'irreducible observation', both object and subject of knowledge, and potentially their relationships. For Walter Benjamin, postcards, ads, street signs, posters and many other artifacts of the late nineteen century Paris were precisely such symbols. To my mind, theme parks are such 'ideal symbols' of the Twentieth Century where 'general reveals itself immediately in a particular form' (Simmel 1918: 57). Theme parks themselves are thus the theory of total landscape.

The question then was how to represent the complexity of theme parks, and especially of urban public space, without simplifying them—how to talk about so many interrelated domains without appearing a dilettante? The resulting narrative is for the most part free from any attempt to work explicitly in either theoretical or critical mode, as well as from attempts to instrumentalize knowledge towards operational aims because this is neither a 'how to make a theme park' book nor a 'how to design public space' manual, although it sheds light on the actual processes of designing and operating both

theme parks and public spaces. In doing so, I have tried to minimize the professional jargon from all fields involved and allow the general public to get a sense of complexities beyond each of the professional practices at work without simplifying their intricacies. In order to open the book to non-design audience, I have also tried to present my theoretical observations within the narrative context and avoid too many normative declarations. This book has been a long time coming and in the process, I have accumulated an impressive amount of research material from a variety of sources and all imaginable academic and professional disciplines. I have met a wide range of people and learned a great deal about things I cared about as well as about topics I could not care less about. At times, I felt that different materials had pulled me their ways and often I felt lost in view of the complexities involved in this kind of research. At the same time I struggled to bring all the relevant material to the eyes that may be different than mine, as I desired to speak to designers of all kinds, to marketing professionals, to sociologists, anthropologists, geographers, and many others including the lay reader. Keeping this ship on its course, whatever the course may have been in the last ten years, was not a trivial task. I believe many of those struggles will be obvious to careful readers, together with the fact that this book does not 'celebrate' either Walt Disney's or other theme parks.

Writing a book on something as complex as theme parks and public spaces without explicitly referencing ways in which their cultural and social meanings are contested on the ground through daily practices was a hard task, but it was done on purpose. The assumption that at this point in time seems realistic is that in-between theme parks and the increasingly privatized urban public spaces, there are subtle differences of degree rather than kind, and the purpose of my effort has been to identify, unearth, and study the common framework of the two in order to eventually learn how to manage it in regard to its most promising possibilities. For promising possibilities are embedded within the grounded and critical social practices of both individuals and social groups inscribed in space and time. Despite all the challenges to be mapped out later in this book, it has been precisely the populist appeal of mass entertainment and mass consumption that potentially, just potentially, carries an energizing force within it for the traditionally marginalized social groups, for women, children, teenagers, people of color, the poor, the old, and many other 'good natured crowds', both as producers and as consumers. Despite all my efforts, I did not find evidence that there is a critical mass of resistance practices that can mount a significant challenge to the condition of total landscape, even though, one could argue, we all simultaneously produce it and consume it. After all, as Christine Boyer rightfully asked, 'who raises a voice in opposition to this corporate organization of culture?' (Boyer 1994: 65) More importantly, there is no evidence that there is *de facto* a meaningful dialogue between those who produce theme parks and public space, and those who 'enjoy' them. The only form of 'exchange' between the two camps is marketing analysis. One of the reasons for that has also been an explicitly materialist conceptualization of both theme parks and privatized public space that tends to disable alternative interpretations and contested meanings potentially generated by varied social and cultural groups. Ironically, total landscape offers a vision of social space without society. But rightly so, because if there is no voluntary, desirable, meaningful and constructive communication between individuals, 'there is no such a thing as society', as Margaret Thatcher famously declared. Thus, by purposefully excluding the point of view of those who 'produce through the act of consumption'—guests, visitors, tourists and citizens—I wanted to be very realistic in identifying the current state of the question.

Through the last few years of working on this manuscript I ended many of the long days by reading stories to our daughter Maya, many of which, on her request, where about Disney princesses. I even promised I would take Maya to Walt Disney World Resort where all of the Disney Princesses, together with Tinker Bell and Peter Pan, live.

After all, her friend Eva is going to visit soon, and what kind of Dad would I be had I not promised we would go too as soon as Daddy finished the book? Very often Maya impatiently asked: 'Daddy, are you done with your book? When are we going to Disneyland?' I then had to explain we are going to Walt Disney World, not Disneyland, because Walt Disney World is bigger and better: it's a whole 'world' not just a 'land', and we can also go to nice places to swim. Of course, as millions of other parents, I was thinking mileage, gas prices, affordable hotel rates along Florida's Atlantic coast, and the AAA discounts on vacations in Walt Disney World Resort! I even got somewhat excited and enthusiastic about the trip. Inspired by what she saw on television and also by her friends's practices, Maya insisted on playing games on Disney web site, and the environment of many such games is the clear metaphorization of the Walt Disney World Resort. Needless to point out, the local mall has a Disney store that enabled Maya to make a leap from the phantasmagoric world of Disney to the materialistic world of retail shopping. The bright red, blue and yellow that made the Disney store stand out, together with the extra large pair of abstracted black mouse ears, created a strong and memorable image. The music that played in the store was the same as that we heard on the website. The environment felt so familiar and friendly, warm and inviting. The Tinker Bell swimming suit, made in China, was particularly interesting and would be an ideal 'present', Maya argued, given our forthcoming trip to Florida to visit Walt Disney World Resort. On the way home we stopped by the local supermarket to get milk, and somehow passed by Disney toys and books, and what a wonderful opportunity presented itself to us: to get a set of five Disney Princess books to be read the same night while drinking the milk we were just about to buy. The milk jar Maya drinks her milk from was also made in China and has Tinker Bell on it. And on, and on, and on this goes, and it is not only about the panoptic effect of synergetic marketing. As this book is about to show, it is much more than that: it is total landscape at work!

1

PUBLIC SPACE

SONY PLAZA

SONY WONDER
TECHNOLOGY LAB

YOU ARE HERE

'O Brave new world', he repeated.

'O Brave new world that has such people in it. Let's start at once'.

'You have a most peculiar way of talking sometimes', said Bernard, staring at the young man in perplexed astonishment.

'And, anyhow, hadn't you better wait till you actually see the new world?'

(HUXLEY 1932)

On a warm summer evening in June 1999, two consecutive news items that appeared on the Japanese NHK's early news-hour caught my attention: first was the information that as little as one percent of all Americans possess more than 50 percent of the entire American non-residential real estate property.[1] The second was that Walt Disney Co. is about to build a new theme park in Hong Kong. Asked whether this is a wise move for the troubled post-colonial economy of Hong Kong, an official in the Hong Kong Government said that although the actual contract with Walt Disney Company predicates large infrastructure and other investments on the part of the Government, the prestige that this project would bring, the number of people who would be employed in its construction and operation, and also the prospect of attracting five million Asian Disney fans a year to Hong Kong, all made the venture desirable and ultimately profitable. NHK news were occasionally interrupted and then followed by advertisements for special ready-made meals, high-tech dishes, exotic tourist destinations, super tools, car polishers, yacht shiners, supreme master cleaners, skin cleansers, moisturizers and softeners, and other such necessities. By discussing theme parks and privately-owned public spaces, this book attempts to understand tiny fragments of a globally emerging socio-economic system that produces and consumes specialized space just as it does with all other commodities. In such a system, the historically dialectic relationship between private and public domains seems to have been replaced by a homogeneous realm which stands close to the base of what Michel Foucault called 'the sanitary society'. For Foucault, the ideas of strict sanitation (hygiene) and discipline, when brought together form the ultimate stage of any panoptic, totalizing social realm. Namely the symbiosis of the political and economic power, and the convergence of governmental and corporate interest have created new bureaucratic bodies based on an ensemble of normative procedures that have since organized the techniques for both the production and consumption of theme parks as well as other specialized spaces. Once such techniques become deeply associated with the human practices they generate—so deeply associated that in fact we confuse the two—they tend to become autonomous and to function independently from the social system they serve (Postman 1992).

Total Landscape, Theme Parks, Public Space unfolds on two parallel levels of discussion. On the first level, the book argues that the production of theme parks is achieved by employing a complex apparatus that simultaneously fabricates consumer fantasies and desires in the media, constructs material routes that lead and transport consumers to theme parks or capitalizes on existing ones and organizes the theme park as material construct, symbolic environment and an experience factory. On the second level, the book employs the theme park in identifying, dissecting and describing the properties of new, hybrid forms of privately owned public space emerging in urban environments worldwide. In that respect the book does not propose that theme parks are (or will ever become) desirable substitutes for democratic public space, but deliberately cuts across the 'theme park model' in order to understand the principle of systematic totality employed when such a 'model' is used to reconstruct public realm in the United States, Japan and Europe, and to discuss what its expansion out of the boundaries of theme parks means for the transformation of the public realm as a whole. Furthermore, by illuminating the relationship between theme parks and public space, the book offers an insight into the ethos, criteria for design and evaluation, and a new set of normative expectations for the increasingly privatized urban public space in the Twenty-First Century.

The theme park industry is today a truly global industry with over 250 million visitors annually at 50 most visited theme parks (O'Brien et. al. 2002b) that generate total revenue of nearly US$19 billion (Benz 2003a). Only Walt Disney theme parks have been visited by over one billion people since the opening of Disneyland Park in 1955 (Marling 1997: 14). Such large theme parks are designed as systems of breathtaking complexity and scale: Disneyland and Walt Disney World were in respective historical periods largest investments into privately owned public facilities in the history of mankind. Levels of investment into large theme parks and complexities of their design, execution and operation can scale-wise be compared only with the largest military installations and with some NASA programs. The complex design challenges that theme parks present are so immense that no single individual or a single disciplinary team can accomplish them successfully. Large theme parks are customarily designed, constructed, and operated by thousands of individuals working in multiple, interdisciplinary teams that simultaneously design its presence in the media, the material and immaterial routes that lead people to theme parks, their material environment, and guest experiences alike. In that sense every material object, sound, smell, or performance, together with the outside factors such are income levels, oil prices or weather, is designed as an adaptable, relational unit within a dynamic system in action whose complexity is symptomatic of total landscape. Miscalculating any of the elements within such a complex system brings the entire system into jeopardy.

Most theme park developments cover thousands of acres of landscape and some work as real towns. Walt Disney World Resort, for instance, is twice the size of Manhattan, has customarily over 25 million visitors a year, and employs over 30 000 people. The unrestrained imposition of the totalizing governing and design principles over such vast landscapes makes theme parks increasingly important case studies especially in regard to theme parks 'inhabited' by permanent residents. In Chapter 4, I will discuss a 'theme park to end all theme parks' (Hendry 2000:43): Huis Ten Bosch (HTB) which was designed and constructed in Japan as a theme-park-town to be inhabited by 30 000 permanent residents. I will try to argue that HTB, as well as all other theme parks, exist within the system of urban spaces and that of social relationships, rendering the theme park simultaneously as a spatial and social machine. Their significance for a critical

understanding of the relationship between design and the key socio-economic processes that characterize the late Twentieth and early Twenty-First Century is essential.[2] In that respect the book will open by exploring a few concepts of seminal importance for understanding the processes and conditions I will then address in the following four chapters.

The Totality of the Artificial[3]

Concepts of 'totalization' and 'systematic totality' are among the key ideas that have marked the Twentieth Century. Totalizing narratives have been built into the core of the modern movement and modernity itself, and could be found in varied discourses ranging from ideological frameworks, to political and military regimes, art discourses, critical theory, market economy, or psychoanalysis. It is indeed the nature of an artifice and every man-made system, from language to traffic signs and to climate-controlled environments, to be totalizing: there is no such a thing as a non-totalizing artifice. The question is only to what extend can the constituents of such a system contest its form, meaning, its practices, and to what extend can they participate in its creation. The Frankfurt School of Social Research used the term 'totalizing' to describe the totalizing capitalist system which attempts to impose its values, structures, and practices throughout social body and social life as a whole in ways that suppress the contestation and offer limited opportunities for participation. The totality this book is attempting to portray in relation to 'total landscape' signifies a largely metaphysical effort aimed at imposing a holistic notion of 'harmony' as normative value, by orchestrating a complete and unified vector-field aimed at perpetually achieving a desired converging effect at desired points in space and time. Total landscape will signify a condition that emerges out of a totalizing convergence of the following three protagonists: first, a socio-economic system organized upon the idea of systematic totality, that embodies a holistic, harmonic, and exclusive worldview, an account that aims at covering everything, leaving nothing undefined; secondly, the artificial system that establishes its dominance 'on the ground' (the theme park proper); and finally, the system designed and operated by the media and entertainment industry that establishes its dominance in the collective consciousness and in cultural imagination. Even though totalization is here understood as a practice of fabricating an ensemble of totalizing narratives that contain an inherent regime of truth designed to offer a totalizing perspective that would relegate ultimate truth to itself, totalization does not necessarily imply a conceptual closure of any kind nor a complete inventory of cultural forms and practices. In that sense total landscape does not propose simply the reconfiguration of the notions of culture, nature, individuality, particularity, public, private, space or time—what it proposes instead is the fundamental change of the principles of socio-economic and narrative mapping that render such conceptual categories relevant. One of the central premises of this book is that theme parks are complex artifacts, designed to spatialize such totalizing narratives; in other words, to enable such narratives to unfold without friction in both space and time. One of the key elements of such a practice of representation is the aggressive rationalization and standardization of landscapes upon which they sit. As with any other apparatus of power, the theme park always needs a proper, a landscape in which to manifest itself, on which to be inscribed (Certeau 1984). The colonization and standardization of landscapes, both symbolically and materially, tends always to extend to the entire social realm and therefore an individual is naturally submerged in such a totalizing system that attempts to invade every area of life, invading ultimately 'the realm of subconscious' (Jameson 1991). However, total landscape does not negate anything, it simply works by emphasizing only those selected features of the landscape that support its totalizing worldview.

By juxtaposing 'total' with 'landscape' my hopes were multifold: I am aware that a singular totalizing schema that reveals the working of society as a whole is *de facto* only possible through great generalizations and through meta-totalization. In that respect, I have been strongly influenced by the writings of Michel Foucault who argued that multiple, often incoherent and discontinuous forces at work in any society generate a range of discursive dependencies: hence my treatment of historical fragments. 'Landscape' is the potential site of such multiple and discursive practices, and I use it accordingly to potentially and hypothetically counterbalance totality. Landscape is also a culture-bound concept and is capable of representing the symbiosis of the 'artificial' and the 'natural' through the so-called 'cultural detail'. The term 'landscape' itself contains multiple and complex layerings: on the one hand, in opposition to the absolute artifice of the apparatus of total landscape, 'landscape' stands as the ultimate depository of beliefs, values and practices that bond cultural groups together. As such 'landscape' is still partly bound to the notion of 'land' and materializes rural values and principles that have to a great extent been also built into the suburban mentality. 'Landscape' indeed ideologically stands in a sharp opposition to the notion of urbanity and to the realm of artifice as a whole. On the other hand, the term 'landscape' as a noun dates back to the late-Sixteen Century Dutch word *landschap* that etymologically derives from the word *land* meaning nature, and the word *schap* meaning either a picture representing a view of natural scenery or the art of depicting such scenery. Sometimes it also signified the act of framing a portion of natural territory that could have been viewed at one time from a particular location. In any case, the origin of the term 'landscape' points at an embedded duality between the notion of pristine nature and that of its framing, or the fabrication of its view. The book will thus employ the term 'landscape' to create a specific tension to follow throughout this discourse, namely the tension between the natural and artificial, between urban and suburban, urbanity and urbanization, between real and simulated, and between privacy and publicity.

By definition, total landscape is a true battlefield, positioned right at an explosive boundary: as the United Nations Global Report on Human Settlements of 2001 (HABITAT 2001) claims, slightly over half of humanity nowadays lives in urbanized areas across the globe, or within the so-called urban systems. Urban system refers to spatial arrangements of urban concentrations on local, regional, national or global scales, interconnected by respective transportation and information networks (Bourne and Simmons 1978, Marshall 1989). Since the political, economic and social relations are spatialized in these systems, they are by definition also complex socio-economic systems (Friedmann 1978, Lefebvre 1991). Within such systems, the notion of total landscape carries a mysterious load, a tension that is simultaneously defined by rural notions obvious through natural claims for the private ownership over land, the establishment and supervision of strict boundaries, the control of access, all based in the principle of territoriality, and yet at the same time the necessity for systematic, global thinking, open and free global market, sophisticated networks within the ever-growing urban systems, and cosmopolitan lifestyles, all interrelational and essentially based in the principle of urbanity. Unlike the process of urbanization, urbanity is a condition of urban life, a function of civility as well as of diversity, an interplay between freedom and necessity, pleasure and risk, as well as of the volume of information an individual receives and processes per unit of time. In that sense, total landscape should be understood as an authoritarian condition of the space-time totality that paradoxically privileges urbanization while it suppresses urbanity. The process of totalization that brings theme parks, landscapes and public space into the same framework is not obvious through formal and aesthetic similarities, but through systematic ones, through the system of values, conditions and techniques that has been systematically extended upon the entire social realm. In that respect, theme parks and public spaces operate according to a shared invisible rationale that may or may not make them visually similar. The aim of this book is not to search for a model according to which a non-totalizing conception of the theme park may be developed, but to expose the search for systematic totality in order to employ it analogically in looking at public spaces and the social realm as a whole. Subsequently, one would argue that the

only way to clearly understand where the lack of adequate public policy, the exercise of governmental power to protect civil rights, and active citizen participation would lead to is to look closely into the mechanisms that bring theme parks into being.

The extreme degree of smudging of the boundaries between the world of media (the cognitive) and the material world (the perceived and/or lived) is absolutely necessary in a totalizing system such as the one described here. The mode of production that facilities such a flow and softening of boundaries is entertainment. As Neil Postman argued, not only has entertainment become a major form of public discourse and the dominant model of cultural production, it also made itself the natural format for the representation of all human experience (Postman 1985). As the theme park is indeed a part of the system of specialized spaces and signifies both the space of consumption and the consumption of space, someone always has a clear interest in (re)producing it. Such a 'power' creates the mode of representation of its proper by the media (fabricated by television, radio, film, internet), determines physical and symbolic venues that lead people to its proper, and constructs the theme park environment which determines human interaction through a system of 'prescribed syntactical forms'. It also has the power to alter or fabricate interpretative codes upon such an environment is interpreted (Gottdiener 1997). Thus, if total landscape conditions a general conception of life based in consumption, theme parks are designed to operate as a 'scholastic program for the naturalization of commodity form' (Fjellman 1992: 402). Within such an arrangement, total landscape establishes and naturalizes the economic value of cultural goods and the cultural value of consumer items (Zukin 1991: 241–250). In order to assure the precise functioning of such a coordinated ensemble of techniques, both the material and symbolic environment of the theme park simultaneously employ an elaborated system of control mechanisms. These mechanisms of control are aimed at manipulating the behavior of visitors to achieve desirable outcomes, and very often they are totalizing. This book will not argue that the technology of control employed in theme parks cannot induce individual pleasure in visitors. On the contrary, the 'exchange value' of a theme park visit is in the individual pleasure that it commonly generates, together with reassurance and the reaffirmation of social norms and expectations summed up with the phrase 'having fun'. Ironically, thus, the theme park is presented as a collective fantasy of escape and entertainment, whereas at the same time it is being employed as an ideal vehicle of social control due to its ability to spatialize social relations and instrumentalize space through the arrangement of seemingly benevolent technical procedures. What one experiences in a system of totalizing forces is a set of 'entertaining experiences', 'once-in-a-lifetime adventures' that are 'comfortable', recognizable (through familiar images or music), perfectly organized, predictable and controlled 'for your convenience', apparently apolitical, seemingly culturally diverse and economically pragmatic 'for your benefit'. The attributes assigned to theme parks are the ones usually prescribed by the media invasion of colloquial speech: they are 'true adventures', 'trouble-free', 'safe', 'irresistible', 'everything is at hand and nothing is lacking', the service is 'generous and attentive', and after all they 'accelerate the feeling of freedom'. Finally they are generously presented by some anonymous identity formation such as 'World Networks Inc.', that is represented by an image of a smiling crew composed of people of different ethnic origins. Paradoxically, every attempt to define a meaningful principle of identity rebounds upon one and the principle of technical intelligibility is the only thing that one encounters. Namely, any encounter of this kind instantly reveals a three-fold structure: there are those who present the theme park to us, those who serve us on behalf of the presenter, and there is 'us'. They are hierarchically-controlled environments catering to fabricated needs of people in specifically designed space-time arrangements. The transparent *tour de force* of this designed space- and time-bound totality is Total Customer Satisfaction: 'Was everything all right?' is measured, quantified and reciprocally compared to the average answer. One's tip is calculated relative to the amount of the bill and as a code assigned to the name of the server and one's ticket. The effect of Muzak on one's mood is quantified by the amount of money one has spent and finally, the effect of: 'May I have your attention, please: you are about to leave the premises of the World Networks Inc. We hope you have enjoyed your stay and please, come visit us again. On behalf of the World Networks Inc. I wish you a pleasant trip', is quantified by the number of repeat visits. If necessary, the grain of the voice or the speed of narration may be adjusted to achieve the 'optimum response' from the target customer population. These conditions are not only characteristic of theme parks, but have increasingly come to characterize our experience of the world as a whole. The numbness of one's senses achieved by an overall control of environmental conditions and by the banality of dispassionate comfort provoked William Whyte's confusion of walking in downtown Los Angeles of which he wrote:

> Where, indeed, is here? And when? Is it night or day? Is it spring? Or winter? You cannot see out. You do not know what city you are in, or if you are in a city at all. Perhaps it is a complex out by the airport or at new interchange. It could be on the West Coast. It could be on the East. It could be in a foreign country. The piped music gives no clue. It is the same music everywhere. You are in the universal controlled environments. (Whyte 1988: 221)

Like all artifice, theme parks are also subject to the transcendental obsession with systematic totality. In terms of customer needs, they cater to the time/space bound needs of customers, anticipate and when possible choreograph customer's behavior within a complete and unified effort especially orchestrated to achieve a desired effect: one that implies that everything has been counted, weighed, measured, considered and anticipated in the production of desirable human experiences. In that respect, theme parks are empirically quantifiable and measurable by temporal and monetary units, as is obvious through timetables given to visitors in order to plan the 'visit' and inform them that the trip, for instance, from Tokyo Station to the Huis Ten Bosch theme park in Kyushu will take 5 hours and 36 minutes:

'If the weather allows we should be able to see Mt. Fuji on our right,' while moving at the speed of 160 miles per hour. Once there, it will take an additional four minutes walking South-East to arrive to theme park's gates. The schedule, however, extends into the structure of the destination through precise timetables that regulate consumption of the location and strictly determine visitors's practices: the *how, where*, and *when*. Due to that particular 'quality', once visitors experience one theme park, they know what to expect and how to behave in any other theme park because they all seem to be organized following an invisible rationale, an anonymously established set of standards and normative expectations. In that respect, theme parks have a rather phantasmagorical quality for one always *a priori* assumes one understands them easily and can make a perfect sense in describing them. Few would disagree regarding the significance of the sensory impact they make on visitors by building memorable environmental images. Visitors easily memorize strong environmental images, and organize their experiences into a clear narrative form. Nonetheless, every serious attempt to define a meaningful principle of any such environment unmistakably reveals solely the principles of technical and economic intelligibility, 'the systematics of the inconceivable' to employ Roland Barthes term. The key element of that ensemble is a chain of environmental conditions with an underlying thematic framework that implies narrative structure, sequential sensory stimulations, story line, and syntax all spatialized by the chain of multidimensional units. The conditioning of such an environment is so overwhelming, that the objectification of the public is precisely what its visitors desire, because it implies an ultimate control over experiential outcomes. Theme park designers and operators have developed ingenious mechanisms to achieve this goal, from gates and entrance fees to the mechanisms of social control established by the mass media. Such a desire for perfection and totalization on the part of all constituents, management as well as visitors, is what George Ritzer has called the 'paradigm of McDonaldization' (Ritzer 1996). It stands for 'the process by which the principles of the fast-food restaurant are coming to dominate more and more sectors of American society as well as of the rest of the world' (Ritzer 1996: 1). Ritzer identifies four basic premises for the proliferation of this type of rationality: efficiency, calculability, predictability and control.[4] Efficiency means choosing the optimum means to a given end, a procedure that relies on employing optimum means that have been previously invented and tested in a variety of social settings. Calculability stands for an emphasis on the things that can be quantified and refers to the processes of production, services and the final products. Quantity has not only become an alternative for quality but the substitute for it. Predictability, argues Ritzer, is privileged in a rational society that emphasizes discipline, order, systematization, formalization, routine, consistency and methodical operation. Moreover, 'in such a society people [...] neither desire nor expect surprises' (Ritzer 1996: 21). Control stands for the arrangement of increasingly effective technologies that prescribe normative expectations from both customers and employees and demand their fulfillment. As Ritzer suggested, the greatest source of uncertainty and unpredictability in such a rational system are the people and 'hence the efforts to increase control are usually aimed at people' (Ritzer 1996: 27). He effectively shows how the paradigm of McDonaldization not only namelessly rationalizes any given social context, but also ironically provokes a desire for social engineering. Both are immanently linked to economic studies and help realize that economy is not just a technique of production, distribution and consumption but more importantly, as Jacques Ellul has written, economic technique encounters *homo economicus* 'in the flesh [as] the human being is changing slowly under the pressure of the economic milieu; he is in the process of becoming the uncomplicated being the liberal economist constructed.' (Ellul 1967: 219) In sum, a socio-economic system described by Ritzer attempts to govern many or all aspects of social life first by constructing a totalizing theory that will see the entire world through its own goggles, and will then methodologically proceed to design the world according to such an image.

The Production of Total Landscape

As indicated above, the main rationale of the total landscape is economic in nature. Both David Harvey (Harvey 1985, 1989, 1989a) and Henri Lefebvre (Lefebvre 1976, 1991) have argued that one of the dominant aspects of post-industrial capitalist production is the transformation of space into time through the mediation of money. Space is turned into a function of distance, distance a function of time, and time a function of money (Traganou 2004: 59). Since space is a function of money, and can be defined in monetary or economic terms, it is obvious that space can indeed be produced; moreover, since 'space' has been historically used to describe, categorize and organize the experience of human senses, and human experience in the world as a whole, one can assume that both space and human experience are indeed socio-economic artifacts. The question, however, is: can both space and human experience be commodified, and just how could that be done? Here, one must step away from the Marxist notion of production that had been based in the industrial production of material goods and saw the only source of economic value in labor itself. Neither space nor experience can be produced as material artifacts and yet both indeed have been produced as commodities within complex processes that place varied constituents, simultaneously both producers and consumers, into socio-economic arrangements that form the base of the post-industrial capitalism. I subscribe here largely to the writings of Jean Baudrillard (Baudrillard 1975) and Henri Lefebvre (Lefebvre 1976), specifically to Lefebvre's notion of 'social production' (Lefebvre 1991). As Gottdiener noted, since the mid-1960s, the problem of capitalist system was no longer situated within processes of manufacturing and distribution (Gottdiener 1995, 1997). In other words, the production of material goods was brought to a very high level of rationalization and efficiency, and distribution systems were greatly improved by the advances in transportation and communication networks. Both Lefebvre (Lefebvre 1976) and Baudrillard (Baudrillard 1975) realized that by the early 1970s, capitalism was facing the most serious crisis of its internal contradictions that could have no longer been resolved by improving either production or distribution processes. Lefebvre claimed that capitalism has managed to surpass the contradiction and to achieve growth by producing and occupying space: more precisely, by the production, colonization, fragmentation, specialization and commodification of space (Lefebvre 1991). Baudrillard suggested that one has to take into account the changing dynamics of capitalist accumulation, coupled with the redefined position of the human subject, and argued that the crisis that capitalism began facing in the post-World War II years was in the realm of realization of capital and therefore was to be found within the processes of consumption (Baudrillard 1975). He argued that the process of consumption carries within a process of production, or 'self-realization', within the symbolic processes aimed at resolving the realization problem of capital.[5]

Key to Lefebvre's production of space (Lefebvre 1991) is the shifting of the discourse from the notion of 'product' to the notion of 'productive activity', or from an idea of social space being a static social product to the construction of social space as a perpetual process of production, induced by the interplay between the triad conceived-perceived-lived. The triad is spatialized by the three fields of forces (the physical, the mental and the social) into three spatial concepts: Representations of Space (space conceptualized by planner, policy makers, social engineers, all with the realm of the conceived), Representational Spaces (spaced directly lived through images and symbols, the space of inhabitants, users, all with the realm of the lived), and Spatial Practices (daily practices unfolding within the realm of the perceived). Practices of the production of space within total landscape are greatly facilitated by the dissolution of boundaries between the realms of perceived-conceived-lived, since one moves in-between them through total landscape 'without friction'. One of the aspects of the production of space crucial to the subject matter of this book is what Lefebvre calls 'ludic space', a space designated for leisure and amusement. The production of 'ludic space' has facilitated the reproduction of the capitalist organization of production and its 'colonization [of space] as a whole' and has turned some of the basic principles of industrial capitalism upside-down. Namely, instead of the circulation of commodities to locations of consumption (places where people lived), post-industrial capitalism has since 1960s involved the circulation of people to specific locations that are consumed as commodities.

> Leisure spaces are the object of a massive speculation that is not tightly controlled and is often assisted by the state (which builds highways and communications and which directly or indirectly guarantees the financial operations etc.). This space is sold, at high prices, to citizens who have been harried out of the town by boredom and the rat-race. It is reduced to visual attributes [...] it is rigidly hierarchized [...] Thus leisure enters into the division of social labor—not simply because leisure permits labor power to recuperate, but also because there is a leisure industry, a large-scale commercialization of specialized spaces, a division of social labor which is projected 'on the ground' and enters into global planning. (Lefebvre 1976: 84)

Indeed, Lefebvre's abstract ludic space extends as *tabula rasa* throughout a measurable terrain homogenizing natural and cultural characteristics of landscape. On the other hand, the same production mode is characterized by a desire for hierarchical ordering, fragmentation and specialization. In some ironic way, capitalist space can simultaneously totalize entire landscapes not necessarily by the extermination of the intrinsic qualities of landscape and the cultural and social habits of local dwellers—a framework in military theory called 'cultural detail'—but by rendering 'cultural detail' invisible and therefore irrelevant. As we have argued earlier, it can also achieve differentiation by the amplification and caricaturization of only those selected features that can promote both the symbolic and material consumption of total landscape.

Like space, human experience can also be instrumentalized within the framework of 'experience economy' as the fourth type of economic output, after commodities, goods and services (Pine and Gilmore 1999). Not surprisingly, Pine and Gilmore trace the beginnings of the 'experience expansion' to one man and the company he founded: Walt Disney. For Pine and Gilmore, while experiences are still a largely unarticulated genre of economic output, through their capacity to transform 'guests' (human subjects experiencing economy in flesh) they will become the dominant mode of economic output in the Twenty-First Century. Analogically to Lefebvre's argument that a monetary or economic definition of space demands differentiation as a marketing tool, they have argued that staging experiences has forestalled the commoditization that was rapidly driving down the differentiation, relevancy and price of so many goods and services at the close of the Twentieth Century. In direct opposition to the phenomenological approaches to the subject matter, Pine and Gilmore have argued that from an economic point of view 'there is no such thing as an artificial experience. Every experience created within an individual is real, whether the stimuli be natural or simulated.' (Pine and Gilmore 1999: 36) Moreover, staging experiences is not about entertaining customers, it is about engaging them within a process that may begin to 'describe the kind of connection or environmental relationship that unites customers with the event or performance' (Pine and Gilmore 1999: 30–31) in either immersive or absorbing ways. Thus, unlike conventional malls that commodify normative social experience and offer it as entertainment, theme parks offer an ensemble of distinct, differentiating experiences that would be based in the 'total involvement' with the environment. Pine and Gilmore employ Mihaly Csikszentmihalyi's notion of 'optimal experience' of this kind as 'the process of total involvement with life' that Csikszentmihalyi calls 'flow' (Csikszentmihalyi 1990). The experience of the theme park visitor would thus be the polar opposite of the pure escapist entertainment experience one finds in shopping malls and cinema halls. As Pine and Gilmore subsequently argued, those who charge for the activities are in the service business and those who charge for the time customers spend with them are in the experience business (Pine and Gilmore 1999: 2). Theme parks obviously charge for both. The extreme rationalization of such procedures provoked journalist Bob Garfield to coin the neologism 'cost per fun hour' (c.p.f.h.) and quantify his family's five-day experience in Walt Disney World Resort for the *Washington Post* in the following way:

> We luxuriated in 113 hours and 47 minutes of eating, sleeping in our 'affordable' Disney accommodations, riding on buses and standing in line, punctuated by a cumulative 6 hours and 47 minutes of fun, fun, fun. That amounts to $261 c.p.f.h. (cost per fun hour). (Bryman 1995: 93–94)

Although it is obvious how Garfield felt after the 'family adventure', he missed the 'experience economy' argument that 'journey is the destination' by which all 114 hours were a part of his total experience, thus reducing the cost per fun hour. But how does one know what kind of experience a guest has had? Was it satisfactory? How can an experience be both qualified and quantified? In general, guest experience is quantified through the economic performance of the theme park and is customarily evaluated based on the conventional marketing research and customer satisfaction methods which are interested in the quantification of consumer practices as a process of determining the economic quality of the theme park as a commercial environment. In that sense, the degree of market penetration and visitor per-capita expenditures are two key criteria for evaluating theme park performance. Per-capita expenditures are most commonly expressed through the purchase-volume (or 'dollar-volume') of the theme park that specifies the volume of purchases per square foot of the facility. The experiential dimension of the theme park is hard to qualify. Literature on customer satisfaction suggests that, besides being directly affected by the product and service quality, consumer behavior is also affected by the *a priori* expectations regarding those performances (Anderson et. al. 1993, Barsky 1995). Moreover, several studies have suggested that customer satisfaction also depends upon the environmental experience in which the product is obtained (Hempel and Rosenberg 1976) and that in order to generate the 'total degree' of customer satisfaction, every product, service or experience must be designed, produced and delivered in the context of 'total offering' (Brown and Fern 1981). Gottdiener suggested that the reason for the proliferation of themed environments lies precisely in the melding of fabricated environmental themes with the world of mass media, giant entertainment corporations and control of consumer fantasies, which taken together as a system indeed construct the 'total offering' of goods, services and experiences alike (Gottdiener 1997: 155). In the last decades of the Twentieth Century, a professional field called 'experience engineering' emerged out of a keen interest of entertainment corporations to advance knowledge and expertise in fabricating and reproducing human experiences in order to improve chances for economic success. The emergence of 'experience engineering' is only a continuation and rationalization of the tendency that Daniel Boorstin had traced back to the late Nineteen and early Twentieth Century (Boorstin 1962). He claimed that newspapers and, later, other mass media outlets have established a practice of fabricating fake events ('pseudo-events') in order to entertain and manipulate the public. For Boorstin a pseudo-event is a synthetic novelty, a simulation etymologically derived from the Greek word *pseudo* meaning 'false', intended to deceive, coming more remotely from the noun *psema,* meaning 'lie'. A pseudo-event is not spontaneous but a planned occurrence arranged for intelligibility and the convenience of reproduction, thereby being more intelligible, more reassuring and even more dramatic than spontaneous occurrences. Since pseudo-events are costly constructs, someone always has the interest in advertising and repeating these events, hence they tend to become ritualized. The consequences of the deliberate production of pseudo-events and human experiences as socio-economic artifacts are highly problematic and will be discussed in Chapter 3 in terms of production and in Chapter 5 in terms their implications on the reconfiguration of public space. As Alvin Toffler wrote in 1970:

If consumers can no longer distinguish clearly between the real and the simulated, if whole stretches of one's life may be commercially programmed, we enter into a set of psycho-economic problems of breathtaking complexity. These problems challenge our most fundamental beliefs, not merely about democracy or economics, but about the very nature of rationality and sanity [...] One of the definitions of sanity, itself, is the ability to tell real from unreal [...] we shall become the first culture in history to employ high technology to manufacture the most transient, yet lasting of products: the human experience. (Toffler 1970: 208)

Cycles of systematic totality may as well be symbolically and materially closed by the ability to produce human experiences, as such an ability in fact implies the power to treat the entire social realm as an object of systematization that has to be closed in order to be complete: hence the totalizing logic of the total landscape.

Historico-Etymological Notes

In many ways, also etymologically, the theme park is a combination of the conceptual categories of 'garden' and 'park'. Garden is a pluralistic concept that changed profoundly during its history. Besides its originally utilitarian role it has come to signify an 'attempt to establish meaning by giving form to the nature' (Tuan 1974). Tuan argued that Renaissance and, to some extent, Baroque Gardens worked as miniature recreations of the cosmos, models of an ideal world made from the real stuff. This role of gardens was made possible by a shared symbolism, a 'unified code' (Lefebvre 1991: 64), a consensus regarding the shared set of values, beliefs and meanings layered upon each other over centuries of design and use. However, by the end of the Eighteen Century, distinctions between gardens and parks had blurred. The difference between the two was initially one of scale and the role of nature. As Riley argued, the essence of garden was not only in controlling nature, but in demonstrating that control (Riley 1998). Parks lack such control of natural processes and have historically stimulated the vision of nature as a setting for moral lessons, framed through ensembles of harmonious human activities. By the beginning of the Nineteen Century, when these distinctions became obsolete,

PUBLIC PARKS IN THE UNITED STATES FROM 1850S THROUGH 1950S

The term 'park' in the late Eighteenth-Century United States meant an enclosure into which animals were driven for slaughter, a corral or a level valley among mountains.[1] Since the beginning of the Nineteenth Century, it meant a large territory set apart as national property for public benefit (recreation and pleasure) or for the preservation of wildlife (such as national parks).[2] Park-making methods were brought from Europe during the Nineteenth Century by F. L. Olmsted, among others, and until the 1930s, its development went through two main phases: first as Pleasure Garden and subsequently as Reform Park.[3] The Pleasure Garden, later called 'pleasure ground', was an antidote to industrialized, polluted urban environments usually situated at the edge of the city where land was cheaper. As Cranz wrote, the pleasure ground was a landscape of freedom and choice 'within the context of industrial order' (Cranz 1982: 249). Fear of epidemics and diseases was the major factor in making these parks after 1850s. A typical example is Olmsted's Central Park in New York City, a wilderness as an antidote to the urban grid of Manhattan. Inspired by the works of Paxton, Nash and Repton, Olmsted designed Central Park as a pastoral landscape with an emphasis on the kinesthetic experience organized through sequencing of different settings. Buildings were kept minimal in size and decoration. Olmsted also adopted Paxton's separation of pedestrian from vehicular traffic, first utilized at Birkenhead Park. Central Park was a site of a controllable social mix with an emphasis on passive observation, initially without a strong participatory character. In the early 1900s, ice-skating and various sport fields were introduced and the park became partly a recreational facility. Museums and exhibition halls were introduced as educational devices and proved successful, if experimentational, in offering educational experiences not conventionally offered by schools. Folk dances, athletics, games and football were parks' constant features. As Cranz pointed out, if the most characteristic element of pleasure grounds was class, gender, and age segregation, in the reform park, such exclusions were weaker and less revealing (Cranz 1982: 23) since commissioners needed the parks to appear nonsectarian and apolitical in order to justify public spending. In order to be able to cope with rising tensions among the social and economic classes, races, ethnic groups and gender differences reform parks provided 'consensus entertainments' that effectively mediated social conflicts by money (Warner 1993). Consensus entertainments such as ice cream stands, beer gardens, band music, and wild animals worked as social distractions: everyone was allowed to take part as long as they could afford to participate in the cycles of consumption. Since early 1920s, reform parks had specialized in athletics and sport, and such playgrounds were then moved farther to terminal points of cheap trolley lines or other transportation means. Days were broken into parts according to temperature changes and schedules of school children, mothers and workers. Through strict programming, reform parks were deliberately instrumentalized as vehicles of social control. The reform park gradually gave way to recreational facilities in the 1930s as the 'ideal of apolitical machine-like efficiency in the context of a society fighting for economic and political hegemony' (Cranz 1982: 249).

1. *Chambers English Dictionary.* (1988) London: W&L Chambers Ltd.: 1050.

2. The alternative colloquial use of 'park' (as in 'to park') was in the Nineteenth Century based on the notion of depositing military vehicles and artillery into an enclosure usually within a military camp (*Chambers English Dictionary.* London: W&L Chambers Ltd.: 1050).

3. After the late-1930s, Reform Park went through another two phases in its evolution: namely the Recreational Facility and the Open Space System (Warner 1993).

Central Park, New York City

gardens and parks merged into 'landscape garden', a model transferred from the United Kingdom to the United States by F. L. Olmsted. Both gardens and parks have historically mediated between two dialectically opposed realms: the private realm, traditionally linked to the institution of family (sacred, secluded, protected) and the public realm, traditionally linked to social and political realm (the space of the *other*). While gardens remained essentially private in terms of ownership, and often in terms of accessibility, parks have mutated from the notion of wilderness (Jackson 1980)[6] to the notion of communal space, and increasingly (since Eighteen Century) to a form of public space. The English word 'park' is of Teutonic origin and comes from the Celtic, especially Gaulish (also referred to as Barbaric), word *perh* meaning an enclosure.[7] This gave the Primitive-Germanic *parrak* that also influenced the Medieval-Latin word *parricus* which dates from the Eight Century ('Lex Ripuaria'[8]) and later was contracted into *parcus,* meaning a small tract of land. The Italian word *parco,* the Spanish word *parque* and especially the Old-French word *parc* are of direct Latin descent.[9] In its Thirteen Century use, the English word *park* meant an enclosed ground held by royal grant or prescription for the chase. Occasionally it meant a tract of land surrounding mansions kept as a pleasure ground and sometimes used for recreation. Since the second half of the Nineteen Century, 'park' has been conventionally understood as a large territory set apart as national property for public benefit, often recreation and pleasure. After the mid-Twentieth Century, it has also been used to indicate an area designated for a particular kind of development (industrial park, science park, business park or theme park).

The English word 'theme' comes from the Greek word *thema,* which means a proposition, the subject of an argument or something to put down.[10] Its roots lead to *tithenai,* a Greek word meaning to place or to lay down,[11] a distant origin of the English *Do.*[12] *Thema* also gave *thematikos,* meaning pertaining to a theme. English acquired the word *theme* most directly from Latin *thema.*[13] In its contemporary English sense, the word 'theme' conventionally refers to 'the topic of a work of art or of a discourse'.[14] This suggests that its extended meaning, later signifying even character of an urban milieu or a restaurant chain, has presumably come into use with the phrase 'theme park'. The phrase 'theme park' has been in colloquial use after the opening of Disneyland, California in 1955. Nevertheless, it was 30 years later that this term entered slang dictionaries, and dictionaries of new words and phrases. In 1993, the term 'theme park' entered the *Oxford Dictionary of New Words,* which describes it as an amusement park in which 'the structures and settings are all based on a central theme'.[15] Likewise, *Chambers English Dictionary* defines it as 'a large area with displays, fairgrounds, rides, all devoted to or based on one subject'.[16] The word 'theme' is not integral to the concept of the 'park', therefore 'theme' expands the conventional meaning of 'park' beyond its conceptual boundaries by adjoining new scopes to its idiosyncratic features. Together, they offer a rationale for formal idiosyncratic attributes and a hint of the narrative and semiotic code upon which the theme park could be instantly denoted. In addition, Jones and Robinett of the Economics Research Associates (ERA), a leading consulting firm in the theme park industry, came to recognize that all theme parks share the following primary characteristics: theme parks have a family appeal; they contain one or more themed environments; they have some form of 'ambient entertainment' (strolling, musicians, street performers, costumed characters and the like); they also have a high investment level per unit of ride or show capacity; they have high standards of service, facility maintenance, and overall hygiene; they contain enough activities (entertainment content) to create an average visitor length of stay of typically five to seven hours; and theme parks will usually have a pay-one-price admission policy (Jones and Robinett 1999).

Although it is relatively simple to conceptually define what is commonly meant by 'theme park', it is, as it will be clear in what follows, nearly impossible to do the same for 'public space'. Besides the fact that there is no conceptual closure on what the term 'public space' commonly means, there was also never a proper theory of public space. Instead, what one finds in literature are more-or-less powerful descriptive models that could be professional, academic (disciplinary-based), political, legal or commoner's in origin. What they provide, sometimes successfully, is an inventory of forms and practices that may exist in public space, they may even create a discourse on public space, but rarely would they advance the knowledge on public space or make claims to provide a proper theory of public space. As Lyn Lofland (Lofland 1998) wrote, vast areas of the historical development of 'public realm' and 'public space' are still *regiones incognitae.* The root of English word 'public' comes from Latin *publicus* (close to Latin *populus* meaning the people) and as an adjective, it dates back to the Fourteen Century, when it signified something that has an affect upon or relates to 'all the people'.[17] As a noun it enters colloquial usage in the Fifteen Century, signifying commonly either a place accessible or visible to the public (in public) or the people as a whole (populace).[18] As Richard Sennett (Sennett 1977) claimed, by the end of the Seventeenth Century the opposition of 'public' and 'private' assumed the general properties it still holds to until this day.[19] 'Public' meant 'open to the scrutiny of anyone', whereas 'private' meant 'a sheltered region of life'. Every human being was thus defined by and through these oppositions simultaneously as a 'private' and as a 'public' individual. By the same time in France, the term *le public* had gradually evolved into meaning a 'region of sociability'; especially applied in discussing audience. As Sennett further indicates, in the Eighteen Century the sense of 'public' evolved into a more generic concept of 'public geography', one more closely related to the growing urban areas, cosmopolitanism, the establishment of public parks, of the promenades and a wide diversity of strangers and acquaintances one would meet in 'public regions' of social life (Sennett 1977: 38). In a sense, the public realm was seen as something to be made, whereas it was in the private realm, as Sennett claimed, that Eighteenth Century man would realize his natural claims: '[...] while man made himself in public, he realized his nature in the private realm' (Sennett 1977: 18). Hannah Arendt also referred to 'public realm' as an artifact, a 'fabrication of human hands' and minds (Arendt 1958). Thus, it is in the Eighteenth Century that the notion of public comes to signify a realm of social life that is deliberately 'designed' by varied constituents: people/ users at large, as well as the center of political, religious and economic power. After all, as Senett claims, it is the capital city that had favored and enabled such changes through economic mechanisms such are cash economy, credit, investment, profit and accounting procedures. During the Nineteenth Century, and especially in the early Twentieth Century, capitalism had profoundly changed relations of power invested in the notion of 'public', and 'public' (both as a noun and as an adjective) became regarded as morally inferior and something to be afraid of, to stay away from. As a result, citizens have lost interest in investing into it, in taking part in the process of designing. It is precisely to the same type of fear that in the 1940s Walt Disney referred to Coney Island and Manhattan as a 'malaise' he wanted to oppose by building a new type of public space oriented towards family entertainment. Paradoxically, 'public' came to connote more (in terms of what it potentially conceptually embraces) as it came to denote less (in relation of what it actually offers in terms of social realization). Sennett claimed that this is a result of the superimposition of 'public' over 'private' that came as a consequence of behavioral and ideological confusion between the two realms that originated in the Nineteenth Century, whereas Habermas saw it as the 'interlocking of the public and private domains' that caused a 'refeudalization of public sphere' (Habermas 1989).

It is already obvious from the above that the adjective 'public' has been in use since the Fourteenth Century, and that since the Eighteenth Century it will often appear next to the nouns 'sphere', 'realm' and 'space'. The English word 'space' comes from Latin *spatium* (via French *espace*) which meant an empty area, an interval of space or time.[20] Before the Seventeenth Century, 'space' (just as 'time')

belonged to the Aristotelian tradition within which it was used to describe, name and classify the evidence of the senses. As Lefebvre (Lefebvre 1991: 1–9) argued, Descartes brought this tradition to an end by moving his concept of space into the realm of the absolute: Cartesian space came to dominate, by containment, both senses and bodies, both the cognitive and the perceived.[21] This rationalization of space presented space as a boundless three-dimensional extent in which objects and events occur and have relative position and direction. Before the Twentieth Century, 'space' (worldly space, that is to say not the outer space, nor the cosmological representations) was either defined in geometrical terms as an 'empty area' (Euclidean geometry), as a conceptual category that facilitated the rationalization of the evidence of human senses (Aristotelian tradition), as a transcendental, 'mental' category separated from the empirical (Kantian space), or as a set of mathematical entities with a set of axioms of geometric character (such are metric space, topological space, or vector space, all within the Cartesian tradition). With the advent of modern science and contemporary academic disciplines such as anthropology, ethnology, sociology, political science, linguistics and later computer science et, as of the early Twentieth Century one can talk of anthropological space, political space, the space of the language, cyberspace and so on. Michel Foucault proclaimed that as the Nineteenth Century was preoccupied with history, the Twentieth Century was preoccupied by space (Foucault 1985).[22] As indicated earlier, the lineage of space put forth by Henri Lefebvre will be instrumental to the argument I develop in this book. Lefebvre (Lefebvre 1991) had divided the development of space into three stages: Absolute space, Abstract space and Differential (contradictory) space. Absolute space is a historical space, also a natural space because the natural claims of those who produced it were better (or only) articulated than their social claims; it was also religious and political in character. Since the Renaissance, Absolute space has been slowly replaced by the Abstract space, although it still exists suppressed and as an undercurrent in places escaping the reach of globalization (the global market). Especially since the Eighteenth Century, Abstract space 'smashed naturalness forever' and established the space of accumulation of wealth, knowledge, power, technology and money. In relation to my earlier argument that similarities between theme parks and public spaces are not formal and visual, but above all systematic, Lefebvre asserts that Abstract space cannot be understood and defined on the basis of what is perceived and it cannot be reduced to a transparent logic or strategy. The real subject of Abstract space is the post-bourgeois bureaucracy, the symbiosis of corporate and state power. Finally, Abstract space is instrumental, institutional, political and homogeneous in intent and appearance as it extends over measurable terrain as *tabula rasa*. Differential space is a sub-category of Abstract space in that the Abstract space has to create differentiation in isolated segments in order to perpetuate its homogeneity. The best example of this practice, and of the production of Differential space, is the practice of producing entertainment space, or what Lefebvre called 'ludic space,' the space of leisure pursuits of all kinds. In this scheme of things, theme parks are representational spaces whose production is facilitated by the representations of space and related spatial practices.

It is impossible to find the exact moment in history when the phrase 'public space' was used for the first time except to assume that in its modern form it comes into colloquial use in the Eighteenth Century. The notion of public space as a manifestation of a general political and social consensus was established by the bourgeois culture and its institutions in the Nineteenth Century. In the Twentieth Century, multidisciplinary discourse on public space developed into three distinct directions that could be roughly summarized into the aesthetic, the technocratic, and the naïve approach,[23] although many authors could fall into more than one of these directions. The aesthetic approach argues that public space is an urban artifact designed to simultaneously satisfy cultural, social and particularly political concerns, and it often idealizes the processes of its social production while it emphasizes the theatrical character of public space. Authors such are Erving Goffman (Goffman 1963), Jane Jacobs (Jacobs 1961), Jürgen Habermas (Habermas 1989), Richard Sennett (Sennett 1977), William H. Whyte (Whyte 1988), and later Lyn Lofland (Lofland 1998) all in one way or another fall predominantly into this direction. The aesthetic approach emphasizes in many ways the 'view from below' and places value on the public spaces as lived and perceived, or in Lefebvre's terms on representational spaces and spatial practices. The technocratic approach is interested in the functional aspects and instrumental power of public space, and not coincidentally most architectural and planning discourse on public space falls into this direction. Authors such are Camillo Sitte (Sitte 1945), Lewis Mumford (Mumford 1942, 1961), Sigfried Giedion (Giedion 1949), Jose Luis Sert (Sert 1942), together with avant-garde institutions such as CIAM (Tyrwhitt et. al. 1952) all fall within this approach that often emphasizes the 'view from above', or in Lefebvre's terms is interested in the production of the spaces of representation. This is largely a discourse initiated from the position of power, whether real or imaginary, that, for example, addresses the importance of open, public space for the quality of public life. The naïve approach is somewhat simplistic and largely nostalgic, typically claiming that 'public space is the stage upon which the drama of communal life unfolds.' (Carr et al. 1992: 3) The naïve approach is also often characterized by subjective, impressionistic and anecdotal accounts that document or illustrate practices (or the lack of the same) of specific social and cultural groups in public space (Betsky 1997, Sudjic 1992, Zukin 1995). Despite all differences in approach, by 'public space' most authors have assumed static notions of public space grounded in traditional sites of public interaction where public comes together in face-to-face situations such are plazas, squares, streets, parks, atria, beaches, but also airports, shopping malls, festival marketplaces and theme parks. The aggressive commercialization and privatization of the public realm that had occurred in the 1980s as a consequence of Thatcherism (in Europe) and Reaganism (in the United States) brought about the privatization of major state-owned enterprises in the areas of mass-transportation and mass media and communications. One could argue that not only have these developments redefined our understanding of public realm and our ability to shape it, moreover they have fundamentally re-mapped the very principle of civility. Consequently, the socio-economic framework of post-industrial capitalism has enabled a creation of hybrid forms of public space in which previously rigid relations between producers and consumers have been questioned, and in which the character of citizen participation is never certain. Towards the close of the Twentieth Century, public space has acquired a new symbolic dimension as it becomes seen by many as the last vestige of resistance against the aggressive processes of globalization and privatization of public resources. In that respect, an idealized operational definition of public space would define it on the tactical level as an environment designed to allow for [open and unrestricted] citizen participation [on equal footing] forms and practices of which have been defined by public law and policy as well as by the cultural, political and socio-economic milieu. On the strategic level, public space can be defined as a complex, dynamic, multi-dimensional system in action composed of constituents and stakeholders of all kinds (both producers and consumers) together with ensembles of social relationships and practices (formed by public policy, law, cultural patterns, values and beliefs, economic order, division of labor) as well as by material artifacts (buildings, greenery, cell phones, benches) and immaterial environmental stimuli (sound, smell, taste, light, color). We can also assume that people attend public spaces in order to satisfy their psychological, biological, emotional, social, economic or political needs-and-wants through socializing, shopping, commuting, self-realization or exchange. At the same time, many citizens have fears and concerns in relation to public space that may be related to the presence of others, lack of privacy, safety, comfort, choice, freedom of movement, desirable orientation, control, selection or overcrowding. A common set of normative characteristics that most public spaces share can be distinguished here in order to help develop a systematic understanding of public space, to establish a simple comparative framework, and in order to help develop a discourse on public space: ownership, modes and types of accessibility, degrees of enclosure, types and degrees of control, and its purpose.[24] In that respect, an interesting definition of public space is provided by the United Kingdom Parliament, House of Commons, and its Commission for Architecture and the Built Environment (CABE). They define public space as 'space that is normally accessible to the public and from which private ownership of land is excluded in the interest of a public good' (CABE 2002). In terms of accessibility, CABE's working definition of public space excludes space that is not accessible to the public at any time, but it does not require public access to be unlimited, that is public space should be normally but not always accessible to the public. In terms of the concept of public value, the definition also implies that some public benefit—not necessarily material—derives from public space, which means that there must be some social, environmental or even (actual or potential) economic value accruing to the public from the existence of public space. The difference between public space and open space in CABE's view is that open space can be privately-owned and can offer no, or very limited, access to the public. Some cities indeed accrue profits by renting out their public spaces: Washington D.C.'s Public Space Rental Act of October 1968 allows private property owners to lease public spaces that D.C. Public Space Committee determines are not required for use by the general public. The updated act of 1999 has the established public space rental fees of US$5.00 per square foot of public space used for unenclosed sidewalk cafes, and US$10.00 per square foot of public space used as an enclosed sidewalk cafe, while there is no charge for tables and chairs placed in public space as long as 'the general public is authorized the unrestricted use of such amenities'. The right to lease public space is granted only to applicants who clearly demonstrate that the primary purpose of the lease 'is for the public good rather than private gain.' (DC 1999)

In relation to the character and treatment of historical data related to the diachronic development of theme parks and public spaces, this book proposes that the rationale for both theme parks and public spaces emerges neither out of a singular culture nor out of a singular historical period. Unlike common approaches to the history of material form, the book does not trace back the historical trajectory of the theme park (neither public space) as material form (such a task would necessarily lead back only to Disneyland) because the main trust of the book is that both theme parks and public spaces are complex, dynamic systems in action composed of material forms as well as of immaterial stimuli, constituents of all kinds and their relationships. The book therefore traces a history of the inventions and applications, procedures and techniques, tendencies and ideas, forms and practices that have given both the theme park and public space concepts in the Twentieth Century. Historically speaking, their evolution has been diachronic rather than synchronic, ephemeral rather than transcendental, sporadic rather than linear and has usually unfolded over generations through repeated trial-and-error attempts. Such attempts have been proven effective and have been appropriated from a variety of past, historical experiences of different origins and could be related to the design methods, social engineering, communication and transportation techniques, the control of large crowds and other relevant issues. Each such historical configuration will be called a 'fragment', and such fragments will always be placed within their respective historical arrangements, that is to say, the systems of social relationships and that of urban spaces. A non-exhaustive continuum of fragments will be found in parallel with the main body of the text throughout the book. Just as I have argued earlier that, synchronically speaking, the process of totalization that brings theme parks, landscapes and public space into the same framework is not obvious through formal analogies but through the systematic ones, I will also argue that what brings contemporary theme parks and the fragments in this book into a common framework are not formal or morphological diachronic analogies but the systematic ones, those related to entertainment experience, economic framework, accessibility, control, and a variety of other relevant issues. Finally, the method by which fragments will be studied and their principles brought to bear upon the contemporary theme parks and public spaces is that of conduction.[25] The conductive logic is not native to literacy but it subsumes the modes of inference that have been formalized by the apparatus of literacy: induction, deduction and abduction (Ulmer 2003). Conductive inference operates by means of metaphor and thus the reader should not expect to find either the study of historical 'cases' or direct analogies between formal or aesthetic aspects of theme parks with those of the fragments studied. Thus, I will not abstract the rules out of fragments and use those to 'explain' the theme park or public space. Instead, the metaphoric terms will be juxtaposed, brought together so that they can be identified, contrasted or associated with each other within a new, emerging pattern. In fact, by using conduction as a mode of inference, I am trying to break the solidity of the common notion that theme park is a 'model' and discover patterns of relationships that would allow me to move heuristically.

Outline and Arrangement of the Book

The arrangement of the material that follows is a reflection of the belief that the only way to understand manifold processes outlined above is to expose the data that reveals not only the design aspect of theme parks and privatized urban public space, but also clearly presents evidence of their economic, political, cultural and social capacity. In order to facilitate further explication and understanding of the complexity of such a complex, dynamic system in action, the book will introduce two major domains of conceptualization and operation of theme parks: Themeparking and Themeing. Through the following chapters, the reader will encounter a plethora of minute detail, hundreds of specific practices, methods and procedures described together with their effects, each with its own logic of exposure. At times it may seem that the material will take its own course and lose the reader in too many details. Reasons for that are twofold. Firstly, I wanted each of the examples I discuss or document to have a voice of its own, and have attempted not to exercise excessive force in order to bring the material into my narrative. In other words, I attempted to enable each example to argue for itself, to expose its own argumentation. It is precisely for such reason that many parts of the book are free from my immediate critical reflection, because I tried to create a high degree of flexibility in my overall totalizing narrative. I believe this is a critical stance and will be discussed in the book's closing. Secondly, the experiential logic of reading this book is aimed at coaxing the reader towards an understanding of a profound complexity of the subject matter. My argument is that such a complexity has to be encountered face-to-face, and has to be fully experienced in its immense intricacies and totalizing convergences. It has been my belief that when the critical mass of the examples unearthed reaches the point of no return, the world itself opens up to an understanding that may potentially lead to action. There is no critical action, and no change in the world of total landscape, if there is no understanding of how that world works. In that respect, I could not have made the same argument with a third of the examples I use, and that is precisely where this book substantially differs from all other books on the subject matter.[26] Namely, in the way in which it attempts to construct a critical trajectory, not a position, in relation to its subject matter by exposing the production processes of the world it criticizes. At quite a few points the trajectory will leave the encyclopedic format and move deeply into specific cases (both diachronically and synchronically) in order to expose data and practices that will contribute to the overall understanding of the subject matter. The rationale for that is that power relationships at play in the production of total landscape are not always demonstrable across the scales; sometimes in smaller-scale projects it is hard to visualize their interplay. Thus, in many ways opportunistically, I dive into specifically giving examples in order to bring to the surface images of the seabed topography they produce. It also has to be noted, as a way of preparing the reader for what is to come, that some of the examples I discuss in the book have indeed brought both economic and social well being to their communities. Therefore, the world I will attempt to portray here is neither static nor black-and-white.

Themeparking, discussed in Chapter 2, is a framework commonly referred to as geo-political or in military terminology referred to as strategic. It is a 'panoramic view', to employ de Certeau's term (Certeau 1984), a view concerned with geo-political goals and socio-economic strategies and the design of complex strategic systems on either regional, national or global scale or all thereby simultaneously. Since themeparking reveals the symbiosis of strategic political and economic decision-making (at the macro level) that has appropriated both space and methods previously belonging to the military realm (the defense), this chapter will discuss the intersections of military, planning, geographic and economic (location) theories. Themeparking attempts to delineate the convergence of the realm of media with the material world of theme parks aimed at the socio-cultural fabrication of consumers's desires and the construction of routes that facilitate its fulfillment. It also discusses the 'engineering of leisure', a professional discourse on leisure that determines normative procedures that organize circulation of people to theme park locations to be consumed as spaces of leisure and amusement. In that respect, Themeparking will initially define the notion of 'trade theater' and then discuss strategically important input variables such are demographic data, traffic networks and accessibility, site selection, attendance projections, theme and concept developments, marketing and branding, tourist arrangements, and finally cultural patterns that also greatly determine strategic decision-making within the domain of themeparking.

Themeparking is extremely marketing sensitive because one of the key concepts within total landscape directly relevant to marketing is the dissolution of the boundaries between the world of media and the material environments of theme parks. In fact, in many ways it is through the process of marketing that the two are brought together into an inseparable whole. Since boundaries of thematic environments are no longer defined only by their geographic locales but also by their media presence, mostly on television, the concept known as 'marketing synergy' enables theme parks to promote movies, movies to promote merchandise and merchandise to promote theme parks so that cycles of synergetic marketing expand endlessly into entertainment space. As a consequence, theme parks are used as backdrops for a variety of television programs, movies, sport competitions, conventions and convention-related television broadcasting, and at the same time the confluence and interdependence of theme park industry, the airline industry, the cruise industry, the railway industry, the car rental business, drivers associations, the hotel industry, the tourist industry, telephone and communication companies, the credit card industry, incentive travel programs and many other interests is increasing exponentially with the consolidation of the theme park industry and as themeparking grows in scale. These developments will be discussed also in relation to the fabrication of thematic frameworks within themeparking that relies on the synergy of cultural, political and socio-economic factors that are inseparable in the contemporary world of media and synergetic marketing controlled by multinational entertainment and media corporations.

The most complex group of input variables within the themeparking equation are those that establish the relationships between cultural references and thematic frameworks. Some common ways of fabricating bridges between cultural contexts and thematic frameworks will be discussed. This plays directly into the discussion of categorizing theme parks in terms of the scale of operations involved in their design, construction, and operation. Besides the cultural narratives they employ and the complexity of their thematic frameworks, expressions of theme park's complexity can be read by understanding levels of investment, target populations analysis, anticipated and realized volumes of attendance, and so on. In relation to the above, the distinction will be made between regional theme parks, networks or regional theme parks, and global theme parks, and I will subsequently also discuss specific examples. A true systematic approach to the design of theme parks configures both themeparking and themeing simultaneously by taking into account complex variables related to the design of infrastructure, the design of the physical facility, visitors's experience, marketing, operations and management and so on. All aspects of theme park design are heavily interdependent and can only be successfully designed and operated if the entire ensemble outlined above is brought into the condition of absolute perfection that reduces and progressively eliminates all uncertainty until the synergetic accumulation of forces in the theater clearly exhibits a desirable totalizing configuration.

Themeing, discussed in Chapter 3, begins by delineating two ideas crucial for bridging the domains of Themeparking and Themeing: first, the idea that theme park as a material environment represents an extension of the public realm of television, advertising, films, retail and mass-tourism; and second, that for such an extension to work a homogeneous human experience had to be fabricated across multiple scales. The chapter will discuss ways in which Walt Disney created an unknown fusion of the previously entirely separate domains of human experience. If the task of themeparking is to identify all variables in a complex theme park equation and chart their interrelationships, the task of themeing is then to systematically reduce the number of variables in the theater of operations until key variables are identified, until final objectives of the environment are agreed upon, and finally until only one of many possible alternative designs is identified and brought into a desirable configuration. In that sense, themeing symbolically, materially and logistically sustains trade-theater objectives established at the strategic level and sets in motion a frictionless procession of tourists through predetermined 'spending routes'. The key to themeing is the understanding that designing assumes not only the configuration of material aspects of environment and its operational logic, but a multitude of environmental clues and stimuli that affect the experience of visitors: themeing is *de facto* a deliberate attempt at designing an environment configured to produce specific behavioral outcomes in visitors. The design of theme park's layout, phone-answering system, web site, marketing campaign, light fixtures, transportation system, operational budget or staffing scheme are all acts of designing that in different ways contribute to the total quality of user experience and theme park's overall economic performance.

The theme park environment as a whole will be assumed to operate as 'theater of operations' (TOP). TOP is composed of four basic elements of the theme park environment: the internal pattern, the harlequin dress, sensory stimuli, and scores. Within the environmental system established by these four elements, TOP is also configured through a complex arrangement of individual environmental modules such are food outlets, retail outlets, rides, attractions, storage spaces, or offices. Clusters of such modules unified by a concept will be called 'theatra'; for instance, Adventureland is a typical example of a theatron. Themeing thus produces the theme park environment by defining material attributes of the environment (scale, color, layout, costumes), all sensory environmental stimuli (visual, aural, tactile, olfactory), commodities sold (arts and crafts, food, souvenirs) and the practices of all constituents (both on frontstage and backstage). On the operational level, themeing is concerned with the maneuver and support of field operations that involve a web of constituents including visitors, employees, managers, or suppliers in complex operations such are daily staffing, supply, maintenance or control.

The product of the parallel workings of themeparking and themeing is what I will call 'total environmental image'. Theme park environments are deliberately designed to operate on the subliminal level, affecting visitors's emotional states and inducing high affective and low cognitive involvement with the environment. The 'total experi-

ence' of an environment is always the result of a composite of layered clues, a combination of cognitive and emotional processing. Cognitive processing assigns meaning, whereas affective processing assigns values to our experiences of the environment. Successfully designed interplay of the above clues facilitates perception of the theme park environment as an interrelated, singular image. An environmental image is also an accumulated, layered impression that combines influences generated by the media world with those related to the theme park visit. I will employ the term 'environment' to represent the immense complexity of such efforts and the multidimensionality of human experience in the man-made world. It will be argued that theme park environment commonly denotes the totality of circumstances, objects and conditions within which an individual or an artifice is embedded, and the combination of complex external and internal conditions that affect and influence its experience and behavior. The experience of visitors is directly linked to the evaluation of the theme park environment by two variables: how frequently people visit and how long they stay, two variables undeviatingly linked to how much they spend ('dollar volume').

What *de facto* puts the entire theme park apparatus in motion on the daily basis are scores that connect different constitutive elements of the environment into a coherent arrangement of forces in the theater of operations. The score takes into account people, space, time and their mutual interrelations and configures them through a chain of pseudo events, fabricated and heavily scripted performances that occur within pre-determined time-frames and pre-programmed 'scenes'. Themeing will discuss the rationale for the fabrication of pseudo-events and ways of doing it, including the Rent-an-Event companies that mass produce a variety of performances including wedding ceremonies. Together with pseudo-events, the chapter will close by discussing ways in which theme parks operate as environmental labs and deliberately manipulate sensory clues in order to influence the behavioral responses of visitors. The speculative employment of visual, tactile, aural and olfactory environmental stimuli is also aimed at affecting visitors on the visceral level, much before it can be cognitively interpreted. I will discuss the use of fragrances through mechanisms such is the 'affect infusion model,' and also sound patterns as an important aspect of environmental design in terms of stimulating visitors's affiliative behavior in theme parks. Successful, cumulative layering of emotional and functional environmental clues facilitates the creation of desirable total experiences in visitors, and it directly translates into the creation of optimal environmental images, moods, and traits.

Chapter 4, Departing, discusses departures from the standard theme park formula. The most common departures from the theme park are Retail Entertainment Centers, a combination of retail shopping and themed entertainment in a themed, gated, sometimes indoor environment. The chapter will discuss a few examples, including the largest REC of all: Las Vegas. In 1972, Tomas Maldonado noted that Las Vegas is 'the final product—one might even call it almost perfect of its kind—of more than half a century of masked manipulatory violence, directed toward the formation of an apparently free and playful urban environment.' (Maldonado 1972) Another noted type of departure are those locally-bound, regional theme parks that focus exclusively on cultural, historic or geographically defined themes such are ethnographic and heritage centers, or theme parks promoting particular religious world-views. The chapter discusses the construction of restoration villages and open-air architectural museums such are the Polynesian Cultural Center, Shikoku Mura, Window on China, The Dracula Land, and Taiwan Folk Village. Since the mid-1980s, a stream of religious theme parks have been proposed and constructed: the chapter will discuss Heritage USA, the Holy Land Experience, Aparecida, and the Krishna-Lila theme park constructed as 'a spiritual Disneyland' to accommodate a newly formed township for families that relocated to Vrindavan 'for the purpose of either retirement or to do service in the Holy Dhama'.

The second type of common departure is when such environments are turned into living-history theme parks, where a specific historical moment, or religious setting, is carefully detailed and preserved for the enjoyment of visitors and often permanent residents alike. The book places such nostalgic and profitable drives into a historical perspective by discussing Dreamland, Coney Island, Henry Ford's Greenfield Village, and Colonial Williamsburg, Virginia, all virtual, nostalgic, fictional communities where people have inhabited an idealized, yet personal vision of the past. Similar drives have motivated many developers and entrepreneurs to develop contemporary living theme parks, such as the one based on the ex-East Germany as a thematic framework proposed in Prenden, twenty miles north of Berlin. Subsequently, the chapter discusses Huis Ten Bosch and Celebration as ideal examples of the escalating process of fabricating desires for living and working within the strict boundaries of theme park territories. Celebration is initially discussed within Walt Disney's ideas related to the 'city-making', and then in more detail in relation to its rationale and design.

The main emphasis in Chapter 4 is placed on discussing Huis Ten Bosch. Following the method established in Chapters 2 and 3, the discussion of Huis Ten Bosch will be framed through Themeparking and Themeing. By its size and capital budget, Huis Ten Bosch (HTB) is one of the largest private facilities ever built in Japan. The discussion places HTB within the system of urban spaces and that of social relationships in Japan. It also discusses the historical trajectory of HTB's invention: the origin of its thematic envelope and the reasoning behind its development and promotion. Political and economic factors that underlie its conceptualization will be discussed in relation to its trade theater, the regional and national traffic infrastructure, and both the macro- and micro-economic impact that HTB had in the region. In order to make HTB's impact on the region comprehensible, I will form a comparative framework between data from its first year of operation (the period between 1992–93) with the trends established at the peak of its economic performance (1996–97). The data for 1992–93 also include the impact that had occurred during the construction process that had taken place in the period from 1989–92. Socio-economic statistics clearly show the production capacity of the theme park apparatus: HTB has significantly improved the socio-economic environment not only in terms of the number of tourists and the level of expenditure in the area, but also in terms of other significant socio-economic factors such are employment, regional and national migrations, restructuring of the work force, tax revenues, and the supporting service industry it had generated.

With respect to the themeing of HTB, the chapter initially focuses on the displacement of visitors by the force of an alien visual and spatial ordering system, and the impact of an 'exotic' narrative theme. This clear semiotic distinction from the environment, enhanced by the mechanisms of social displacement, is maintained throughout the theater of operations and organized into eight principal theatra: Entrance theatron, Kinderdijk theatron, Mauruts square theatron, Nassau square theatron, Alexander square theatron, World Bazaar theatron, Utrecht theatron, and Palace theatron. Theatra are linked into a chain of environmental units by an intriguing example of the loop-plan, together with bridges and canals. Each theatron is then discussed in terms of its place within the loop pattern, its harlequin dress, sensory stimuli employed, and its role in the overall score. Each theatron is the site for a series of pseudo-events whose space and time of occurrence are strictly determined by the master score. From the nature of pseudo-events and socio-cultural processes of their production, the discussion moves towards the instrumental role of pseudo-events in organizing the spatio-temporal consumption of HTB, and in enhancing the control over its proper. Furthermore, the convergence of the 'event-schedule' with the three other elements of the theater of operations (internal pattern, harlequin dress, and sensory stimuli) is also discussed in relation to HTB Company's dis

tinctions between 'software' (event programming) and 'hardware' (physical planning) aspects of the theme park apparatus.

HTB provides a desirable introduction into the discussion of dialectic relationship between theme parks and cities because it was designed as a theme-park-town to be initially inhabited by 30 000 permanent residents. Due to economic recession and financial problems including undercapitalization, HTB is today inhabited by about 750 people living in Huis Ten Bosch Hills. These issues are discussed as a way of closing the discussion of theme parks and opening the discussion on the specific type of departure from the conventional theme park formula to what is usually referred to as the imposition of 'the theme park model' onto the existing urban fabric, that is the process of expansion of the theme park apparatus beyond the strict boundaries of theme parks as a vehicle for the production of total landscape.

Chapter 5, Becoming, thus brings the discussion to a dialectic relationship between theme parks and cities, and to the ways in which the two merge into a generation of conceptual hybrids. It discusses the imposition of 'the theme park model' upon urban, public spaces across the world, and the resulting production of PROPAST: privately-owned publicly-accessible space typically organized around a specific theme, the archetypal manifestation of total landscape in urban public space. I will employ the metaphor of 'healing' in order to speculate on what may happen when the 'theme park model' is employed towards the 'healing' of urban, public space. I will also claim that, in order to properly understand and frame urban, public space as a public resource, a systematic understanding of both the external variables and its complex innerworkings is a must. I show that public agencies, elected public officials, and promoters of public space commonly see and present isolated sites and sporadic manifestations of public space and provide simplistic schemes for their (re)design. Even when they understand public space holistically they often come to predictable 'solutions' that challenge the idea of public space as a public good. As a result, public space is compartmentalized, individualized, and privatized through the 'rhetoric of therapy'. Such a 'therapeutic ethos' of total landscape prefers varied forms of private ownership and management, some of which will be discussed in detail in this chapter (such are the public-private partnerships). It will be also argued that just like Henry Ford had set standards of assembly-line based industrial production, Walt Disney had set standards for the production of 'public experience' enveloped in the therapeutic, family-value themed narratives.

PROPAST is typically produced through a mechanism called Urban Entertainment Project, that has been naturalized as the way to 'revitalize problematic' urban areas. Most revitalization projects revolve around a flagship project such as waterfronts, sports arenas, museums or entertainment districts, including Walt Disney Co.'s projects for the transformation of 42nd Street in New York City. In many ways, PROPAST is *de facto* a theater of operations and similarly to theme park it is woven into the framework of total landscape by the interlocking of the domains of media with that of material environment, by the elimination and denial of social conflict through private management and private security forces, by consensus entertainments, and other characteristics. Some forms of public-private partnerships will be discussed, such as Business Improvement Districts (BID), and more specifically the Bryant Park BID in New York City as a typical example. The other form of privatization discussed is the inauguration of privately owned public spaces by the New York City in 1961, with the adoption of a new zoning resolution that had enabled the city to trade off with developers by offering extra floor area bonuses to developers willing to construct open spaces for public use designed by following the Zoning Resolution standards. Other forms of developing PROPAST will also be discussed, such as Times Square in New York City or the Japanese examples like Festival Gate in Osaka and Canal City in Fukuoka. All of them came into being through the rhetoric of therapy and healing.

Like theme parks, PROPAST is also extremely marketing sensitive. Many PROPAST are symbolic projects linked into an intricate web of cross-marketing schemes and, just as theme parks, they are not core-generating revenues but a vehicle for diversifying corporate portfolios. What puts the PROPAST apparatus in motion are scores, by effectively connecting different constitutive elements of the environment into a coherent arrangement of forces within the theater of operations. Scores determine, among other characteristics, the character of pseudo-events, their environmental disposition, the time of occurrence and duration, frequency, number of performers, and the way they interact with tourists. Urban tourism is the single largest source of revenue for most PROPAST developers. Realistic challenges that cities encounter in face of urban tourism, such the problem of controlling an escalating influx of tourists that goes beyond the carrying capacity of historic urban centers, has in many cities been resolved by mechanisms that move the experience of urban public space closer to total landscape. Tourist cards, explicit and strict behavior codes, way-finding systems that disperse the urban tourist to highly predetermined locations, and urban safaris are just some ways in which urban communities across the world strive to find sources of economic revitalization within the framework of competitive urbanism. Economic benefit of all the above is questionable to all but PROPAST developers. In fact, the data shows that many such 'healing' projects usually suffer from profit-leakage and have a negative sum economic effect on the micro-economic environment. Thousands of small business and individuals are evacuating areas immediately surrounding emerging PROPAST in search of a more affordable place to live and do business. Finally, as with the theme park industry, when the urban entertainment industry reaches the point of maturation, the PROPAST market will be consolidated by multinational media and entertainment conglomerates buying out smaller property owners, such are varied redevelopment corporations and revitalization agencies. In that respect, the door is currently wide open to those who would have an interest in potentially owning entire cities.

In its concluding part, Chapter 5 will discuss a common notion that PROPASt operates as a behavioral laboratory and exhibits restrictive interest in human behavior as well as a restrictive menu of possibilities for human interaction. That has a direct effect on physical, visual, social, and psychological accessibility. But the control exercised in theme parks and PROPASt cannot be placed on entirely different grounds from the control exercised in the society as a whole, where varied policies of exclusion are the norm. In that sense, PROPASt offers a vision of civility bounded by consumption (Zukin 1995: 55), and protected by gates, entrance-fees and private security forces in an aggressive attempt at combining general access with social control. A boom in the number of private security forces in the 1990s has been followed by the sophistication of surveillance technology and a parallel erosion of public authority. Partnerships between state police and private security agencies have now grown into a security industrial complex that commodifies 'security' in the name of public safety (Jennings 2005). The use of biometric technology in all this has marked a quantum leap in the convergence of surveillance technology, laws that enable fast data collection and analysis, and dehumanization of data, all inevitably leading towards a 'total information convergence' in all aspects of contemporary life (O'Harrow 2005). Given that the authority of the security apparatus over public spaces and public life is growing exponentially, the above are terrifying developments that, without doubt, point at the militarization of public life through PROPASt. Finally, Becoming addresses the question of representation of 'desirable urbanity' across scales that can be identified in the ways in which PROPASt, public art, galleries, museums, sport halls, theaters are all linked in a never-before-experienced ways in terms of the aestheticized urban public experience. Dimensions of human experience in the public space have been radically remapped as PROPASt fabricates notions of new civility by spatializing new propositions for civic life and configuring them into a web of social relationships and processes, which are then represented by public art, mass media, edutainment and other practices that reconfigure the cognitive, perceptual and lived aspects of civic life.

NOTES

1. For an interesting discussion of the same statistical data see Drew 1998.

2. It goes without saying that this most accurately applies to the leading economies, namely to the United States, Japan (as well as emerging Asian economies), and the European Union.

3. In terms of the meaning of the term 'artificial' I subscribe to Herbert Simon's definition by which he distinguishes 'artificial' from 'natural' by the fact that artificial is 'man-made', and also by the following four characteristics: artificial is synthesized (forethought); artificial may imitate appearances of natural things; artificial can be characterized in terms of function, goals, and adaptation; and, artificial is always discussed in terms of imperatives as well as descriptives (Simon 1969: 55–83).

4. For a detailed analysis of how each of the four principles applies to Walt Disney theme parks see Alan Bryman's analysis (Bryman 1999).

5. This approach, due to its focus on self-realization, results in studies that stand for a generalized experience of the human subject and the way in which theme park environment is 'consumed'. One such study is Mark Gottdiener's *The Theming of America* that understands the proliferation of themed environments as a result of corporate strategies aimed at finding new ways for the realization of capital through consumption (Gottdiener 1997).

6. For Jackson, the opposite of garden is wilderness (Jackson 1980).

7. *An Etymological Dictionary of the English Language.* (1884) Oxford: Oxford University Press: 422.

8. *The Oxford Dictionary of English Etymology.* (1966) Oxford: Oxford University Press: 652.

9. Until the Eleventh Century Southern Italian (Sicilian) gardens and parks have been directly inspired by Arab principles although much of the Eastern influences came through the Greeks (Lasdun 1991: 1–20). Direct Arab influences were certainly a consequence of the Arab conquest of Sicily as well. In the Eleventh Century Normans occupied Sicily and found there much of the parks and pleasure gardens that Arabs had left behind. It is through Norman's conquest of Sicily that Western and Northern Europe learned about classical and Islamic gardening, and the experience they acquired has slowly penetrated through Europe. Returning to England, Normans also became familiar with French gardens and parks, simple enclosures at the time, meant to be distinguished from forests and surrounding fields. They inherited the French word *parc* that has been in use in France since the Eleventh Century and has also influenced the formation of the English word *park* in the Thirteenth Century. There are how-ever other hypotheses for the origin of this word: one claims that *park* is a contraction of the Middle English word *parrok* (1200 A.D.–1500 A.D.) which comes from the Old English word *pearroc* (the Native-English in its earliest form). (Sources: *An Etymological Dictionary of the English Language.* (1884) Oxford: Oxford University Press: 422 and Lasdun 1991: 1–20).

10. *An Etymological Dictionary of the English Language.* (1884) Oxford: Oxford University Press: 635.

11. *Origins: A Short Etymological Dictionary of Modern English.* (1979) London: Routledge & Kegan Paul: 711.

12. Ayto, J. (1990) *Dictionary of Word Origins.* London: Bloomsbury Publishing Ltd.: 527.

13. *Ibid.*

14. *Longman Register of New Words.* (1989) London: Longman Group UK: 382.

15. *Oxford Dictionary of New Words.* (1991) Oxford: Oxford University Press: 287.

16. *Chambers English Dictionary.* (1988) London: W&L Chambers Ltd.: 1523.

17. *An Etymological Dictionary of the English Language.* (1884) Oxford: Oxford University Press: 565.

18. *Ibid.*

19. *In The Fall of Public Man* of 1977 Richard Sennett gives a precise account on the dialectic development of terms 'public' and 'private' (Sennett 1977: 3–27).

20. *Chambers English Dictionary.* (1988) London: W&L Chambers Ltd.: 1234.

21. The discussion here in large part follows Lefebvre's account on the history of space (Lefebvre 1991: 1–9).

22. Foucault had further delineated the history of space into three stages: the space of 'localizations' (Middle Ages), the space of 'extension' (post-Galileo), and the space of 'arrangements' (Twentieth Century) (Foucault 1985).

23. These categories were inspired in part by George Teyssot's attempt to summarize research programs that have been carried out in 1990s regarding general attitudes towards urban public parks (Teyssot 1991: 21).

24. The five categories are a reworking of the four categories employed by Charles Goodsell in order to distinguish civic space 'from other kinds of architectural space' (Goodsell 1988: 10).

25. I am following here the writings and teaching of Gregory L. Ulmer who uses the conductive inferences to construct his notion of the apparatus of Electracy. Within Electracy conduction is the dominant mode of inference that subsumes induction, deduction and abduction as modes of inference formalized by the apparatus of literacy (Ulmer 2003).

26. A book based on the implicitly similar idea is Steven Fjellman's *Vinyl Leaves: Walt Disney World and America* (Fjellman 1992).

THEMEPARKING

Sir John Grugeon, an energetic Englishman, has just toured u.s. theme parks for 10 days to mine ideas for [...] turning waste lands into profitable, publicity-generating theme parks on the model of Disney World and other American theme parks [...] for the first international garden festival ever staged in Britain, on 250 acres of long-abandoned dock yards in Liverpool, between April and October 1984. The Queen is expected to attend. Sir John, festival director, expects 3 million visitors. Eighteen countries, ranging from Italy to Japan, have already agreed to create various types of display gardens. In his U.S. tour, Sir John said he learned the importance of high-quality souvenirs, efficient car parking and transport from parking lots to exhibition sites, strict cleanliness and hygiene, and smiling hotel-staff that put the tourist first. (WILLIS 1982: 12)

~~~~~~~~~~~~~~~~~~~~~~~~~~~~~~~~~~~~~~~
ST. JAMES PARK
~~~~~~~~~~~~~~~~~~~~~~~~~~~~~~~~~~~~~~~

In 1660, Charles II invited Le Nôtre to redesign the St. James's park as a forum, a 'theater of politics and power' meant to gather the political and noble elite (Lasdun 1991: 74–76). He wanted the park to become a public meeting place by means of which Charles II wanted to meet the new 'social subject' and establish control over it in order to re-establish the power of monarchy. Long, shady promenades (also called 'parades') were new architectural devices that took into account new social rituals and placed them in the beautiful scenery that formed the visual background for this social intercourse. In 1661, Charles II opened St. James's Park to the public and it is at this point, for the first time, that the word 'park' came to mean an enclosed, ornamentally landscaped tract of land for public use. The term 'public', however, signified the 'polite society'. Organized refreshments, places designed for sports and games, together with exotic birds and animals formed a stage-set that was colloquially defined through the new name, the Mall, and the time-denominator: *park-time*. These events had inspired private developers to capitalize on the new formula and commercial pleasure gardens and parks, such as Vauxhall Gardens, began appearing in England in the late 1660s. St. James's Park was redesigned in the Eighteenth Century and following the taste of the period, many pavilions and walks were added. As Lasdun noted, the hours of promenade had been established to midday until 2 P.M., and at 7 P.M. (Lasdun 1991: 76). In the Nineteenth Century, park-time moved to 4–5 P.M. and 8–9 P.M.

The Panoramic View

It is not an exaggeration to claim, as Paul McCracken Chairman of Silicon Graphics did in a Business Week interview, that 'the entertainment industry is now the driving force for new technology, as defense used to be.' (BW 1994) As we enter the Twenty-First Century, it would be more precise to claim that the differences between the way the entertainment industry and the military-industrial complex drive the development of new technology is that of degree rather than of kind. It would indeed be very hard to draw a precise line indicating the end of the influence of the former and the beginning of the influence of the latter, as it would be to draw a line demarcating the boundaries of state engagement, venture capital, private investments and public interest in both. The same can be said in relation to 'entertainment space' and total landscape, as all the above interests have high stakes in its design and production. As indicated in the previous chapter, in a world in which entertainment has become a major form of public discourse and the dominant model of cultural production, it is difficult to define such an overwhelming category as entertainment space. Provisionally, it could be defined as a product of the relations of socioeconomic production characteristic of total landscape whose *modus operandi* is entertainment. The apparently entertaining aspects of ontological hybridity between stealth fighters, hi-tech boots, high-definition television and film, ride simulators, virtual reality, roller coasters, GPS devices, mobile phones, theme parks and other such artifacts further points to a never-before experienced condition in which differences between entertainment space and military space have been blurred, or in a most desirable scenario have been layered upon each other to the point of no recognition. Numerous writers have pointed to the expansion and appropriation of the previously military realm of operation by the entertainment and media industry and the consequent similarities between the military space and entertainment space, among them Marshall McLuhan (McLuhan and Powers 1989), Guy Debord (Debord 1983), Henri Lefebvre (Lefebvre 1991), Michel de Certeau (de Certeau 1986), Paul Virilio (Virilio 1989, 1994),

Neil Postman (Postman 1992) and Michel Foucault (Foucault 1977) to name but a few. Specifically, since Paul Virilio's *Bunker Archeology* (Virilio 1994) and *War and Cinema* (Virilio 1989), the interpretation of advanced technology in the context of its original military application has been frequent, particularly in relation to the interpretation and analysis of media technology. If, as Paul Virilio has brilliantly shown, fortifications and bunkers were once upon the time expressions of the military understanding of territory, time and subsequently of the concept of 'military space', what are the expressions of the concept of entertainment space today and of its equally militant understanding of space and time?

As the military focus has since World War II moved to outer space, military strategies for defining and controlling 'territory, communication and speed' have been appropriated by political and commercial daily interests. Moreover, it could be argued that the void caused by this displacement of military interest and operations has *de facto* enabled and conditioned the total landscape within which the symbiosis of governmental and commercial interests play a major role in producing entertainment space. Within such a condition, parallels between military space and entertainment space are unavoidable. The major premise we will reintroduce here (from Chapter 1) is that total landscape is, as a condition, enabled by the tripartite structure that represents the above concerns: firstly, the production of entertainment space within the realm of the cognitive by media and entertainment industry as well as by state laws and regulations (normative expectation, fabrication of desires, timetables as well as labor divisions, maps, cartography, marketing, branding, economic rationale); secondly, the production of entertainment space by the establishment of new material infrastructure and also by the appropriation and use of the existing infrastructure: together with the traffic infrastructure, engineering of leisure manages the flow of people to and from constructed locations that are consumed as prescribed by the rationale of total landscape; and finally, the production of entertain-

ment space by the establishment and production of locations, target destinations such as theme parks, where one encounters total landscape 'in flesh'. These three realms always develop simultaneously, as such is the logic of entertainment space, although they have not always been homogeneous in appearance. As indicated in the first chapter, in order to facilitate further explication and understanding of the complexity of such a multi-dimensional system in action, I introduced two domains called Themeparking and Themeing. A true systematic approach to the design of theme parks configures both Themeparking and Themeing simultaneously, meaning it simultaneously takes into account complex variables related to the design of infrastructure, the design of the physical facility, visitors's experience, marketing, operations, management and so on. All aspects of theme park design are heavily interdependent and can only be successfully designed and operated if the entire ensemble outlined above is brought into the condition of absolute perfection that reduces and progressively eliminates all uncertainty until the synergetic accumulation of forces in the theater clearly exhibits a desirable totalizing configuration.

Themeparking implies the level of understanding and decision making that is commonly referred to as 'geo-political' (Certeau 1984). It is a 'panoramic view' to employ de Certeau's term, a view concerned with geo-political goals and socio-economic strategies, and the design of complex strategic systems on either regional, national or global scale or all thereby simultaneously. Since Themeparking reveals the symbiosis of strategic political and economic decision-making (at the macro level) that has, as we have indicated earlier, appropriated both the space and methods previously belonging to the military realm (the defense), we will discuss in what follows the intersections of military, planning, geographic and economic (location) theories. On its most basic level, military theory would define Themeparking as the strategic realm (O'Sullivan and Miller 1983: 8). In terms of economic theory, Themeparking operates on the macro economic scale that customarily takes into account the spatial variations of production, distribution and consumption (Themeparking is not commonly concerned with microeconomics although HTB provides a different example). Planning theory has historically been inseparable from military theory, as it is today in relation to contemporary economic theories and practices; for instance, both utilize the intelligence previously restrictive to the military discourse on geo-politics (such as geo-political maps, detailed data on national and global traffic/transportation infrastructures and detailed demographic and cartographic data). Besides, this chapter will also discuss socio-cultural mechanisms (of attendance for example) that negotiate the meaning and role of theme parks and entertainment space within any given socio-economic and political realm.

Breaking points in the overall complexity of themeparking were certainly the World Wars, and these coincided with the shift from an essentially two-dimensional military investment into the notion of 'territory' ('field') to a three-dimensional notion of 'space' (volume) and later in a multi-dimensional notion of 'theater' ('theater of war'). One can indeed trace the production of entertainment space and the positioning of amusement installations before the Nineteenth Century by looking at the relationship between the military and political systems that had in most cases defined planning principles, and socio-economic systems that had in most cases reflected religious beliefs. For example, the Seventeenth Century public walks in Europe were rendered possible by the organization of national territories and defense systems, a process that had generated clusters of attractions outside the medieval walls of Paris. Numerous attractions offered the city crowds modes and types of entertainment that were otherwise prosecuted within the city walls, due to a void caused by the move of the defense away from medieval fortifications and city walls to the boundaries of newly formed national territory. As a result, the territory outside the city walls was in a different juridical realm not yet properly defined and understood, and therefore out of the reach of political and religious clerks who demanded religious purity in the city. The same practice was known in England and had been utilized for medieval fairs, such as Bartholomew's Fair. Pleasure Gardens such as Vauxhall also functioned as a mass escape for the population of large cities in permanent need of healthy recreation, but they already relied on the means of public transportation (railway) that was constructed in order to facilitate defense needs in the first place. The occasion of the first Great Exhibition held in Crystal Palace in 1851 gave rise to a paradigmatic practice, not as much in its original setting in London as it was in its second and final setting at Sydenham. Sydenham was the first modern large-scale private investment in an entertainment destination, made possible by a homogenization and privatization of political and economic interests obvious also through the use of railway network with the aim of facilitating the rush of urban population out of London for 'health and educational purposes', and thereby realizing massive profits.

It was not coincidental that levels of complexity changed with Sydenham, following the developments in military theory and practice in the late Nineteenth Century. Sydenham signifies the move from 'territory' to 'space' and from 'visibility' to 'accessibility'. In the pre-Sydenham times, the military systems and weaponry demanded visibility in order to be effective, and military theory reflected such technological and technical (also practical) concerns: we thus had the relationships embedded in the military notion of 'territory' and in the geographical arrangement of forces that can be described in terms of three fundamental, two-dimensional formations: line, column and square (Hart 1954: 52). The understanding here was two-dimensional and the essential problems underlying this thinking were of visual nature. Sydenham marked a breakthrough also because it moved the discourse into the realm of the abstract, mathematical, logical and above all Cartesian, both in the realm of cognitive (maps, timetables) and in the realm of perceived (significant distances, railway traveling). The military thinking of the period as well as military practice moved beyond visibility to include the nexus of concerns including mobility, timetables, accessibility and probability (Peltier 1966: 162). These introduced a new ensemble of relationships by treating the interaction system as a field, and thus patterns of inter-action as a field phenomena (rather than as a point or place phenom-ena) that can be pictured as a set of vectors within an arrangement that has the map as its basic format (O'Sullivan and Miller 1983: 81). Since 'vectors have no face' and since military theory implies that there is no objective without an object, an objectification of 'public' and its institutionalization as an economic and political object had through modernization preceded these events. One could thus argue that the modern entertainment space, as well as entertainment loca-tions within it, are represented as much by the modern traffic net-works as they are by maps and timetables that assign entertainment and other programs to specific space-time locales. The notion of 'timing' and 'timetables' were derived from probability considerations and from the military requirement for coordinated action. They relate to the estimate of time that should be allowed for the probable and unforeseen events so that a coordinated group action can unfold without friction. It consequently applies to the development of a real-istic schedule of flow, movement and other activities in which initial and terminal locations, accessibility and resource-values play impor-tant roles (Peltier 1966: 165). Such destination-oriented planning reduces space to its temporal dimension by taking into account only the time involved in crossing certain spatial distance and arriving to the destination. The speed of movement plays a pivotal role and rail-way transport was instrumental in that respect. The production of emerging entertainment space thus appeared as a balance between two essentially military concerns: 'the path of minimum time' that puts pressure on the speed of movement as it aims at reducing travel-time rather than distances, and 'the path of optimum time' that would maximize economic efficiency of such a movement through the emerging entertainment space (Williams 1994).

Maps appear as signs of such modernizing procedures as well as of modern entertainment and traveling practices: first commercial maps appeared on the occasion of the Great Exhibition in 1851 together with Thomas Cook, the first professional tourist agency that began facilitating adequate traveling practices. Since military activities require sophisticated access to topographic information in a variety of forms, military maps have to be properly detailed, precise, concise and ready to be acted upon. For military purposes, topographic map-ping is combined with the so-called 'cultural detail' that gives an officer more precise idea on the nature, routes to use in troop move-ment, the demographic data such is size and distribution of popula-tion, landmarks, cultural symbols and so on. The world-view of the late Nineteenth Century and early Twentieth Century officer was indeed framed by such a map and by the landscape he saw before him and acted upon (Dorling and Fairbairn 1997: 90). Although mili-tary maps had to be abstracted before being offered to mass audi-ences for the purpose of regulating their traveling practices, the prin-ciple remained the same: tourist maps of the period contained a com-bination of topographic elements and cultural detail. For instance, the official London map produced in 1851 renders topographic ele-ments, the network of street and buildings, railways lines and stops as well as landmarks and cultural symbols: Crystal Palace appears as an out-of-scale perspective rendering that clearly stands out on the map's otherwise flat surface.

The creation of first amusement parks in the United States and Japan went through similar processes. In the mid-1800s, rapid industrial-ization, urbanization and the defense strategies gave rise to contem-porary transportation networks, as well as both public and private transportation companies. Although weekdays kept electric trolleys and railway busy, transportation companies searched for ways to stimulate traveling and commuting during holidays and weekends. This effort resulted in the creation of the first amusement parks typically built at the end of trolley and railway lines. The illustrative

example to parallel Sydenham is that of Coney Island. Coney Island began as a leisure-destination targeting the population of New York City. Leisure seekers initially walked over the bridge built by the Coney Island Bridge Co. in 1823 in order to reach Coney on the other side of the channel, a practice that required significant efforts which eliminated Coney Island's mass impact. In 1865, the first railroad crossed the bridge and reached the island, bringing in thousands of people during weekends and holidays. This event enabled the beginning of Coney Island's transformation into a large entertainment environment developed by a variety of private investors and divided into smaller contiguous units. The development process culminated with the con-

struction of the Brooklyn Bridge in 1883. This was thus a threefold relationship: on the one hand it made Coney Island a rapidly and successfully developed amusement park and a precious leisure-destination for New Yorkers in search of recreation and fresh air; it also multiplied the capacities of transportation infrastructure bringing in enormous profits to privately owned transportation companies; and finally it benefited the state, not only by allowing the labor force to recuperate and therefore to renew the production capacity of the socio-economic system, but also by employing thousands of people in the construction industry, through tax revenues and so on. It should be noted that before the 1920s on the occasion of such large projects

Official 1851 Map of London issued on the occasion of the Great Exhibition in Hyde Park. Coney Island Station in 1890s.

of public interest (defense, tax revenues, social order) as Brooklyn Bridge, a company in charge (such as the Coney Island Bridge Co.) would be allowed by the state, through a special procedure, to 'incorporate' a number of private companies for the purpose of accomplishing the objective in a timely and efficient manner. Upon the completion of the project such incorporation had to be taken apart. That way the state had a supreme control over the growth of (in)corporations and, in fact, largely kept it until World War II (Carey 1996).

In an illuminating brief article on the relationship between the entertainment industry and the military, Tim O'Brien claimed that there are historical references showing that the German, French and the United States armies studied the transportation and movement methods of the Barnum Bailey and other circuses as early as 1892 (O'Brien 2002). Two United States Army officers joined the 1906 Barnum Bailey Great Show in Baltimore for several days to study some of the problems they shared with the great circus, such as the rationale for distribution of people, animals and goods across vast territories within strictly limited timetables. Reportedly, the military also studied how the circus kitchens operated and fed thousands of people on the move. As O'Brien further indicates, *Hagerstown (Md.) Herald* reported at the occasion that this was 'the first time in the history of the United States government where they have found a private organization of

sufficient size and system large enough or organized in such a manner as to be the object of close study on the part of any of the government departments.' (O'Brien 2002)

The last decades of the Nineteenth Century and the early decades of the Twentieth Century gave rise to a significant development of the Japanese railway system initially built, as in Europe and the United States, to facilitate military operations, namely the distribution of goods and men across the national territory. This system brought along the rise of amusement parks. The first amusement parks were modeled upon the European and American examples, such as Hanayashiki built in 1887 in the Asakusa Park in Tokyo (Ishimori 1995). Luna Park was another 'American-style' amusement park built in Tokyo in 1910 as a replica of Coney Island's Luna Park. As in the United States, large Japanese Railway companies at the time were state owned, whereas medium- and small-size lines were privately owned. They realized that building amusement parks at the end of lines would improve the volume of commuting and traveling and ultimately increase profits. Many amusement parks were also built along the railway lines, including famous Tamagawaen built by the Musashino Electric Railway Company in 1907 and Toshimaen built by Seibu Railway Company in 1926. Since railways in Meiji and Taishô Japan implied westernization as well as modernization and progress, similar instruments of rationality were introduced to regulate the traveling practices of Japanese entertainment seekers. Timetables were combined with maps, whose characteristics were similar to the ones offered in England, but at the same time also carried numerous characteristics of maps offered in Japan's early modern era, namely the Edo period. Such maps combined details of transportation networks with exaggerated, caricaturized topographic elements (often the obligatory Fuji Mountain), cultural symbols and natural resources all in the service of emerging consumption practices. Despite their iconographic character, these early railway charts and maps were instrumental in introducing an idea of space that derived from the newly-established logic of capitalism, according to which space and time are transformed through the mediation of money (Traganou 2004: 59). These maps participated in the change of spatial perception from one possessing absolute values to one of abstraction. At the same time, elements of absolute values (such as Mt. Fuji, 'famous places,' famous products, tradition) were incorporated within the space-time-money system of undifferentiated homogenization (Traganou 2004: 62) and together with the era's new fascinations (technology, westernized practices) were also proposed as ideal objects of consumption.

From Place to Theater

Strategies for placing amusement parks in Europe, Asia and the United States had radically changed after World War II, due to a number of related developments within the nexus of ideas in the military geography, urban planning and economic theory. The most important for this narrative was surely the opening of Disneyland Park in 1955. Disneyland was an embodiment of a new philosophy, a new paradigm, as it combined all of the principles, techniques and methods to be used later by theme parks across the globe. Disneyland Park opened on 17th July 1955 in Anaheim, California during the period Tomas Hine called 'Populuxe' (1954–64), a materialistic 'golden age' through which America 'enthusiastically adopted a new attitude towards itself, the world and towards consumption.' (Hine

1986) Disneyland Park initially featured 18 attractions in five themed areas at a cost of us$17 million. In terms of the methodology used in its design, Disneyland was in fact very modern for its time and up-to-date in terms of the work and theory of architectural avant-garde of the day, including the CIAM (Tyrwhitt et al. 1952, Newman 1961) and the Situationists International (Sadler 1988, Gilles 1953, Nieuwenhuys 1959). It was based on the merging of the material environments with the world of mass media and telecommunications, on an absolute reliance on rapid transportation networks (express freeways, the system of interstate highways and airports), on the tabula rasa approach to planning, and finally on the principle of zoning on a significant scale. Not surprisingly, 'the greatest of all pieces of Populuxe architecture' was a theme park: Disneyland (Hine 1996).

Disneyland was the first built environment ever designed in parallel with a national television channel that familiarized national audiences with the environment of Disneyland and its thematic novelties before ever stepping into it. Due to its media presence, Disney imagery had become globally present through aggressive worldwide promotion: Disney's movies, cartoons and merchandise had conquered the planet. Besides its firmly established 'location' in the world of media, Disneyland Park was strategically situated along the route planned for the Santa Ana Freeway (Interstate 5) in the midst of the orange groves located 25 miles South-East of Los Angeles. Disneyland Park was a masterpiece of zoning because it operated on two levels. In a wider sense, Disneyland as a whole was an entertainment zone within the dispersed megalopolis of Southern California, and at the time it served as a major 'recreational' facility in the larger area of Los Angeles. In the stricter sense, Disneyland Park used zoning principles to structure the environment, and further elaborated this method by the use of 'enveloping by theme' strategy (Fjellman 1992).

The semiotic distinction between the zones was facilitated by the homogeneity of a particular visual and narrative theme, as well as by

Aerial photograph of Disneyland Park, 1955.
© Anaheim History Room of the Anaheim
Public Library.

Christaller's hexagonal diagram representing
a system of central places, 1933.

Melvin Webber's overlapping pattern of urban
realms diagram, 1964.

visual and spatial ordering systems. By September 1955, Disneyland attracted one million visitors, most of which were residents of Southern California. During the first 30 years of operation more than 60 percent of Disneyland's visitors came by car from the State of California (Findlay 1992: 89). Since Santa Ana Freeway (Interstate 5) opened just prior to the opening of Disneyland Park, Walt Disney had a major traffic corridor which brought those visitors to the gates of his park without investing a penny (Findlay 1992: 58). With the advent of air travel towards the mid-1960s, the number of visitors coming by airplane had steadily increased. As a social proposition, Disneyland signified a shift from metropolitan forms of entertainment oriented towards bachelors to a suburban form of entertainment aggressively orientated towards families. The orientation towards 'family adventure' is an important contrast not only to the existing forms of leisure and entertainment in the United States (amusement parks such as Coney Island, Frontierland, et al.) but also to a hypothetical European leisure society emerging at that time. If Coney Island was about the institutionalization of misbehavior through a seemingly reformist framework of leisure, Disneyland was about the re-institutionalization of the conservative notion of 'proper family entertainment' on a significant scale. One of the most important qualifying factors of Disneyland was that Disneyland was a private enterprise, a vast privately-owned, publicly accessible space and, at that time, the largest private investment in a 'public' leisure facility ever. Walt Disney's interest in the social and cultural aspects of leisure were pragmatic: not only had Disneyland emptied the expectations of what leisure in a commercial environment could be, but by setting the new standards it naturalized itself as the model for the commodified pursuits of leisure. As Colin Rowe suggested, Disneyland is precisely the product of a social situation where evidence of the public realm was never certain and it came to furnish the void caused by the deficiency of the formal power of the state (Rowe 1978). Namely, the growth of corporations went hand-in-hand with the crisis of capitalism, capital restructuring and the production of space as described in the previous chapter, and the decline

of state power in all spheres of life. By the early 1970s, some corporations became economically (and thus also politically) at least as powerful as some nation-states. The growth of venture capital went together with these developments, as did the consequential effort of both to control large areas of public realm, particularly in the areas of transportation (railway, air transport, car manufacturers, and gas prices) and communication (mass media and entertainment industry). Consequently, these events had created a void between the space previously occupied and controlled by the power of state, and the emerging power of private capital and its need for establishing control over public realm.

In parallel with above developments, by the late 1960s, Ludwig Von Bertalanffy's Systems Theory (Von Bertalanffy 1968), Paul Zwicky's morphological thinking (Zwicky 1969), advances in the fields of formal morphology, behavioral and environmental studies, as well as the work of the Design Methods Group (Jones 1970, Alexander 1964, 1977) had influenced much of design thinking across disciplinary boundaries. The Megastructure discourse developing in Japan by Kenzo Tange and Fumihiko Maki, together with Jean Gottman's concept of Megalopolis (Gottman 1961), had pushed further the idea of human environment as a complex system increasingly based on the geographic and socio-economic rationale of distribution and circulation of goods, people, information and wealth among different geographic locations. The demands that massive retailing operations, new forms of mass consumption, new degrees and modes of mobility, emerging patterns of wealth distribution, and advances in mass communication and mass transportation have placed on old conceptual systems based upon the Euclidian-Newtonian order (that relied on bounded, stable and fixed categories) had began to profoundly challenge the notions of 'land', 'place' and 'boundary'. The nexus of economic, military, urban planning and design theories that, until the second half of the Twentieth Century, had seriously invested into the notion of 'place' began to change significantly. Geographers like Jean

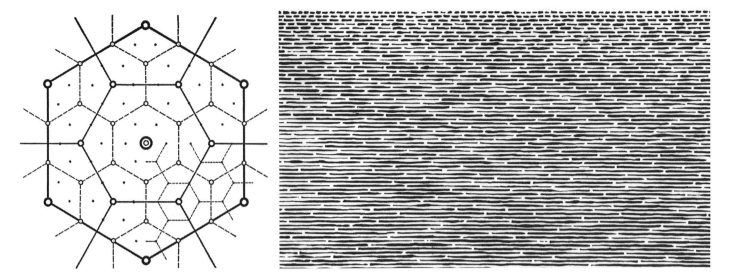

Gottman played a key role in understanding and instrumentalizing these developments. As Harvey's discoveries regarding the circulation of human blood have influenced a 'circulatory thinking' that has subsequently affected urban design for several centuries thereafter (Sennett 1994), analogically geographers in 1960s had carefully followed new discoveries in military theory and military geography, but also in studies of human nervous system, biology, plant and animal ecology, hoping that advances in these fields would help redefine human notion of 'the sense of place'. Subsequently, they had developed the notion of 'location' that rationalizes a possible synthesis between the conceived, perceived, and lived: it began by explicating a geographic location in terms of its internal characteristics and in terms of its connectivity with other locations within the systems of circulation. Besides, the location might potentially integrate the elements of nature, culture, and man's individual beliefs by creating a special internal ensemble that distinguishes one location from another. Thus, unlike purely phenomenological view that promotes an autonomous, introvert and transcendental notion of 'place', this view explicated a location simultaneously in relation to its internal ensemble and in relation to the urban and social system within which it resided.

Making a dramatic departure from the investment in 'place', much of urban planning and economic theory has basically refocused between the 1920s and 1960s from the Central-Place Theory nexus to the Nonplace Urban Realm principle first put forward by Melvin Webber. New definitions also emerged as a result of inadequacies of old theories such as Reilly's Law of Retail Gravitation of 1931 (Reilly 1931) and Christaller's Central Place Theory of 1933 (Christaller 1933, 1966, Vining 1954) to explain the role of consumer behavior in the restructuring of urban concentrations. Christaller's theory was economic in approach in that it attempted to predict how an optimal, centralized settlement pattern emerges out of the competition for resources, as in the case of Southern Germany were he lived and worked. Reilly's theory stated that two commercial targets (centers) attract trade from an intermediate area in direct proportion to their sizes and in inverse proportion to the distance of those centers from any given location within the intermediary area (Golledge and Stimson 1997: 350). Reilly's, Christaller's and other early theories were static, place-bound, Euclidian, non-behavioral, and thus unable to respond to the changing socio-economic dynamics. In the 1950s, behavioral-based and customer-based models emerged and fundamentally challenged the notion of central place: in 1962, David L. Huff published his model of Retail Gravity (Huff 1962, 1964). Huff's contribution was that he moved retail gravity models out of a deterministic mode and into a probabilistic mode that reflected both consumer and behavior concerns, and introduced 'time' as a key determinant in configuring urban interactions.[1] He was also the first to formulate a mathematical framework that helped explain what previously appeared to be 'irrational' spatial and economic behavior of people (consumers) in what he termed 'demand surfaces' that contained potential customers for a specific product, service or distribution center (Golledge and Stimson 1997: 352). All of these theories and models appeared as a result of cross-disciplinary interest of their authors and as a common effort as it may be between geographers, economists and planners.

In 1964, Melvin Webber (Webber 1964) coined the Non-place Urban Realm concept that proposed the universal *tabula rasa* condition for the ceaseless development of liberal capitalism (Frampton 1980). Webber's theory developed precisely out of his conviction that by the mid-1960s 'a frame of reference' had developed that applied uniquely to the large urban developments never before seen, rather than to traditional urban settlements of small scale. Webber wrote he was 'struck by the inadequacies of the place concept of settlement and of region for dealing with the spatial patterns in which [...] the functional processes of urban communities are not placelike or regionlike at all' (Webber 1964: 108). Traditional urban settlements, he claimed, were necessarily bound into a definite place due to the unfortunate immobility of people who formed them: hence, within such 'urban-place' formations the concept of 'unitary place' had developed. For it had become apparent to Webber that it was accessibility rather than propinquity that had generated a new condition he called 'community without propinquity'. As accessibility became further freed from propinquity, cohabitation in a territorially-defined place became less relevant for the constitution of social communities. Webber set out to search for a holistic conception that can sharply distinguish between 'the physical patterns, the spatial activity patterns, and the spatial

interaction patterns that are the expression of economic and social behavior' in the 'social system in action' (Webber 1964: 93). Most importantly, since he looked at urban communities as 'spatially structured processes', he attempted to find a way of dealing with form and process simultaneously. Thus, unlike Christaller's Central-Place Theory that regarded urban unit as a regional phenomenon (urban place/center and its hinterland), Webber proposed a spatial network of functional interdependencies that brought various social groups into 'operating systems' for which the traditional idea of propinquity was no longer valid. He thus proposed that such an urban conglomeration could be understood by looking into three heavily interrelated factors: A. spatial flows of information, money, people and goods (human interactions); B. locations of the physical channels that facilitate and enable flows and activities (physical plant); and C. locations of human activities (activity locations). Obviously, Webber was an extraordinary analyst and he was right in identifying the processes taking place in the mid-1960s, the very same process that, although immensely intensified, are still at play today. In many ways, his analysis was analogous to the one made by Lefebvre in his *The Production of Space* of 1974. However, his misfortune was in his technocratic mentality, and his unfortunate attempt to create an operational theory of planning based on what he correctly observed but uncritically acted upon. Webber was also criticized for categorically divorcing 'land' from 'use' in his theory, and for treating landscape as a source of commodities (soil, source of minerals and oil, etc.) or as a commodity itself in an economic sense, nevertheless an important determinant in what he called the 'total ecology' (Webber 1964: 101). The fear of such a 'total ecology', especially among true humanists,[2] was best expressed by Kenneth Frampton's suggestion that, having increasingly accepted a set of normative technical procedures in order to take part in such a community without propinquity, 'we might have eliminated, once and for all, the possibility of ever being anywhere' (Frampton 1974). Kenneth Frampton was in many ways right also in arguing that Webber's slogans have ever since been instrumentalized in rationalizing 'the total loss of civic domain in "motopian society".' (Frampton 1988) The uncritical expansion of such slogans and planning practices prompted David Harvey to suggest that, as of the early 1970s, planning and urban design have become 'shamelessly market oriented' and directly in the service of 'urban entrepreneurialism' as a means of attracting capital investments and human resources within emerging megalopolitan areas (Harvey 1989: 77–92), specifically concentrated within the two coasts of the United States, Tokaido region in Japan and the so-called 'banana' megalopolitan region in Europe.

That the place-concept has still been so rigidly implanted in theories and research methods across the Humanities and design disciplines alike has been made clear by the works (specifically among the phenomenologists) that appeared in the early 1970s and in the revival of the idea of 'non-place' that appeared in mid-1990s (mostly among anthropologists). The initial idea of 'placelessness' was employed in 1974 by the geographer and phenomenologist Edward Relph, who claimed that there is an ongoing erosion of the distinctive places of the United States by 'making of standardized landscapes that result from an insensitivity to the significance of place' (Relph 1976). In his view, vast previously unexplored landscapes have lost their chance of ever becoming meaningful places due to 'placeless developments'. Drawing on Jacques Ellul's concept of 'technique', Relph suggested that placelessness leads to functional efficiency, objective organization and manipulative planning, all based on a set of procedures determined by the 'technical nature of social engineering and planning'. The exemplars of this attitude are what he called 'other-directed places' and 'other-directed architecture' geared towards consumers, passers-by, outsiders and spectators and designed as tourist resorts, entertainment districts, commercial strips and 'Disneyfied places': sites of mass consumption. Whereas Relph's placeless developments restricted the possibility of a phenomenological experience of place, what for the anthropologist Marc Augé (Augé 1995) fundamentally distinguished such a 'non-place' from a

'place' was its relation to history: 'place' assumes layering of historical coatings whereas 'non-place' does not integrate the earlier places but locates them as places of memory and turns them into monuments. Augé suggested that 'non-places' are products of Supermodernity, which is in turn characterized by an overabundance of events, spatial overabundance and the individualization of references as materialized in large shopping malls, vast parking lots, highways, leisure parks and airports. He further suggested that Supermodernity actually bypasses the existing places and turns 'the old (history) into a specific spectacle, as it does with all exoticism and local particularity.' Since 'non-place' descriptions are language based, they work through negation and thus clearly marginalize the question of how 'non-place' conditions are materially and culturally produced and reproduced, both internally and externally. If 'place' can be defined as inner-directed in Relph's terms and also 'relational, historical and concerned with identity', then the 'other-directed' 'non-place' may be also seen as relational (in relation to the urban system, patterns of human interaction and to other environments within it), historical (by fabricating its own 'understanding' or 'reading' of history and therefore breaking the code of potentially undesirable historical meta-narratives) and very concerned with identity (as it relates to the identity of the complex system it is a part of whether it is corporate, national or communal). In other words, the 'non-place' discourse does not contribute to a better understanding of the conditions of production of the world it apparently criticizes.

Since theme parks are largely retail operations, theories used in the daily practice of themeparking are coming out of the nexus of Economic Location Theories (such as Retail Gravity Theory or the Market Saturation Theory) together with a number of related methods and techniques (such as the Buying Power Index). Retail Gravity Theory suggests that there are underlying regularities in shopping and leisure behavior that can be analyzed and anticipated by mathematical analysis and prediction methods based on the notion of gravity and leads

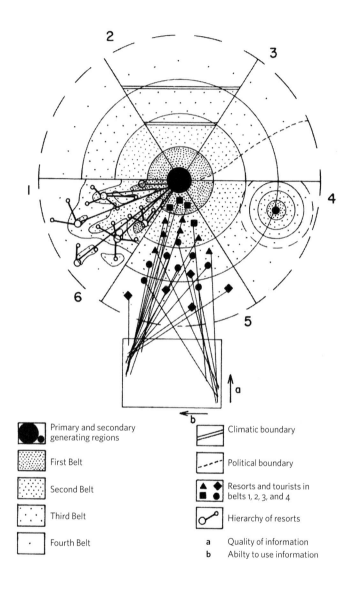

Primary and secondary generating regions

First Belt

Second Belt

Third Belt

Fourth Belt

Climatic boundary

Political boundary

Resorts and tourists in belts 1, 2, 3, and 4

Hierarchy of resorts

a Quality of information
b Ability to use information

Miossec's model of tourist space grounded in the deterministic central place hypothesis modified for concentric belts. Source: After Miossec (1976) and Pearce (1987).

to the identification of trade areas for retail locations. Trade area of a theme park is defined as an adjacent geographic area that accounts for the majority of a theme park's sales and visitors and is customarily divided into zones: primary trade zone generates up to 60 percent of visitors, secondary trade zone 25 percent of visitors and tertiary trade zone usually 15 percent of all visitors. Conventionally, these zones are represented by circles whose radius determines the so-called 'target population'. However, the zones are rarely concentric and two-dimensional, and subsequently their volume and the corresponding percentages alike depend on a number of variables including the so-called 'market penetration rate'. In reality, trade areas are in fact dynamic, multi-dimensional environments, essentially analogous to the military concept of the 'theater of war'. 'Theater of war' is a strategic environment that represents a composite of the conditions, circumstances and influences that describe the military situation, affect the employment of forces and affect the decisions of the chain of command (DOD 2004). 'Theatre of war' is also defined as a multi-dimensional system in action that includes air, land and water and may contain more than one 'theater of operations'. A 'theater of operations' is, on the other hand, defined as a system component that enables a conduct of specific combat operations and is geographically distinct from other 'theaters of operation' within the same 'theatre of war' (DOD 2004). Theaters of operations are usually of significant size, allowing for operations over extended periods of time. The concept of 'theater' reflects a shift in military world-view towards a dynamic notion of military space as a multi-dimensional system in action. Contemporary satellite technology, Geographic Information System (GIS), Geographic Positioning System (GPS), mobile communication technology, wireless technology and an ever increasing air power have transformed the mid-to-late Twentieth-Century military world-view by, to say the least, enabling it to analyze and visualize relevant data into complex multi-dimensional maps due to the ability of new technology to store the location, shape and spatio-temporal properties of information. Based on such a multi-dimensional map, military analysts can identify spatial boundaries of conditions, circumstances and influences and define the 'theater of war' and its environment (DOD 2004). In such a complex, systematic, and convergent world-view, the meaning of each element within the theater of war is heavily dependent on its relations to all other elements within the system, to such a degree that one can almost argue that individual elements have no inherent meaning other than the relational one; that is to say, other than the one they obtain through the interactions with the system as a whole. In light of the book's main thrust, and in order to bring the two into a desirable framework that will facilitate further discussion, I will coin the term 'trade theater'. Trade theater will signify the shift in the scale of themeparking after mid-1960s, and with it also the shift from a static two-dimensional notion of 'place' to the dynamic and multi-dimensional notion of 'theater'. Having thus argued that for the condition of total landscape to emerge, an abolition of formal expressions of humanistic values invested into the notion of 'place' was a must, one can also note that total landscape has *de facto* turned traditional representations of humanistic values into a monument to be visited as Yesterday's Land. In what immediately follows, I will attempt to explain how that particular aim has been practically achieved.

Themeparking Infrastructure

Based on the principles derived from the nexus of planning, economy and military theory, one can distinguish four categories of scale related to types of decisions to be made and actions to be undertaken within the domain of Themeparking: global, regional, local, and operational. Within the global scale, one could distinguish various levels, in respect to the geo-cultural, economic, and other goals as well as the in relation to the strategic scope of operations: Walt Disney Company is the case in point and will be discussed in Global Theme Parks. Regional scale is predominantly concerned with the cumulative strategic employment in the theater of operations. Local scale is the scale of the theme park, concerned with tactical domain such is design

URBAN PUBLIC WALKS IN PARIS—TRAVEL REDEFINED

In Seventeenth Century France, most of the urban concentrations were confined within medieval perimeter walls. National defense system devised by Vauban caused the proliferation of citadels and fortified towns as its key components (Rabreau 1991: 308). Defensible city-fortresses, with a couple of gates usually placed along main access routes, were areas of distinct juridico-political identity and thus different from the hinterlands in-between them. A walk out of the city walls was an act of traveling to other juridical territory. Upon crossing the boundary of the city walls, avenues extended into the surrounding fields often as organized gravel walks. Although avenues were intended to anchor the city territorially and expand the virtues of urban culture outwards, they actually facilitated a proliferation of alternative behaviors that originated outside the city walls. Freedom of behavior and a relief from the confinements of the social norm imposed by political realities and religious clerks was facilitated by the establishment of pleasure grounds that began appearing along the avenues in the Seventeenth Century. Pleasure grounds initially offered cheap popular entertainments with a few simple attractions which were otherwise forbidden in cities, such as prostitution and alcohol.

The first ephemeral structures to appear were simple stands or kiosks that later became more sophisticated and were turned into bars, coffee shops and even dance halls (Auricoste 1991). Cheap drinks, lower moral standards and an emphasis on entertainment were among the key factors that quickly transformed these playgrounds into alternative but organized entertainment facilities. Pleasure grounds soon became pleasure gardens and offered a variety of attractions. The layout was similar to that of the landscape garden with weaving paths and attractions placed along them. In the early Eighteenth Century, many of these pleasure gardens became specialized and offered a specific range of attractions and very distinct novelties. Tivoli was far the most popular of these gardens. It had an informal layout, few controlled entrances and a range of spectacular attractions placed along its walkways. The Game of Chinese Rings and the Tower of Aeolus flights were clearly the early roundabout rides and were powered manually. 'Switchbacks'

The Tower of Aeolus at Tivoli Gardens (with Switchbacks in the background), Paris. Lithograph by C. Motte, c. 1800. Musée Carnavalet, Paris.

was an early roller coaster ride that started from an artificial hill created in order to accelerate carts carrying visitors along a 100 feet-long driveway, running through a cave-like scene and finishing at the flat terrace. Workers then pushed the carts back to the top of the hill, where new customers waited in line for the next ride. Most of the rides were mechanical, and although participatory in character, they engaged the visitor only on the level of novel bodily experience. Similar developments took place outside of the walls of numerous European cities: in London such public areas and houses were called 'liberties' (Boyer 1994: 88).

of the theme park environment or the control of large crowds. Operational scale is concerned with the maneuver and support of field operations that include daily staffing, supply, control and so on. What is obvious here is the division between the fundamental domains of problem-settings that are military in origin: the strategic domain and tactical domain, both geographical in nature (O'Sullivan and Miller 1983: 7). Like in a military 'theater of operations', relations between intelligence, logistic and action can be viewed in terms of geographically-specific informational and logistic constraints on the freedom of visitors's action. The choice of action is dependent upon a set of variables commonly grouped as physical-sphere variables and psychological-sphere variables (O'Sullivan and Miller 1983: 81). Physical-sphere variables are related to the anticipated visitors's movement within the theater that can be summarized as 'the line of least resistance.' Such variable domains would include topography/terrain, latitude/longitude, land/water masses, rainfall/snow levels, rivers, lakes, mountains, forests, average anticipated temperature, possibilities for group transport, time, protected environments, demographics, man-made structures such are freeways, industrial facilities, cemeteries, and numerous other variables. Psychological-sphere variables are commonly related to visitors's surprise and can be summarized as 'the line of least expectation': it depends on precise calculations that involve manifold conditions and data including socio-economic variables (consumption patterns, work patterns, leisure behavior, 'the other side of the tracks' syndrome, purchasing power, lifestyle affinities), political variables ('the other side of the tracks' can also be seen as a political variable in the United States similar to the crossing of a symbolic political boundary between two states in the European Union) as well as cultural variables (times of attendance, eating habits, language barriers, humor affinities, or resonance of the thematic framework in a given cultural milieu). For successful themeparking, both physical and psychological variables have to be identified and calculated into the theme park equation, either by removing them from the environment as clear obstructions, by neutralizing them by attention-diverging methods, or turning them into a real or symbolic capital by acknowledging their existence and often by caricaturizing their presence. Since the ultimate aims in establishing and controlling a theater of operations are dislocation (creating an opportunity) and exploitation (exploiting the opportunity and create effect) (Hart 1954: 349), variables are treated in ways that would effectively enable optimal frictionless access to identified targets within the theater. That is why both physical and psychological variables (operating as either obstacles or opportunities) have to be brought into an ideal balance with the trade area characteristics through the careful selection of

Significant changes in the national defense system that took place in the late Eighteenth Century had caused changes in the organization of the national territory of France. Cities like Paris, at the safe distance from national borders, did not have to maintain perimeter walls for safety and defense reasons. Walls immediately gave way to the city's expansion. With territorial expansion and changes in the juridico-political system, avenues previously linking the city with surrounding landscape, became parts of the city of Paris. Social codes and modes of behavior promoted at pleasure gardens, as well as their social status, became intolerable.[1] Although the combination of old and new walks created a previously unknown kind of social mix, in 1833 the architect J. I. Hittorff was commissioned to make a plan for conversion of the Champs-Élysées, Place Royal and Place Louis xv (de la Concorde) in order 'to impose order and civic behavior' onto these territories (Von Joest 1991). Fountains, new uniformed lighting, benches, gates, fences, a circus, a Panorama, a parade ground, coffee shops, bars and museums were all part of this newly organized and ordered 'architecture of leisure'. This rationalization of urban and political space was an attempt to impose centralized power and to extend municipal territory symbolically and physically through new architectural means. Hittorff suggested that the elements of urban uniformity (lights, gates, fountains, water works and paving) should be done at the expense of the city, whereas the actual entertainment architecture should be left to private enterprise. It was assumed by Hittorff that profit making and leisure enterprise are not the business of government and should be controlled by private capital, whereas civic order (imposed by visibility as well as by the uniformity of 'urban furniture' such are lights and benches) was believed to be in the realm of government's control and jurisdiction.

Hittorff's and Alphand's elements of urban design and uniformity for *Squares des Batignolles,* 1867.

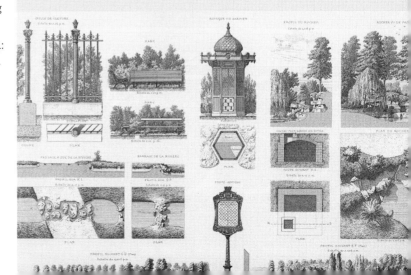

When in 1850s Haussmann became in charge of the next phase of the reconstruction of Paris he first created the *Service des Promenades et Plantations* and appointed a *Ponts est Chaussées* engineer, Jean Alphand, as the head of operations (Giedion 1949: 667). Alphand immediately transformed the old Pleasure Grounds and created new ones such are the Bois de Boulogne, the Parc Monceau and others. In 1959, Haussmann created the *Direction du Plan de Paris* and made Barillet-Deschamps its head. Within the new plan Hittorff was ironically asked to design some of the profit making leisure facilities that were part of his previous plan. Jean Alphand was made the Commissaire Général of the 1889 World Exhibition in Paris (Giedion 1949: 667).

1. At this time most of the heterotopian models became intolerable: hospitals and cemeteries too were pushed outside the medieval city walls.

possible sites. Accordingly, theme park development projects are practically structured through the so-called 'hard' and 'soft' costs (in Japan it is called 'hardware' and 'software' costs). The budget for 'hard' expenses commonly assumes expenses on the material realm of themeparking such as the purchase of land, construction of infrastructure, the material aspects of theme park environments, installation of rides and shows and so on. The budget for 'soft' expenses commonly includes the themeing budget, design expenses, legal and other expenses, pre-opening expenses such as marketing and media promotion, staff training, event design and other miscellaneous expenses. How theme park industries across the world invest in these two realms varies: in the United States, 'hard' costs usually represent about 70 percent of the total project development cost, whereas in Europe and Japan the figure is often as low as 30 percent (Robinett and Braun 1999).

Themeparking can be initiated in a number of ways and each design team has its own way of approaching the front end of the design process. Imagineering design process used to start with the 'Blue Sky' phase, where 'the sky is the limit' to ideas and concepts. For the occasion of conceptualizing Disney's California Adventure Park, Michael Eisner planned a 'concept charrette' that included both in-house and guest experts at an outside location (Aspen, Colorado). From this charrette, three distinct concepts emerged out of which one was developed further: the idea of a park based on 'the dreams, the myths, the iconography and the reality of the Golden State of California.' (Sklar 1997: 17) As Sklar noted, in Disney's design process, Design Development (DD) is followed by Schematic Design (SD) and Feasibility Study (FS). Other companies typically begin with the Feasibility Study that commonly determines the targeted geographic trade area ('target population' or 'target radius') of the theme park, demographic analysis, infrastructure, traffic and site study, the impact of existing and projected tourist capacities and flows, industry and competition analysis, the overall thematic framework, the 'design day', entertainment and operating capacity, theme park utilization plan and size requirements in relation to attendance projections, definition of the 'mix' of major component, attractions, programming and operational characteristics, staffing in relation to operational projections, per capita spending projections and capital budget together with revenue projections. The industry standard for the investment value of a FS is up to two percent of the total development costs. In order to control such a complex and dynamic design and construction process successfully, large theme park developers whose significant source of revenue is generated by the theme park business conduct most of the above-described process in-house. Walt Disney Company is known for taking absolute control over the entire process, due also to the fact that the in-house group, Walt Disney Imagineering, does all design and detailing within the company. Theme park developers without design departments commonly commission so-called 'producers' who take control of the design, construction and often also marketing process for them. Producers customarily oversee multi-disciplinary production teams that include all the disciplines of feasibility, design, development, marketing and management. Depending on the complexity of a project, a producer company such as White Hutchinson may form a production team including architects, interior designers, landscape architects, acoustics designers, graphic designers, civil engineers, QS engineers, market feasibility experts, financial experts, a variety of staff trainers, business experts, child development experts, education specialists, professional writers in charge of storyline and theme development, menu and food designers, safety engineers, electrical engineers, experience engineers, as well as many other experts including contractors and subcontractors.[4] FS also determines types of thematic and conceptual frameworks to be employed. Large corporations, such as Walt Disney Company or Six Flags Inc., commonly determine the concept for a new theme park by capitalizing on their varied properties and pre-existing discourses that could be related to movies, cartoons, or fictional characters. Smaller theme park developers/operators often have vague concepts that need elab-

oration and definition and they may have no *a priori* presence in the media. Once the FS is completed and capital budget is approved, a Project Development study, Master Plan and Design Development are undertaken. Typically, a Project Development study includes, but it is not limited to the following items: evaluation of the proposed location and the site plan; preliminary Master-plan; selection of the appropriate mix of attractions and supporting equipment in relation to theme park's entertainment capacity and attendance projections; definition of equipment sizing and volume requirements; definition of the operating layout; schematic design drawings for building and themeing elements; thematic framework and brand design; preparation of technical specifications; and cost estimates and the analysis of revenue projections and investment returns. Managing the project development is a very complex task, as it implies turning actionable insights derived from the Master Plan into effective action by determining the following three domains: the Master Program that outlines all elements to be included in the theme park in terms of size, capacity and cost; the Master Schedule that translates the Master Program into a timetable with the aim of distributing development operations over the development cycle of the theme park; and Value Engineering that involves the analysis of each component of the project in order to determine the most economic way to design it, build it, or buy it ready made.

A complete design of a theme park, including storyline, brand development, complete themed architecture, interior and site design, equipment specifications and procurement assistance, management consulting and start-up assistance, usually costs up to 15 percent of total development cost (White 1995). Given the inverted curve of design cost in relation to other costs and also in relation to the lifespan of a theme park, design expenses can consume up to 80 percent of the operating costs during the lifetime of a theme park (White 1993).[5] It follows that a high early investment into themeing may preclude later investments into new attractions as well as into new themeing down the line, and that is precisely what commonly happens in a majority of European and Japanese theme parks. Huis Ten Bosch theme park in Japan had to file for bankruptcy in December 2003 precisely due to miscalculated investments into themeing, design development, construction and the pre-opening budget.

The domain of Themeparking encompasses strategically important elements of PD. Thus, in what follows in this chapter, I will discuss location theories, demographics, traffic network and accessibility, site selection, attendance projections, theme and concept developments, marketing and branding, tourist arrangements, and finally cultural patterns that also greatly determine strategic decision-making within the domain of Themeparking.

Location Theories

In addition to what has already been discussed earlier in this chapter in terms of determining potential locations for the trade theater, an important aspect is how the demand for amusement, entertainment and leisure (AEL) of a potential trade theater location is being served by current AEL establishments in comparison with other potential markets. The Saturation Theory examines precisely such concerns.

Index of AEL saturation can be calculated as the ratio of demand for an AEL service/product (households in the geographic trade theater multiplied by annual AEL expenditures per household) divided by available supply (the cumulative surface of AEL facilities in the trade theater). Buying power index (BPI) is an indicator of a market's overall retail potential and it is composed of the measures of effective buying income (personal income including all non-tax payments minus all taxes), retail sales and population size. BPI effectively measures market's ability to buy and is expressed as a percentage of the total market potential.[6]

Demographics

Potential trade theaters are also identified and initially compared through the demographic data. Demographic data is usually composed of the data on population and household base, population growth potential, income potential, age makeup, populations of daytime workers, students, tourists, occupation mix and so on. Such data is used for the analysis of population composition, wealth and spending levels, age groups, ethnic breakdown, housing information and population concentrations. How this type of data influences the design of theme parks is very obvious: for instance, in the late-1990s, the ageing of 'baby boomers' brought theme park operators in the United States to identify a need for a more balanced entertainment offering with much more emphasis placed on shows, 'street performances' and generally higher quality entertainment compared to roller-coaster and other aggressive rides emphasized in the early 1990s. The success of Disney's California Adventure Park, which opened in 2001, is a proof of that trend. Demographic data can nowadays be purchased from demographic data vendors that specialize in repackaging census-type data coupled with the Geographic Information System (GIS) technology. Demographic data vendors analyze and visualize (spatialize) information about customer demographics, buying behaviors (BPI), lifestyles and other relevant data into multidimensional maps that enable the analyst to identify boundaries of the trade theater and isolate target demographic groups.

Traffic Networks, Sites, Accessibility

Once potential trade theaters are identified, one of the key steps in qualifying them is to analyze the potential locations of the theme park within the theater as well as available transportation networks meant to enable the flow of people, goods and information between the new trade theater and the theater of operations. Therefore, a part of the framework of Themeparking is the engineering of leisure, a professional discourse on leisure that coalesces with the world of media and with the procedures that determine the circulation of people to specific theme park locations. Subsequently, the feasibility study and trade theater analysis determine the existence of major vehicular traffic corridors and airports, the quality of accessibility from the primary traffic arteries, the visibility of the signage or the facility from such traffic routes, the layout of the site in relation to incoming traffic, parking areas and the theme park's entrance, the existence of possible pedestrian traffic and the availability of the means of mass transportation to the site (subway, buses, etc.), traffic density and congestion and the ease of access for delivery. These are all key elements in determining the quality of a site. It goes without saying that high population-density is customarily followed by a high density of transportation networks. There is, however, a significant difference between the population density parameters in Europe as opposed to those in United States or Japan. Whereas in Europe or Japan, it would be easy to locate a 150-mile radius out of major urban concentrations with a population of 20 million people, in United States that would be a difficult task. Thus, a regional theme park in Europe and Japan, as opposed to those in the United States, would have a major impact and a significant number of visitors due to the density of both population and transportation networks. The comparative average densities of railway infrastructures, road networks and numbers of cars between Japan, United States and Belgium show radical differences (HABITAT 1996: 522–525): Belgium has a railway infrastructure density of over 186mi/1000mi^2, Japan of 86.3mi/1000mi^2, while United States has 36mi/1000mi^2. Similarly, Belgium has a highway infrastructure density of 7500mi/1000mi^2, Japan of 4775mi/1000mi^2, while United States has nearly 1073mi/1000mi^2. In terms of the number of individual vehicles (cars), Belgium has 430 cars per 1000 citizens, Japan has nearly 480, and the United States leads with nearly 800 cars per 1000 people. Although other European countries, such as The Netherlands, Germany and France, follow the figures for Belgium with similar values, other Asian countries, such as China or Korea, are far behind the figures of Japan.

The purpose of traffic study is to determine the key access routes to the site and to obtain traffic count information, as well as actual drive times and distances from urban concentrations within the target theater for the purpose of identifying the target population for the proposed theme park. Although issues at stake are much more complex for global theme parks (as it will be discussed later in this chapter), traffic networks, flows and accessibility for regional theme parks can also be determined by a set of simplistic techniques, such as traffic counts on arteries from which the theme park is visible or accessible, or other 'spotting techniques', such are license plate surveys, customer surveys, customer records or customer activities in the theater (contests, sweepstakes and so on).

How people drive is also culturally and economically determined. For some cultures, driving time is much more important than driving distance, for others, the opposite is true. In densely populated trade theaters, driving (or travel) time can be excessive, although distances crossed are not significant. In loosely populated trade theaters, travel distance can be excessive, but the speed of movement can be higher therefore reducing travel time. Excessive travel time or distance can also be a form of psychological obstacle, sometimes an economic obstacle too. In a study titled *The Impact of Motor Fuel Prices and Availability on Theme Park Attendance* (Evans 1981), Christopher Evans identified the impact that price and availability of motor fuel have on the attendance patterns to Knott's Berry Farm theme park. He concluded that opportunity and option to travel to the theme park could be restricted by the cost of motor fuel in ways that psychologically reduce the freedom of movement and the choice of leisure destination, thus the boundaries of entertainment space.

Successful site selection and careful Competition Analysis are directly proportional to the attendance figures. The adequate mix and critical mass of AEL offerings within a trade theater generates high levels of attendance at all targets that multiplied by per-capita expenditures gives total revenues for the entire trade theater. As will be shown later in this chapter, Huis Ten Bosch Co. in Japan is a case in point. One of the benefits of Competition Analysis is also the recognition of the existing web of movement within and in relation to the trade theater. Namely, this analysis identifies competing or complementary AEL and shopping nodes (other theme parks, shopping malls, restaurants, cinemas and other tourist targets) and recognizes regular patterns of movement in relation to such nodes. Depending on the concept, theme and size of the theme park, its location can be either complementary (as a secondary target close to an existing node) or competitive (as a primary target that pulls the web of movement away from existing patterns). If an existing web of movement is related to a large, regional shopping mall, locating a theme park in its vicinity or within the mall can be advantageous to the theme park developer (The Mall of America or West Edmonton Mall are cases in point). Other examples include joint ventures or promotions with local competition so that everyone in the trade theater enjoys the benefits of collaboration, coexistence and simultaneous engagement.

Site selection within the trade theater is also important in terms of normative regulations, such are building safety code restrictions, types of zoning practiced and zoning restrictions, the history of the theme park site, environmental regulations, signage regulations, licensing requirements and so on. In many countries where building codes are highly regulated, zoning determines how a particular site can be used, whereas building codes determine possible types of buildings, sizes or types of parking lots and so on. Sign restrictions can be very detrimental to a theme park's success because sometimes the theme park is not visible from the access route and signs are necessary to lead travelers towards the site. When environmental codes do not allow for signs to be posted at key intersections, the theme park will stay out of the dominant pattern of movement: if the target is not clearly marked and not located along the penetration route, it will be missed. That is why having the right to establish new codes is essential for many large theme park developers, a key example of which is Walt Disney Co.'s government in Florida called Ready Creek Improvement District.

The traffic infrastructure utilized for theme parks is commonly constructed by state funds. Initially, the economic speculations of theme park developers simply utilized the existing infrastructure (Disneyland utilized Interstate 5), whereas the paradigmatic changes that occurred in the 1980s have created a new set of economic and political mechanisms that have allowed large theme park developers (such as Walt Disney Company) to design partnerships with local or national governments based on mutual financing of a regional infrastructure needed for theme park operation in return for promised new jobs or expected tax revenues generated by the presence of these playgrounds. As Steve Schmidt reported, the State of California invested nearly US$1 billion to widen and reconfigure Interstate 5 (Santa Ana Freeway) and other freeways in the area near Walt Disney Company properties, to add a new interchange to funnel guests directly into Disney's parking structure, to plant 15 000 trees and shrubs, to expand the convention center and make many other improvements during the three-year construction of the US$1.4 billion Disney's California Adventure Park (Schmidt 2001). This US$1 billion investment (that came mostly from hotel-room taxes) was supposed to bring over 8000 new jobs to the area and generate a US$6 million in annual revenue to the State, money spent on police and other basic services. By the theme park's opening on 8th February 2001, Walt Disney Company and the State of California (including the local governments) invested collaboratively over US$3 billion into this project. The new resort features the theme park, a 750-room luxury resort hotel and Downtown Disney, a district of restaurants, shops and clubs including House of Blues, ESPN Zone and Rainforest Café (Snyder 2001).

A general awareness of the importance of traffic/transportation networks for the circulation of people to theme parks is also obvious through the economic mechanisms developed to facilitate the collaboration of theme park operators with airline carriers, railway companies, car rental companies, travel agencies, hotel industry, credit card companies, long-distance telephone companies and other adjacent business and industries. It is of major importance for the success of themeparking that the trade theater includes or is located in the vicinity of an airport. The quality and scale of the airport, number of flights through the airport, range of available airfares and the availability of the airport as a destination within the frequent flyer programs, may greatly influence the success of a theme park in terms of attendance. It has become a worldwide practice that major transportation companies figure as shareholders of large theme parks. Delta Air Lines paid US$40 million to Walt Disney Company to replace its previous partner Eastern Airlines in 1987, and to become its official airline and shareholder (Knowlton 1989: 124). Since 1998, a similar arrangement exists between Anheuser-Busch and Southwest Airlines: on Southwest Airlines's official web site, guests can find maps and descriptions, operating hours and schedules, and also purchase admission tickets to all Anheuser-Busch theme parks. Some Southwest Airlines airplanes have been covered with the image of Sea World's mascot. In Japan, ANA (All Japanese Airlines) and JR Kyushu (Japanese Railways Kyushu) are major shareholders of Huis Ten Bosch Co., the owner, developer and operator of Huis Ten Bosch theme park in Kyushu. Some transportation companies, due to size and economic capacity, still employ early modern methods and develop theme parks in order to stimulate commuting along their own lines: Japanese Kintetsu Group, a major national railway company, developed in 1994 Shima Spain Village at the end of its regional Kintetsu line in order to stimulate the use of trains from Nagoya to Kashikojima. The confluence and interdependence of theme park industry, the airline industry, the cruise industry, the railway industry (not in the United States), the car rental business, various drivers associations (such as the American Automobile Association-AAA or the German Allgemeiner Deutscher Automobil Club-ADAC), the hotel industry, the tourist industry (travel agents and tour operators, the engineering of leisure), the telephone and communication companies, the credit card industry, incentive travel programs and many other interests is increasing exponentially with the consolidation of the theme park industry and as themeparking grows in scale.

Attendance Projections and Entertainment Capacity

As Jeff McNair of Forrec wrote, 'attendance projections [and the resulting capacity calculations] are the DNA of a theme park.' (McNair 2000) Using information obtained through demographic, economic and geographic research on the trade theater, as well as traffic study and site analysis, calculations can be made as to the volume of targeted population and theme park attendance thresholds, as well as the anticipated frequency of attendance. The maximum visitor flow, capacity levels and visitor cycles are then used in order to anticipate the peak usage often called the 'design day'. The 'design day' is an estimate of the number of visitors during peak attendance periods that the park will be designed to efficiently accommodate. According to the industry standards, the 'design day' is in practice calculated based on attendance levels of 25 percent below peak attendance. Peak attendance is commonly calculated as up to two percent of the projected annual attendance. Conceptualizing and designing the theme park around the concept of 'design day' allows designers to achieve a critical balance between the size of the theme park environment and the corresponding attendance projections: gates, parking spaces, circulation spaces, sitting and rest areas, retail facilities, supporting facilities (such are restrooms or daycares) as well as the overall mix and the capacity of attractions. Based on the above, designers calculate overall operating capacity of a theme park that defines the capacity of each aspect of the theme park environment. These tactical decisions will be discussed further in Chapter 4 and belong to the domain of Themeing. For instance, food concessions are commonly

HUIS TEN BOSCH
a resort with many museums, attractions and events
International performances bring excitement and wonder.

HUIS TEN BOSCH
one of the biggest resort and theme parks in Asia

While visiting Huis ten Bosch, you will not be bored for even one minute. Besides the various museums and attractions, special festivals are held throughout the year. In spring, during the **Tulip Festival**, 300,000 blooming tulips can be found. During the **Windmill Festival** from the end of April till the end of May, many street performances can be seen. Other festivals are: **Hydrangea Festival** (June-mid July), **Ocean Festival** (mid July & Aug), **Harvest Festival** (Sep-Nov), **Christmas** (Dec), **New Year** (Jan 1-5) and **Chinese New Year**. (Feb 1-14: fireworks etc, etc.).

During all these festivals, special events take place to make your visit a memorable one.

Regular events are:

Huis ten Bosch Royal Horse Parade
A magnificent parade of Frisian horses from The Netherlands, traditional European carriages, and decorated cars can be seen daily.

In the evening you can see the **"Bon Voyage De Liefde,"** a spectacular show using water, smoke, light and sound with a ship as its stage, and the **Sound Galaxy**: the grand sounds of a synthesized orchestra and brilliant laser beams piercing the sky, adding another page to your memories.

For more information, please contact: HUIS TEN BOSCH RESORT & THEME PARKS, INTERNATIONAL DIVISION

6 DAYS TOKYO/HUIS TEN BOSCH/OSAKA

Hightlights:
Tokyo City - Mt. Fuji - Tokyo Disneyland - Nagasaki City - **Huis ten Bosch** - Osaka City - Nara City - Todaiji Temple - Kyoto City - Kiyomizu Temple - Handicraft Centre - Nishijin Textile Centre

Departure:
Nov : 7, 14, 19, 21, 26, 28.
Dec : 3, 5, 10, 12, 17, 19.
Jan : 2, 9, 16, 23, 30.
Feb : 3, 6, 13, 20, 27.
Mar : 6, 13, 20, 27.

7 DAYS COLOURFUL KYUSHU

Highlights:
Nara Deer Park - Todaiji Temple - Tenmangu Dazaifu Shrine - Beppu Hot Spring Resort - Kumamoto City Tour - Mt. Aso - Suizenjikoen Garden - Kumamoto Castle - **Huis ten Bosch** - Nagasaki: Peace Park - Atomic Bomb Museum - Glover Mansion.

Departure:
Nov : 3, 10, 17, 24.
Dec : 1, 8, 15, 22.
Jan : 5, 12, 19, 26.
Feb : 2, 9, 16, 23.
Mar : 2, 9, 16, 23, 30.

ANA
ALL NIPPON AIRWAYS
JAPAN'S BEST TO THE WORLD

SINBA 270 7779	SIN CHUNG 533 9888	INTER TRAVEL 538 2268	ADVENTURE TOURS 538 3733	NEWSMAN 534 5678
UNIVERSAL 535 5577	MORNING STAR 292 9009	DINERS 292 5522	TRAVELINK 336 3555	AIRELATED 532 5686
HONG THAI 533 1788	SIAKSON 331 8213	GASI 733 2228	RELIANCE 532 2222	JETABOUT 734 1818
EXPERIENCE TOURS 277 1665	SAFE-KNT 227 8660	B & L 339 6383	SCAN TOURS 339 7733	ANANDA 535 1138

Contact your agent for prices.

8 DAYS BEST OF JAPAN

Hiroshima Peace Park - Fukuoka - **Huis ten Bosch** (daytrip) - Nagasaki: Glover Garden - Madam Butterfly Statue - Oura Church - Kumamoto Castle - Suizenji Park - Mt. Aso - Beppu - Cruise to Osaka - Nara: Todaiji Temple - Kyoto: Kiyomizu Temple - Toyohashi - Bullet Train - Mt Fuji - Tokyo - Disneyland.

Departure:
Nov : 8, 22, 29.
Dec : 20, 27.
Feb : 5, 6, 7.
Mar : 7, 21.

6 DAYS KYUSHU

Stay at 5-star hotel in **Huis ten Bosch**
Direct flight Singapore - Fukuoka - Singapore

Fukuoka - Tenmangu Shrine - Kumamoto Castle - Suizenji Park - Mt Aso - Nagasaki: Peace Park - Atomic Bomb Museum - Glover Garden - Madam Butterfly Statue - Oura Church - **Huis ten Bosch**

Departure:
Nov : 22, 29.
Dec : 6, 13, 20.
Jan : 31.
Feb : 5, 6, 7.
Mar : 7, 27.

KEN AIR 332 5850 — **Fly By Singapore Airlines**

TRADEWINDS TOURS 533 1313	PRIME TRAVEL 222 6522	SIAKSON 331 8213	TOURIST MOBILE 334 1940
NEW SHAN TRAVEL 220 4924	SA (UIC) TOURS 535 2611	COMMONWEALTH TRAVEL 532 0532	CHAN BROTHERS 535 5333

Contact your agent for prices.

HOTEL DEN HAAG
This is one of the hotels, located within the resort, used for visitor who join the **6 Days Kyushu Package**. Overlooking Omura Bay, this hotel stands in the quiet depths of Huis ten Bosch. The dining room Excelsior, is specialised in Mediterranean cuisine, using fresh fish caught from the nearby sea. A glass of wine in the Vinotheque is the perfect conclusion of the day.

Since its opening in March 1992, Huis Ten Bosch has been recognized as one of Asia's largest res. This city is designed for everyday living and is place where one can relax with the sense of bel ing. It suggests a new style of resort-living in th quality seeking world. Omura Bay connects th four locations—Huis ten Bosch, Holland Villag Bio Park and Huis ten Bosch Country Club, forming an extraordinary resort area where pe and nature can live together in harmony.

Spend a relaxing day, enjoy the museums, attractions, restaurants, shopping and shows till 9 in the evening.

HORIZON ADVENTURE
Many attractions contain some educational elements. Her you can see what happens when you waste water; Ran, th goddess of the sea introduces a great flood, like the ones t have plagued the Netherlands for centuries. Within the se of a typical Dutch town you will witness the destructive f of a terrifying rampage of water. The latest in high-tech fl and wave-making equipment is used, including 800 tons water, to provide this realistic simulation.

Access:
Singapore Airlines has daily flights to Fukuoka

Flight No.	Singapore	Fukuoka	Singapor
SQ 990	01:05/01:20	08:00	
SQ 989		12:00	17:00/16:

Fukuoka to Huis ten Bosch: By charterbus: 1:45 hour

By public Transport:
Bus : Airport : 09:00 - Huis Ten Bosch : 10:45
Train : Fukuoka Airport - Fukuoka Train Station:
5 min by subway or 10 min by taxi.
Fukuoka Train Station - HTB Station:
Japan Railways Huis ten Bosch Express: 105 min

1-1 HUIS TEN BOSCH, SASEBO CITY, NAGASAKI 859-32 JAPAN TEL: 81-956-27-0526 FAX: 81-956-27-

calculated based on the empirical observation that 35 percent of the 'design day' in-park guests will eat during peak meal periods, and they are called 'peak-time diners'. Based on the peak-time diners, basic types of service are calculated in relation to the length of service per outlet type. Subsequently, the number of seats can be derived which would finally give volume projections for both frontstage and backstage. Based on the above calculations, theme park designers determine through the Master Plan an ideal mix of rides, shows, events, entertainment facilities and their relationships.

The above methods for anticipating attendance determine the size of the theme park, its relationship to the trade theater and its population as well as the capital budget. However, many other variables can also act as input factors in the theme park equation, such as weather patterns and the number of season days, and they can seriously affect attendance and per capita spending values. As Vogel argued, the techniques used in achieving the perfect mode of operation, while taking into account all variables and input factors in the theme park equation, are similar to those of an assembly line within the industrial mode of production: sophisticated mathematical modeling techniques such are Linear Programming, Production-Function and Queuing-Systems Estimators are used in order to amortize the effect of each input factor on other variables within the system and on the cumulative output of the theme park system as a whole (Vogel 1986: 343).

Thematic Procedures

Thematic frameworks of theme park environments within the total landscape are often more closely related to the world of media and marketing described above than to the actual landscape in which the theme park sits. As will be shown in this section, the fabrication of thematic frameworks within Themeparking relies on the synergy of cultural, political and socio-economic factors that are inseparable in the contemporary world of media and synergetic marketing con-

trolled by multinational entertainment and media corporations. Georges Van Den Abbeele wrote that 'the most postmodernly radical project of all [is] the outright separation of the attraction from its site [...] such extreme cases are rare, yet they do assert the primordiality of the cultural designation of a site over its physical or even historical features.' (Van Den Abbeele 1994: 240) The detachment of thematic envelopes from the landscape has also been enabled by a common practice of locating theme parks on abandoned industrial sites and wastelands, strategically positioned within the theater as well as in relation to the existing and anticipated traffic infrastructure. Walt Disney Company utilized Florida swamps and made enormous investments to change soil quality for the purpose of constructing Walt Disney World. Huis Ten Bosch utilized an abandoned industrial site previously reclaimed from the sea with the necessary infrastructure already built in. Landscapes put to use for theme parks often lack inherent cultural, social and material context and consequently their organizing principles are effortlessly directed by a fictive, visual theme. For Edward Ball, the essence of thematization lies precisely in the priority of 'image' over the phenomenological experience of 'place' (Ball 1993: 33). The procedures of framing the experience of landscape through appropriate cultural mechanisms and respective technical devices has been known since antiquity. Subordinating a world-view as well as the principles of design to the rationale of representation was imposed in the Eighteenth Century by new optical devices such as *Camera Obscura*: a landscape garden viewed through these optical devices became a meta-garden, since it reduced the phenomenological experience of garden to a two-dimensional image. Analogically, the totalizing principles at work within the procedures of Themeparking turn any given landscape into a meta-landscape by imposing a fictive, alien and after all irrelevant thematic content upon it, and by simultaneously erasing all traces from it except those that can support its production process and can be manipulated as sources of revenue generation.

The most complex group of input variables within the themeparking equation are those that establish the relationships between cultural references and thematic frameworks. Cultural references are the least tangible factors in the theme park equation since culture is a dynamic concept that changes over time in ways difficult to anticipate. All designed environments are culture-specific and since culture is variable, they must respond to variables of needs and priorities as shaped by 'cultural templates' (Rapoport 1980: 7). Thematic frameworks of small, regional theme parks are commonly designed based upon the culture of the local area. Since larger regional and global theme parks commonly utilize sites devoid of direct cultural references, a broader cultural milieu that influences every aspect of individual and group environment and behavior is taken into account. Each cultural milieu chosen contains a treasure box of symbolic values that can be used for the fabrication of a theme park's thematic envelope and storyline. For Pierre Bourdieu, 'symbolic capital' consists of 'culturally appropriate intangibles' such are honor, pride, trust, youth, integrity, national history, cultural heritage, vernacular architecture, democracy and so on (Bourdieu 1977). These intangibles can be stored, re-packed and manipulated as sources of real, tangible capital. In that respect, theme parks may capitalize on the symbolic political events not necessarily directly related to their operation as in the case of Animal Kingdom Park's opening and President Clinton's visit to Africa in 1998. Six Flags over Texas capitalizes on the dramatic history of Texas, Huis Ten Bosch capitalizes on the historical ties with The Netherlands, Warner Bros. Movie World capitalizes on the German film history, Las Vegas plays on the symbolic load of gambling along 'the American frontier', Colonial Williamsburg utilizes the inheritance of all-American values, Polynesian Cultural Center employs vernacular architecture and traditional songs and dances, Bush Gardens capitalizes on the symbolic value of the Wild-West and so on. All these examples show how symbolic values, cultural intangibles, can play a significant role in the cycles of themeparking. Large corporations have created pop-culture properties and symbolic values of their own

that can also be perpetually capitalized upon: Walt Disney Company has a high reputation for safety, public order, cleanliness, safe fun and 'the American way' as well as Mickey Mouse, Hercules and other popular properties.

Each thematic framework employed thus identifies, isolates, manipulates and capitalizes on certain symbolic values that already exist within the chosen cultural milieu (regional culture, pop culture, global culture, corporate culture) either by exploiting them for the fabrication, enhancement or diversification of theme park's brand, or as a treasure box of ideas and concepts that marketing procedures utilize as symbolic capital.

Marketing and Branding

Themeparking is extremely marketing sensitive, and in a highly segmented market it requires very precise targeting achieved by the identification of 'target markets'. After the trade theater is identified, marketing strategies are employed to define (or fine-tune) the theme park concept and its thematic framework. Marketing studies use data related to the demographic analysis as a way of quantifying population-data that relates to the trade theater (such as income, age, ethnicity, marital status, education) and some sort of psychographic segmentation system that predicts consumer behavior based on the understanding of consumers values, beliefs, attitudes and motivations. PRIZM system by Claritas is one of the existing systems that categorizes social constituents into unique Socio-Economics and Lifestyles groups (SEL segments) by identifying over 60 distinctive SEL segments in the United States. The SEL analysis describes qualifying factors of the population defined both as group/individual social and economic standing (socio-economic profile) and as group/individual values and beliefs (lifestyle affinities). Another commonly-used psychographic tool is the SRI's Values and Lifestyles Program (VALS system). Psychographic segmentation systems commonly identify social groups based on their belief systems, values, 'needs-and-wants', as well as expectations and desires such are pleasure and adventure seeking, learning and discovery, relaxation modes and affinities, self-realization affinities, group affinities and so on. Although each region in the world has a marketing segmentation system adequate to its socio-economic milieu, the (ab)use of customer data for psychographic and marketing purposes is in many countries illegal. These segmentation systems are then used for the Market Feasibility studies that identify, quantify and qualify the following factors: focus factors identified through geo-demographic analysis (boundaries of the target population within the theater), motivation factors identified through a psychographic analysis (motivating variables that would explain reasons for attendance), hauling factors identified through traffic study and site analysis as well as through elements of psychographic analysis (means of attendance such are time-distance relationship, comparable travel costs, group affinities), time factors identified through psychographic analysis, demographic analysis and an analysis of socio-cultural patterns (determine periods, length and frequency of attendance) and market factors identified through industry and competition analysis as well as through psychographic analysis (identifies other potential tourist targets in the theater that attract the same target population).[7] Based on the conclusions drawn from the above analysis, an adequate concept and a thematic framework are designed to target the specific audience(s), and marketing then proceeds by establishing the 'value' of the theme park's offer or the estimate that customers make in relation to the ability of a theme park to satisfy their desires and expectations. As Morrison has suggested the so-called eight 'P's are characteristic marketing factors that determine marketing strategies or the so-called 'marketing mix': product, place, promotion, price, people, packaging, programming and partnership (Morrison 1997: 21). The success of theme park marketing is dependent on the marketing mix as well as on the marketing environment as a whole.

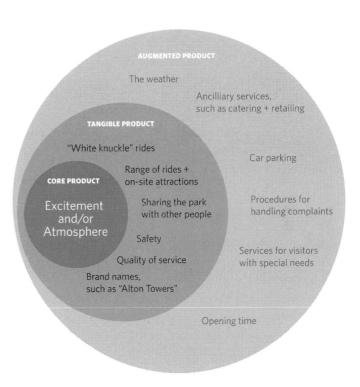

Diagram depicting a common management approach to the holistic notion of the theme park as product: core product (intangible values), tangible product (tangible values), and augmented product (tangible and intangible values). Source: after Kotler (1994) and Swarbrooke (1995).

One of the key concepts within total landscape directly relevant to marketing is the dissolution of the boundaries between the world of media and the material environments of theme parks. In fact in many ways it is through the process of marketing that the two are brought together into an inseparable whole. Walt Disney and the ABC television network introduced this paradigmatic move: in 1953, Roy and Walt Disney made an agreement with ABC to supply a weekly Disney show in return for a line of credit needed for the completion of Disneyland Park (Marling 1997: 72–74). Walt Disney organized the weekly show titled Disneyland by a set of themes corresponding to the imagined 'lands' of the future theme park. Each theme, framed thus by a 'land', combined news reports from the Disney studio together with technological innovations, corporate research and films from Disney's personal animation library. Disney described each element of the future theme park in detail and shared with his audiences the excitement. The message that clearly came across is that the experience of Disneyland Park will be substantially different from anything the audience had seen before, that in fact their experiences would be closer to that of watching television through a series of discontinuous narratives. Thus, every Wednesday evening Tomorrowland, Adventureland, Frontierland and Fantasyland were turned into the 30-minute television narratives. In April 1955, ABC announced it would broadcast a live television show featuring Walt Disney introducing his new theme park, which was anticipated to open on 17th July the same year. Corporate sponsors were eager to capitalize on product tie-ins, offering paper castles before Disneyland Park was actually opened. Ninety million Americans watched the opening show. Following Disney's example on 21st May 1955, CBS covered the seasonal opening of Steeplechase Park in Coney Island and NBC covered the seasonal opening of Rockaways Playland (Mooradian and Benz 2002). As Mooradian and Benz wrote, the trade magazine *Billboard* estimated that within this greatest mass exposure the amusement industry has ever achieved, over 28 million people saw the CBS's and NBC's television shows and dubbed them (Mooradian and Benz 2002). Before these events took place Morris Lapidus designed his Fontainebleau Hotel in Miami Beach, in 1947, to gimmick stage sets designed in Hollywood for contemporary soap operas and television shows. Ever since, boundaries of thematic environments are no longer defined only by their geographic locales but also by their media presence, mostly on television. The use of theme parks as backdrops for a variety of television programs, movies, sports competition, conventions and convention-related television broadcasting has become increasingly more present as a direct result of marketing efforts. The concept known as 'marketing synergy' enables theme parks to promote movies, movies to promote merchandise and merchandise to promote theme parks so that cycles of synergetic marketing expand endlessly into entertainment space. As Peter Rummell of Disney Design and Development Company said:

> The worlds that are going to come into your home through a wire may be connected to a three-dimensional world that we create outside the home. There will be environments that you can explore and enjoy that will come into your home but that are reproduced in a three-dimensional form in a place that you can visit. Simplistically, you could go to Disneyland by getting in your car and driving there or you could go to Disneyland on your home television by accessing a Disney channel of some kind. (ULI 1997: 387)

Rummell calls this 'an interesting confluence'. Theme park developers and operators invest large portion of operating expenses towards marketing: major theme parks in the United States spend up to 15 percent of total operating expenses on marketing, whereas European and Asian theme parks spend up to 10 percent (Robinett and Braun 1999). Sometimes in a new, emerging theme park market heavy general marketing efforts are required in order to establish industry's identity and to construct the desire for theme parks: Huis Ten Bosch's aggressive marketing campaign throughout Asian markets (besides Japan particularly in Taiwan, Hong Kong and Singapore) is the case in point. In fact, the key to successful marketing efforts is the creation of the theme park's concept that also outlines the thematic framework and the 'storyline'. In many ways, this means the creation of brand identity. Companies like Walt Disney have a strong brand presence in the global market and represent most clearly the confluence of the company name, logo, storyline, theme and characters (that together fabricate the company's mythology) with the media presence (movies, advertising) and the physical presence of Walt Disney theme parks, retail locations, urban entertainment centers (Disney-Quest) and the themeing (physical, visual and sensual environment). Disney's brand identity thus fabricates emotional bonding that connects the experience in each Disney facility with its media presence.

An enormous growth of marketing and the increasing globalization in the media business are characterized by an ever-increasing consolidation and control of the theme park industry by multinational corporations. In 1995, Walt Disney Company invested US$1.296 billion in a global media promotion of its products including theme parks. Contemporary marketing strategies with the synergetic functioning of television, newspapers, magazines, advertising, movies and movie previews, music television, the Internet and a variety of related material commodities also successfully fabricates and promotes specific social and cultural relationships framed by appropriate themes and brands. Within such a synergetic framework, theme parks spatialize these fabricated relationships: by the instrumentalization of space they prove that such fictitious relationships can be real even though strictly speaking they are fabricated and ephemeral. In addition, the ability of contemporary marketing to accomplish such complex tasks has been facilitated by a departure from the traditional features-and-benefits approach to marketing, to the design and management of holistic experiential outcomes. As Schmitt writes, Experiential Marketing fabricates synergetic holistic experiences across scales and domains through a global supremacy of corporate brands together with the converging effects of information technology, integrated communications, and entertainment (Schmitt 1999). The extent to which the principles of synergy are utilized for marketing purposes was strikingly apparent on the occasion of the opening of Disney's Animal Kingdom Park. Namely, President William J. Clinton had toured six African countries from 23rd March to 2nd April 1998 in order to confirm American influence in the region (BBC 1998). Media images of the President dancing and singing with the natives in typically ethnic settings circled the globe during that week while the world attentively observed the imagery. Just as media attention around President Clinton's tour was dissolving and late reflections appeared in the media calling it an 'African Odyssey' (PBS 1998) or an 'African Safari' (Okumu 1998), Disney's Animal Kingdom Park opened on 22nd April 1998 with all the appropriate media attention usually

BARTHOLOMEW'S FAIR

Commercial feudalism brought the medieval country-fair, a form of entertainment essentially different from medieval markets. Country fairs were cosmopolitan in character and gathered people from far away, lasted up to two weeks, and sold finished goods as opposed to raw materials and raw food sold at markets. The major difference, however, was that country fairs were placed outside the medieval city walls, an element of displacement that was essential to their success: for their visitors they meant 'travel' outside of the territory of everyday life while for the officials it meant 'order' since the territory out of the city walls belonged to another juridical realm. Since the closing of Roman theaters in the Sixth Century until the Middle Ages, the Catholic Church had vigorously censored popular entertainments and so dancing, drinking, and playing risky games were strongly forbidden within the city walls and in all regions under its strong control. Early Twelfth Century fairs were associated with funeral ceremonies and thus cemeteries were among the places where public entertainment and fairs initially took place (McKechnie 1969: 29–54).

Bartholomew's Fair was initiated in 1120, and it took place every year on a site initially marked by civic and religious rituals.[1] The site would be initiated by building a wooden stage where heretics were burnt (Morley 1869: 62), a practice that lasted until 1611 (Morley 1869: 113). The act of transformation of the heretic's bodies into ashes marked the beginning of fair-time. In the Sixteenth Century, Bartholomew's fair was the most popular fair in Europe. Like many other medieval fairs, Bartholomew's Fair was also based on a kind of grid system, with booths featuring food and commodities in the core of the site and amusement installations marking its perimeter (Braithwaite 1968: 21–29). Peasants and artisans brought to the fair the surplus they acquired due to a gradual dissolution of feudal system. Iron, clothing, hats, gloves, food, silk, toys, were sold at the fairs's booths. Bartholomew's Fair was a typical example of the so-called 'pleasure fair' offering special commodities: merchants from Genoa would bring silk, from Catalonia leather, from France clothes, making the fair a true international trading event. Besides trading, Bartholomew's Fair also offered live entertainment: wax figures of famous people, freak shows, jugglers, clowns, etc. After the mid-Seven-

given to such an event (OBJ 1998). One of the Kingdom's 'lands' was naturally Africa and, in addition, an African Safari was designed for the 'guests'. The same day the first visitors reported live on a major cable television channel: 'It is unbelievable, it looks just like Africa, and my husband asked me in the middle of this Safari-tour: "Is this Africa or what?" [...] And all those wonderful animals. Real thrill!' For US$40, everyone could have the presidential experience without leaving the comforts of home.

Similar strategies are used in Japan. In 1988, the NHK (national television station) aired an historical drama *Takeda Shingen* based on famed historic events of significance for the national identity that took place in the Shizuoka Prefecture (Shirahata 1995). The drama was staged at different locations in adjoining Nagano and Yamanashi Prefectures, and prior to its airing regional tourist businesses boosted the birth and development of tourist attractions that were to employ the same set of historic narratives. Once the drama aired on a high viewer-rated channel, local theme parks (such as Tsumakoi) and adjoining attractions were overwhelmed by millions of incoming tourists. Thus, an historic event was transformed into symbolic capital through its use by the national television station for the purpose of educating the Japanese public about national history. The same symbolic capital was simultaneously activated by the tourist and theme park industries and transformed instantly into the source of real revenues.

Marketing is also heavily dependent on daily affairs: the best example for this is Walt Disney World Resort's attraction called Mission: Space, an updated version of Disneyland Park's Rocket to the Moon attraction built within Tomorrowland in the late-1950s. In 2000, the Walt Disney Company intended to offer an attraction that would build on the growing interest in the Space Program and NASA, and also capitalize on the proximity of the Kennedy Space Center located only 70 miles away. It was also an attempt to boost the attendance at EPCOT whose visitors have been steadily declining. The plans were well underway for the official opening scheduled for spring of 2003 and NASA acted as a consultant for this attraction (Jackson 2003). As Mike Schneider wrote, the space shuttle Columbia disaster that occurred on 1st February 2003 has fundamentally challenged Disney's idea: Disney could have moved out of this impossible marketing situation only by turning the attraction into an homage to the Space Program, while losing the ability to advertise the attraction as a thrill-seeking experience which also meant leaning the ride to some sort of museum exhibit (Schneider 2003). Disney naturally postponed the opening, arguing that discussions on how to market the attraction had not even begun in February 2003 so that marketing executives had not even considered at that point how the Columbia tragedy would affect their plans. The attraction finally opened in October 2003. As Schneider further indicates, EPCOT is not the first theme park to have a major tragedy collide with its idealized world: Universal Studios in Orlando had also delayed the opening of the Twister ride in 1998 following tornadoes that killed 42 people in central Florida.

The Walt Disney Company provides the best expertise in cross-marketing in the industry due also to its size: most of the cross-marketing is done within the corporation and in-between various Disney departments. It applies cross-marketing as a base of its business and not as a final promotional step after the product is ready. Some examples include the appearance of over 80 Hollywood stars such are Jennifer Garner, Jim Belushi, Dennis Franz and George Lopez at Disney's California Adventure Park in September 2003, an event covered fully by the ABC (Disney owned media company) Prime-time Preview Weekend that used the event as a promotional tool for the upcoming fall season and its new shows to be launched just a few days later (Rice 2003a). Visitors were allowed to interact with the stars through Q&A sessions, photo sessions, acting sessions (were visitors could act in a scene next to one of the stars) and a concert featuring Jim Belushi and his Sacred Hearts band. Access Hollywood, Entertainment Tonight and TV Guide also covered the event,

teenth Century, its duration extended to two weeks (Morley 1869: 294).

Although the first dramas were performed there in the Fifteenth Century, in the Eighteenth Century the fair began featuring organized theater performances called 'stage-plays'. Stage-plays were 'expensive entertainments', because they produced popular theater pieces showing in London in a format adjusted to the masses. Serious and lengthy dialogues would be replaced by efficient scenic effects, the use of machines, projections, light-effects, transparent paintings of giant sizes and stage-set composed of a couple of iconic facades formed this open-air setting. Plays lasted for about 30 minutes. The most popular show was The Siege of Troy, designed by Elkanah Settle in 1707 (McKechnie 1969: 41). It had four scenes: in one of them a 17 foot tall, excessively decorated Trojan horse enters the stage and 40 soldiers jump out of its body setting the whole town on fire. At that moment, windows and doors of the surrounding buildings all painted on large transparent sheets began burning in flames spreading from one house to another—a simulated stage-set effect perfected by Settle. In the concluding scene, Greek soldiers triumphantly occupied the scene. In the foreground there was a peep-show, food store, dog dressed in elegant clothes, a man flying from the tower, and many other amusements.

Unlike the designs of garden-buildings and pavilions in the prevailing English Picturesque Garden that employed archi-

The Siege of Troy performance at the Bartholomew's Fair. Lithograph by William Hogarth, c. 1707.

tecture as an associational device *par excellence,* fair buildings were complementary to an artificial arrangement (stage set) and could have been observed from a set of fixed viewpoints. They were thus reduced to two-dimensional, iconic representations and had operated on an iconic level in order to complement the narrative of theatrical performance. Architecture of amusement installations became no different from that of theater stage: facades were relatively elaborated and made of wood and plaster, on the back held by triangular wooden supports. In the early Nineteenth Century, free trading became more organized, especially following the Industrial Revolution. Trade shows and organized commodity exhibitions moved to city galleries, arcades, Market Halls and other more appropriate settings. The demand for a clear view of goods, lots of light and convenient communication made a paradigmatic break in the traditional association between trading and amusement through the form of pleasure-fairs. This paradigmatic shift had forced pleasure fairs to focus on pure amusement. As Morley noted, 'its vulgar appeal to an idle curiosity answered the taste of London better than the highest efforts of the dramatist and the comedian.' (Morley 1869: 300) At Bartholomew's fair, the roundabouts, stages and other amusement installations moved from the periphery of the site to its center (Braithwaite 1968). Subsequently booths featuring food, drinks and some commodities were aligned marking the perimeter of the site. The decorative 'architecture' that originated at fairs was also utilized in pleasure gardens, such as Vauxhall and Ranelagh that existed in parallel with Bartholomew's Fair until 1850s. Bartholomew's Fair was abolished in 1851, the year of the Great Industrial Exhibition in London.[2] As consumer goods moved to market halls, the institutionalization of 'technological invention' caused 'technological wonders' traditionally promoted at fairs to be moved to other, institutionalized settings such as Great Industrial Exhibitions.[3] In the Nineteenth Century, pleasure fairs gave way to a number of typological variations that also focused on pure bodily pleasures, such are amusement parks that began appearing towards 1870s. Coney Island is a typical example of that tradition.

1. The following is Samuel McKechnie's account of establishing the place for the Bartholomew's Fair in 1598 described in his *Popular Entertainments Through the Ages:* 'It is worthy of observation that every year, upon St. Bartholomew's Day, when the Fair is held, it is usual for the mayor,

adding to a spectacular media coverage. Another example is Disney's attraction Who Wants to Be a Millionaire-Play It! developed in parallel with the ABC's prime-time television show. The attraction opened on the 7th April 2001 at Disney-MGM Studios as a clear attempt to boost both the television ratings of the ABC show and attendance at the Disney-MGM Studios, both declining at that point.

The inventiveness of the Walt Disney Company's brand strategies is also obvious through its attempt not to re-design the brand itself but to reposition it in relation to the existing target audiences (e.g. market segmentation). In other words, the Walt Disney Company wisely creates different value propositions for customers that would customarily fall outside of its primary target audience:[8] couples with no children, minorities, gay and lesbian audiences, pre-family markets and so on. As Mike Branom indicates, the Gay Days in Disneyland Park started out in 1991 when gay tourists informally decided to get together at Disney's Magic Kingdom Park (Branom 2003). For many years, Walt Disney Company fought the battle against the Gay Days, including the placement of warning signs to alert straight tourists that homosexuals were in the theme park. Nowadays, both Disneyland Gay Days that run during the first week of October and Walt Disney World Gay Days that run during the first week of June are an attraction welcomed by Walt Disney Company. Nearly 150 000 gay visitors get into Disney theme parks during each of the two weekends. Al Weiss, President of Walt Disney World Resort, explained the management's move this way: 'What we try to do every day is deliver a product—whether it's entertainment, attractions, cleanliness, architecture, great service—that would appeal to a broad range of people across this whole globe no matter how old they are, how young they are, whatever their ethnic background is.' (Branom 2003) In the words of Linda Warren, the Executive Vice President of Marketing and Brand Management at the Walt Disney World Resort, Walt Disney Company is in fact indeed simply 'reinventing the brand by making it relevant' (Rassmuson 2001). In 2000,

Warren's team designed a scheme within which advertising and collateral materials were created for four distinct groups: families with young children, families with teens, empty nesters, the pre-family market and Hispanics/African-Americans market. This move had brought an estimated 600 000 new visitors through Walt Disney World Resort's gates the same year.

The symbiosis of the material world, the world of media and the synergetic cross-marketing behavior of corporate patrons is also obvious through an aggressive attempt by Universal Studios in 2001 to develop new entertainment areas in the Universal Studios Hollywood by partnering with two cable television networks: Viacom and Discovery Communications. Through Viacom, Universal has developed programs in collaboration with its Nickelodeon cable television channel, whereas through Discovery Communications, it has collaborated with its Animal Planet cable television channel. This move brought to Universal Studios Hollywood a massive exposure to over 60 million viewers through promotions on Viacom's and Discovery Communications's networks (Morell 2000). As Natasha Emmons reported, Brian Pope, Vice President of marketing for Universal Studios Hollywood said: 'It's all part of us being the world's largest movie studio and theme park. We try to link all the attractions to top brands in film and television. Nickelodeon and Animal Planet are both extremely popular and compelling brands now and into the future.' (Emmons 2001) The attractions added to the Universal Studios Hollywood were The Nickelodeon Blast Zone, a 30 000 square-foot interactive playground with a few sub-themed areas and Animal Planet Live! inspired by Animal Planet's television shows. Animal Planet Live! combines live animal acting, video clips from Animal Planet television shows, personal appearances by stars from Animal Planet programs, and walk-through interactive experiences. Along with the two play areas guests are also offered both Animal Planet and Nickelodeon merchandise: namely the merchandising agreement between the parties anticipates both Animal Planet and

attended by the twelve principal aldermen, to walk in a neighboring field, dressed in his scarlet gown, and about his neck a golden chain, to which is hung a golden Fleece, and, besides, that particular ornament which distinguishes the most noble order of the Garter. When the mayor goes out of the precincts of the city, a scepter and sword and a cap are borne before him, and he is followed by the principal aldermen in scarlet gowns with gold chains, himself and they on horseback. Upon their arrival at a place appointed for that purpose, where a tent is pitched, the mob begin to wrestle before them, two at time; the conquerors receive rewards from the magistrates. After all this is over, a parcel of live rabbits are turned loose among the crowd, which are pursued by a number of boys, who endeavor to catch them, with all the noise they can make.' (McKechnie 1969:30)

2. Officially, the fair was proclaimed for the last time in 1855, but it was as of 1851 that no Mayor accompanied the opening ceremony (Morley 1869: 389).

3. A case in point are 'mechanical automatons', mechanical dolls performing various tasks: writing, drawing, moving around, walking, such as Pierre Jacquet Droz's Writing Doll of 1770. It had the mechanism similar to those of contemporary watches, packed in a wooden body, with fake hair and clothes. A sophisticated version of it was exhibited at the *Premiere Exposition Des Produits de l'Industrie Français* (Giedion 1949: 166).

Nickelodeon selling its themed toys and children's clothing through a global network of Toys'R'Us retail locations, while the same branded items will also be sold at Universal Studios Hollywood. Besides these, a live show based on the animated film Shrek was also added to the theme park's offer in parallel with the national release of the film in May 2003. These attempts go hand-in-hand with fabricated visitors's expectations and desires for a theme park version of 'the real working film and television studio'.

The Tourist Experience

The view of theme parks as pilgrim sites and visitors as pilgrims is a common one: utilizing Victor Turner's concept of liminality (Turner 1969, 1978) and Dean MacCannell's tourist theory (MacCannell 1976), Stephen Fjellman argued theme park visitors are both pilgrims and tourists (Fjellman 1992: 223). MacCannell's *The Tourist: A New Theory of the Leisure Class* of 1976 was one of the first consistent attempts to theorize contemporary mass-tourism constructed as a criticism of Daniel Boorstin's early notions (Boorstin 1962). The basic assertion of MacCannell's work was that contemporary tourist is a middle-class sightseer, world-traveler in search of authentic experiences. He finds no such phenomena in the world since those who package tourist experiences into ready-made, risk-free experience-packages have transformed every available landscape into a gigantic stage-set. MacCannell further argued that tourist's inability to experience authenticity generated 'tourist shame' because one is aware of the fake scenery one is brought to admire. In *The Image or What Happened to the American Dream* of 1962, Boorstin adopted a fundamentally different point of view as he argued that tourists are no travelers: they are middle-class admirers of the pseudo-eventful 'adventures' (Boorstin 1962, 1964). When traveler's risks are insurable, argued Boorstin, he becomes a tourist. His tourist expects risk-free, lifetime adventures in two weeks where the 'exotic' and the 'familiar' are a matter of choosing a different *oeuvre* within the very same menu:

Expecting all this, he demands that it be supplied to him. Having paid for it, he likes to think he has got his money's worth. He has demanded that the whole world be made a stage of pseudo-events. And there has been no lack of honest and enterprising suppliers who try to give him what he wants, to help him inflate his expectations, and to gratify his insatiable appetite for the impossible. (Boorstin 1962: 80)

It is from Boorstin's 1960s notion of tourist that the notion of 'post-tourist' has developed, where 'post' refers both to its links to post-modern world as to its historical ancestor 'the tourist'. Post-tourist is aware of the tourist condition as he realistically adopts the condition of an outsider and stops struggling against it (Feifer 1985, Urry 1990). Total landscape thus is not only produced by those engaged in themeparking, but also by the tourist, who having adopted this condition deliberately sets himself the cause and the sole consumer of tourist attractions and joyfully understands the whole cognitive and sensory overload staged for him as an end in-itself (Boorstin 1962). The tourist does not search for authenticity in theme parks and other tourist targets within the total landscape, it is precisely the fabricated that he expects to find there. As Umberto Eco has argued, 'once the "total fake" is admitted, in order to be enjoyed it must seem totally real [...] because the public is meant to admire the perfection of the fake and its obedience to the program.' (Eco 1986: 44) In fact, Eco argued that the acknowledgement of the production of illusion stimulates the desire for it as well as an ultimate dissatisfaction if fake is not clearly declared. Rojek has summarized the main characteristics of the 'post-tourist' as follows: an awareness of the commodification of tourist experience, the denial of the idea of progress in tourist experience (as related to self-realization) and a positive identification with intertextuality (Rojek 1993: 177). Gottdiener has argued that mass-tourism today facilitates the consumption of specifically assigned 'tourist spaces', drawing on Lefebvre's notions discussed in the first chapter (Lefebvre 1991), particularly that instead of the circulation of commodities tourism nowadays involves the circulation of people to specific locations that are consumed as spaces of leisure or amusement, within the cycles of the production of entertainment space (Gottdiener 1998: 13). The consumption of space is promoted by exotic spatial experience in a themed mode that works as a tourist attraction in itself.

Marketing is heavily dependent on the developments in the travel and tourism industries. One of the tie-in arrangements the Walt Disney Company made in February 2002 was with Travelocity.com, an online, tourist discount-package business for the sale of vacation packages, including hotel reservations and theme park tickets online in an obvious effort to move out of the post-11th September 2001 attendance crisis (Johnson and Pack 2002). Within this arrangement, Travelocity.com bundles Disney vacation packages with discounted airline tickets, rent-a-car arrangements and travel insurance deals (that it obtains separately), and markets them under its own brand Travelocity Vacations. The Walt Disney Company also has an agreement with the American Automobile Associations (AAA)[9] and American Express to include Walt Disney destination resorts and theme parks in their travel packages. Given that Travelocity.com has over 30 million Internet subscribers and AAA has 45 million members, the exposure of Disney properties has been greatly increased. Other theme park giants use similar cross-marketing deals. For instance, in view of ever increasing lines in theme parks, especially during busy weekends and holidays, Universal Studios Hollywood and MasterCard International have developed a program that offers a print-at-home option for guests who purchase their tickets online at the Universal Studios Hollywood Web site 'presented by MasterCard'.[10] In order to make the purchase, future visitors have to use a major credit card (MasterCard or alternatively VISA, Discover Card, American Express or JCB). Visitors print tickets with the unique bar code information on regular paper that is then scanned at the theme park's entrance (Rice 2003). Universal promotes these ideas in the following way: 'You'll receive your tickets in advance, so you won't need to stop at a ticket booth line when you arrive at the park. Go straight down

the red carpet and begin enjoying your day!'[11] At most times, Universal Studios Hollywood offers print-at-home users a discount off regular park admission: in spring 2004, it offered 'buy a day get a year free' deal that offered an annual pass for a price of one day admission.[12] The types of annual passes the park offers are Front of Line Pass, VIP Experience Pass and the Celebrity Annual Pass.

The stability of the tourist industry is densely interwoven with fluctuations of the global market. The tourism industry is one of the largest industrial complexes in the global economy with over US$400 billion in revenue and over 10 percent of the world's income and employment (ULI 1997: 384). When the theme park industry in the United States went through its initial development phase in the 1960s and 1970s, most theme parks were designed and marketed as regional attractions (with the exception of Walt Disney World Resort to be discussed later in this chapter) to be visited by population living within a day-drive radius. With the rise of significant levels of disposable income, free time and discretionary travel in the 1980s and early-1990s, many new theme parks were designed and marketed as international tourist destinations, thus changing the one-day-market into a week-long-market. This also meant that directed and targeted marketing focused increasingly on package tours, promotions, special events and often group sales programs. Due to group marketing, theme parks in the 1990s based up to 50 percent of annual attendance figures on group visits. Package tours complemented theme park visits with other destination activities, often visits to other theme parks in the area, shopping malls, museums and other targets. Large theme park operators invested heavily into hotels and other accommodation facilities. In fact packaging, as a combination of related and complementary services into a single-price offering, has together with programming changed the theme park industry. Programming adds value to packaging by designing special events and activities that reconceptualize the presence of individual theme parks and increase tourists's per capita spending. Morrison recognized the benefits of packaging and programming for all constituents: customers, travel trade intermediaries (tour operators, travel agents, and incentive travel planners), suppliers (lodging, restaurants, car rental, cruise line, individual attraction operators including theme park operators) and carriers (airlines, bus and train companies) (Morrison 1997: 287–295). As he further suggested, for customers, programming implies greater economy and convenience, implicit assurance of quality, an ability to budget for trips, satisfaction of special interests and added dimensions to traveling. For the industry, it means increased business in off-peak periods, enhanced appeal to specific target markets and attraction of new ones, flexibility to capitalize on new market trends, use of complementary events, attractions and facilities, easier business forecasting and improved efficiency, stimulation of repeat and more frequent visits, increased per capita spending and lengths of stay, publicity, and 'increasing awareness' value of unique packages (for theme parks that promote issue of great public interest) and very often also increased customer satisfaction.

In view of such developments, packaging becomes even more critical to theme park attendance because it also presents opportunities for homogenization and cross-marketing of tourist offerings either within or without the theater. A case in point is a strong trend that began in the 1990s as large theme parks offered new incentives for extended stays: convention and conference facilities, sports facilities (mostly golf, tennis and swimming), diversified shopping opportunities, a variety of themed dining experiences and many other options characteristic of a resort destination. The leader in these developments has been Walt Disney World Resort. Although Walt Disney World Resort has the capacity to offer a great variety of experiences through mass-customization of experiences and targeted marketing, smaller theme parks are better positioned to cater to a variety of specialty markets looking for environmentally and culturally sensitive environments: eco-tourists, heritage tourists, educational tourists and pilgrimages of various kinds. For example, Huis Ten Bosch Co. in Japan, the owner and operator of Huis Ten Bosch theme park, had in 1997 founded the Kyushu Sightseeing Company in order to link the existing and new target destinations in the trade theater into a network. As a result of this successful operation, the length of stay was increased and per capita spending was doubled (see Themeparking Huis Ten Bosch): in relation to hotel occupancy, Hotel Amsterdam in Huis Ten Bosch had in 1997 an AGER (Average Guest Expenditure Rate) value of US$80 800 per room annually while the average AGER value for Japan the same year was US$40 500. The construction of resort-like environment within a theater brings about the key economic benefit of themeparking: overnight stays. Commonly in such an economic environment, day-visitors generate up to 20 percent of the economic impact whereas the remaining 80 percent is generated by destination tourists, overnight stays and related services.

Tourism and Theme Park Marketing after 11th September 2001
The late-1990s have brought great economic and other uncertainties and consequently a desire for shorter travel times. The early years of the Twenty-First Century are bringing ever more serious threats such as that of international terrorism. Regardless of the immanence of such threats, they now constitute a serious psychological barrier to international tourism. In the five weeks immediately following the 11th September 2001 terrorist attacks, Walt Disney World Resort reported a 25 percent drop in attendance (O'Brien 2001a). Other destination theme parks in the United States experienced similar developments due to the decline in air travel and fears of terrorist attacks. However, regional theme parks during the same period experienced a rise in attendance volumes: Busch Gardens in Williamsburg, Virginia as a part of the drive-in tourist market had its record fall season (O'Brien 2001a). Longer vacations have been replaced across the world by more frequent shorter travels to regional destinations, even in countries like Italy where previously the entire month of August was used for vacationing. Breaks are becoming shorter and more frequent and are usually woven into holidays and longer weekends. New

entertainment venues built in the late 1990s are 'closer to home' and commonly located in shopping centers or urban areas such are Family Entertainment Centers (FEC) or as Retail Entertainment Centers composed usually of small theme parks located in shopping malls (REC).

Even before the 11th September 2001 terrorist attacks, the North American theme park industry had began to show signs of decline. Theme park operators often attempted to boost attendance levels by introducing value packages mostly centered on discount admission tickets.[13] Various industry-commissioned studies in the United States showed that over half of the theme park visitors in 2001 did not stay overnight which meant the industry was already shifting towards a day-market and their tourist and marketing policies reflected that fact. Local advertising was a new trend. At the Californian Sea World, the management created an eight-state Shamu Across America campaign in which customized VW Beetles toured the North American West in the spring to promote the theme park in order to boost attendance in the summer, especially in the wake of the opening of Disney's California Adventure Park (Cain 2001). The trade journal *Amusement Business*'s 2001 Family Price Index (FPI)[14] showed the increase of national average for seven percent to US$163.22 (AB 2001) which in addition to the weakened American economy, gasoline prices at record highs, the strong U.S. dollar, overall hotel occupancy off six percent nationwide and undesirable weather meant a disastrous season for the theme park industry (McDowell 2001). Even Disney theme parks that had never previously offered discounted admission reduced adult ticket prices in June 2001 from US$43 to US$33 for Southern California residents, and allowed one child in free with each adult ticket (Freeman 2001).

By the end of 2001, *Amusement Business* reported a decline of theme park attendance of two percent at average to 170 million tourists. Although, for instance, Disneyland Resort's overall attendance fell 11 percent, international visits at Walt Disney World Resort were down about 20 percent, while international traffic at the Orlando International airport was down nearly 25 percent (Hopkins 2002). At the same time, European theme park market-analysts claimed that figures showed European regionally conceived theme parks depending on local tourists were not damaged by the terrorist attacks and fears of travel (Koranteng 2001). Overall worldwide theme park attendance had hit a record of 250 million visitors to the world's top 50 theme parks, an increase of nearly 300 000 tourists over 2000 (Schneider 2002). By June 2002, 64 percent of North Americans attending theme parks that summer decided to drive and only one third of all Americans decided to fly that year (Rice 2002). Out of the nearly 30 million tourists that had visited Orlando in 2002, over 21 million drove according to the Orlando Convention & Visitors Bureau: Orlando's biggest drive markets have been New York, Chicago, Philadelphia, Boston, Houston, Detroit, Washington, D.C., St. Louis and Charlotte, N.C. Seventy five percent of North American theme parks seeking to make up losses from fewer international visitors began marketing directly to people within driving distance and offering bargains and discount packages. As Kate Rice reported, Orange County and Orlando Convention & Visitors Bureau, Inc. offered a discounted Orlando Magic Card to be used at area attractions, accommodations, restaurants and transportation companies in order to reduce the FPI (Rice 2002). Florida residents purchasing a full-price admission ticket to any Florida theme park received a Florida Fun Card good for free admission throughout the year: at the Universal Orlando Florida residents saved US$25 on a two-day two-park ticket by bringing in specially marked Coca-Cola products (Schneider 2002). Dolly Parton's Dollywood offered the After 3 program that granted visitors attending the theme park after 3 P.M. free admission to the park on its next operating day. Other theme parks offered seasonal passes costing less than two days worth of admission tickets, reduced admission for children and seniors citizens, free children meals, some even included free breakfast and free transportation to theme parks. On the 1st February 2001, Universal Studios launched a free bus service called Universal Studios

Express from Anaheim just one week before the opening of the competing Disney's California Adventure Park. The shuttle-bus stopped at major Anaheim-area hotels four times a day to collect visitors and carry them to the Los Angeles Universal Studios and could be ordered by calling 1-800-UNIVERSAL. Advertising for the campaign was aggressive and was seen in television ads, flyers and brochures in the hotels, in bus shelters, wrapped buses and elsewhere in the area.

In 2003, fears of SARS, the possibility of a war in Iraq and a declining economy worldwide had caused many theme park operators into bankruptcy. As Disneyland Paris Resort experienced a steady decline in attendance that dropped another 600 000 in comparison with 2002, French theme-park operator Euro Disney S. A. reported record losses that had brought the overall company's debt to more than US$2.3 billion, a cost that brought uncertainties between Euro Disney and the banks that had invested in the theme park's restructuring in 1994 (AB 2003b). As attendance volumes declined across Japan, Huis Ten Bosch's attendance also fell to 2.3 million visitors in 2003 and together with unsold housing capacity, the company arrived at a US$1.92 billion debt and listed a negative net worth of US$31 million. Accordingly, Huis Ten Bosch Company had to file for bankruptcy in December 2003. North American theme parks still suffered from the terrorist fears as the federal government announced it prohibited all flights directly over Walt Disney theme parks in Florida and California in fear of attacks, and especially as Homeland Security's threat level warnings became publicized daily in the media. In February 2003, Homeland Security raised the threat level from yellow to orange (high) for the first time and as a result 'the phones stopped,' as Michael Eisner, CEO of Walt Disney Co. put it, causing severe damage to destination theme parks (Benz 2003). Attendance at the 50 most-visited theme parks in North America fell in 2003 to 168 million tourists, two million below the 2001 level (Schneider 2003a). In October 2003, *Amusement Business* reported Walt Disney World Resort offered free admission for children, given that a four-night family package is purchased at any level of Disney resort: within this arrangement one child is admitted free for each paying adult, if the purchase is made with a VISA Card (AB 2003a). In parallel with the addition of Pop Century Resort in December 2003, Walt Disney World Resort had almost 25 000 guest rooms that stayed mostly empty. The company offered the 'pay for four days and get seven' promotional package to regional markets in order to incite tourists to utilize its facilities (Blackerby 2003). Once the campaign was successfully launched and tourists arrived, it was relatively simple to restore revenues potentially lost through bargain accommodation and discount admission by increasing per capita spending on food, merchandise, parking and the like. Some Disney attractions fell victim to the drop in attendance: as of 2003, Wonders of Life attraction in EPCOT at the Walt Disney World Resort would operate on a seasonal basis catering to periods of anticipated peak attendance (Balancia 2003). Similar moves were made by a majority of theme park operators, particularly regional theme parks that were hesitant to invest and to build new rides given the uncertain world economy and unpredictable travel habits of both regional and international tourists. Many preferred to capitalize on already made investments and preferred cross-marketing efforts to new investments: Universal theme parks in Florida and California offered multi-day multi-park passes with the Sea World parks and other regional attractions. Likewise, for a purchase of two-day ticket good for Universal Studios and Islands of Adventure in Orlando tourists received a third day free of charge.

Because almost every region in the world that can support a large-scale theme park catering to vacation tourists already has one, the global market has absorbed the critical mass of large theme parks. This is especially true for North America, Europe and Japan, and is increasingly true in the rest of Asia as well as South America. The solidification in the theme park industry has also brought a global control over the entire market into the hands of a handful of corporate entertainment giants. Given the above developments, the only feasible line of development in the Twenty-First Century will be growth of themeparking operations in the so-called 'drive-in' market where Location Based Entertainment (LBE), Retail Entertainment Centers (REC), Urban Entertainment Centers (UEC) and community entertainment facilities have already become the new frontier. As Harold Vogel, the Vice-President of Merill Lynch Capital Markets, has suggested, 'although it is improbable that industry can achieve above-average gains in productivity, it appears that no matter what the financial or operational structures that evolve, national demographic trends will support growth of admissions from people at both ends of the age spectrum.' (Vogel 1986: 348)

Unlike in the early-1990s, when trade theaters located outside of major urban concentrations began acquiring resort-like forms, in the early 2000s, trade theaters located within large urban concentrations providing steady influx of tourists are capitalizing on an increasingly prevalent idea of visitors to stay 'closer to home'. Many previously exclusively day-market theme parks are trying to extend the tourist stay by expanding into a resort-like environment: a case in point is Oriental Land Company's attempt to turn a day-trip experience to Tokyo Disneyland Park into a three-night four-day experience by creating a resort destination. The 177-acre DisneySea that opened in October 2001 has completed the resort, together with two hotels and an additional ten contracted hotels in the area that take care of the overflow since all 4200 guest rooms within the resort have been steadily booked (Emmons 2002a). By 2004, all Disney theme park destinations have been renamed into resorts. Six Flags Ohio had purchased in 2001 its complementary destination SeaWorld Ohio in order to create the Six Flags World of Adventure resort and increase both per capita spending and the length of stay. Once again, turning the theater into a resort environment generated overnight stays, the key economic benefit of themeparking.

Cultural Patterns

Cultural patterns play a significant role both in the circulation of people to theme parks and in relation to the design of thematic frameworks. One of the key purposes of the Economic Feasibility Study is to identify the trade theater, while one of the key purposes of Market Study is commonly to analyze socio-economic and cultural factors. The problem in employing market studies to identify cultural variables is that trade theaters and cultural spheres do not necessarily overlap. This is particularly important for regional theme parks. In other words, whereas cultural spheres have unique cultural qualities, trade theaters have unique socio-economic qualities. Psychographic segmentation systems that attempt to identify cultural values and affinities with the trade theater can only be partly precise as they can roughly identify only major socio-economic groups. Thus, to develop a relevant thematic framework and storyline that will affect both dominant cultural groups and also subgroups is a complex task that requires both quantitative and qualitative research in the targeted socio-economic groups in order to further understand how geo-cultural locales influence people's perceptions, values and expectations, and how a unique concept can be constructed so as to create relevance in the target market (Robinett and Braun 1999).

As to the cultural patterns that relate to the circulation of people to theme parks and their consumption, the most illustrative ones are those related to the introduction of theme parks in Europe and Japan. Unlike American tourists, European tourists treat theme parks as pleasure gardens and are usually willing to drive or ride a train (rarely to fly) for up to two hours in order to reach a theme park destination. Japanese are unable to make long drives to reach the theme park destinations simply because of the lack of leisure time. Nevertheless, by airplane or the 'bullet train' (*Shinkansen*) they are able to reach remote destinations in Kyushu (remote southern island) or Hokkaido (remote northern island) within a couple of hours. The shift from private means of transport to public, an unprecedented economic pros-

perity, a relative increase in leisure time and a shift in orientation from regional leisure centers towards the national ones, caused a 'leisure boom' in Japan in the mid-1980s. This was followed by the privatization of the Japanese National Railways (JNR) in 1987 and the construction of thousands of new leisure facilities, including hundreds of theme parks.

European tourists generally attend theme parks on weekends, particularly Sundays: at Asterix Parc, design days equaled 15 percent of annual attendance indicating a weekend preference not experienced in the American theme parks (Robinett and Braun 1999). As Robinett and Braun clearly further indicate, European themes are overly intellectual when compared with American themes, and cross-themeing would not work since inadequate themes cannot create emotional experiences meaningful to visitors. In other words, themes that may create positive responses in Europe would not affect the American public the same way and vice versa. One of the most difficult things about opening an American theme park abroad is adapting nuanced communication with audiences (such as humorous phrases) to foreign cultural milieus. Norm Elder, Senior Vice President of International Marketing at Universal Studios Recreation Group in Los Angeles, pointed out that one of the most complex tasks in conceptualizing

Universal Studios theme park in Osaka, Japan was adapting the American humor to the Japanese audience: some jokes or story lines that ordinarily would have been conveyed verbally were instead performed physically or were subtitled (Schneider 2001a).

Since the late-1970s, the American theme park industry has had a very difficult time establishing standards for the theme park industry across the world mostly due to cultural differences. This has been especially true for developing economies. The non-American public did not understand the fundamental principles of the American theme park concept, from technical difficulties with rides to the obligatory one-admission-price to all attractions. Moreover, the concept of 'park' in Europe and Asia has traditionally a different meaning. The enclosed nature of the theme park and the lack of flexibility in terms of movement and behavior patterns made many stay away from these playgrounds. As Robinett and Braun argued, in North American theme parks, visitors generally spread the lunch peak-time over a three-hour period, whereas in Europe and Asia peak lunch service occurs in a one-hour period (Robinett and Braun 1999). Generally, European and Asian tourists have much stricter eating-time habits than their American counterparts. Such concerns often carry over to the design of menus at American-owned theme parks abroad, although the food in American-owned theme parks abroad is predominantly American with a variety of contextualized offers. Universal Studios tested nearly 4000 different menu entries over a three-year period to get the right menu configuration for its restaurants in Osaka. Although Tokyo Disneyland Park now has a Japanese restaurant, originally it did not. This was the result of a request made by the executives at the Oriental Land Co., Walt Disney Company's partner in Japan. As Martin Sklar, Vice Chairman and Principle Creative Executive of Walt Disney Imagineering, remembered: 'The Japanese told us from the beginning, "Don't Japanese us." What they meant was: "We came here for Disney. We came for America. Don't give us Japan because we know Japan."' (Schneider 2001a) Sklar also reported on a very different experience Walt Disney Imagineering encountered in France: 'The French said: "We are very important. Therefore, don't forget you have to pay attention to our culture."' (Schneider 2001a) Disneyland Paris Park thus had to incorporate a strong presence of French culinary culture and also to initially offer entirely French restaurants such as the restaurant *Auberge de Cendrillon* in Fantasyland.

A curious example of cross-cultural referencing is the design of the Hong Kong Disneyland Resort, for which Walt Disney Company had to commission a Chinese Feng-Shui master. As Mike Schneider reported, as a result, the theme park's environment incorporates a number of Feng-Shui elements such as its location between a hill shaped like a white tiger and another hill resembling a dragon, courtyards with rocks and small ponds, and doorways aligned so that no sharp objects point at them (Schneider 2001b).

Ideological reasons are also not to be underestimated: in low-end, developing markets, the presence of an American theme park has had the same impact as Hilton International hotels had in the 1950s. As Annabel Wharton writes, in the post-World War II world, the Hilton Hotel was quite literally 'a little America' (Wharton 2001). The Hilton was a space of luxury that fabricated desires for the American-type of modernity, while at the same time establishing the powerful global presence of the United States. During the Populuxe period, Hilton International (a contemporary of Disneyland) built 16 luxury hotels abroad and, as Wharton writes, they were all designed as significant Modern structures, unprecedented in their host cities in terms of scale and striking visual contrast to vernacular fabrics. By offering a powerful synthesis of American technology in an entertaining form and elements of American popular culture (swimming pools, air conditioning, ice water tapped to guest rooms, individual telephones, cheeseburgers, milkshakes, soda fountains, radios and the appearance of the building itself), Hiltons dramatically outlined the difference between a traditional culture and a desired American modernity. Most importantly, in relation to (and in parallel with) our concern with the global expansion of American theme park industry and the production of entertainment space, the United States government played a central role in the international expansion of Hilton, whereas the capital for the construction of the early Hiltons, as Wharton brilliantly points out, was not provided by the Hilton Corporation but by the American Economic Cooperation Administration, with the support of the United States Department of State and, much more often, by institutions in host countries that most commonly used pension funds, state lottery funds or formed joint stock companies to facilitate construction. It goes without saying that hotel design, as well as much of the sensitive construction and interior work, was done by American companies.

Analogically, as Wasko indicates, Walt Disney Company and other American entertainment and media corporations 'move with agility' in foreign markets also due to a significant assistance from the United States government (Wasko 2001). It will suffice to cite one obvious example: the Walt Disney Company has very strict rules on copyright protection for their products in foreign markets and relies heavily on the United States government to enforce these rights using whatever means are necessary. A common way of fabricating bridges between cultural contexts and thematic frameworks of theme park is through the so-called High Concept inference, conductive in essence and operating by means of metaphor (Ulmer 2003: 196–97). Michael Eisner and Barry Diller have been credited with inventing the High Concept (as heads of the Twentieth Century Fox) as one-liner captions used for pitching new movies. The essence of the High Concept is that there is a significant amount of concept in the theme park and that all action within the park centers around that one critical metaphor that is often called 'a hook' (Kosberg 1991: 60, Ulmer 2003: 197). Once the target audience becomes 'hooked' on the pitching line of a theme park, all of the other components of the theme park's 'total offer' become transparent through the power of metaphoric linking; in such a situation audience is drawn to experience every single aspect of the theme park, every single variation on the theme 'until they see them all'. They never see them all, hence the rationale for repeat visits. High Concepts are commonly used to fabricate themes and narratives for theme parks, in critical situations when alienation between a theme and the cultural context is drastic.

In theme parks that use regional cultural references and have a regional effect, the use of Hollywood-type hooks is not common. Such theme parks commonly re-interpret regional historical narratives or local political and ideological struggles. They are sometimes based on regional novelties that have a global appeal. For example, the Taman Mini Indonesia theme park in Indonesia, originally conceived and financed by President Suharto's wife, uses local mythologies and a manipulated version of regional history in order to show that the contemporary state of Indonesia, although immensely culturally and religiously diverse, is a 'natural' and historically justified formation. That was achieved by the juxtaposition of miniature reproductions of the scenes from daily life of thousands of islands that form the contemporary state of Indonesia. Similar 'folk villages' exist throughout Asia such as those in Taiwan (Taiwan Folk Village and Window on China) or the AsiaPark in Kyushu, Japan. What is impor-

tant for these theme parks is that they are geo-culturally bound to an indigenous locale used as a source for the storyline, thematic envelope and a base for the High Concept linking of essentially fundamentalist regional narratives with the 'proper' image of a wider region.

A variation on this typology was Splendid China in Kissimmee, Florida that opened in December 1993 off Highway US192, adjacent to the Walt Disney World Resort theater. Splendid China was also curious example because it was owned by China Travel Services H. K. Ltd., the largest Chinese government-owned travel agency. China Travel built its first theme park in Shenzhen, China in 1989. Two years later, China Travel announced plans to build Florida Splendid China in Osceola County. In a typically Disneyesque style, between 1990–93 China Travel had acquired land and developed the US$100 million theme park through its subsidiaries: initially through American Eastern International Corp. based in Los Angeles and then Hwang's International Inc. based in Florida. In January 1994, they acquired all the holdings from subsidiaries and assumed full ownership over the Splendid China theme park, together with a Days Inn motel nearby. This theme park used traditional Chinese mythologies, regional cultural references and a manipulated version of regional history in order to boost the national pride, but also to show that Tibet and Taiwan are 'natural' parts of the Chinese national entity. The difference, however, was that this theme park displaced regional novelties into a different geographic and cultural context—the Sunshine State. By doing so, it increased the visitor flow and made its political and cultural message globally present. Especially in view of the fact that it deliberately rendered itself a secondary tourist target in the larger Orlando area (and within the Walt Disney World Resort theater) that attracts over 30 million visitors every year. Therefore, this theme park promoted the presence of regional novelties on the global scene. Splendid China featured more than 60 detailed replicas of China's historic landmarks on its 76-acre site including a half-mile long Great Wall, the Forbidden City, the Terra Cotta Warriors and the theater

遊びながら、アジアを体験・体感。

ASIA PARK
アジアパーク

アジアパークのマスコットキャラクターです。
られた、たくさんの応募作品の
れました。

ジアの
険と味」を体験する、
感覚テーマパーク。

り、九州はアジアとの交流が盛んに行われていました。その
を、もっと深く体験することをコンセプトとした「アジアパー
びながら、アジアの歴史や文化、そして味に出会う、新しい
溢れたテーマパークです。水辺の景観を楽しみながらアジ
の遺跡・観光名所めぐり…そして迫力のサウンドと映像で
れた不思議な洞窟の世界をボートでクルーズする（全長
トル）「アジアクルーズ」。そして、アジアの雰囲気が楽しめ
ラン街や民芸物産ショップ、迫力の映像ホールなどが集
、全天候型の施設「アジアモール」。この2つのゾーンから、
な国際交流が始まろうとしています。

アジアクルーズ

アジアモール

centuries, Kyushu, in Japan has maintained good relations with
sian countries. "Asia Park" is an amusement park where, while
g it, you can learn about the histories, the cultures and the foods of
sian countries through pleasurable experiences.
Asia Park" there are two special features, "Asia Cruise" and "Asia
From the boats of "Asia Cruise" visitors are enabled to see repro-
s of famous tourists spots and ruins. They can also go through the
us artificial cave while riding the boats. In "Asia Mall", an all-
facility, there are many Asian handicraft shops and restaurants as
a movie theater. All these should help promote new types of
onal exchanges.

MESSAGE

世界へ羽ばたく子供達へ
夢を伝えたい。

21世紀のアジアへ、そして、世界
へ飛び立つ子供たちに輝く夢
と希望を届けたい。アジアパー
クは、そんな思いを込め
てゲストの皆様をお迎え
します。アジアという素晴
らしいステージの中から、
自然を愛する優しい心を、
感じ取ってください。

こんにちは。みんなで夢を語りましょう。

インドネシア Selamat sing. Marilah kita berbicara
tentang cita-cita.

韓国 안녕하세요！ 우리 모두 꿈을 이야기합시다.

フィリピン Halina, at ating pag-usapan ang ating
mga pangarap.

中国 你好！
大家一起来暢谈理想吧

シンガポール
Hello! Let's chat
about our
dreams!

production The Mysterious Kingdom of the Orient featuring the largest Chinese cast ever assembled outside of China. In addition, Splendid China also offered a shopping, dining and entertainment complex called the Suzhou Gardens. The area of the park was the site of permanent protest by a variety of political and citizen organizations, including Tibetan monks, who argued that such a fabrication of historic and geographic facts was unacceptable in the state of Florida, and should be closed down as a clear example of the Communist propaganda. School children and their parents were warned not to attend, and school teachers were particularly vocal in protesting against this theme park. It was mostly due to the orchestrated efforts of these citizen groups that Splendid China closed the gates on 31st December 2003 after its attendance dropped to about 70 000 visitors a year (Mervine 2003).

Another striking variation is Huis Ten Bosch in Kyushu, Japan (See Themeparking Huis Ten Bosch). This theme park is composed of a set of one-to-one replicas of Dutch architectural monuments and various distinct parts of both the cultural and material landscapes of Holland. Besides the displacement of cultural icons, this theme park was constructed by a Japanese company in Japan. This typology is very much a part of the Japanese cultural context and the tradi-

tional Japanese tendency to isolate and re-contextualize influences of foreign cultures. Besides Huis Ten Bosch, in 1990s the Japanese have also built a Russian Village, a Spanish Village, a Turkish Village and numerous other 'foreign villages'.

Unlike the smaller parks that use regional (sometimes ethnic) novelties, larger theme parks tend to use global, cross-cultural, pop-cultural or corporate references and mostly have a global cultural impact. Disneyland Paris Resort employs globally recognized Walt Disney properties as the source for its novelties. Because of broad American cultural influences after the World War II and a global acceptance of *Americana,* Walt Disney Co. is able to attract 97 million people worldwide into all the Walt Disney theme parks annually. The fact that people around the world can relatively easily identify with Walt Disney popular properties as emblems of *Americana* does not mean that the same ensemble of properties and novelties would not successfully attract also millions of Americans who understand them as being authentically American. Despite the fact that Walt Disney theme parks outside the United States, attract regional population on the basis of High Concept 'exoticism' each of these intercultural theme parks has customized attractions designed to fit into a regional cultural milieu: as Yoshimoto points out, Tokyo Disneyland Resort has an attraction called Meet the World, which enthusiastically represents Japanese encounters with foreigners and historically misrepresents the Japanese-Korean conflict (Yoshimoto 1994). Moreover, along Tokyo Disneyland Park's World Bazaar, there is a Japanese restaurant, Hokusai, with a typically Disneyesque lobby and a neo-traditional Japanese interior.

Similarly, Warner Bros. Movie World theme park in Germany has all the typical attractions of the American West: a conventional Main Street, Wild West street scenes, a film production studio and a series of attractions based on the Warner Bros.'s popular properties: Batman, Superman, Looney Tunes and others. However, there is also a strong reference to both its locale and the owner: a museum of German film history. This theme park was advertised as 'Hollywood in Germany', an indication that sheds light also on the success of the previous examples. As discussed previously, all of the Warner Bros. fictional properties are promoted through cycles of synergetic marketing. Likewise, Walt Disney's popular properties are promoted through comic books and movies, they promote theme parks, theme parks promote merchandise, these promote movies and the cycles of synergetic marketing expand. In a similar way, Busch Gardens theme parks are based on a set of local novelties that celebrate life in the Wild West, with street scenes, fights and other simulations.[15] Although this theme has been historically linked to the American Wild West, thanks to the Hollywood invasion in the post-World War II years, and the fact that Hollywood Westerns used such regional historic narratives as plots for a generation of internationally successful movies, these narratives came to have a global appeal and to appear 'exotic' to both American and international audiences alike.

Scales of Themeparking

There are a number of ways to categorize theme parks in terms of the scale of operations involved in their design, construction and operation. Expressions of their complexity can be read by understanding levels of investment, target populations analysis, anticipated and realized volumes of attendance, by whether they cater to destination-market or daily-market (destination market parks can generate demand for lodging facilities, other overnight accommodations, related entertainment attractions and commercial and retail development), by the cultural narratives they employ and the complexity of their thematic framework (discussed above), by whether they are ride-oriented or show-oriented, by whether they operate year-round or seasonally and so on. In relation to the above, the distinction will be made in what follows between regional theme parks, networks or regional theme parks and global theme parks.

JOSEPH PAXTON AND THE NINETEENTH-CENTURY XANADU

In the early 1850s, the density of urban fabric around Hyde Park, the proximity to major traffic lines, its fine informal landscaping and its size turned Hyde Park into a favorite picnic destination for Londoners. On the occasion of the Great Exhibition of the Works of Industry of All Nations, Hyde Park was chosen as the exhibition site. In 1850, an international competition was announced for the design of the exhibition building. Requirements imposed for the use of the site by the Exhibition Commissioners were strict: the site was not to be altered in any way, the existing trees were to be kept in the current state of condition and the building should have been quickly build as well as quickly demolished upon the closing of the exhibition. A great number of architects took part, but the result was hundreds of conventional buildings that were hard to build and very hard to take apart. Since no competition entry had been selected by the Committee of Commissioners in May of 1850, they proceeded to create their own design by combining the elements of different competition entries. (Chadwick 1966)

After Paxton learned of their intention, he promptly sent in a design proposal describing a structure made of modular steel elements, enclosed by large glass panels that had just been made commercially available. His design could have been assembled on-site and taken apart in a matter of days. The project itself was groundbreaking neither in terms of structure nor in terms of program. Similar structural principles had already been utilized for railroad construction and the roofs of shopping arcades in Paris. What was truly groundbreaking and ingenious, though, was the way in which Paxton combined the potential, implied modularity of the structural system with the specific requirements of the Hyde Park project. In June 1850, Paxton was officially commissioned to submit an alternative design proposal.

Paxton then teamed up with steel manufacturer, Fox & Henderson, and made the following offer to the Commissioners: the first option was that Fox & Henderson construct Crystal Palace for a fixed amount in which case the Commissioners would hire another company to take the building apart and clear the site. Since this was a pricey option the Commissioners accepted its alternative. The second option,

View of the Crystal Palace and Park at Sydenham. Lithograph signed by Joseph Paxton, 1854. The Victoria and Albert Museum, London.

designed by Paxton, was that Fox & Henderson erect the building within the schedule for half of the initially projected cost, dismantle the building and remove the material at their own expense after the exhibition is over, keep the building material and bring the site to its original state. That way the Commissioners actually leased the building from Fox & Henderson (Chadwick 1966: 92). This deal was a phenomenal move on both parts that rendered the exhibition financially feasible. The Exhibition opened on 1st May 1851 and remained open until 11th October the same year.

> The Inexhibitable, then, must never be forgotten, amidst all the attractions and wonders of the Exhibited or Exhibitable. (Excelsior 1851)

In the five months it was visited by more than six million people and it had made a profit of £186 000. The commissioners had leased, for the period of five months, a 1048 feet-long and 408 feet-wide building with an extension on the North side measured 948 feet by 48 feet. The height of the nave was 63 feet and of the transept 108 feet. Within the building, there were some 100 000 exhibits from nearly 14 000 exhibitors from all over the globe demonstrating human inventiveness and Nineteenth Century

Regional Theme Parks

Among the regional theme parks, one can distinguish between the small regional theme parks that are commonly family-owned and operated, and the larger ones owned and operated by larger corporate patrons. Family-owned theme parks individually have an insignificant share of both the national and international tourist markets. Such theme parks rely on regional transportation networks and smaller trade theaters commonly covered by one-hour drive radius. They are usually started with an investment level of up to us$10 million and with the size of approximately 20 acres, followed by an attendance level of up to 200 000 visitors annually. The narratives they are based on are usually linked to local heroes and historic battles, regional mythologies or fairy-tales. Since these theme parks operate as communal leisure destinations, they rely heavily on repeat visitors: over 90 percent of their overall attendance is generated by repeat visitors. In order to attract local population, they are forced to develop a variety of seasonal events and festivals. A good example of such a theme park is Shikoku Mura (see page 175).

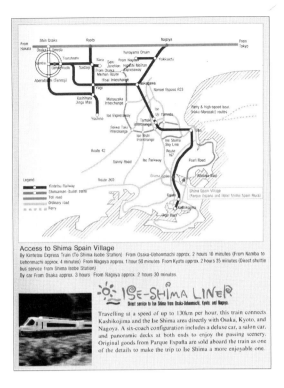

Access to Shima Spain Village
By Kintetsu Express Train (To Shima Isobe Station) From Osaka-Uehonmachi approx. 2 hours 10 minutes (From Namba to Uehonmachi approx. 4 minutes) From Nagoya approx. 1 hour 50 minutes (Direct shuttle bus service from Shima Isobe Station)
By car From Osaka approx. 3 hours From Nagoya approx. 2 hours 30 minutes.

ISE-SHIMA LINER
Direct service to Ise Shima from Osaka-Uehonmachi, Kyoto, and Nagoya.

Travelling at a speed of up to 130km per hour, this train connects Kashikojima and the Ise Shima directly with Osaka, Kyoto, and Nagoya. A six-coach configuration includes a deluxe car, a salon car, and panoramic decks at both ends to enjoy the passing scenery. Original goods from Parque España are sold aboard the train as one of the details to make the trip to Ise Shima a more enjoyable one.

Parque España

A different scale of regional theme park operation is exemplified by Shima Spain Mura, a regional theme park in Mie Prefecture in Japan also called Parque España. Parque España employs 'Spain' as its thematic framework and it contains, among other imitations, a full-scale copy of Gaudi's Parc Guell in Barcelona and a part of Santiago de Compostela in North-Western Spain. It is owned and operated by the Kintetsu Corporation and its subsidiary Shima Spain Village Co. Ltd. It was designed and constructed by the Takenaka Corporation. The level of investment into the park was us$600 million for the 45-acre operation. Land used for Parque España was mostly agricultural fields along the edges of Matoya Bay.

One of the most distinctive attributes of Parque España is its attachment to the world famous pilgrim site Ise Shrine. The major railway line that links Nagoya (regional capital) with Ise Shrine is owned and operated by the Kintetsu Group. Kintetsu group is one of the largest transportation companies in Japan owning railway and bus lines,

Kintetsu map depicting railway access routes to
Spain Mura. © Shima Spain Village Co., Ltd.

NEXT SPREAD
Map of Spain Mura. © Shima Spain Village Co., Ltd.

British achievement in particular. It was meant to house every machine known to man and the exhibits ranged from mechanical reproductions of exotic animals to technical achievements of the period, such as a steam-driven combine. The British Committee of Commissioners proposed a system of classification that included five major divisions with numerous subdivisions used to put all exhibits into appropriate categories. The Thomas Cook Company, to mention but one, is an exemplar of related services that the Exhibition generated: the Great Exhibition in fact established the foundations for the modern tourist industry. The paradigmatic physical and economic format of the Great Exhibitions was discovered. That this physical format was applicable within different economic frames was proved by the following events.

Ah, there lies the mighty difference. 'Here we have no continuing city;' nothing is stable, nothing abiding. Soon shall the Palace of Glass be demolished, and all its pomp and splendor fade from the view, and be as though it had never been. But there you have a tabernacle that shall never be taken down—a house not made with hands, eternal in the heavens. The felicity will be perfect, and permanent as perfect; and on the whole scene, so complete, so enduring, ETERNITY will place its crown.[2] (Clayton 1851: 36)

In May 1852, six months after the Great Exhibition was over, Paxton, Fox and Henderson established a public company called The Crystal Palace Company. Paxton convinced Fox & Henderson that the building, once dismantled, should be re-erected at a new site. Paxton had invited directors of major Railway companies such as London, Brighton and South Coast Railways to join the board of directors of his company. It was no coincidence that the director of Brighton Railway Company was the original owner of the new site at Sydenham, located within a short distance from rail access. The company bought a new site in Sydenham, took apart the building in a matter of weeks and moved it to the new site.

The major limitation of the London site for Paxton was the fact that he had no right to alter the site. If imploding in Hyde Park regardless of its transparency, Crystal Palace simply exploded in Sydenham making the building and the garden a homogeneous spatial experience. The building was 50

CIUDAD TIERRA MAR FIESTA The park

CIUDAD (City) is bursting with joy and energy.
TIERRA (Land) is surrounded by lush greenery.
MAR (Sea) is a seaport recalling the Age of Discovery.
FIESTA (Festival) is colorful and dynamic.
Parque Espana has distilled all the charm of Spain in four areas set in beautiful natural surroundings. In addition, there are exciting attractions, cultural facilities, shops, and restaurants to match the theme of each area. The parade and a variety of other live shows performed in the streets give the park an even stronger Spanish flavor.

HOTEL SHIMA SPAIN MURA

Carnival House

Splash Montserrat

Gran Montserrat

Gaudi Carousel

Battle of the Alcazar

Parking area

Fiesta Train

Don Quixote
Sancho Panza
©SHIMA SPAIN VILLAGE CO.,LTD.

Pearl Road

ur areas are filled with the charm of Spain.

PARQUE ESPAÑA

Adventure Lagoon

Colon Plaza

"Castillo de Xavier" Museum

a Cruz Street

Roman Ruins

Donkey's Sherry

Colosseum

en Hall

"Puerta del Cambron" Theater

od Court

Plaza Mayor

Cibeles Plaza

Casino House

Musical Circus

España Avenue

Flying Don Quixote

Swing Santa Maria

Entrance

Amigo Balloon

Tierra

Windmills

Super-Express Iberia

Ciudad

Shops outside the park

Bus parking area

Fiesta

Attraction - Museum
Restaurant, shopping area
Other facilities

Lower-level Station at the Crystal Palace site at Sydenham, 1854.

percent larger than its early Hyde Park version, although it was based on the same 24-foot girders.[3] Initially the site had one railway station at the Lower-level, but in 1856, the High-level Station was built within the building. The new Crystal Palace Line was introduced from Victoria Station at Pimlico. After the construction of the High-Level Station that brought visitors into the building, visitors could have stayed permanently inside during the winter and, in summer, they would experience the interior of the building first and then proceed towards the garden.

Mechanical installations were brought from London's site, but here, Paxton had another problem: in Hyde Park the major feature was cooling while at Sydenham Paxton had to heat the environment for the exotic plants and birds. He then invented and introduced a low-pressure, hot-water heating system. Water was generally one of the main concerns at Sydenham. The large number of fountains, water-works, two lakes, secondary basins, water-temples, cascades, the supply for the green system and the required amounts for fire-fighting required a constant pressure in the sophisticated water-system powered by four powerful engines. This revolutionary water system could only be compared to that sophisticated system designed by Bountalenti to animate fountains and the automata at Pratolino in the early Sixteenth Century.

Instead of organizing exhibits upon national denominators as in Hyde Park, plants and animals were exhibited upon the regional and climatic origin: there were sections with tropical plants and aquatics, orange trees from France, exotic birds from the South, and so on. Famed bands performing popular music were a regular feature at Sydenham, together with a variety of other events such are fireworks

department stores, resort centers, spas and theme parks. By linking Nagoya with Ise Shrine, Kintetsu monopolizes the symbolic capital of this national monument and turns it into the source of real revenues. Besides linking Nagoya with Ise Shrine, the Kintetsu line also links Nagoya and Ise Shrine with other secular regional attractions farther South, one of which is also Parque España. This type of procedural arrangement was initiated in the 1850s upon the introduction of the railway for pilgrimage and commercial purposes. In 1889, Sangû Railway Company was established for the purpose of linking Ise Shrine with major urban centers and facilitating the circulation of pilgrims to Ise Shrine. Moreover, it was introduced for the purpose of linking Ise Shrine with other popular, small-scale pilgrim sites situated South-East of the famous shrine such are tea-houses, brothels and play-houses nearby (Vaporis 1995). The North-South link weakened in the post-WW II era when the Megalopolitan East-West (Tokyo-Kyoto) axis became stronger after the development of the bullet train (Shinkansen) in 1964, run today by Japan Railways (Traganou 2003: 300). Drawing on Turner's analysis of the similarities between tourist and pilgrim behavior ('A tourist is half a pilgrim, if a pilgrim is half a tourist'. Turner 1978: 20), various authors have suggested that the Japanese have historically combined elements of traditional pilgrimage with visits to modern tourist attractions within the same trip (Graburn 1983). The relatively transparent rationale behind this agendum is that the Japanese are inclined towards combining the educational and spiritual aspects of tourism with the earthly pleasures of popular entertainments. Thus the contemporary arrangement of tourist targets is not coincidental: by placing Parque España in the vicinity of Ise Shrine and by linking the two by its own under-utilized railway line, Kintetsu utilizes the existing resources and takes advantage of the historically rooted apparatus of pilgrim-tourism by constructing the 'total offer'. A comparison of the figures for 1994 would give an insight into the relationship between the two tourist targets: Ise Shrine was visited by 6.7 million tourists, whereas Parque España had 4.3 million visitors the same year. Nearly half of them had come from

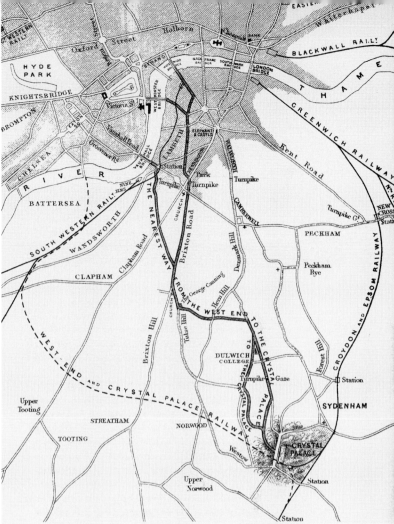

or through Nagoya city by the Kintetsu Ise Shima Liner, while almost 90 percent came from Nagoya and Osaka Prefectures (Kansai region). Prior to the introduction of the railway in the early Eighteenth Century, Ise Shrine had been frequented by as much as one million pilgrim-tourists a year coming from all over Japan. An average travel on foot to Ise Shrine would have taken up to five months (Noritake 1995). Nowadays most visitors stay in the region for one-night two-days and visit a number of networked tourist sites in the theater.

The fact that the thematic framework of Parque España has little to do with its commercial prosperity is apparent from an interview I conducted in August 1997 with one of the founders and the Manager of the Operation Division in Shima Spain Village. When asked why Spain was chosen and if there is a special interest among the Japanese for Spanish culture he answered:

> Well, quite frankly, we decided to copy Spain because in Japan at that moment we had Turkey, Holland, Russia, New Zealand, Germany, but we haven't had Spain. So we decided to be Spain. After the decision was made a market study was conducted to investigate whether Spain would be of any interest to the Japanese people and it was positive. But after all the real interest was created by the creation of this theme park, by us.[16]

that enhanced the visual spectacle made on the ground by artificial lighting, exhibitions and displays of most varied kinds, dog shows, flower shows, Handel music festival and so on. It is at Sydenham that the real Paxton came to exposure. The size and location of the site and the capital of the newly formed public company gave him the impetus for ambitious dreams. A late Medici and an early Disney, Paxton's ambitions to make a Xanadu of the Nineteenth Century were serious:

> In this Winter Park and Garden the trees and plants might be so arranged as to give great diversity of views and picturesque effect. Spaces might be set apart for equestrian exercise, and for carriage drivers; but the

Map depicting railway access routes to the Crystal Palace site at Sydenham in relation to the its original site in Hyde Park, 1854. From: Phillips, S. (1854) *Guide to the Crystal Palace and Park*. London: Bradbury and Evans. Tav. 1.

main body of the building should be arranged with the view of giving great extent and variety for those who promenade on foot. Fountains, statuary, and every description of park and garden ornament, would greatly heighten the effect and beauty of the scene. Beautiful creeping plants might be planted against the columns, and trailed along the girders, so as to give shade in summer, while the effect they would produce by festooning in every diversity of form over the Building, would give the whole a most enchanting and gorgeous finish. Besides these there may be introduced a collection of living birds from all temperate climates, and the science of Geology, so closely connected with the study of plants might be illustrated on a large and natural scale, thus making practical Botany, Ornithology, and Geology familiar to every visitor. (Chadwick 1961: 139–40)

It is obvious from this passage how transparent was the neutral vitro-ferrous frame idea for Paxton. It allowed for the encyclopedic format of his park within which a great variety is displayed: Crystal Palace was not more than a structural support and environmental envelope for the park and the garden. The formal layout and symmetrical ordering was reversed from that of the 1851 building: instead of Crystal Palace being the focus of attention and the main visual anchor as in Hyde Park, at Sydenham the building occupied the top level of the terraced gardens and the formal, central axis extended from the building outwards. Three central stairways led to the next terrace 15 feet lower. The central axis led to the circular pool surrounded by sculptures and down to the Eastern entrance. Half-way through, on both sides, there were water cascades leading form the water temples to the main water displays with large water-jets in the middle. Two lakes functioning as water reservoirs were hosting the geological collection composed of full-scale plaster reproductions of prehistoric animals. The visual effect of this collection was emphasized by placing it out of reach of the main central walk and connecting it with the central walk by wandering paths extending through woods.

Sydenham was a curious assemblage of different influences: the formal layout derived from Versailles (which Paxton deliberately wanted to outrival), the informal influence from Italian landscapes he had visited in 1830s, the idea

As a matter of fact, the real interest was generated by the socio-cultural patterns upon which people behave in such constructed situations: if properly set up, how they respond to what is offered is always highly predictable. Thus, the real interest is actually produced by the cognizant fabrication of Parque España as a supplementary tourist target within the trade theater of Ise Shrine.

Network of Regional Theme Parks

The best example of a large theme park developer operating a series of regional theme parks is that of Six Flags Inc., a Time Warner Entertainment Company that figures as the second theme park company in the U.S.A. (after Walt Disney Company) and the world's largest regional theme park company. In 1947, a wealthy oil typhoon, Angus Wynne, and the Great Southwest Corporation founded Six Flags Theme Parks Inc. in Arlington, Texas. In August 1961, they opened their first theme park titled Six Flags Over Texas in Arlington; the park was acquired by Premier Parks Inc. in 1998. In 2000, Premier Parks Inc. changed its name into Six Flags Inc. and became the world's largest regional theme park company, possessing through its subsidiaries 39 parks in eight countries around the world. As the nation's largest regional theme park company Six Flags operates 31 regional theme parks in the United States located strategically around the country.[17]

Six Flags theme parks are located within 35 of the 50 largest metropolitan areas in the United States and an estimated 90 percent of all Americans live within an eight-hour drive of each of the Six Flags's theaters. Because of such an elaborate system of trade theaters, overall attendance at North American Six Flags parks was approximately 35 million in 2003 generating total revenues of approximately US$1 billion (Burke 2003). Its worldwide attendance in 2002 was over 50 million (AB 2002). The ingenuity of this strategy becomes apparent upon looking at the map of the United States and the system of Interstate highways. The overall North American attendance parallels that of Walt Disney Company's North American theme parks and yet Six Flags theme parks rely on regional circulation of people (with conservatively defined trade theaters), the government owned Interstate system of highways and individual vehicle transportation. For example, in comparison with Movie World in Germany, whose primary trade theater is populated by 30 million people, and Disneyland Paris Resort with a primary trade theater populated by 41 million, North American Six Flags network of theme parks has the cumulative trade theater of 252 million people, all living within a drive radius of eight hours. Nevertheless, precisely because of its reliance on daily markets, regional theme parks can be heavily affected by changes in local political or economic climate, changes in microclimate, weather and other issues that do not affect globally appealing theme parks catering to tour-markets. As Tim O'Brien of *Amusement Business* indicates, regional theme parks had a hard time in 2001 and again in 2003 when compared with destination parks like Walt Disney World Resort and Universal Studios because of weather: 'The big reason was the weather [...] people going to go to Disney World have been planning that trip, so they'll go whether it's raining or not. If it's raining when you wake up on Saturday morning, you're not going to go to your regional park'. (Wood 2003)

Despite the cumulative effect that Six Flags Inc. achieves by operating a sophisticated network of regional theme parks, each regional Six Flags theme park logistically operates as a regional attraction whose rationale is derived from the High Concept symbiosis of Warner Bros. capital (movies, characters and entertainment properties), some of the symbolic capital of the Six Flags Inc. (largest and fastest roller-coasters or water-based fun), as well as by the usually caricaturized regional character that caters to regional audiences. For instance, Warner Bros. Movie World in Germany is enveloped by a general theme defined as 'Fascination with Film' with sub-themed areas such as the German Film History Museum, whereas Six Flags Texas in Arlington has had as its underlying theme the 'Six Flags of Texas' based on the six different flags that have flown over Texas:

of the Picturesque park from the current local taste (Nash and Repton), but after all, Sydenham was not a copy of any of these examples. The garden at Sydenham became so large that it simply blurred the boundaries between itself and what was supposed to be the park. This confusion of scales and formal features rendered the underlying aesthetic principles of the Picturesque obsolete, finding a conceptual base in the scientific knowledge of horticulture and making way for new landscape movements (Lasdun 1991: 178).

Although Paxton persistently emphasized the educational aspect of the project, the commercial was not less emphasized in practice. The Crystal Palace Company arranged travel and accommodation for visitors willing to stay longer at Sydenham. After the construction of the High-Level Station, a series of hotels was planned although only four hotels were built near the Palace offering more than 400 rooms. Initially, Paxton designed a scheme for converting the public street leading to the Palace into a glazed walkway (Chadwick 1961: 155). Despite all that, Crystal Palace was not a highly successful business venture until the early 1920s when commercial features were placed along its walkways: a dance-hall, roundabouts, a cricket field, race-tracks and many others. The great fire of 1936 destroyed the building and its grounds. The whole project was culturally a phenomenal success that brought Paxton professional fame and commissions all over Europe. In 1862, the French Emperor met Paxton regarding the forthcoming Great Exhibition of 1867 in Paris, but there is no evidence that Paxton influenced its design.

1. It had actually happened in May 1852.

2. A sermon on the Great Exhibition preached in York St. Chapel, Walworth, 1851.

3. Sizes of both buildings and their differences is a speculation of George Chadwick (Chadwick 1961).

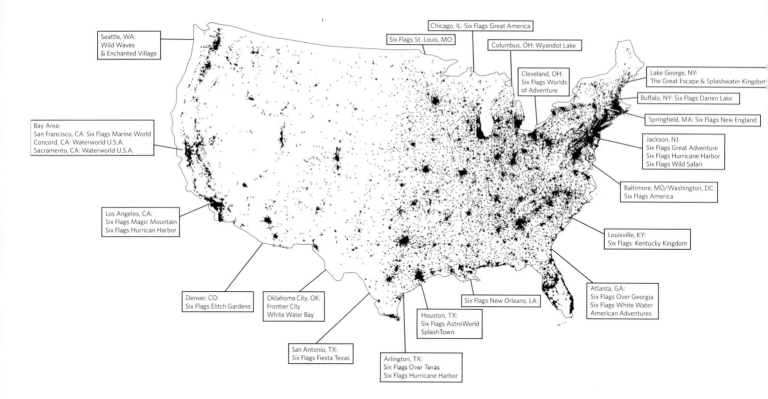

Seattle, WA:
Wild Waves
& Enchanted Village

Chicago, IL: Six Flags Great America

Six Flags St. Louis, MO:

Columbus, OH: Wyandot Lake

Cleveland, OH:
Six Flags Worlds
of Adventure

Lake George, NY:
The Great Escape & Splashwater Kingdom

Buffalo, NY: Six Flags Darien Lake

Springfield, MA: Six Flags New England

Bay Area:
San Francisco, CA: Six Flags Marine World
Concord, CA: Waterworld U.S.A.
Sacramento, CA: Waterworld U.S.A.

Jackson, NJ:
Six Flags Great Adventure
Six Flags Hurricane Harbor
Six Flags Wild Safari

Baltimore, MD/Washington, DC:
Six Flags America

Los Angeles, CA:
Six Flags Magic Mountain
Six Flags Hurrican Harbor

Louisville, KY:
Six Flags Kentucky Kingdom

Denver, CO:
Six Flags Elitch Gardens

Oklahoma City, OK:
Frontier City
White Water Bay

Six Flags New Orleans, LA:

Atlanta, GA:
Six Flags Over Georgia
Six Flags White Water
American Adventures

Houston, TX:
Six Flags AstroWorld
SplashTown

San Antonio, TX:
Six Flags Fiesta Texas

Arlington, TX:
Six Flags Over Texas
Six Flags Hurricane Harbor

Spanish, French, Mexican, The Republic of Texas, Confederate and the flag of the United States of America. As a rule, operating a network of regional theme parks and relying on day visitors is a much safer and more conservative business proposition than operating a global tourist destination such are Disneyland Resort, Walt Disney World Resort or Universal Studios Orlando. The industry standard for North American regional theme parks is that 90 percent of their attendance is regional visitors coming from a 100-mile radius. A case in point is Six Flags over Georgia that mostly operates from Memorial Day through Labor Day with over 90 percent of its visitors come from a 100-mile radius within the state of Georgia (Ward 2002).

Warner Bros. Movie World

In 2000, Warner Bros. Movie World in Germany changed hands from Warner Bros. to Six Flags Inc. management.[18] Two companies entered a long-term license agreement that grants Warner Bros. licenses to Six Flags Inc. providing it with exclusive theme park rights and

the usage of the Looney Tunes and DC Comics characters in Europe, North America and South America. In return, Six Flags operates the theme parks as licensee under the name Warner Bros. Movie World Germany and Warner Bros. Movie World Spain. As part of the Time Warner family, Six Flags Inc. acquired the opportunity to use Warner Bros. movies, characters and entertainment properties such as Batman, Superman and Looney Tunes in its parks around the world. As a result, the Six Flags European Division became the largest regional theme park company in Europe with eight major theme parks. Other Six Flags European parks were bought from the Walibi group in 1998.[19] From 2000–02, all of the Six Flags parks in Europe were modernized and made to comply with Six Flags standards.[20] Today the Six Flags European Division includes six regional theme parks.

The Warner Bros.' Movie World in Germany that opened in June 1996 is an indicative example of a regional theme park conceived on a more complex regional scale, and also in terms of its positioning regarding

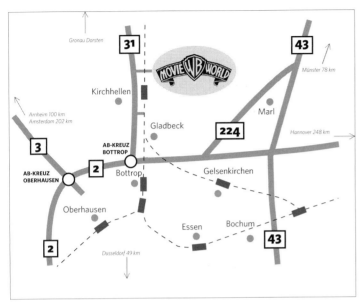

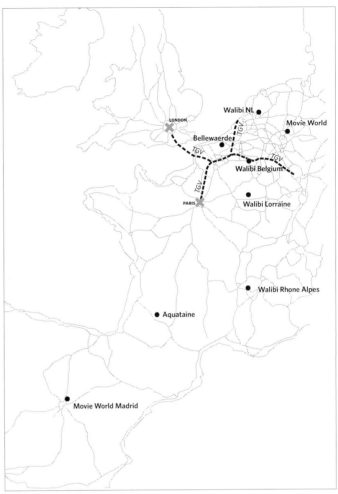

Map of the network of Six Flags theme parks in the United States, in relation to population density.

Map depicting railway and highway access routes to WB Movie World, Germany.

Map of Six Flags/Time Warner theme parks in Europe, within the network of highways and the TGV.

to the density of population, traffic networks, cultural patterns and economic factors in the trade theater. Warner Bros. International Recreation Enterprises and its German co-partner invested nearly US$250 million in this project, making this park not only the largest investment Warner Bros. has ever made outside the North American market (Walker 1996), but also the largest investment ever made by a German company into the German leisure industry. The German market's demand for amusement and recreation services was at that point estimated to US$40 billion and equaled roughly 20 percent of the overall demands of the European market.[21] The park is located in the German town of Bottrop-Kirchhellen (population of over 120 000) on an area of 112 acres previously utilized as a public recreation park. It is enveloped by a central theme of 'The Fascination with Film': it includes a conventional Main Street, four movie-related attractions, nearly 30 rides, Wild West street-scenes, two large production studio halls with offices and workshops used for German and European film and TV productions, as well as a reference to both its locale and the owner—Museum of German Film History. Its trade theater is located within the heart of North Rhine-Westphalia, Europe's most densely populated area (HABITAT 1996: 60–69) with a radius of 150 miles and population of nearly 30 million people. Movie World's location unmistakably generates a considerably high and steady visitor flow and a high repeat-visitor rate within the trade theater that includes Amsterdam, Brussels and many other European financial and tourist centers that belong to the so-called European Capitals Region, the highest per-capita income region in Europe. Within the primary trade theater, a guest population of 15 million can reach the park within one hour by train or by car. Special packages are created for railway passengers (the so-called VRR Kombi Ticket) so that for a surcharge of nearly US$2 on the regular admission price, one can get a 'free' return ticket to any destination within the region on all VRR means of transport. Such tickets can be purchased at advance sales points of the VRR Transport Companies, including Railway Travel Centers or at the theme park's gates. The Feldhausen railway station is within a short walking distance, while immediately in front of the theme park's entrance there is a bus stop along the major traffic corridor A31. Because of the relative proximity of Disneyland Paris Resort and the traditionally unpredictable French public, Warner Bros. estimated that the major flow of visitors would come from Germany (regional visitors), Belgium and The Netherlands. Their commonly broad cultural acceptance of *Americana* was certainly one of the basic assumptions for this plan.

In early 1990s, German government has designated previously agricultural and heavy-industry region (metal industry) of North Germany primarily as a service-industry region (HABITAT 1996: 60–69), thus creating conditions for a major regional restructuring in capital investments (land, service and entertainment capacities). The US$250 million investment was a low-level investment for a major company such as Warner Bros. since in the mid-1990s, an average investment level into a major theme park was between US$400 million and US$700 million, with investments in theme parks such as Walt Disney World Resort or Universal Studios closer to US$1 billion and beyond. It is a general rule that European theme parks have significantly lower levels of investment and development budgets than American theme parks. In the time of major capital restructuring, Bottrop welcomed an international investment in the entertainment and experience industry due to park's tax-revenues, tax-revenues from adjacent services, enhanced capacities of the regional transportation infrastructure, worldwide tourist promotion, new jobs in service, construction and entertainment industries, and most of all because this projects symbolizes the desirable political and economic shift towards new type of industrial complex to be developed in this region.

The flow of tourists to Warner Bros. Movie World has also been facilitated by the development of Northern-European high-speed rail system (TGV), linking all the major metropolitan centers into the European Capitals Region (including Paris, London, Amsterdam, Brussels,

Cologne and Frankfurt). Moreover, the construction of the Channel Tunnel in 1993 linked both the rail and road systems of the United Kingdom and France, extending the possibilities for expansion of tourist markets on both sides of the Channel. The tunnel links the United Kingdom with France through Dover and Calais respectively. From Calais, both the road and rail networks develop in two major directions: Paris Interconnexion and the Belgium traffic network that further extends into The Netherlands and Germany. A large number of regional theme parks developed successfully in Europe since 1990 (Warner Bros. Movie World included) due to these new European traffic networks and also due to the fact that the European Capitals Region has 25 percent of the total European Union's population and 30 percent of its GDP (HABITAT 1996: 60–69). Various studies also confirm that the new traffic expansion in Europe has produced a boom in the short-stay tourist market that will benefit all tourist destinations (especially theme parks) situated by the major traffic routes and urban concentrations in The Netherlands, Belgium, Northern France and Northern Germany (Ruhr-Rhine area) that form the core of the European megalopolis. As Roger Vickerman argued (Vickerman 1993), Disneyland Paris Resort was the first major leisure development in Europe whose positioning was influenced by the above developments: 17 million people live within a two-hour drive from the park, 41 million within four-hour drive, an estimated 100 million within six hour-drive (including visitors from the United Kingdom coming though the Channel) and over 300 million within a two-hour flight (Greenhouse 1991). Figures for 1996 prove this to be true: 41 percent of all visitors came from France (regional tourists), 20 percent from The Netherlands, Belgium and Luxembourg, 15 percent from Germany, 10 percent from United Kingdom, three percent from Italy, three percent from Spain and six percent from Switzerland (Reuters 1997).

Global Theme Parks

Global theme parks obviously rely on global transportation networks and international tourism flows. Their design, development and management require high level of geographical abstraction and the perfection of organization and execution, matched only by military strategies for the control of global interests. They rely on complex constellations within the fluctuating global markets, such as international tourism, global air networks, control of local labor markets worldwide, global market potential for amusement and recreation services and so on.

The case of Six Flags Inc. and their monopolistic configuration on global scale is a typical sign of the consolidation of control that occurs in any industrial complex at the point of its maturation: it begins unfolding when major multinational corporate capital consolidates the industry by buying or taking control over smaller businesses. Since the mid-1990s, the global theme park industry has been dominated by Walt Disney Company, Six Flags Inc./Time Warner, Vivendi/Universal, Anheuser-Busch (Sea World) and Viacom/Paramount (Kings Entertainment-KECO), corporations that control the dominant share of attendance and revenues in the industry (Braun 1998). One of the main reasons for the imperialistic move of these American corporate giants is the saturation point of the domestic market, because a few significant opportunities have been available for major theme park development within the continental United States. In 1998, the North American market had about one theme park for every 10 million people, whereas European market had only about one theme park for every 20 million citizens (Robinett and Braun 1999). European markets are larger and European trade theaters are very densely populated: in such a dense market theme parks are located within close proximity and with often overlapping trade theaters. By all industry indicators the new, developing theme park markets will emerge in Asia (besides Japan also Korea, Hong Kong, Taiwan, China, Singapore, Malaysia and Indonesia), Latin America (Brazil and Mexico), India, Thailand and the Middle East. In 2003, the government of Dubai announced plans to begin the construction of an US$18 billion theme park project called Dubailand, set for completion in 2006 (AB 2003b). Although all of the entertainment corporate giants mentioned above are aggressively present at the global scene, the contemporary global theme park industry has been disproportionately influenced by Walt Disney Company. As Jones and Robinett have indicated, Walt Disney Company often educates the market by introducing the idea, value and the quality of the theme park experience as well as the management expertise, the need for target marketing and adequate positioning strategies (Jones and Robinett 1999).

The 2002 Icon Group Ltd. world outlook for amusement and recreation services across over 200 countries has shown that global market potential for amusement and recreation services is expected to reach US$737 billion by 2005.[22] Besides, in the United States, leisure businesses would account for one half of the Gross National Product after 2015 (McNair 2001). Within these estimates, Europe will have the highest market potential of approximately 36 percent of global market value whereas North American market is anticipated to decline to nearly 30 percent of the potential global market value. Asian markets are anticipated to reach over 21 percent of the world market. That in effect means that a company such as Walt Disney that targets these three regions of the world within its theaters captures an accumulation of over 86 percent of the global demand for amusement and recreation services. The same year, Walt Disney theme parks and resorts had nearly 97 million visitors worldwide (Emmons et al. 2002c) and the year prior Walt Disney Company's theme park division alone had generated US$1.9 billion in revenues (Herubin 2001). PriceWaterhouseCoopers' (PWC) Entertainment and Media Outlook: 2003–2007 also anticipated that amusement and theme park market in Asia will grow from US$5.3 billion in 2002 to US$7.4 billion in 2007 (Zoltak 2003b). It is not surprising that major theme park operators are moving aggressively into the Asian market: Hong Kong Disneyland Resort opens in 2005, DisneySea opened in Tokyo in 2001, Universal Studios Japan opened in Osaka in 2001,

and Universal Shanghai will open in 2006. As much as these new theme parks are driven by existing needs for recreation and entertainment, once in operation, they will additionally totalize landscapes and drive spiraling needs, spending and expectations in the never-ending cycles of themed consumption. In many ways, the developments in Asia-Pacific region in the 1990s are analogous to the 1950s developments in the United States in terms of an expanding economy (despite the mid-1990s crisis), and a booming middle-class with significant increases in leisure time and rising discretionary income (Hannigan 1998: 177).

For many giant, global entertainment and media corporations theme parks are not core-generating revenues:[23] for Anheuser-Busch, Viacom, Walt Disney Company, and Vivendi Universal theme parks simply act as a node in the network of cross-promotional and interlocked marketing schemes and provide important revenue diversification. As Benz reported, Anheuser-Busch, the world's largest producer of beer, had revenues of US$1.71 billion in 2001 only six percent of which was generated by its theme parks (Benz 2002). Benz further cites Walt Disney Company reporting that its theme parks and resorts had generated 27 percent of its total revenues in 2001.[24] An enormous growth and increasing globalization in the media business is characterized by an ever-increasing consolidation and control of the industry by transnational corporations, some of which are listed above. Generally less than 500 multinational corporations, a majority of which are media and entertainment giants, control over two-thirds of global trade and up to 40 percent of this trade occurs within these corporations (HABITAT 1996). This means a control of the global division of labor and direct influence on the stability of job markets in its most promising sectors: service (entertainment and tourism) and media/information industries (both regional and global). They also control a large share of both the global tourist market and business convention market. Walt Disney Company has a significant and stable share of both markets.

Disney Resort California:
California Adventure Park
Disneyland Park
19 M

40 M
● Walt Disney World Resort

● Disneyland Paris Resort
10 M

25M
● Tokyo Disney Sea Park
● Tokyo Disneyland Park

● Disneyland Hong Kong Resort
(opens Fall 2005)

Ogden Corporation can indicate the direction of development of entertainment conglomerates (Hannigan 1998: 127). Even though Ogden's sales revenues are only ten percent of that of Walt Disney Co., the breath, the depth and the scale of integration of its services and business activities is stunningly unique: Ogden focuses on power generation from solid waste (as well as a general solid waste management), aviation, services (concession food and beverage services at recreational and convention facilities, janitorial services, security, parking, facility management) and entertainment (themed attractions, theater productions, gaming, performance arts management, broadcast production service, music and video production). As Hannigan speculates, Ogden Corporation is capable of owning its own airline fleet, fueling the planes from solid waste it processes, flying guests to its own theme park, preparing the food guests consume throughout their journey (at the airport, on the plane and at the destination), and producing all pseudo-events including those that occur beyond the physical boundaries of the theme park. Such a synergetic coordination is *de facto* the aim of all entertainment conglomerates as they proceed in solidifying the global market.

As to the control of labor markets, it is a dominant trend for multinational corporations with theme park businesses to employ labor in low-wage countries of Asia or the Caribbean through their subsidiaries or subcontractors for jobs such as information processing, accounting, invoicing and manufacturing, but also for all kinds of merchandise offered at theme parks and chains of retail outlets. Walt Disney Company generates a vast number of related manufacturing jobs worldwide and, through its subsidiaries worldwide, produces Disney clothes, toys, calendars, notebooks and other products for consumption in Walt Disney theme parks and in the extensive chain of Walt Disney retail outlets. As Janet Wasko points out, Walt Disney Company often designs its products, then licenses the rights to its intellectual property to contractors at relatively high rates who then seek subcontractors that will manufacture products for the lowest possible cost (Wasko 2001). That usually means that products are manufactured in over 3000 factories worldwide in places where labor costs are low: China, Hong Kong, Macau, Vietnam, Taiwan, Dominican Republic, Mexico, St. Lucia, Malaysia, Brazil, Thailand, Colombia, El Salvador, the Philippines, Indonesia, Sri Lanka, Honduras, India, Bangladesh and elsewhere. Wasko cites a credible source that claimed at least 80 percent of Disney toys and merchandise that require manual labor are manufactured in the above countries while over 90 percent of media products that rely on digital technology and specialized automated production were produced in industrialized nations including the United States. Moreover, due to new communication technologies, European companies controlling large 'public' facilities (theme parks and other publicly accessible environments) are now employing highly skilled Asian security firms to moni-

THE GRAND TOURS AND THE PICTURESQUE

By the mid-Seventeenth Century, the social status gained by the ownership of a park was further emphasized when the word park became the suffix of the name of the estate, replacing previously common suffixes such are 'manor' or 'hall' (Lasdun 1991). Although the term 'landscape' had been in use since the early Seventeenth Century, at the turn of the century after the influence of French landscape paintings, both gardens and parks came to be called 'landscape'. Dutch landscape paintings of the Seventeenth Century became too realistic when compared with the work of Rosa or Poussin.[1] The Eighteenth Century was the era of travel, as famous Grand Tours led English aristocracy to Italy, Germany, France and The Netherlands. Ruins of Roman villas and picturesque landscapes, Italian *campagna* and Dutch *rust*, together with the discovery of the paintings of Nicholas Poussin and Claude Lorrain, set the tone for the sensibility they tried to recreate upon their return to England (Lasdun 1991: 80). As a result, a symbiosis of real (vineyards and ruins) and idealized (classical, idealized allusions of Poussin) gave form to most of the English gardens and parks during the Eighteenth Century. Both gardens and parks were deliberately designed to appear 'more like nature' in terms of both layout and scenery. In fact, they merged into the so-called Landscape Garden. Physical boundaries between them blurred as the walls that previously separated gardens and parks were pulled down. This was facilitated by the invention of a new device called a 'ha-ha',[2] brought to England in the early Eighteenth Century as an invisible boundary between the garden and the park (Lasdun 1991). This gave the appearance of the garden being virtually open to the park and surrounding land, while keeping animals within the boundaries of the estate. The new landscape garden embodied the philosophy of Enlightenment as a critique of the geometric, Cartesian, French garden. As opposed to the view of nature as subordinate to the mastery of mathematical ordering and regularity, the new view adopted a romantic, nostalgic, almost Arcadian sensibility of unity between man and landscape. New elements were introduced into garden design:[3] rocks, waterfalls, grottos, woodwork,[4] statues with classical inscriptions, canals, artificial rivers and lakes, seats and benches. Within the informal pattern of these devices, new categories of formal buildings were introduced including temples, baths,

tor their properties. The lower paid staff in China monitors a facility in Europe through a live-feed generated by a set of video cameras placed around the park that instantly transmits the image to China. Remote security groups are able to alert police or other security agencies in Europe within seconds if an inhibited activity is detected. This practice also lowers wages significantly because night-time surveillance in Europe is a day-time job in Asia (HABITAT 1996: 9).

The rapid growth of international trade, particularly in the area of specialized services and finance, caused the total capitalization of the world's stock markets. The increasing mobility of capital during the 1980s and 1990s resulted in the domination of direct foreign investments over export trade. After the economic peak and 'theme park boom' during the 1980s, Kabushikikaisha Dentsu and other Japanese corporations, led by the Japanese Amusement Association, became major investors into Chinese theme parks and leisure centers (together with investments in other areas such as information industry). Since 1993, China was the world's largest recipient of direct foreign investments, estimated at almost 30 percent of total direct foreign investments worldwide (HABITAT 1996: 10). One of the most important factors in attracting direct foreign investments in theme park industry and tourism is the quality of existing transportation infrastructure and generally economic growth is accompanied by a demand for high-quality infrastructure. Many countries have improved their infrastructure in order to attract direct foreign investments. In 1991, China had a density of $9mi/1000mi^2$ of its railway network and $172mi/1000mi^2$ of the road network (HABITAT 1996: 522–525). The same year, Japan had a density of $86mi/1000mi^2$ of the public railway network and $4750mi/1000mi^2$ of its road network, whereas the number of cars was estimated to 473.3 vehicles/1000 people. Generally, there is a much lower automobile ownership per household in Asia and Europe than in the United States, the fact that greatly limits accessibility of regional theme parks. Eastern Europe, the Caribbean and Latin America experienced similar growth in direct foreign investments. Although seemingly economically efficient and benevolent, direct foreign investment suffers from the so-called 'profit leakage'. This actually means that profit never stays in the region where the actual operation takes place, but in the region/country of investment's origin. Therefore, the region where the theme park's theater of operation is located does not fully benefit from its economic performance. This is possible even within the same national territory: as Novak-Branch argued, Walt Disney World was a Californian investment into Florida and the profit of its operations went to California (Novak-Branch 1983). Florida thus did not immediately benefit from Walt Disney World's 'economic multiplier' and studies have shown that at the micro-economic level conditions worsened. As will be discussed later in this chapter, Huis Ten Bosch has created a different economic effect on the micro-economic level.

Direct foreign investment cannot happen without a direct government support and an especially favorable economic climate for such investments was created during the period of Thatcherism and Reaganism in the 1980s, respectively in the United Kingdom and the Unites States. During this period, significant privatizations of major state-owned enterprises in the areas of mass-transportation and mass-media were conducted, and an aggressive development on a scale perhaps not yet fully comprehended in collaboration between public and private sectors occurred in order to create the legislative and other infrastructure and services that can handle large international investments. During that period, the Walt Disney Company entered a partnership with French Government and various other private investors, investing US$16 million and its copyrights into Disneyland Paris Resort, together with a promise of 30 000 new jobs in the service sector. Christopher Knowlton's account of this arrangement is indicative of the tactics that the Walt Disney Company employs, in many ways similar to Hilton's: first, they designed a two-tiered corporate structure for this US$2.5 billion project, composed of a limited partnership and a publicly traded corporation. During

roman bridges and viaducts, ruins of Roman buildings, churches and chapels, and mausoleums.

Edmund Burke's *Philosophical Inquiry into the Origin of Our Ideas of the Sublime and the Beautiful* of 1756 was the most influential work of the Eighteenth Century, in which Burke identifies natural phenomena like mountains, craters, storms, thunders and night skies as 'sublime' (Burke 1756). This notion of sublime beauty, combined with the experiences from Grand Tours, and with the new term *picturesque*, initiated the replacement of Landscape Garden by the Picturesque Garden by the end of the Eighteenth Century. The term *picturesque*, referring to a scene in the real world that could be viewed as a part of a picture, has its origins in Italian and French. It meant a garden conceived of a set of scenes to be framed and organized into a coherent chain of experiences, in the same way in which Poussin's paintings provided scenery for a hypothetical action-scene. Such gardens introduced a double role of the visitor, as both spectator and actor. The difficulty of this position was facilitated sometimes by textual inscriptions placed in the garden at various points in order to make understanding tangible (Teyssot 1991: 359). Although initially an intellectual game of reading garden as text, the textual inscriptions and explanations reduced the knowledge necessary for understanding the garden and transformed the intellectual game into popular entertainment.[5] Parallels between garden and theater were often made during this period, as to the theatricality of a garden conceived as a set of scenes, compared to the metaphorical employment of garden as a thematic framework in theater productions of the period. Since reading the garden as text implied a linear narration, many gardens had one-way paths leading from one scene to another. This popular format of conveying meanings reunited spectator and stroller in these illusionary stage-sets.

Military terminology and formations were often used in the arrangement of biological material. Long avenues leading into the countryside had trees planted in *platoons*, symmetrically arranged on both sides. The use of military technology emphasized the duration of the building process: instant result and effective execution were demanded and subsequently satisfied by new machines for transport and replanting. Treatises on planting and garden management were a popular literature of the period. Ready-made trees

and plants in specified sizes and shapes would be brought to the site and instantly planted, facilitating quick changes in style and taste.

1. In his famous paintings such are *Landscape with the Ashes of Phocion* and *Christ Healing the Blind Men,* collage backgrounds are composed of the *objects à réaction poétique:* Palladian villas, elements of Christian anthology, early Christian basilicas, Arcadian peasants, and mythical animals (snakes). They always form the stage set for a mythical action taking place in the foreground (Hunt 1991: 234).

2. Ha-ha originated in France during the Seventeenth Century. Initially, it was a military device invented to surprise the enemy and keep it out of a territory: in this early stage it was a wide and deep ditch behind the lowered wall (sometimes ornamented), invisible to the enemy until approached at a very short distance. Later, it had been utilized in some of the formal, walled gardens to keep the unwanted animals out (Source: Lasdun 1991).

3. During the Seventeenth Century, a new emphasis was placed on kines-thetic experience, which meant that the previously static viewing subject was now in deliberate motion. Walking became fashionable, and provoked an interest in surrounding fields, forests and hills; thus, the creation of the static garden elements changed to an arrangement of multiple focal points and strategically placed visual attractors: teahouses, terraces, grottos, canals, cascades with water, temples, or sport fields. Novelty and entertainment in park design were among the revolutionary new features of these leisure-oriented territories. Teahouses became quite a fashionable addition to the gardens. Paille-Maille (pall-mall), the game that originated in Italy, was brought to France and England, and places specially designed for it came to be *de rigueur* in park design. During long winters, aristocracy would amuse themselves with ice-skating along the canals and lakes, a fashion that came from Holland and became especially popular in England (Source: Lasdun 1991).

4. A large formal terrace densely planted with trees, also called *wilderness.*

5. As Teyssot wrote, in the *Observations on Modern Gardening* of 1770, Thomas Whately distinguished between two essential principles of gardening: emblematic (didactic and allegorical), and expressive (meta-phorical) gardening. The emblematic represents the syntax and grammar of garden as a text, while the metaphorical expresses emotional side of the process only possible when observer's reading is independent of the didacticity of inscriptions and statuary (Whately 1770 quoted in Teyssot 1991: 359).

the construction process, the limited partnership created operating losses used as 'tax shelters'. The public corporation deal gave European shareholders the ability to profit, but only out of theme park's operational revenues. The initial contract with the French government that gave Walt Disney Company 49 percent equity and operating control over Disneyland Paris Resort in return for a US$200 million investment was canceled, and Walt Disney Co. finally invested only US$16 million of its own money into the project (Knowlton 1989).

Similar business arrangements have been made in the case of Hong Kong Disneyland Resort, a 300-acre theme park located on Hong Kong's Lantau Island, scheduled to open in 2005. Initially, the Hong Kong government invested US$1.7 billion in the necessary land reclamation and infrastructure for this US$3.5 billion project. Simultaneously, the Hong Kong government and Walt Disney Company formed a joint venture company, Hong Kong International Theme Parks Ltd. The company received financing from the Chase Manhattan Bank, Hong Kong in the level of US$423 million to finance the construction of the theme park, according to *Amusement Business,* which included a US$294.92 million term loan and a US$128.22 million revolving credit with a maturity of 15 years (AB 2000). Walt Disney Company contributed US$314.15 million in equity to the project whilst the Hong Kong government provided US$416.73 million in equity as well as a US$782.17 million loan, according to *Amusement Business.* In November 1999, Hong Kong International Theme Parks Ltd. announced the deal, claiming that the Hong Kong government owned 57 percent of the company while Walt Disney Company held the remaining 43 percent (AB 2000). The theme park's trade theater covers nearly 80 million people in surrounding areas that include Guangdong, the Pearl River Delta, and Guangzhou.

Global travel patterns reflect changes in consumer behavior, economic strength of source markets, new destinations, stable oil prices, economic and political stability of the OECD countries, low air

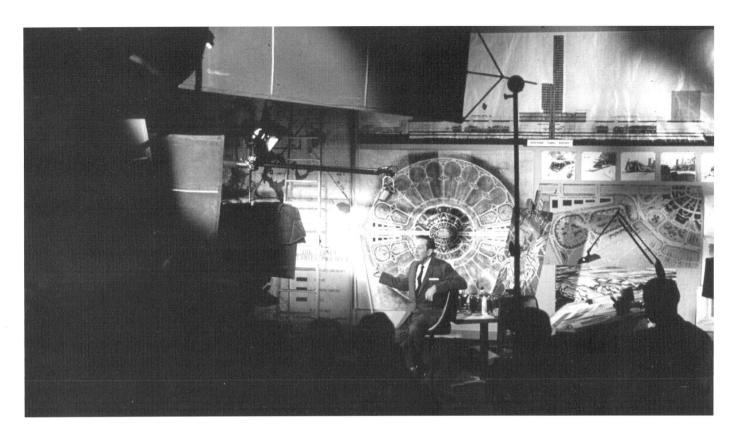

fares/ travel costs, safe political climate and political realignments, extended vacation times, good public health and wellness, education and numerous other factors. How important international tourism is to a national economy is clear in the case of the post 9/11 United States: as Gallen reports, the 42 million international tourists that had visited United States in 2000 had spent over us$88 billion dollars and had generated and sustained over one million jobs in tourist, travel and service industries. In two years following the all-time peak in 2000, the number of international tourist had steadily declined, causing a loss of nearly half a million jobs in the above-mentioned industries (Gallen 2003). New United States Security measures installed in 2003 in the face of the War in Iraq and other concerns have pushed this trend even further.

Global weather can also have a significant impact on international theme park attendance: Reuters reported in December 2003 that global theme park attendance fell 1.5 percent in 2003 due not only to travel fears and weak economy, but also to bad weather across the Western world: Europe experienced an eight percent drop and visits to the largest 50 North American parks fell also by 1.5 percent in 2003 (Reuters 2003). One of the ways in which theme parks resolve the problem of seasonal attendance is weather and climate control. Numerous 'artificial environments' have been created to complement the existing theme parks (Kajima Corporation's Ski Hill near Tokyo Disneyland Resort) or to expand the tourist offer in the trade theater: indoor ski centers, indoor tropical beaches and lagoons, as well as simple solutions such as the massive roof-structure erected over the World Bazaar in Tokyo Disneyland Park.

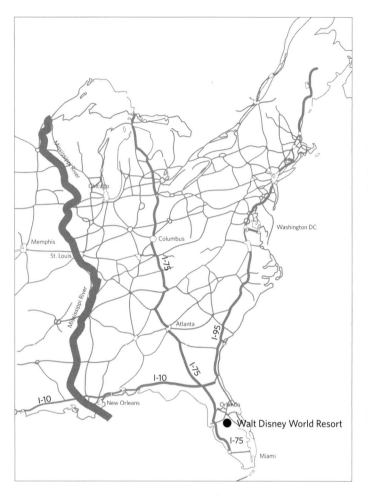

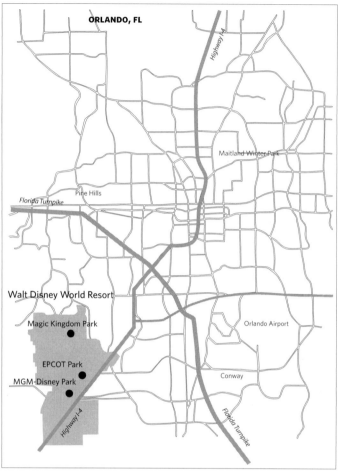

Walt Disney World Resort, Florida

Based on the above criteria, one could say that global theme parks are those that have a critical mass of facilities necessary for attracting a significant volume of international tourism that measured in annual visits reaches 20 million, investment levels of us$1 billion and more, and direct relationship with issues listed above such are global traffic infrastructure, global market, global divisions of labor and so on. In 1981, Walt Disney World Resort (WDW) alone had attracted ten percent of the total number of international tourists to the United States. The scale of operation within global themeparking involves a high level of geographical abstraction and an absolute perfection of organization and execution across the scales. WDW's and Disneyland Resort's official airline, Delta Air Lines, facilitates the tourist flow in various ways: through various promotional materials, showing Touchstone movies (Touchstone Pictures is a Walt Disney Co. subsidiary) and short films advertising Walt Disney novelties and Walt Disney World Resort on its intercontinental flights to Florida, through the 'interlocked' discount-ticket system, and through package-tours designed in partnership with various associated companies worldwide.[25]

Map depicting the position of Walt Disney
World Resort within the system of Interstate
Highways East of Mississippi River.

Map depicting the position of Walt Disney
World Resort within the Orlando area.

107

Walt Disney World Resort in Florida is arguably thus the only true global theme park destination. At the time of its initial development in 1965, Walt Disney World was an island of fertile land in the midst of endless Florida swamps and in the vicinity of the under-developed city of Orlando. The late Walt Disney intended to place the project within a densely populated area East of Mississippi River. However, all such areas were in cold climates that would not have allowed for a year-round type of operation Disney intended to develop. The next logical decision was to look into three factors: traffic systems that would facilitate a significant flow of tourist to a remote destination, a climate that would enable Walt Disney to keep the theme park open in full operation throughout the year, and a tract of land large enough to avoid the parasitic developments that have occurred around the Disneyland Park's California site (Findlay 1992).

The chief-example of 'know-how' in acquiring land for development is Walt Disney Company's business deal in Florida (later somewhat repeated in Paris and Hong Kong): an analysis of company's polices towards land development and planning makes obvious the fact that what Walt Disney had established as standards in selecting, purchasing and developing sites for future Walt Disney parks is still a set of strategies to which the company strongly adheres. After a highly selective process of primary selection, two sites are always 'finally' chosen and made to compete with each other as to which one will host the future Disney operation. This tactical game gives the company the possibility of realizing promising business deals and has been proven right from the early competitions between Anaheim and Long Beach in California in the 1950s to host Disneyland Park, to the late ones in-between Spain and France for the hosting of (at that time called) Euro Disney. In Florida, the situation was a bit different: the final two sites in Florida were Ocala and Orange/Osceola Counties. At the time, Florida's swamp-land that had not been used for agriculture was very inexpensive, approximately us$180 per acre. Very early on, in 1964, Walt Disney made the decision of placing the park in

the Orange and Osceola Counties and his collaborators secretly purchased 27 000 acres of central Florida land. Small, local landowners sold the land to Walt Disney Company's subsidiaries, and local authorities, unprepared for such a serious business operation, had extended to the company the right to found Reedy Creek Development Agency (later Improvement District), which had more rights on governing this major piece of Florida's land than Florida's elected officials and its public institutions. Moreover, regarding most legal issues, Florida waived its rights to control this land. For example, Disney Company acquired a total control over zoning and building codes, taxation and governance, wildlife protection policies, fire protection services, internal infrastructure development, (roads, bridges, sewage) making in fact an autonomous administrative, political and economic unit. The importance of this decision is obvious through a comparison of sizes: the surface bought and designated for the future Walt Disney World was twice the size of the island of Manhattan. The estimated initial investment of us$230 million (all of it Walt Disney's own money) for the 27 000 acres of property was at the time an unbelievable sum to be spent on a leisure-related project.

At the time of initial development Walt Disney World's theater was located within an existing but underutilized state and federal traffic systems that connected the region of the United States East of Mississippi River with Florida. It included I-75 national highway linking South Florida (down to Florida Keys) with the Mid-West, I-95 linking Florida with the North-East United States, I-10 linking central United States with the South, regionally important I-4 linking both coasts of Florida (Gulf Coast with the Atlantic Coast), Florida Turnpike linking central Florida with the Palm Beach megalopolitan area and Miami, and the vicinity of the Orlando Airport. At the time, Orlando Airport was not an international port and had only national significance unlike Miami, already a major tourist destination and an air-gateway to Europe and Latin America. Being closely linked to the intersections of the major Interstate highway system and two significant airports,

Walt Disney's ambitions were to attract tourists from Eastern United States (east of Mississippi River), Latin America and Europe, while Disneyland Park had already attracted tourists from West of Mississippi River and had developed programs to attract Asian tourists (Findlay 1992). The tourist flow into Walt Disney World's trade theater could not have been planned solely by the population-radius parameters or conventional trade area analysis: for example the population of Florida has been considerably smaller than its annual visitors flow (in 1995 it was 23 million). On the other hand, Walt Disney World Resort abides within the network of Walt Disney theme parks worldwide and the pattern of its global visitor flow shows a very intricate diagram.

On the micro-economic level, including Osceola County and greater Orlando area, Walt Disney World has made a dramatic impact. A comparative overview of different economic indicators for greater Orlando area shows the dramatic increase in the number of airline arrivals in the period from March 1971 (just after Magic Kingdom Park at the Walt Disney World opened) to one year later (1972) and until

a decade later (1981) is indicative for the type of operation involved and the scale of infrastructure serving this theater. In 1971, Orlando airport had recorded slightly over 50 000 airline arrivals whereas a year later, in 1972, it had recorded a number of nearly 115 000 arrivals. Ten years after the opening, in 1981, the number of airline arrivals had jumped to nearly 2.3 million. Over 400 000 of those passengers were international tourists to Walt Disney World, the number of which rose in 1990 to 2.7 million as the total number of visitors rose to 26 million (Greenhouse 1991). Statistics for air-freight, daily vehicular traffic on I-4, gasoline sales and employment had also shown a similarly dramatic increase.[26]

Besides Walt Disney's own investment and the 14 000 jobs in the construction industry his project had generated (currently Walt Disney World Resort employs over 30 000 people), the project also caused unexpected investments on the part of Orange County. It is estimated that Orange County had to spend US$14 million on the Walt Disney World project (before the park opened in 1971) in order to improve the traffic infrastructure and housing capacities (Burt

Access Road to Walt Disney World Resort,
Florida. Used by the permission from Disney
Enterprises, Inc.

109

1982). Most of these changes were felt by taxpayers of the Orange County, where the so-called 'Disney effect' had devastating consequences. In 1970, the population of Orlando was just under 500 000 people, whereas it had doubled from 1970–86 as it rose to one million. The rapid increase in population had caused an immense demand on housing capacities as well as on the entire public and private infrastructures: prices for food, gas, insurance soared even years before the theme park opened. As Disney employees and people related to the development of Disney's theme park moved to the Orlando area, thousands of people evacuated the area in search of a more affordable place to live (Fjellman 1992).

Today, approximately 5000 acres of the total WDW land has been developed leaving 15 000 acres for future development and over 7000 acres as a wilderness preserve. Since the site for Disneyland in California was large enough only to accommodate the park itself, the developments that have occurred along the road linking Disneyland Park with Santa Ana Freeway were out of Walt Disney's control. Low-cost motels and other attractions undermined Disney's efforts in terms of lowering the overall standard and reducing the economic effect that Disneyland Park might have generated with overnight stays. The strategy employed in Florida disabled such developments and allowed Walt Disney Company to take total control of tourist flows in and out of its theater. Hotel capacities at Walt Disney World Resort have expanded steadily over the years so that with the addition of Disney's Pop Century Resort in December 2003, Walt Disney World Resort had accumulated nearly 25 000 guest rooms.

NOTES

1. For discussions of the role of time-function in shaping urban structures see Lynch 1972 and Bobić 1990.

2. Kenneth Frampton defined humanists as 'those whose vocation is to analyze and postulate the fundamental superstructure of the society.' (Frampton 1988: 51). The humanists, argued Frampton, 'are the ones who find themselves enmeshed in the almost inexpressible aporias of the postmodern condition.'

3. This is a rough approximation of standard items such as a FS report would contain. More precise insight into the process of industry leaders such are Economics Research Associates (ERA) and Amusement and Entertainment Management (AEM) can be obtained by checking their official material or their web sites: of ERA (http://www.econres.com/) and AEM (http://www.aemllc.com/) (both accessed on 1 May 2004). Raymond Braun of ERA had outlined the planning process for Fiesta Texas as a typical development cycle for a theme park as follows (Braun 1998): Concept, Feasibility Study and Master Plan; Public approval process; Design Development (DD); Financing; Construction drawings; Construction; Procuring rides and other equipment; Installing rides, show facilities and other equipment; Pre-opening (including the operating plan for the park); Park opening. As Braun further indicated the planning and development process was a very complex affair and it had involved a number of different groups for this project. The owner-operators were USAA and Opryland while the overall project management was performed by Project Control of Texas based in San Antonio. ERA was the economic consultant on the project and was involved in the early stages of project planning and financing. The concept and Master Plan were developed by Forrec International based in Toronto. They handed over detailed design drawings of the project to San Antonio-based architecture and engineering groups Benham-Jones-Kell and Pape-Dawson who did design development and construction drawings in collaboration with general contractors Lyda/Manhattan and HB Zachery. Besides these major consultants and contributors to the project numerous other consultants, designers, suppliers and contractors also participated in the project in important ways (Braun 1998).

4. This information appears on White Hutchinson's official web site and is a part of their standard offer. At: http://www.whitehutchinson.com/ (Accessed on 1st May 2004).

5. These figures are the industry average (White 1993).

6. BPI for the United States is published annually in 'Demographics USA', *The Census and You*, United States Department of Commerce, Bureau of the Census. At: http://www.census.gov/epcd/www/97EC44.HTM (Accessed on 1st May 2004).

7. The five factors mentioned here are in part inspired by Randy White's discussion of the five categories that 'define the dimensions of the mix' (White 1997).

8. A successful marketing move was also The Magic Kingdom Club (MKC) originally created as Disney's courtesy to those who lived near Disneyland Park and wanted to visit park often back in 1970s. In mid-1980s, it grew into a world-wide program. Walt Disney Company had established a few types of MKC memberships for individuals and companies alike. Companies could have enrolled into the program only if they employed more than 500 people. Employees of such companies would get benefits such are discounted accommodation, reduced prices on selected ticket options in Disney parks, and so on. Individual members of this no-fee based club had similar options including also discounts on merchandise and meals in Disney parks, a small bag, pens, a free video and luggage tag, and so on. In 2000, Walt Disney Company had discontinued the Magic Kingdom Club and established a new fee-based program called the Disney Club. Disney Club basically worked the same way and also in return for the initial annual fee of US$39.95 provided its members with special discounts on selected Disney books, home videos, merchandise from the Disney Store, discounts on some Disney theatrical performances, annual subscription to Disney Magazine, and more. Disney Club was also closed in December 2003.

9. In 1994, AAA teamed with Walt Disney World Resort to open the Ocala Travel Center in Ocala, Florida just off I-75 and a few miles from the gates to Walt Disney World Resort. The center has been providing travel services including theme park tickets, vacation packages and hotels accommodations. After 11th September 2001, AAA Vacations offered specially priced packages to Walt Disney World Resort that included three nights accommodations at Disney's All Star Resort and an Ultimate Park Hopper Ticket offering unlimited admission to all Disney theme parks and water parks (Calcagni and Cheske 2001). In 1997, AAA signed an initial partnership agreement with Walt Disney Company, and in 2002 two travel industry giants extended the partnership agreement for another five years, until 2007, so that AAA members received benefits with Disney vacation packages and special discounts on lodging, whereas AAA Club received increased revenue opportunities through sales of AAA Vacations and Disney Cruise Line products, as well as extensive marketing support. Besides Walt Disney Co.'s subsidiaries, AAA's partners include Anheuser-Busch Adventure Parks (Sea World, Busch Gardens, Adventure Island and Water Country), Best Western, Carnival Cruise Lines, Days Inn, Hertz, Hilton Garden Inns, Hyatt Hotels & Resorts, LaQuinta Inns & Suites, Marriott, Princess Cruises, Radisson Seven Seas Cruises, Royal Caribbean International, Six Flags Theme Parks, Universal Studios Hollywood, Universal Orlando, Universal Studios Vacations, and many others. AAA Club sales through AAA Vacations operated by Walt Disney Travel Company increased over 100 percent between 1997 and 2002 (Cheske 2002). The same year, AAA Travel presented its Preferred Partner of the Year Award, the Best Marketing Award, and Best Member Satisfaction Award to Walt Disney Travel Company (Cheske 2002b). In January 2004, AAA Travel celebrated the 'Disney Month' that once again provided AAA members with 'significant savings' on theme parks tickets, airplane and train tickets, rental cars, hotel rooms and restaurants, that in 2001 alone amounted to a total of US$315 million (Cheske 2002a).

10. The arrangement between Vivendi Universal and MasterCard International is yet another example of the synergetic cross-marketing of international corporate giants. The agreement between the two corporations has been obvious to North American television audiences through the Priceless campaign that involves multiple Vivendi Universal properties related to film, music and theme parks. The campaign was designed by the advertising agency McCann-Erickson and was broadcasted internationally promoting simultaneously both brands. In addition to this campaign, the arrangement of the two corporations has been evident in print ads publicizing promotional tie-ins, at point-of-sale advertising, at specific promotions, at MasterCard member banks and elsewhere (Zoltak 2003).

11. At: http://www.universalstudioshollywood.com/ (Accessed on 1st May 2004).

12. It is very common in the theme park industry that average admission revenues in regional theme parks are generated only up to 10 percent by admissions from the posted prices. The rest of the attendance revenues come from a variety of incentive admissions, such are seasonal passes, group sales, promotional discounts and so on. As Amusement Business reported in 2003, group sales tickets account for approximately one third of all admission revenues in the North American theme park industry (AB 2003a).

13. As Tim O'Brien reported, in April 2001, Busch Gardens in Tampa Bay, Florida estimated that 90 percent of its five million visitors used some sort of a discounted ticket (O'Brien 2001). Paramount Parks reported the same trend: 185 million Coca-Cola cans distributed in the summer of 2001 had discounts printed on them ranging from US$4 to US$10 for all five of the Paramount Parks. The Florida Busch and Sea-World parks were in 2001 in the second year of discounting programs: as O'Brien indicated, once tourists attended a park multiple times many upgraded their passes to include free parking, food and merchandise discounts. Since 2001, discounting through promotional partners who distribute money-off coupons on soft drink products, at fast food restaurants, travel discount packages and elsewhere has became an industry-wide trend as coupon-tie-inns have become a proven method of boosting theme park attendance (AB 2003a).

14. The annual FPI lists prices at 25 theme parks across the United States for parking, posted admission for two adults and two children, two hot dogs, two hamburgers, four orders of French-fries, four small soft drinks and two kid-size souvenir T-shirts.

15. These vary depending on location.

16. The interview with Mr. Tokuoka Tateru was conducted at Mr. Tokuoka's office in the Shima Spain Village in August 1997.

17. California (Six Flags Magic Mountain, Los Angeles; Six Flags Hurricane Harbor, Los Angeles; Six Flags Marine World, San Francisco; Waterworld USA, Concord; and Waterworld USA, Sacramento), Colorado (Six Flags Elitch Gardens, Denver), Georgia (Six Flags Over Georgia, Atlanta; Six Flags White Water, Atlanta; and American Adventures, Atlanta), Illinois (Six Flags Great America, Chicago), Kentucky (Six Flags Kentucky Kingdom, Louisville), Louisiana (Six Flags New Orleans), Maryland (Six Flags America, Baltimore/Washington, DC), Massachusetts (Six Flags New England, Springfield), Missouri (Six Flags St. Louis), New Jersey (Six Flags Great Adventure, Jackson; Six Flags Hurricane Harbor, Jackson; and Six Flags Wild Safari, Jackson), New York (Six Flags Darien Lake, Buffalo and The Great Escape & Splashwater Kingdom, Lake George), Ohio (Six Flags Worlds of Adventure, Cleveland and Wyandot Lake, Columbus), Oklahoma (Frontier City, Oklahoma City and White Water Bay, Oklahoma City), Texas (Six Flags Over Texas, Arlington; Six Flags Hurricane Harbor, Arlington; Six Flags Fiesta Texas, San Antonio; Six Flags AstroWorld, Houston; and Splash Town, Houston) and Washington (Wild Waves & Enchanted Village, Seattle). Besides Six Flags Inc. owns and operates parks in Canada (La Ronde, Montreal), Mexico (Six Flags Mexico, Mexico City) and Europe (Six Flags Belgium; Bellewaerde Park, Belgium; Walibi Lorraine, France; Walibi Aquitaine, France; Walibi Rhône-Alpes, France; Six Flags Holland, The Netherlands; Warner Bros. Movie World, Germany; and Warner Bros. Movie World Madrid in Spain). This information has been used by Six Flags Inc. since 2004, and included in their regular press material package and their web site.

18. If not otherwise indicated the data used in this section comes from the Six Flags Inc.'s press packages.

19. The Walibi group was founded in 1975 in Belgium with the opening of its Walibi Wavre park. The group has steadily grown to an overall attendance of over three million visitors in 1997. In 1998, Premier Parks Inc. purchased the Walibi Group and kept all of its parks except Mini Europe and Océade which were sold to the Meeús family the same year.

20. In 2002, the new Warner Bros. Movie World Spain theme park opened in Madrid under Six Flags Inc. management.

21. France was second with US$27 billion followed by Italy with a demand of US$24 billion. Source: Icon Group Ltd., Copyright 2000. At: http://www.icongroupedition.com/. Chapter 4: Europe: Amusement And Recreation Services—Market Potential for Amusement and Recreation Services in Europe: 57 (Accessed on 1st May 2004).

22. At: http://www.icongroupedition.com (Accessed on 1st May 2004).

23. Anheuser-Busch owns Sea World, Busch Gardens, and Sesame World. Besides, Anheuser-Busch is also the world's largest beer producer (Budweiser, Bud Light, Michelob, Busch and a variety of specialty beers). Viacom owns Paramount Parks plus Cable channels such are MTV, VH1, BET, CMT, TNN, and Nickelodeon, television channels CBS and UPN television, Paramount Pictures, Blockbuster, Simon & Schuster, etc. Walt Disney Company, besides theme parks, owns and operates film studios, ABC television network, Disney Channel, ESPN and multiple cable networks, a chain of retail stores, Touchstone Pictures, etc. Vivendi Universal owns Universal Studios theme parks and all Vivendi International properties including television and cable channels, film production, publishing, retail, and more.

24. In 1989, when Walt Disney World Resort scored record attendance figures of 26 million visitors, theme parks accounted for 56 percent of Walt Disney Company's revenues (Knowlton 1989).

25. Similar strategies are employed by Air France, the official airline of Disneyland Paris Resort, and since 1997, by Japan Airlines the official airline of Tokyo Disneyland Resort.

26. The data was adapted from Marlowe 1972 and Fjellman 1992.

THEMEING

'Men and women must have their adrenals stimulated from time to time'.
'What?' questioned the Savage, uncomprehending.
'It's one of the conditions of perfect health. That's why we've made the V.P.S. treatments compulsory'.
'V.P.S.?'
'Violent Passion Surrogate. Regularly once a month. We flood the whole system with adrenin. It's the complete physiological equivalent of fear and rage. All the tonic effects of murdering Desdemona and being murdered by Othello, without any of the inconveniences'.
'But I like inconveniences'.
'We don't,' said the Controller. 'We prefer to do things comfortably'.
'But I don't want comfort. I want God, I want poetry, I want real danger, I want freedom, I want goodness. I want sin'.
'In fact,' said Mustapha Mond, 'you're claiming the right to be unhappy'.
'All right then,' said the Savage defiantly, 'I'm claiming the right to be unhappy'.
'Not to mention the right to grow old and ugly and impotent; the right to have syphilis and cancer; the right to have too little to eat; the right to be lousy; the right to live in constant apprehension of what may happen tomorrow; the right to catch typhoid; the right to be tortured by unspeakable pains of every kind'.
There was a long silence. 'I claim all that,' said the Savage at last.
(HUXLEY 1932)[1]

It is a common understanding that what bridges the gap between the domains of Themeparking and Themeing, or the strategic with the tactical domain, is means of transportation. What actually bridges the two is the fabrication of tourist experience. 'Guest experience,' or what Walt Disney Imagineering calls 'the art of the show' (Hench 2003: 2), is a nearly theatrical experience of tourists as they progress through the narrative that links together the domain of Themeparking with a great variety of attractions within the theme park. Walt Disney has to be credited not for inventing, but for perfecting the method of layered narrative procession through a multitude of scales including the orchestration of large crowds of visitors on the ground. Disney's use of 'enveloping by theme' strategy implied that neither cultural nor topographic conditions played significant roles in determining the design of the theme park environment, but the way in which Disneyland bridged the domains of television, film, animation, and retail. That was accomplished by designing a smooth, frictionless procession from the realm of television and film to the realm of theme park and retail by designing above all a totalizing environmental experience. Disneyland, the first theme park, was a complex, multidimensional and multilayered environment that had to be experienced in a way that preserved its complexity, but nevertheless, maintained its legibility in relation to the desires and interests of the middle class America. The design of Disneyland Park had to respond immaculately to the images and experiences that preceded, those that Americans observed on Wednesday nights a year prior to the opening of the actual theme park. Walt Disney knew that in order to create such an environment, he would have to use a number of production techniques acquired from a range of sources, such as film, miniature period rooms at museums, historic villages and others. The techniques employed in Disneyland Park were developed through the use of mathematical and geometric ordering systems in 1930s, when Jean Perrier designed film techniques that created appearances of great depth or height in order to enable camera to 'see' a desirable image: relationships of actors in relation to the background were easily exag-

gerated, some characteristics were overemphasized, some neutralized, and so on (Wasserman 1978: 33). Secondly, miniaturization appealed to Disney as an introduction to playfulness, but also as a way of playfully introducing the American heritage lost by 'progress'. In that respect, he was inspired by Henry Ford's Greenfield Village he visited a few times prior to 1955 (Marling 1997: 45).

Walt Disney was also aware of numerous historical examples researched and documented by Walt Disney Imagineering, such are Pleasure Gardens and Great Exhibitions, where thematization was adopted to convey national character, induce pleasurable experiences by simulating travel, and achieve cohesive narration. As Christine Boyer noted, Great Exhibitions were simulated travelogues that combined iconic, architectural images with modern amusement technology within a time-frame programmed and planned for commercial advantage (Boyer 1994). At the Paris Exhibition of 1889, Charles Garnier designed the History of Human Habitation exhibition that consisted of full-scale reproductions of traditional structures and adjacent national restaurants where visitors could have tasted and consumed ethnic foods. Thus, the thematic environments of Great Exhibitions were composed not only of visual stimuli but also of other sensory stimuli, such as the smell and taste of food. This type of procedure developed into an 'exhibitionary technique' employed excessively by the end of the Nineteenth Century in museums and ethno-villages.

WED designers took the problem of controlling pedestrian flows very seriously. In 1954, on the occasion of conceptualizing the flow of people to, from and within Disneyland Park, Disney brought in the manager of Copenhagen's Tivoli Gardens to advise the design team on methods and techniques of crowd control (Marling 1997: 64). A quantum leap in controlling the movement of large crowds for commercial purposes was also first encountered in the Great Exhibitions. It was first mastered at the Paris Great Exhibition of 1867, where the main building was organized as seven concentric galleries encircling the open-air Palm Garden placed at the core of the scheme. Early amusement parks and pleasure gardens had encountered the same type of problem: Vauxhall Gardens were organized into walkways that ended in large thematic settings such as the Chinese Garden or the Ruins of Palmira. Distant settings were constructed along the procession routes in order to achieve a dynamic cinematic experience in moving through the garden. Most of the techniques employed in Pleasure Gardens were derived from country-fairs or medieval fairs. Both were initially based on the grid system, with booths featuring food and commodities at the core of the site, and with amusement installations marking its perimeter (Braithwaite 1968: 21–29). In the Seventeenth Century, most fairs had a roundabout at each of the site's corners. In the early Nineteenth Century, when the emphasis shifted from trade to amusement, the roundabouts (or a carousel), stage sets and other amusement installations moved from the periphery of the site to its center. Subsequently, booths featuring food, drinks, commodities, stalls, shows and joints have now been aligned marking the perimeter enclosure on three sides of the site. The fourth side was usually reserved for the entrance or the so-called exchange area. Entrances worked as funnels with vistas on the roundabout in motion, whereas booths and joints created a vortex around attractions dispatching visitors on to the spending routes. Such a basic layout was also employed at early Great Exhibitions and World Exhibitions as well as in amusement parks, and the economic and spatial logic still stands at the base of theme park design. The essence of most of these examples is in designing a controlled circulation system with a series of interconnected nodes where each has a capacity to function as a sub-node in order to dissolve large groups of visitors into smaller ones.

DEFINING THE OBJECT OF VISION

Oblique perspective was a representational technique invented in the Sixteenth-Century Italy in the art of drama, theaters and gardens in order to stimulate the movement of observer's eye and his body from one scene to another (Cereghini 1991). The frame of vision would always contain the central object together with at least two marginal objects on both sides, enhancing the spatial dynamics and unifying different scenes into a visually comprehensive whole. The technique was based on the notion that human eyes are always aware of peripheral visual stimulus, even at times when such information is not the focus of our observations. Oblique perspective was a purely optical technique that focused on the simulation of observer's eye when following a narrative procession. The same technique was used in France and in England, beginning with the Seventeenth Century.[1]

With the introduction of new military technology in the Seventeenth Century, the previously static point of view was replaced by a dynamic experience of space one still based on vision but also on movement. Le Nôtre's avenues at Versailles, introduced in order to facilitate fast riding and hunting through gardens, changed the perception of space of those who participated in the hunts. Hunting deer was also replaced by hunting foxes, faster and smaller animals, thus visibility and speed became crucial (Lasdun 1991). The garden's layout depended on the speed of movement and the height of observer's eye (walking vs. riding). Therefore, the role of the horse, or riding, was important in understanding the new notion of cinematic experience of a dynamic space the quality of which depended on the dynamics of vision and thus of movement.

The Eighteenth Century provided a set of peculiar optical devices that redefined the viewing subject and his visual apparatus. The Picturesque garden that so accurately resembled the Arcadian landscapes of Poussin was an ideal stage-set to be frozen, framed and viewed at will. This separation of the observer from the garden, thus the reduction of kinesthetic bodily experience to visual one, was first facilitated by the Claude Glass, a device named after the painter Claude Lorrain (Lasdun 1991: 82–83). The Claude Glass was a hand-held convex mirror within an ornamented and darken

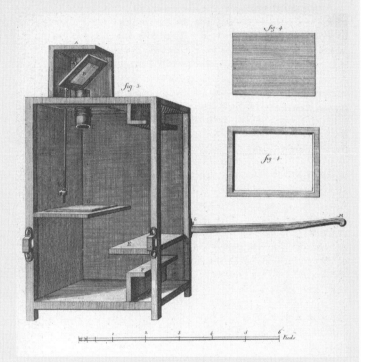

A rendering of *Camera Obscura*, c. 1770.

wooden frame, which was to be used at specifically marked places in the garden, known for their beautiful vistas. The viewer would turn his back on the scene and look at it reflected, reduced (in miniature) and framed as if it were a Lorraine painting. The Claude Glass operated on a level of plain, two-dimensional representation and often included a hint of the subject's body. This was a popular form of entertainment for nobility. As Edward Ball has argued (Ball 1993), the garden viewed through the frame operates on

Theme Park as Environment

And then came the movies, radio and television, which carried the message that what you experienced had nothing to do with where you were [...] The movie down the street brought images from of all over the world, all times in history [...] Television made this far more dramatic by bringing into people's houses a succession of experiences that they found as intense and vivid as life itself. (Hine 1986: 147–8)

For the construction of Disneyland, two ideas were therefore crucial: firstly, the idea that theme park as a material environment represents an extension of the public realm of television, advertising, films, retail and mass-tourism; and secondly, that for such an extension to work, a homogeneous human experience had to be fabricated across multiple scales. WED designers were aware of the thematic work in retail and leisure design such were William L. Pereira's Robinson department store in Beverly Hills of 1952, in which shops were organized around 'wide-vision sales theaters' (Marling 1997: 58) or Lapidus's 1954 Fontainebleau Hotel in Miami Beach. Morris Lapidus was the first designer to incorporate symbolic universes fabricated by Hollywood and television systematically into the design of leisure environments outside of Hollywood. Lapidus designed Fontainebleau as a modern version of 'French Provincial' by gimmicking stage sets of famed television shows and blockbuster movies and thereby creating one of the most successful attempts to blur the boundaries between the emerging and largely symbolic world of mass media with that of the material world in which the newly born mass-tourist searched for the confirmation of sanity. Both Rayner Banham (1961) and Venturi and Scott-Brown (Venturi et al. 1972) discussed the convergences of architecture and mass-media in 1950s and 1960s, particularly in the case of Las Vegas and the branding of architecture, but in a Lapidusian sense, in terms of an architecture that gimmicked the world of television. But the level of homogeneity that Disney exhibited in converging his media presence with his own leisure environments was groundbreaking: since Disney's ideas were also born out of television, film, and animation his interest were *de facto* aimed at creating a complex dynamic environment where the narratives, images, desires and expectations previously fabricated by the media would be supported by experiences in the material world, creating in the process an unknown fusion of the previously entirely separate domains of human experience. His belief in technological progress and free enterprise ensured him that such an aim was indeed realistic and above all desirable. Disney attempted to design a totally artificial 'environment' whose logic was to be found in a systematic attempt at understanding the desires and interests of 'users' (the middle class America), and in a subsequent effort to capitalize on that understanding. Disney's emphatic abilities were legendary, and the combination of understanding people, together with his professional knowledge in film and animation, led to a strong ability to anticipate and control behavioral outcomes in his audiences. He was always keenly observing people, the choices they made in public spaces, the paths they followed, and the range of emotions they communicated to an observer. Walt Disney led members of Walt Disney Imagineering in visiting cities, zoos, parks and in measuring walkways, observing pedestrian flows, and studying patrons's reactions. He insisted they always assume guests's position and point of view and observe visitors's behavior in relation to specific tasks, in order to gain a better understanding of the space and time guests need in a story environment (Hench 2003: 21). His method of designing theme parks has best been summarized by 'Mickey's 10 Commandments', authored by Marty Sklar, President of the Imagineering Division:

> Know your audience; Wear your guests' shoes, meaning don't forget the human factor; Organize the flow of people and ideas; Create a 'visual magnet;' Communicate with visual literacy; Avoid overload, create turn-ons; Tell one story at a time; Avoid contradictions, maintain identity; For every ounce of treatment provide a ton full of treat; Keep it up. One more: never distract guests' attention unintentionally! (Dunlop 1996: 43–44)

two levels: on the first level, there is the actual garden with its landscaping and the labor that went into its creation and maintenance, while on the other level, there is the 'meta-landscape,' an actual landscape viewed through the frame as a vehicle of detaching landscape from the land into a source of two-dimensional imagery. The crucial relationship is that of the frame and the content, a condition that already contains the presupposition for thematization. For Ball, the essence of thematization lies in the priority of image over phenomenological experience of space. Thus, a Landscape Garden viewed through the Claude Glass is a meta-garden, an evocation of garden.

Replacing the Claude Glass in popularity was the *Camera Obscura,* first theorized and perfected in Italy in 1558 by Giovanni Battista della Porta. At first, the *Camera Obscura* was a dark room to be entered with the whole body. Portable devices were constructed from the Seventeenth Century, and the device became increasingly smaller during the Eighteenth Century. Although the *Camera Obscura* was generally seen as a new machine of scientific inquiry because of its supposed objectivity, it was also increasingly used in artistic practice by those not concerned with the truthfulness of its representation. 'Those that are in the Chamber shall see Trees, Animals, Hunters, Faces, and all the rest so plainly, that they cannot tell whether they be true or delusions' wrote della Porta in 1558 (Della Porta 1658: 365). This is precisely what Joseph Addison, one of the first Englishman to write about observing natural scenes through a *Camera Obscura,* had in mind when he wrote in 1712 that the 'prettiest landskip' he ever saw was 'drawn by camera obscura' (Addison 1712 quoted in Lasdun 1991: 83). It was not any more about gimmicking Lorrain's or Poussin's paintings in creating a Landscape Garden, the process was now extended to include the representation of the garden by way of creating an image mediated through the new optical device. Thus, it was a move to representing garden that had already been conceived as the representation of an Arcadian landscape, mediated by the apparatus of painting. One could only speculate as to the use of the *Camera Obscura* as a design tool in conceptualizing the Picturesque Garden of the early 1700s, however, the fact is that Alexander Pope had a *Camera Obscura* installed in his garden at Twickenham designed in 1719. Some of the scenes in Twickenham, particularly the Riverside Scene and the Park

Scene, might have been designed through the use of a *Camera Obscura* (Hunt 1991, Lasdun 1991). Addison discussed the issue of appropriateness of different types of gardens as to the aesthetic quality of their representation. He argued that, when viewed through a *Camera Obscura,* French and Dutch Formal Gardens look much better than the English Landscape Garden (Lasdun 1991). This was due to the strict geometric patterns and mathematical ordering that allowed for better images when represented through a *Camera Obscura,* while the English garden, due to its soft lines and diffusion of strong shapes and contours, gave less clear image and without apparent depth. It was thus a call to subordinating the principles of design and consequently a whole world-view to the rationale of representation imposed by the new optical device. This view was an accurate expression of a general stance that had to do with the profound redefinition of the human subject and its relations to both 'nature' and 'culture'. Unlike the Claude Glass that activated the subject's presence within the garden and his experience of it, the *Camera Obscura* secluded the subject not only from the external world but also from his own natural mechanism of vision.[2]

1. William Kent used oblique perspective in the design of his gardens.

2. As Jonathan Crary wrote: 'For della Porta's natural magic, the use of the camera obscura was simply one of the number of methods that allowed an observer to become more fully concentrated on a particular object; it had no exclusive priority as the site or mode of observation. But to readers of della Porta several decades later, the camera obscura seemed to promise an unrivaled and privileged means of observation that was attained finally at the cost of shattering the Renaissance adjacency of knower and known. Beginning in the late 1500s the figure of the camera obscura begins to assume a preeminent importance in delimiting and defining the relations between observer and world. Within several decades the camera obscura is no longer one of many instruments or visual options but instead the compulsory site from which vision can be conceived or represented. Above all it indicates the appearance of a new model of subjectivity, the hegemony of a new subject-effect. First of all the camera obscura performs an operation of individuation [...] At the same time, another related and equally decisive function of the camera was to sunder the act of seeing from the physical body of the observer, to decorporealize vision.' (Crary 1992: 38–39).

In parallel to Disney's quest, the knowledge of biomechanics and an increased interest in human psychology was brought by mid-1950s into the design and planning discourses by researchers who had an interest in the application of methods from social sciences to the analysis of human behavior in built environments. Their belief was that a wide range of data that modern research practices within the field of social sciences had come up with had not been utilized by designers in shaping the man-made environment. Research of the Behaviorists group, and later the Environment-Behavior Studies, had produced, directly or indirectly, a number of significant results:[2] most of their research attempted to understand environments (situations, conditions) in which humans make choices and the mechanisms under which human choice-behavior occurs. Many of the studies applied field-research methods used in social sciences (observation techniques, questionnaires, and photo or film documentation) in order to obtain data on use and user behavior. The chief objective of such efforts was to improve the design process itself, namely to make the design process more effective by bringing in data and knowledge generated by both theoretical and field research. In that respect, WED designers and researchers in the fields of behavior and environment studies aimed at the very same objective, often though from different ethical positions. The term 'environment' was found to be adequate in representing the immense complexity of such efforts, the multidimensionality of human experience in the man made world, as well as the techno-optimistic scientism of the period. As Kenneth Frampton notes, 'the euphemistic use of the term "environment", with its "life-science" connotations, is symptomatic of the time.' (Frampton 1988: 53) The term itself dates back to early Seventeenth Century, and comes from the French term *environ* meaning to encompass, encircle or surround.[3] Scottish writer Thomas Carlyle used it in 1827 to render German term *umgebung* as conditions in which a person or things live.[4] Since the early 1920s, it has been used in psychology and since the late 1960s, within the ecological discourses ('environmentalism'). Regardless of whether the term indicates an ontological unity of 'natural' and 'nurtured,' clear distinctions between nature and artifice, or the inner workings of the computer system, 'environment' commonly denotes the totality of circumstances, objects and conditions within which an individual or an artifice is embedded, and the combination of complex external and internal conditions that affect and influence its behavior. In military as well as in computing theory, environment represents the total set of conditions under which a system operates. The term 'environment' thus represented a systematic, dynamic and multi-dimensional approach to designing artifice that presented an opportunity to bridge the gap between form and process through a research-based practice. In that sense, the design of an environment takes into account built forms, landscape and topographic elements, the subliminal field of environmental stimuli, and practices of its constituents (Rapoport 1980). Environment, as defined by Amos Rapoport, stands for a culture-specific, orderly set of relationships 'between things and things, things and people, and people and people'; (Rapoport 1980: 11) when environments are designed four general elements are being organized: space, time, meaning and communication (Rapoport 1982: 178).

In opposition to the modernist dogma 'form follows function', another notion had developed by early 1950s which maintained that both the material and symbolic aspects of environment operate as 'interfaces', mediating between human beings and their surroundings. The 'value' of an environment can in that respect be assessed by scrutinizing the balance between the degree to which an individual reacts to an environment, and the degree to which he also acts through it (Kattsoff 1947, Woodworth 1958). Finding an ideal balance between the two variables is still the biggest challenge of any design practice. The 'value' of an environment, then, is in mediating successfully between its own form and the social processes it enables. The work of Lawrence (urban planner) and Ann Halprin (dancer/choreographer) in 1960s was instrumental in bridging the gap between urban form and urban process (Halprin 1969).[5] They used scores in order to cho-

reograph playful citizen action in urban environments. In doing so, Halprins made direct connections between scores utilized in performance arts and music with the algorithms used in system-engineering and military science, and argued that grounds for similarity can be found in clear objectives and control over the process of performance. In addition to that, argued the Nobel laureate Herbert Simon in his book *The Sciences of the Artificial,* the success of any such artifice will be the function of its 'adaptability' (Simon 1969: 55–83). In that respect, Simon proposed that the only way to represent the full complexity of an artifice and its ability to adapt successfully, is to design it by systematically integrating 'state descriptions' with 'process descriptions'. Plans, as we know them, are examples of 'state descriptions', because they characterize the world as sensed. Recipes are examples of 'process descriptions', because they characterize the world as acted upon, they provide the means for producing or generating artifacts having the desired characteristics. The task of any adaptive system (artifact) is to develop correlations between goals in the sensed world and actions in the world of process, so that differences between the two states are progressively diminished. The mathematical logic and Cartesian rational, analytical attitude promoted by modern science since the 1800s have traditionally been to substitute 'process descriptions' for 'state descriptions' and downplay performative and symbolic aspects of human environment in the process of design and subsequently of use. Needless to say, the reductive rhetoric of the Modern Movement and modernist, pseudo-scientific planning have been based on such notions. By the term 'environment', I will thus assume a man made, multi-dimensional adaptive system in action, whose logic is to be found in a constant interplay between 'state descriptions' and 'process descriptions'.

Arranging Theme Park Environments

Taking the previous into account, theme parks are peculiar environments because the 'process' is in theme parks 'result oriented' and often totally controlled, but also because their boundaries expand beyond their territorial confinements. Since they are so intricately embedded in a complex ensemble of relations within the trade theater, the experience of visiting a theme park begins much before one actually enters its geographic confinement. Media do not only construct a desire to visit a theme park, but also to a significant degree predetermine one's experience of it. Theme parks are thus material (physical) as well as cultural (symbolic) constructs. The desirable blend of expectations (images) fabricated by the media with the experiential attributes of theme park environments determines the design of both the material and psychological aspects of the theme park environment. As was mapped out in the previous chapter, the task of Themeparking is first to identify all variables in a complex theme park equation, and chart their interrelationships. Hence, Themeparking took into account demographic data, market analysis, physical-sphere variables and psychological-sphere variables, and a myriad of other variables in the trade theater. The task of Themeing is then to systematically reduce the number of variables in the theater of operations until key variables are identified, until final objectives of the environment are agreed upon, and finally until only one of many possible alternative designs is identified and brought into a desirable configuration. In military terms, the task of Themeparking is 'dislocation' or the creation of a 'product' opportunity, whereas the task of Themeing is then to exploit the opportunity by materializing environmental targets and to ultimately create effect. Such an effect, whether material or symbolic, is always economic in nature. Thus, in relation to the strategic level of Themeparking charted in the previous chapter, Themeing unfolds on the tactical level where the tourist experiences theme park environment 'in flesh'. In that sense, Themeing symbolically, materially and logistically sustains trade-theater objectives established at the strategic level and sets in motion a frictionless procession of tourists through predetermined 'spending routes' towards specific theaters of operation. As indicated above, theater of operations is a dynamic, multi-dimensional system in action that enables the conduct of specific, tactically crucial procedures in order to create

an economic effect out of opportunities previously generated at the strategic level. Relationships between trade theaters and theaters of operations vary: the case of Huis Ten Bosch clearly shows that a single trade theater can contain more than one theater of operations, united under the conceptual umbrella of the Huis Ten Bosch Sightseeing Company. In this particular case, the individual theme park (HTB) acts as a theater of operations. In other cases, a theater of operations can be composed of a few theme parks. In any case, the first task within Themeing is to translate and further develop conceptual and thematic frameworks established within Themeparking for every aspect of the theme park environment. The design of theme park's layout, phone-answering system, web site, marketing campaign, light fixtures, transportation system, operational budget or staffing scheme are all acts of designing that, in different ways, contribute to the total quality of user experience and theme park's overall performance. Such a systematic approach to designing also implies an intricate cause-and-effect domain within which all elements have to be brought to an ideal balance. In such a totalizing system, the source of greatest uncertainty is always the human being, both as consumer and as producer, and therefore the effort to keep the system at its optimal state is always aimed at also designing and controlling the practices of all constituents (Ritzer 1996: 27).

The initial stage of themeing unfolds through parallel unfolding of Concept Development, Program, preliminary Master Plan, and Schematic Design.[6] The objective of these conceptual vehicles is to strike an ideal balance between the trade theater, the theater of operations (that is the theme park environment as a whole), theatra, and individual environmental modules. Individual environmental modules are food outlets, retail outlets, rides, attractions, storage spaces, and so on. Theatra[7] are clusters of such modules unified by a concept: Adventureland is an example of theatron.[8] The task of Concept Development is to further develop and instrumentalize conceptual and thematic clues identified in Themeparking (derived initially from demographic and marketing research) and translate them into an operational conceptual framework. The key objective of the Program is to establish an assortment of environmental modules needed together with their spatio-temporal relationships in the theater of operations, in order to meet the projected capacities and sustain the overall concept. The program also anticipates scores that determine the precise timing of environmental activities of all constituents in relation to the spatial distribution of environmental modules and theatra. The task of Master Plan is to connect all environmental modules with a conceptual cohesion that determines every aspect of a visitors's experience from arrival to departure. The Master Plan spatializes and institutionalizes Concept Development, Program and Schematic Design based on the thematic framework defined by Themeparking, through plans, outdoor and interior spaces, circulation spaces, and through every physical and operational aspect of the theater that directly or indirectly affects all constituents.[9] Schematic Design visualizes Concept Development, Program, and the Master Plan and indicates volumes and appearances of environmental modules (buildings, rides), as well as their spatial relationship with the overall concept. It also establishes general thematic issues in conceptual terms and in ways that sustain and reinforce the objectives of the theater. Schematic Design also defines 'configurations,' situations and conditions under which choice-behavior will occur in the theme park environment. It anticipates the 'mood' of each 'scene' and creates taxonomy of sensory clues that will induce visceral, bottom-up behaviors. For example, Walt Disney Imagineering and many other theme park designers, use storyboards to design a sequence of experiences that guide the consumption of the park as they would have determined scenes in a film. Rides are a straight-forward example of how controlled visitors's experiences can be, but visitors's procession through the park can also be successfully determined through storyboards by designing interrelationships of visual forms, high-contrast colors (that suggest action and work best as an incentive to move), environmental activity and all other elements in a configuration that

engages visitors's imagination and appeals to their emotions (Hench 2003: 69). Such schematic situations are then elaborated through models and enacting in the Design Development phase. Design Development specifies connections between the Program, the Master Plan, the Schematic Design, the Operating Plan and the operating layout (frontstage and backstage) through materials, textures, furnishings, equipment, colors, signage, music, fragrances, landscaping, and so on.[10] Through the above outlined process, themeing thus produces the theme park environment by defining material attributes of the environment (scale, color, layout, costumes), all sensory environmental stimuli (visual, aural, tactile, olfactory), commodities sold (arts and crafts, food, souvenirs) and the practices of all constituents (both on frontstage and backstage). On the operational level, themeing is concerned with the maneuver and support of field operations that involve a web of constituents including visitors, employees, managers, or suppliers in complex operations such as daily staffing, supply, maintenance or control.

'The influx of tourists is invariably described by the metaphor of invasion,' wrote Van Den Abbeele, looking at relations between the military understanding of space and time with the world of mass tourism in an attempt to relate the efficiency of group movement in both discourses (Van Den Abbeele 1994). In both military practice and the economy of mass-tourism, objectives are most precisely determined and the success or failure to satisfy them could be accurately quantified. These are precisely the grounds on which the economy of mass tourism derives similarities with the world of military action. In that respect, themeing is necessarily driven by the notion of efficiency derived from probability considerations and from the requirement for coordinated action. One of the strategic objectives of Themeparking, in terms of the massive movement towards theaters of operation, is to 'diminish the possibility of resistance by movement and surprise' (Hart 1954: 337). The essential problem underlying tactical exploitation is in maximizing the effectiveness of the available resources in the theater of operations by arranging them advantageously into the so-called 'active defense disposition' (Hart 1954: 349). Such disposition institutionalizes protected areas from which to organize operations (backstage) as well as environmental targets clearly exposed to the tourist (frontstage). Having determined where the tourist should get to, lines of sight, movement to and from targets, and the speed with which they can be traveled are established by designing 'paths of optimum time' aimed at maximizing economic efficiency of movement through the theater of operations. As Hench wrote, Walt Disney Imagineering has always been highly concerned with 'the spaces through which our guests travel within and between attractions, and the time it takes them to do this [...] How much time will it take to give the guests an experience, and what other experience might precede or follow it? How does one form affect another?' (Hench 2003: 5). This obviously requires a great degree of mobility and flexibility as the form of the theme park has to be directly and dynamically related to the process taking place within it.

Attendance Projections give designers a precise idea of the volume of anticipated influx of tourists. They provide data on maximum visitor flow and its cycles, which are then used in order to calculate the 'peak attendance'. Peak attendance is calculated as up to two percent of the projected annual attendance.[11] Designers then determine the 'design day' as an estimate of the number of visitors during peak attendance periods that the park will be designed to efficiently accommodate. According to the industry standards, the 'design day' is in practice calculated based on attendance levels of 15 percent below peak capacity. Above calculations enable designers to determine capacity levels of the theme park environment ('carrying capacity') and are immensely important because failure to take each input factor into account may dramatically affect the cumulative output of the theme park system as a whole. Conceptualizing and designing the theme park around the concept of 'design day' implies also a direct cause-effect connection between the volume of the theme park

environment and the character of each module within it. Design day thus determines sizes and capacities of parking spaces, gates, circulation spaces, sitting and rest areas, retail facilities, supporting facilities, and so on. It also determines the complexity and capacity of the Program, together with the overall mix and capacity of attractions and 'events,' by calculating the 'entertainment capacity' of the theme park environment. Entertainment capacity is a complex input, because it weaves into the theme park equation complex quantitative and qualitative variables. On the quantitative side, it takes into account the previously calculated 'design day' as well as industry standards suggesting that each visitor optimally experiences 1–1.5 entertainment units per hour (EU/hour) (McNair 2000). Multiplying the anticipated 'design day' attendance by the appropriate EU value gives the total number of entertainment units and the corresponding hourly operating capacity of the theme park. Each environmental module is also characterized by its 'throughput' value. 'Throughput' is a term used to describe the number of visitors that can experience an environmental module in a given operating period. The cumulative throughput of all environmental modules is used to calculate the 'entertainment capacity' of the theme park. Nevertheless, on the qualitative side the 'entertainment capacity' is also calculated based upon demographic and marketing variables as attractions that appeal to different target groups have varied throughputs. Theme parks targeting primarily older visitor groups would place an emphasis on theater shows and more educational attractions. Those targeting a younger population of trade theaters may place an emphasis on rides. The same applies in relation to educational spectra: if the trade theater has a predominantly educated population environmental modules will cater to 'intellectual' experiences, as opposed to those with less educated population where an emphasis will be placed on fast rides and shooting games. Such decisions affect the overall entertainment capacity. An environmental module such as a roller coaster is based on one-minute rides and high visitor throughput, but smaller capacity-per-ride (50 people), whereas a theater-like show can have a larger capacity-per-show (few hundred visitors) but lower through-put, since it lasts for 15 minutes. Because of such a complexity in calculating the entertainment capacity, both operating and entertainment capacities can be calculated for the overall theme park attendance, and also separately for each demographic or socio-economic group and then added to the overall capacity projection. These calculations *de facto* instrumentalize the relationship between the trade theater and the theater of operations and are used to determine capital budget as well as the elements of both the Program and the Master Plan.

In relation to the above, the Program first determines major environmental targets[12] that directly support the concept of the particular theater of operations. Such environmental modules are commonly of large size and with a significant throughput. For instance, Nagashima Spaland in Japan (Mie Prefecture) opened in 2000 the Steel Dragon, the 'world's tallest, deepest, fastest and longest roller coaster' at the time, with 1.5 mile-long course, and the height of 320 feet. Up until then, Millennium Force in Cedar Point, Ohio, was the world's biggest roller coaster. Nagashima Spaland had thus constructed a major environmental target not only within the immediate theater of operations, but also within a larger trade theater. The symbolic value of such an environmental module is immense. Upon calculating the cumulative entertainment capacity and throughput value of such large modules, the Program then identifies supporting, second-level units (medium and small size) that sustain the overall theme or concept, but may also generate conceptual envelopes for theatra. After their cumulative throughput is calculated, designers further determine flexible and commonly mobile environmental units such are smaller rides, live shows, spontaneous performances and museum-like displays that sustain the suspension of disbelief and support the overall concept and theme. Their role in the theater of operations is to fill the entertainment capacity of the theme park environment, as needed, and their cumulative throughput is usually low. Since in most theme

parks, a single price of admission at the gate pays for all attractions, all the above listed environmental units have no capacity to generate direct revenues. In this case, additional environmental capacity is filled by revenue-generating environmental modules such are food outlets (divided into four basic types of service: beverage/snack to go, buffet, counter service or restaurants) and retail outlets. For destination theme parks catering to tour market, hotels would also be a part of the Program and a major source of revenues. Finally, the Program determines capacities of the supporting facilities such are restrooms, drinking fountains, daycares, parking spaces, food-processing facilities, and so on. The economic key to successful programming is to determine an ideal balance between revenue-generating and other environmental modules within the park.[13]

The Master Plan initially considers characteristics of the site, that is to say the location of the theater of operations, and its primary aim is to provide a spatial and conceptual rationale for tactical objectives established by the Program. The Master Plan takes into account operating and entertainment capacity of the theater of operations, together with the cumulative volume and footprint of environmental units anticipated by the Program, and defines their spatial relationships, temporal relationships, as well as their locations within the theme park environment. Industry standards provide a formula for calculating the size of every element of the Master Plan and its relationship with the theater of operations as a whole. For example, circulation volumes are arrived at by multiplying the peak-in-park attendance projection by up to 10 square feet per visitor. Parking volume is calculated by adding peak-in-park projections (divided by 3.5 passengers per vehicle) to the anticipated number of park employees (divided by 1.5 passengers per vehicle), and dividing that number by 50 vehicles per acre: the resulting number will give a surface area (in acres) needed for parking. These numbers depend also on the cultural context, standards of living, and also on the type of theme park. A destination theme park will use different calculations from those that cater to daily markets. Unlike other environmental units, restroom requirements are calculated based on the peak attendance, commonly by dividing peak attendance projection with up to 200 visitors per module. The Program and the Master Plan also enable designers to calculate the Operating Capacity of the theater of operations. The Operating Capacity determines the number of check-in lines, the number of attendant stations at the redemption counter, storage capacities, delivery frequencies, maintenance rationale and so on. Together with the anticipated length of stay and frequency of repeat visits, the Operating Capacity directly translates into the rationale for the Operating Plan that determines operational needs such are the number of employees, hours of operation, volumes of merchandize and food, and subsequently specifies operating hours, staffing cycles and schedules, as well as operating expenses and revenues.

Emotional Conditioning

The key to themeing is the understanding that designing assumes not only the configuration of material aspects of environment and its operational logic, but also a multitude of environmental clues and stimuli that affect the experience of visitors. Themeing is *de facto* a deliberate attempt at designing an environment configured to produce specific behavioral outcomes in visitors. The objective of some theme park designers is to design visitors's experiences. Such attempts are largely illusionary because human experience is a subjective phenomenon and is always influenced by various personal memories, collectively shared assumptions, as well as by the sensory stimuli immediately surrounding the visitor. Others attempt to design theme park environments that enable visitors to participate in the creation of their own experiences: such a humanistic, as well as holistic, approach is much more difficult to manage in daily situations, and thus the tendency is towards applying more control to the production of visitors's journeys and in excluding visitors's creativity in the production of experiences. In both cases, however, the key focus of themeing is visitors's total environmental experience.

Human beings respond to environments affectively before they analyze them and evaluate them in more specific terms, because environments first arouse an emotional, affective response that then governs subsequent interactions (Rapoport 1982: 14). Theme park environments are deliberately designed to operate on the subliminal level, affecting visitors's emotional states and inducing high affective and low cognitive involvement with the environment. Disneyland Park was deliberately designed to arouse intense emotional responses by affecting people subliminally first. As John Hench empirically confirmed, visitors begin to perceive its more obvious architectural attributes and analyze the environment intellectually with a significant delay (Dunlop 1996: 50–53). Such a tendency towards a total control of environmental conditions and user-experience comes also from the traditional film and animation production methods where a producer can successfully determine observers's view and predict their responses. Emotional conditioning is thus a key variable in the usability equation of the theme park design, which is measured as the effectiveness, efficiency, and satisfaction with which visitors can successfully accomplish an ensemble of tasks in the theme park environment. Donald Norman (Norman 2004) has argued that human behavior is expectation-driven and asserted that humans process environmental sensory stimuli (clues) at three different levels: visceral, behavioral, and reflective. Visceral level is biologically prewired, genetic, and it signifies the start of affective processing. Visceral processing is subliminal, it sends signals directly to the motor system and activates adequate muscle groups. On this level, people react to environmental clues such are appearances, crowds, light, symmetry, speed, and so on. Neither visceral nor behavioral levels are conscious and deliberate. The behavioral level is 'the site of most human behavior' and it processes usability, function and effectiveness. The reflective level has direct connection neither to directly received environmental stimuli nor to the motor system, but has the capacity to control or inhibit both behavioral and visceral processing through reflections on immediate experiences. Roller-coaster rides are a good example of visceral fear (adrenalin rush) combined with the reflective pride. The 'total experience' of an environment is always the result of a combination between the cognitive and emotional processing. Cognitive processing assigns meaning, whereas affective processing assigns values to our experiences of the environment. Norman suggests that harmonious soundscapes, symmetrical shapes, highly saturated hues, 'smiling faces,' 'attractive people,' sweet smells and tastes, would all affect people positively and contribute to emotionally judging an environment as pleasant. The multitude of interwoven impressions (or 'clues'), visitors are exposed to can be categorized into functional clues, humanics clues, and mechanics clues (Carbone 2004). Functional clues are related to the operational qualities of theme parks, whether rides work, lines are not too long, parking is available, and so on. Functional clues are processed through the behavioral level and visitors are fully aware of their impact on experience. Mechanics and Humanics clues are more complex because they affect people subliminally and are processed at the visceral level. Mechanics clues are generated by artifacts such are buildings, graphics, scents, landscaping, music, or surfaces people touch directly and they translate into sights, smells, tastes, sounds and textures. Humanics clues emanate from people, both employees and fellow visitors, and are related to impressions generated by the tone of voice, kindness, helpfulness and so on. They are engineered by defining and choreographing the desired behavior of employees involved in the customer encounter, and simultaneously also by inducing desirable affiliative behavioral responses in visitors. The composite of layered clues creates the total environmental experience. Successfully designed interplay of the above clues facilitates perception of the theme park environment as an interrelated, singular image. 'Imageability,' wrote Kevin Lynch, implies a quality of an environment 'which gives it a high probability of evoking a strong image in any given observer' (Lynch 1960: 9). Continuity, repetition, rhythmic intervals, similarity, harmony, analogy, textures, scale, perspective, procession, topography, building details, lighting, audio components, animatronics, environmental activity,

symbols, storyline, mood, and everything else that visitors see, feel, hear, smell and perceive, that is all cognitive, sensory and perceptive inputs participate in the formation of environmental image. Because the image is always a matter of individual negotiations between a visitor and the theme park environment, each theme park environment will fabricate a multitude of images. The objective of themeing is to configure the intersection of all environmental images in order to sustain those previously fabricated by the apparatus of Themeparking. In early 1970s, a speculative field of research on retail atmosphere and shopping behavior emerged called Tactical Atmospherics, through which marketing scholars realized that the tangible commodity to be purchased is a small part of the 'total package' to be consumed, to the extent that 'atmosphere' is the primary product (Kotler 1973). The objective of tactical atmospherics has been the design of retail environments that produce subliminal emotional responses aimed at sustaining the fusion of retail environments and commercial culture, a process where the design of an environment is a way to converge the actual experience of retail shopping with the antecedent experiences of the media world of television, advertisements, travel guides and movies (Gottdiener 1997: 4–5). An environmental image is thus an accumulated, layered impression that combines influences generated by the media world with those related to the theme park visit. Emotional states during the visit are important to the initial formation of an image, but they are ephemeral and therefore easily forgotten. An environmental image is further formed through an accumulation of impressions over time and therefore with the 'mood' that the total environment creates rather than with its immediate appearances. Moods and traits are long lasting, sometimes throughout the entire lifetime (Norman 2004: 32) and thus for the condition of total landscape they are much more relevant than the immediate emotional responses alone.

Interactions between people and the surrounding environment are enormously varied, but visitors's general attitude towards the theme park environment could be characterized as that of 'approach' or 'avoidance' (Mehrabian 1976: 12–13). Approach behavior is also known as 'positive affiliation' and means that an individual is inclined to interact with the environment and others in the same environment. Avoidance behavior generally restricts visitors's ability to interact and communicate. Mehrabian suggested that the two main attitudes, or types of human responses to environmental input, depend on the environmental complexity, which can be described as the information perceived in the environment per unit of time. The information rate of an environment is a universal measure of environmental stimulus, and it is called 'load'. The load of any environment depends on its novelty and its complexity. High-load theme park environments are complex, varied, dense, unknown, surprising, crowded, asymmetrical, and so on. A high-load environment is commonly sustained by additional input that reduces its load: for instance, by introducing a guide-map of the theme park environment, a common practice today, designers reduce its novelty and therefore its load, but not its complexity. The same can be said of Walt Disney's Disneyland television show that introduced the theme park environment to television audiences before they stepped into the 'real' Disneyland park. Three basic visitors's emotional dimensions (variables) mediate between affiliative and avoidance behaviors in theme park environments: pleasure (happiness, satisfaction), arousal (stimulation, excitement) and dominance (when one feels important, in charge). All environmental responses can be measured by these three variables also known by the acronym 'PAD'. As Albert Mehrabian wrote, the emotion of dominance is the major factor in stimulating affiliative behavior and thus the most important factor for shaping the tourist experience. When travel risks are reduced to a minimum, and 'unproductive' environmental stimuli have been eliminated from these self-contained environments, emotions of pleasure and dominance are manipulated to achieve optimal behavioral outputs. Successful theme park designers and ride manufacturers have been capitalizing on a systematic understanding of the 140 human emotional states and their interfacings to create desirable experiential outcomes (Levinson et al. 1999).

As indicated earlier, theme park visitors respond to current perceptive, motor and cognitive (both predictable and unpredictable) stimulus generators, as well as to antecedent patterns of stimuli. Causal relationships between changes in the theme park environment and immediately subsequent changes in visitors's behavior streams could be approximated by the 'stimulus control principle' (Glenn 1997), but the only way such relationships can be predicted is through an empirically derived relationship between a specific stimuli and a specific response (Baer 1997). In that respect, theme park designers, such is Walt Disney Imagineering, have empirically developed response taxonomies that establish direct links between company-specific stimulus generators (such are colors, shapes, winnies) with predictable ranges of behavioral responses. Maintaining and updating this taxonomy is a perpetual task, and it is again a matter of empirical on-site research to determine the stimulus variations that produce changes in the intervening variables and predictable changes in behavior (Donovan and Rossiter 1982). Such field-research falls under the category known in Environment and Behavior Studies as Human-Environment Optimization, which allows for the optimization of predictable responses to environments (Stokols 1977: 25) that ultimately improves the approach aspect of the environment in relation to the specific task[14] (Mehrabian 1976: 6). The aim is to improve the usability of the theme park environment by most directly influencing the experience of visitors, which in turn determines the 'dollar volume' of the theme park environment, that is to say, the evaluation of the theme park environment by two variables: how frequently people visit and how long they stay, two variables directly linked to how much they spend (Woodward 1978). Both variables reach their highest value when approach behavior is optimized.[15]

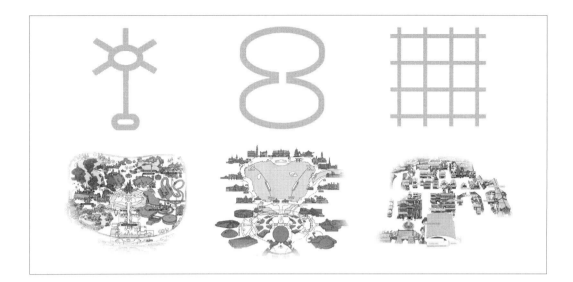

Three major theme park internal patterns: the Magic Wand pattern, the Loop pattern, and the Grid pattern.

Needless to say, visitors's responses to all environmental clues are also culturally driven. As Rapoport maintained, since culture is variable, designed environments have to respond to variables of needs and priorities as shaped by 'cultural templates,' and subsequently, environments are always culture specific (Rapoport 1980: 7). Environmental clues that induce affiliative responses in Europe or the United States may induce displeasing emotional states, offense at the reflective level of processing sensory information, and finally translate into avoidance behavior. For instance, even though color can evoke pleasant emotional responses in visitors, its cultural interpretations can intervene into its decoding. In the Judeo-Christian world, white is the color of joy and delight, whereas in China or Japan white is the color of funerals and sadness; brown implies solidity and power; green evokes nature, health, growth, grass and trees; red implies action, activity and force. Immediate responses to color are visceral and relate to what cognitive scientists call 'pattern matching' (Norman 2004: 29), pre-programmed patterns of responses to learned environmental stimuli. As Norman suggested, such 'bottom-up' activation begins when we 'sense the environment' (realm of perception) and our affective system instantly passes judgment to the brain, which in turn releases neurotransmitters appropriate to our affective state.

Theme parks are masterpieces of bottom-up activation. Unlike bottom-up, top-down activation is driven by reflective processing (realm of cognition) and such activation is systematically downplayed in theme park design. In terms of color, Hench reported that Walt Disney Imagineering used Technicolor White paint (the so-called Navajo White)[16] that allowed them to diminish the influence of bright Florida sun that commonly tends to produce an illusion of formal distortion (Hench 2003: 135). Such a distortion could be used when deliberately caricaturizing a form, but when unintentionally created it can induce uninviting effect on the visitors's reflective processing.

Total environmental image is thus produced by the parallel workings of themeparking and themeing. On the level of themeing, the image is constructed by the combination of four basic elements of the theme park environment, interwoven into a complex system by the Program: the internal pattern, the harlequin dress, sensory stimuli, and scores. These four elements organize five basic components of the environmental image: identity (establishes environmental image apart from other images), structure (establishes spatial and temporal relationships between visitors and the environment), meaning (establishes owners identity and communicates its intentions to the visitor), communication (establishes patterns of interaction between staff and visitors as well as among visitors), and affection (establishes affectionate responses by inducing desirable behavioral outputs through a variety of sensory stimuli).[17]

Internal Pattern of the Theme Park

The internal pattern[18] of the theme park environment is designed according to the characteristics of the site chosen, the type and scale of the anticipated flow of visitors, the conceptual and thematic framework chosen, and the budget. It physically shapes the motion of visitors through the park and it provides a spatial rationale for a set of environmental modules (rides, attractions, shows) and theatra (conceptual clusters), to be framed and arranged into a homogeneous chain of experiential sequences. All theme parks are organized through three basic internal patterns and their combinations: the magic wand pattern, the loop pattern, and the grid pattern. Movie studios, such as Warner Bros. Movie World, are commonly based on the grid patter in order to gimmick layouts of Hollywood production studios. Disneyland has generated a generation of theme parks based on the magic wand pattern. Huis Ten Bosch, Port Aventura and EPCOT are all based on variations of the loop pattern. Many theme parks combine three basic patterns into a variety of modifications: for instance, Spain Mura combines the Main Street entry funnel with the loop pattern attached to it.

The idiosyncratic internal theme park pattern is the magic wand pattern mastered by Walt Disney. Due to its intelligibility, the magic wand pattern is an ideal vehicle for conveying the symbolic content of the theme park environment. The Station—Main Street—Castle axis is a powerful device with no parallel in the other two internal patterns in terms of establishing an immediately identifiable symbolic hierarchy. The magic wand pattern is composed of two basic elements that come in a variety of combinations: the stick-like handle that works as a funnel, and the star at the top of it that works as a

'hub', a focal point and a distribution center, both junction and destination. It was Le Nôtre who invented 'hubs' in the Seventeenth Century and called them *patte d'oie* (goose foot). The form of the magic wand carries a deeply embedded symbolism that visitors internalize on the subliminal level. In that respect, the internal pattern of the theme park is not less complex than famed historical examples such is Claude-Nicolas Ledoux's Oikema project (cca. 1800) for a brothel at Chaux, whose phallic plan represented a communal building intended to serve the ritual of initiation, to *de facto* introduce young lovers to the 'secrets' of sensual life. The symbolism of such a plan asserts a mental image, a code that operates as both the narrative and the means of conveying it. The internal pattern thus generates perceptual patterns and induces symbolic processes along the traveler's journey through the theme park environment.

The Magic Wand Pattern

When conceptualizing Disneyland Park, Walt Disney was looking for an immediately intelligible layout where the symbolic and spatial hierarchies would be so transparent that every visitor would perceive them instantly. He also wanted the Sleeping Beauty Castle as the centerpiece of Disneyland Park, but displaced from the geometrical center of the composition. Walt Disney Imagineering looked at various historic examples, varying from Versailles to contemporary World Fairs, and proposed the magic wand pattern with an arrival square, an entry funnel, and a central gathering place similar to what Walt Disney perceived as an 'Italian plaza' to be located in front of the Castle. The symbolic center of the square was initially composed of flowerbeds, later on the sculptures of Walt Disney and Mickey Mouse were added. Visitors enter Disneyland Park by first leaving cars at the parking lot, then walking through the entrance gate, passing under the Victorian Railroad Station, and finally arriving to the Town Square dominated by the City Hall. From there, the magic wand pattern leads visitors through Main Street, U.S.A. to the Central Plaza. The length from the railroad station to the Sleeping Beauty Castle is 900 feet.

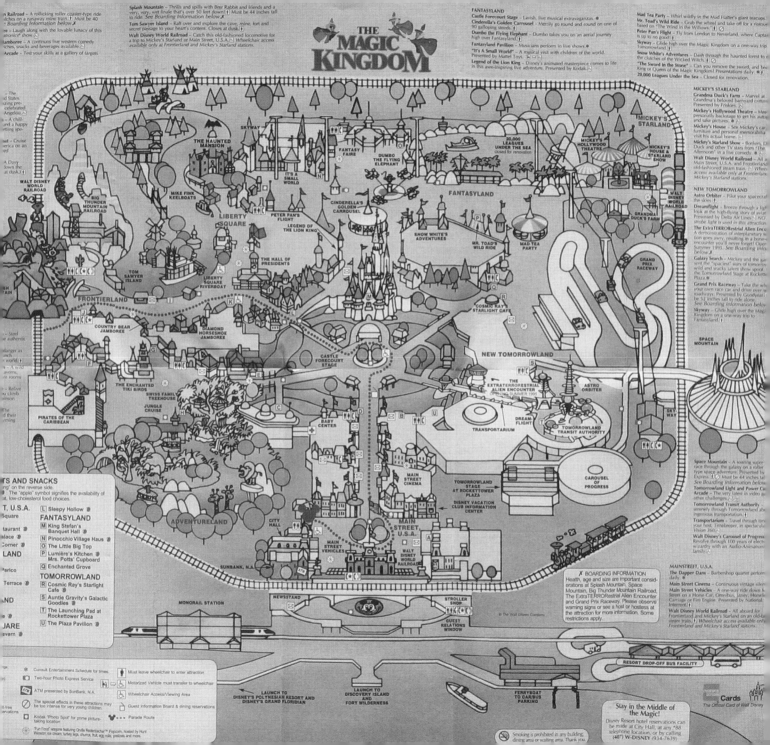

PERIOD ROOMS

The practice of exhibiting artifacts of everyday use together with costumed dolls in period settings was first established at World Exhibitions and began taking place in regular, institutionalized settings by the 1880s. Besides the fact that Great Exhibitions explored the domain of the industry and progress, they also anticipated a trend towards a disappearance of traditional cultural values. Paradoxically, by exhibiting ethnic villages and revivalist national pavilions, by emphasizing the cultural specificities and mapping out differences, they drew on a universal, imperialist drive towards generalization that had rendered ethnicity obsolete if not commercialized. Besides, by emphasizing progress and industrialization they had generated anxiety for the loss of traditional values and distinct ethnic identities (Kaufman 1989).

By the 1890s, many European museums had so-called Period Rooms, composed of daily domestic tools, furniture and sometimes costumed dolls in evocative architectural settings. The stage-set would be composed of three, well-decorated walls while the fourth one would be removed to facilitate voyeurism. Most of those designed settings were full-scale replicas, however, sometimes a house would be dismantled on its original site and brought to a museum where it would be reassembled. Early period rooms in the United States appeared in the early 1900s with the same aim of preserving the disappearing tradition. Early examples were those designed by George F. Dow in Massachusetts in 1907. Dow attempted to simulate the impression of daily occupancy through the placement of various artifacts: a period newspaper would lay opened over a table and the pair of glasses would be placed on it. By 1920s, most American museums had period rooms installed such as the American Wing at the Metropolitan Museum of New York City in 1924, which contained 17 period rooms (Harris 1978).

Period rooms are not authentic: in most aspects, they represent an idealized version of the past. Although in the 1910s museums began buying real period rooms from owners of various types of historic buildings, after being brought to the museums, they would be altered, redesigned and completed so as to fit the pre-established popular image of a particular period (Kaufman 1989). Usually, this would imply

The contrapuntal sequence square—route—square that sets a scene as if it was setting the establishing shot in a movie 'has been an epigram of all of Disney's architecture' (Dunlop 1996: 80). The Central Plaza works as a 'hub' as it affords views in many directions and facilitates decision-making. Hubs make the magic wand pattern more intelligible and comfortable, and reduce the environmental load by enabling visitors to visualize and spatially understand the options they face. That also induces the emotions of pleasure and dominance under which they make choices as to how to proceed, as well as a general positive affiliation towards the environment. Finally, visitors's emotional states are also aroused because at the end of each of the spatial opportunities (vistas), there is an environmental target, a wienie, that draws them to individual theatra. Once visitors enter the four theatra (Adventureland, Tomorrowland, Frontierland, and Fantasyland) paths meander into pre-planned routes around clusters of attractions. The only way back is to pass through Central Plaza back to Main Street, U.S.A., thus making the Main Street experience inescapable for both the incoming and outgoing visitors.

The main concern behind the design of Disneyland Park was the organization of procession. Just like in a film's unfolding, cinematic methods were utilized to generate a system of narrative possibilities by coaxing movement to a number of visual attractors that draw visitors between the predetermined cinematic sequences in a highly restrictive and precise manner. Such a pattern of movement was accomplished by what Walt Disney called the 'wienies', a term he borrowed from the age of silent film (Marling 1997: 66). Wienies are always 'archetypal forms' that imply action, establish a mood, draw the eye and invite visitors to come their way (Hench 2003: 50). They lead visitors through the internal pattern by conveying the narrative through carefully orchestrated environmental clues, such as sequences of interior and exterior spaces, colors, environmental activity and so on. Sleeping Beauty Castle, Matterhorn Mountain and the Tree of Life are all wienies, as is the Space Rocket in Tomorrowland. Tall buildings—such as Sleeping Beauty Castle or large roller coasters—can also be powerful wienies and may have multiple roles in the theater of operations: they can be seen from afar, thereby acknowledging the presence of the theme park (target) in the theater; as such, they draw tourists through the theater of operations. More-over, within the park they sustain the suspension of disbelief because they are the key vehicles for visually unifying all areas of the theme parks at all times—since nearly all theme parks sit on a flat platform, and visitors are immersed in the environment and are rarely given the opportunity to see the park 'from above', they serve the naviga-tional (practical) and psychological (symbolic) function in the theater. Modes of transportation can also function as wienies, such as the Mark Twain Steamboat or the monorail. Different paths within the internal pattern generate a pattern of pseudo-cinematic narratives that together with various environmental stimuli determine the move-ment of visitors and their total environmental experience. Unlike the movies, where narrative sequences are linear, Disneyland Park allows the visitor to participate, in limited ways, in building an interactive narrative experience. Feeling a movement directly through haptic and kinesthetic senses is different than seeing a movement on the screen. The movement itself may arouse the emotion of pleasure and dominance, and together with other senses, enables visitors to navigate through the environment with conviction.

As suggested earlier, Disneyland Park was conceived without a specific reference to its geo-cultural context and the configuration of its internal pattern was designed only in relation to its internal references. Establishing a strong physical perimeter was crucial for sustaining the suspension of disbelief. The railway line enhances the materiality of Disneyland's perimeter by a nearly 1.5 mile-long loop, with its main stop at the Main Street Station located above the entrance area. As opposed to the traditionally induced social segre-gation commonly imposed by the 'other' side of railway tracks, in Disneyland Park the railway generates another type of opposition:

a removal of all the elements of the room that are character-istic of the original house or the site, and the creation of an assemblage of fragments characteristic for all of the rooms of the period. Particularity and site-specificity, so character-istic for rural architecture of Eighteenth and Nineteenth Centuries, were replaced by a desire for archetypal image-making necessary for the popularization of historic narra-tives. Such generalizations rendered period-room-settings so commercially desirable that, by late 1920s, retail venues began utilizing this method in selling traditional goods in period settings.

on one side there is a parking lot, on the other, Main Street, U.S.A. that funnels visitors into the imaginary world. The two realms intersect only at the entrance gate where the interior and the exterior value systems are negotiated by the program of exchange. The realm of exchange provides a terminal point for the theme park experience and sets the mood for it. The arrival through the Town Square hub not only controls the flow of visitors through the internal pattern, but also establishes a receptive state of mind in visitors.

Main Street, U.S.A. is also the most efficient location for retail outlets within the magic wand pattern. The advantage of the magic wand pattern is that visitors are funneled through Main Street, U.S.A. on both their way in and out of the park. Commodities offered along Main Street, U.S.A. thematically refer to theme park's mythological discourse and their exchange value is commonly related to all of the aspects of the theme park experience. Additional retail opportunities within the magic wand pattern are transitional spaces that sometimes include souvenir shops, fast-food kiosks, ice cream, and drink stands. Each environmental module commonly has an adjoining souvenir shop themed to sustain the module's theme and equipped with paraphernalia that captures the experience characteristic of the particular attraction. The exchange value of commodities offered in such retail venues refers both to the novelty of the module as well as to the theme park's overall concept. Out of a total of 55 shops within the magic wand pattern of Magic Kingdom, 16 are placed along the Main Street, U.S.A., 12 in Adventureland, six in Frontierland, eight on the Liberty Square, eight in Fantasyland and five in Tomorrowland (Fjellman 1992: 178, 284).

Main Street

The major constitutive element of the magic wand pattern, and the only place within the pattern where narrative works linearly as in a movie, is the one-directional procession funnel of Main Street. In order to mimic the cinematic experience along Main Street, U.S.A.,

perspective had to be forced by compressing the receding space through an exaggerated proximity of the vanishing point (Sleeping Beauty Castle in Disneyland Park and Cinderella Castle in Magic Kingdom Park at the Walt Disney World Resort) in relation to the viewer's plane of vision (Hench 2003: 74). As in conventional Hollywood movies, a long 'establishing shot' frames the distant Sleeping Beauty Castle with the ensemble of Main Street, U.S.A. facades. The perspectival function of facades within the park is also articulated with the rhythmic disposition of turrets, towers and arieles. This initial framing already pre-establishes elements of narrative displacement as Victorian facades frame a Bavarian castle in the context of Californian suburbs. Main Street, U.S.A. also works as the traditional entry-funnel of the country fairs: it receives incoming visitors and delivers them to the Central Plaza where they make choices as to how to proceeds towards various theatra.

As noted before, Main Street, U.S.A. was a nostalgic, idealized representation of small, mid-Western towns such is Marceline, Missouri where Walt Disney grew up. Although Main Street, U.S.A. in Disneyland Park contains 'authentic' elements, such as old city lamps brought from Baltimore, Boston and Chicago, Victorian facades along Main Street, U.S.A. are neither authentic nor copies of particular buildings or streets: Walt Disney Company calls them 'archetypal truths' (Dunlop 1996). The scale of stage-crafted facades along Main Street, U.S.A. changes from ground towards the roof: first-floor facades are built at 90 percent of full size, second floor at 80 percent, and third floor as nearly 80 percent in order to build the illusion of height (Hench 2003: 74). Such a gradation has a strong visceral affect because it emotionally affects visitors in terms of pleasure and dominance induced by miniaturization. Walt Disney personally selected more than 200 colors for facades and other elements of the Main Street, U.S.A. As Hench recounts, the mood of the 'turn-of-the-century optimism' required a palette of pinks, reds, yellow-greens, and red-oranges, and each shop received a distinct color identity out

View of the midway running under Eiffel Tower at *L'Exposition Universelle* in Paris, 1889.

View of the World Bazaar in Tokyo Disneyland Park towards the Cinderella Castle. Used by permission from Disney Enterprises, Inc.

Aerial view of Main Street, U.S.A., Disneyland
Park, California, 1955. © Disney Enterprises, Inc.

FOLLOWING PAGE RIGHT
Entry sequence through the Main Street in
Spain Mura.

FOLLOWING PAGE FAR RIGHT
Panoramic view of entry sequence and the Main
Street container in Spain Mura.

of that palette (Hench 2003: 110). The width of Main Street, U.S.A. also changes in order to force the framing of the distant castle on the way in, and in order to create an illusion of shorter travel on the way out. On average, Main Street, U.S.A. in Magic Kingdom Park at the Walt Disney World Resort, is wider than the one in Disneyland Park and measures 60 feet. Each façade in Disneyland Park is 23 feet-wide, and doorways are placed at exact intervals of 18 feet (Marling 1997: 79). In Tokyo Disneyland Park, Main Street, U.S.A. was renamed The

World Bazaar and covered with a glazed roof structure. Other cinematic tricks are also employed to optimize the procession through the Main Street, U.S.A. Half way through Main Street, U.S.A., visitors find themselves at an urban intersection where a small, lateral street crosses the main promenade (Francaviglia 1981: 141–156). This theatrical moment, a pause, increases the perceived length of the street and adds to the dramatization of visitors's experience. However, this small street does not lead anywhere, its function is to increase the depth of

Main Street, U.S.A., generate the feeling of multi-dimensionality of the whole setting and (due to its pseudo-residential character) to challenge the essentially commercial appearance of Main Street, U.S.A.. In 1950s and early 1960s, Walt Disney painstakingly maintained a list of tenants of specialized stores along Main Street, U.S.A. because he believed in the variety and vitality of the traditional Main Street (Marling 1997: 90). Also, leasing store spaces along Main Street, U.S.A. helped pay back loans. Today, Main Street, U.S.A. is *de facto* a large shopping mall composed of four containers cladded with visually compartmentalized distinct facade planes. Shops along the Main Street, U.S.A. are internally connected in order to enable a smoother pedestrian flow through Main Street, U.S.A. during peak hours, whereas upper floors are used as storage spaces and offices. The appearance of Victorian 'buildings' along Main Street, U.S.A. is designed in such a way as to sustain the illusion of the traditional Main Street in which ground floors are used as shops while upper floors are commonly residential and offices. These stage-facades are composed of doors that lead nowhere, windows that never open and curtains that hide the indifferent storage and office spaces behind. A glimpse on the other side of Main Street, U.S.A. facing the service areas reveals the utilitarian character of the Main Street container. Nevertheless, as Richard Francaviglia's extensive study of Main Streets shows, the principle of presenting the best facade forward has always been the essence of the Main Street business (Francaviglia 1996: 190).

Besides the visual stimuli created by its cinematic role and its facades, Main Street, U.S.A. conveys the 'atmosphere' of a small town by employing a variety of sensory stimuli. Store barkers, street bands, old tram pulled by horses, a newspaperman and an ice-cream boy are among the performers that entertain the public. As well as the sense of activity they create, they also produce a cacophony of background sounds that enhance visual illusions. Smells of baking, fresh cookies and popcorn coming from the stores complete the environmental sensory experience. Such an immaculate fabrication of environmental clues brought Francaviglia to declare that Main Street, U.S.A. is 'one of the most successfully designed streetscapes in human history' (Francaviglia 1981).

Main Street, U.S.A. also performs a central symbolic function for the mythological microcosm of the Disneyland Park's environment. All of the institutional buildings that sustain the illusion of the 'real place' are placed along or in the immediate vicinity of the Main Street, U.S.A.: the Victorian Railroad Station, the Bank, the City Hall, the fire station, the emporium and the Sleeping Beauty Castle that stands as a symbolic substitute for a religious anchor. The Railroad Station and the Town Square are copies of the equivalents in Marceline, Missouri. City Hall is a copy of the courthouse in Fort Collins, Colorado, as it is the Bank (Francaviglia 1996: 148). Louis Marin argued that Main Street, U.S.A. works precisely as the 'narrative operator' that leads visitors into the center of the text and mediates between reality and fantasy (Marin 1977). A variation on the Main Street theme is Hollywood Boulevard in Disney-MGM Studios theme park, where reproductions of Art Deco facades and other buildings from the Los Angeles area sustain the geo-cultural illusions. Disney-MGM Studios does not employ Hollywood Boulevard as a funnel, but as one of the theatra linked to the exchange program by a variant of the loop pattern.

The Grid Pattern

Both medieval fairs and country fairs were initially based on the grid system (Braithwaite 1968: 21–29). The grid system used in leisure environments has survived for over six centuries to be used in theme park environments today. The grid pattern today though commonly mimics either the urban grid or the layout of Hollywood production studios. In early 1980s cinema attendance alarmed Hollywood, Walt Disney Co. in particular, as worldwide figures suggested that going to the movies became a historic form of amusement, and theme park business represented 87 percent of the company's profit (BW 1984). The idea to merge movie-making (production studio) and the theme park business into 'movie-studio tours' gave birth to the grid pattern use in theme parks, and also marked a major revival project launched in 1984. The US$500 million Disney-MGM Studios theme park was carefully planned throughout the 1980s and it opened in May 1989. The same year, Walt Disney World Resort scored a record attendance figure of 26 million visitors, and by the end of the same year theme parks accounted for only 56 percent of Walt Disney Co.'s overall profit (Knowlton 1989). As Eisner indicated, the interactive 'studio tour' has always been Walt Disney's idea, even prior to Disneyland. On the occasion of Disney-MGM park opening, Eisner said that visitors's involvement in creating experiential outcomes has become the key to success: 'The use of the guests participating as much as possible in interactive entertainment was definitely one of our strategies [...] interactive with the whole family, which is our basic philosophy, our mission' (Sweeney 1989). Even though rhetorically a significant effort has been placed on presenting theme parks as interactive environments, the attempt to control environmental experience and percep-

tions encourages passivity in visitors. Most rides are based on passive involvement that stimulates one's senses rather than the motor system. The ride-through attractions, 'dark-rides', also induce the sense of proximity and active involvement although all possibilities of actual interaction have been systematically eliminated. In that sense, simulated movie-studio sets based on the grid pattern, such as those of Universal Studios, Disney-MGM Studios or Warner Bros., combine both the frontstage and backstage of a conventional movie studio as theme park's 'on-stage experience'. In such a configuration, exteriors of perimeter blocks form 'street facades', while the interiors are used for the studio tour. Facades are always related to the character of the attraction: in Disney-MGM Studios, New York Street has facades of the Empire State building and Chrysler building, whilst Miami Beach has the art deco facades characteristic of South Miami Beach. The difference between the Main Street, U.S.A. in Magic Kingdom and Disney-MGM Studios is in the treatment of the fakery of its scenery: what is carefully hidden from visitors's view in Magic Kingdom is exhibited in Disney-MGM Studios, where visitors can see the back supports of wooden facades painted only on their front ends. As with pleasure and country fairs, the 'backstage' rhetoric is thus complemented by the visual exhibition of the non-exhibitable rendering grid pattern's milieu complex and multilayered. As Fjellman wrote upon attempting an anthropological reading of Disney-MGM Studios, 'the levels of logical typing and cross-reference are very complicated here—complicated enough to dissuade me from attempting an impossible "deep reading" of this theme park.' (Fjellman 1992: 284)

The entry to the grid pattern of Warner Bros. Movie World is reminiscent of Main Street's funnel role. The perimeter of the park is interrupted only at the point where the exchange program is organized. From there, visitors are funneled into the park by a one-directional street-like corridor that contains continuous shops along a two-block long axis. One is then led by different environmental means through the park. Unlike in Magic Kingdom Park, the perimeter line of the park

is never experienced from without, but always from within the park. This renders the grid-plan fruitful in attempts to undermine visitors's sense of scale, proportion, and orientation. Even though in operational terms this internal pattern is an ideal setting for suspension, surprise, and contrapuntal experiences of all kinds, the emotional impact of such an internal pattern could be devastating if not designed or operated properly. That is also the reason why this pattern is increasingly becoming used in combination with loop and wand patterns, and its popularity has decreased.

Although the grid pattern seems to offer unlimited possibilities in organizing retail outlets, quantitatively it is behind the other two patterns due to the fragmentation of facades planes, and ground floors into perimeter blocks. Disney-MGM Studios have 22 shops (13 along Hollywood Boulevard), while Magic Kingdom has 56 and Epcot has 66 shops. In Disney-MGM Studios most retail outlets are concentrated along the entry corridor. The rest are clustered throughout environmental units at the locations where tours begin and end. Such retail outlets are usually called 'catchers'. Catchers can sometimes be located even outside of the theme park itself.

Toei Movieland (TML) in Kyoto, Japan is another example of grid pattern used for a working movie studio that, at the same time, works as a theme park. TML is located in the Uzumasa area of Kyoto that, once upon a time, was called 'the Hollywood of Japan' (Nakajima 1994). It opened on the 2nd May 1926 when famed Japanese actor Bando Tsumasaburo established the first independent film studio in Japan there. In 1980, when it opened its gates to public as a theme park, TML was very active as a motion pictures production studio for both motion pictures and television programs. Its greatest attractions today are precisely its daily operations, because visitors can observe the making of favorite television programs and film productions. Besides its entertainment role, TML also offers the Museum of Japanese Film History that capitalizes on TML's actual role in the development of Japanese cinema. The entire complex is organized through the grid pattern that allows the studio to operate despite the invasion of nearly 1.5 million tourists a year. The grid also enables a clear distinction to be drawn between different segments of the theater of operations, although the thematic framework employed for structuring the environment is that of Edo Japan. This is an important theme in Kyoto because Kyoto was the capital of Japan during Edo period (1600–1868). The theater of operations is mostly used today as a stage set for historical dramas set in Edo period: actors dressed as

Guide map of the Toei Movie World.
© Toei Movie World.

A daily film shooting scene in
Toei Movie World.

A store along Main Street, U.S.A. in Magic
Kingdom Park, Walt Disney World Resort, Florida.
Disney Characters © Disney Enterprises, Inc.
Used by permission from Disney Enterprises, Inc.

139

samurai and geisha are to be found everywhere in this environment as
they walk through pleasure quarters, the Edo town and period shops,
and across the Nihonbashi bridge. Visitors too can rent costumes
and get photographed in the exotic historical settings. As a variation
on the grid pattern, TML is a curious example: visitors enter through a
modern structure that offers restaurants, coffee shops and the information counter, and then proceed towards the arrival square that
distributes them through the park. The actual working studios are
located in the back lots and are open only on weekends when there
is no filming. However, even during the week, visitors can observe
the filming process through glass walls that separate the frontstage
from the backstage of this theme park. In TML, as in all grid pattern-
based theme parks, the great advantage of the internal pattern is that
any given theme or use can occur anywhere in the pattern without
damaging the homogeneity of the whole because all structures are
equally accessible and can accommodate a variety of changes.

The Loop Pattern

The origin of the loop pattern is in English Landscape Garden and in
the principle of organizing pavilions along a one-way path that was
introduced in Eighteenth Century Picturesque Gardens. The loop was
utilized for the initiation ritual where each pavilion was a step, stage
or a scene along the pathway associated with a particular part of the
narrative (historical event, place, or a hero) (Mosser 1991). Such pavilions, or 'show buildings', were also called 'fabriques' and their role
was essentially symbolic.[19] The first modern example of this type of
plan was recorded at the Great Exhibition of Industry in Paris of 1867,
where a labyrinthine web of walkways extended out of the main building into an informal rectangular park, where numerous national pavilions were placed along the paths. It was, however, not before the
Philadelphia Exhibition of 1876 that the pavilion system was utilized
optimally. National pavilions in Philadelphia were designed as full-
scale mock-ups featuring artifacts of daily life and natives involved
in the amusement of the crowds.

N

GERMANY
Treasure – A likeness of Eltz Castle which is pictured on a 500 Deutschmark.
Strolling Accordionist – Traditional polkas and waltzes.
Courtyard Trio – Brings the spirit of "gemütlichkeit" to the courtyard. ✸
Oktoberfest Musikanten – Music and entertainment nightly inside the Biergarten.

Restaurant
Serving Beck's Beer and H. Schmitt Söhne wines.
🍴 **Biergarten** – Sauerbraten rotisserie chicken, traditional German sausages, revelry, fun and entertainment. Lunch, dinner. Table service.
Sommerfest – Bratwurst, pretzels, desserts. Counter service.

CHINA
Wonders of China – Explore the mysteries of the East through CircleVision 360.
Treasure – Hall of Prayer for Good Harvest, where an emperor would go to pray.
"Dragon: Ruler of the Wind and Waves" – Artifacts from Si Zhu.
China Si Zhu – Oriental music.
Red Panda Acrobats ✸

Restaurants, hosted by China Pavilion Exhibition Corporation.
🍴 **Nine Dragons Restaurant** – Regional Chinese cuisine. Dim Sum, Kang Bao chicken. Chinese wine and beer. Lunch, dinner. Table service.
🍴 **Lotus Blossom Café** – Eggrolls, stir-fried dishes. Lunch, dinner. Counter service.

NORWAY
Maelstrom – Treacherous and tricky trolls send you into a North Sea storm. ⚡
Treasure – The Stave Church, itself an architectural treasure, contains Norwegian artifacts.
"To the Ends of the Earth" – Exhibit.
Travel Information – Norwegian Tourist Board.
Trondheim Trio and Fossekallen – Traditional entertainment. ✸

Restaurants
🍴 **Restaurant Akershus** – Royal buffet features hot and cold dishes of meats, cheeses, salads, salmon, and other seafood. Lunch, dinner. Buffet service.
Kringla Bakeri og Kafé – Open-faced sandwiches, pastries. Norwegian Ringnes beer. Counter service.

MEXICO
El Río del Tiempo – Sail through the River of Time. ⚡
Treasure – Serpent-like figure along steps representing Quetzalcoatl.
Art of Mexico – "Reign of Glory".
Marimba Maya Landia and Mariachi Cobre – Traditional music of Mexico. ✸
Travel Information – Courtesy of Mexican Tourist Office.

Restaurants
San Angel Inn Restaurante – Traditional fare. Tacos Al Carbon, Chicken Mole, Margaritas, and Mexican beers. Lunch, dinner. Table service.
Cantina de San Angel – Tacos. Counter service.

✚ ODYSSEY CENTER
Baby Care Center – Hosted by Carnation Infant Formula.

Restaurant
🍴 **Odyssey** – Hot dogs, burgers, and chicken sandwiches. Counter service. Seasonal.

WORLD OF MOTION
Presented by General Motors
Take a humorous tour of civilization's progress in mobility. "It's fun to be free!" ⚡
Transcenter – Preview transportation of the future, and new cars from General Motors. ⚡

FOUNTAIN OF NATIONS WATER BALLET SHOW ✸

WONDERS OF LIFE
Presented by MetLife
Body Wars – Turbulent thrill ride through the human body. Health and size are boarding conditions. ⚡
Cranium Command – Hilarious look at the workings of a 12-year-old's brain. ⚡
The Making of Me – Sensitive film on the beginning of life includes footage of a developing baby. Discretion recommended.
Anacomical Players – Improvisational skits. ✸
Lifestyle Revue – Health survey.
Coach's Corner – Pros evaluate your baseball, golf, and tennis swings.
Frontiers of Medicine – Update on research.
Goofy About Health – Animated show.
Sensory Funhouse – Test your senses. ⚡

Restaurant
Pure and Simple – Low-fat, nutritious waffles, sandwiches, salads, yogurt. Counter service.

ITALY
Treasure – 24K gold-leaf angel on top of the bell tower and in the garden behind the Arcata.
Commedia di Bologna – Audience members are drafted for roles in humorous folktales. ✸
I Cantasuoli – Italian quartet in the courtyard. ✸
Strolling Musiciana – Nightly inside L'Originale Alfredo di Roma Ristorante.

Restaurant
L'Originale Alfredo di Roma Ristorante – World-famous fettucine, veal, seafood, and pasta. Lunch, dinner. Table service. Reservations requested.

THE AMERICAN ADVENTURE
Presented by American Express and Coca-Cola
America Gardens Theater by the Shore – Showcase for "The Magical World of Barbie." Hosted by Mattel. ✸
A moving account of America's incredible struggles and triumphs.
Treasure – Beautiful rotunda typical of Colonial American buildings.
Voices of Liberty – Singing in perfect a cappella harmony. ✸
Sons of Liberty – Colonial Fife and Drum.

Restaurant, hosted by Coca-Cola.
🍴 **Liberty Inn** – Burgers, hot dogs, chicken, apple pie. Lunch, dinner. Counter service.

JAPAN
Treasure – Replica of five-story Pagoda at Horyuji in Nara.
Bijutsu-kan Gallery – Japanese art forms.
Fantasy Dreammaker – Japanese artist creates surprising entertainment. ✸
One World Taiko – Staccato rhythms of traditional Japanese music. ✸

Restaurants, hosted by Mitsukoshi U.S.A., Inc.
Teppanyaki Dining Rooms – Grilled meats, seafood. Kirin beer. Lunch, dinner. Table service.
Tempura Kiku – Sushi, batter-fried meat, seafood, vegetables. Lunch, dinner. Table service.
Matsu No Ma Lounge – Sushi, appetizers, and specialty drinks.
Yakitori House – Broiled chicken, Japanese-style beef. Counter service.

MOROCCO
Treasure – Replica of Nejjarine Fountain located in the city of Fez.
"Treasures of Morocco" – Moroccan art. ⚡
Fez House – Early Moroccan architecture.
Traditional Bellydancing and Musicians – Daily in Restaurant Marrakesh. ✸
Festival Marrakesh – in the courtyard, instruments, music, and dance. ✸
National Tourist Office.
Unisex Restroom Facility ♿

Restaurant
Restaurant Marrakesh – Lamb, chicken, and couscous served in palatial surroundings with traditional entertainment. Table service.

FRANCE
"Impressions de France" – Inspirational music and stunning, panoramic views of France, in air-conditioned comfort. ⚡
Treasure – Replication of French rural street, circa 1800.
Trio Bal Musette – Musicians bring the flavor of Paris to the promenade. ✸
Théâtre du Fromage – Comedy street theater with audience antics. ✸
Alsatier – Magic and mime. ✸

Restaurants, Hosted by Chefs de France of Orlando.
Chefs de France – French cuisine, Coq Au Vin, gracious surroundings. Lunch, dinner. Table service.
Bistro de Paris – Above Chefs de France, cuisine and floor, rack of lamb, salmon terrine, bouillabaisse. Dinner only. Table service.
Au Petit Café – Parisian sidewalk café. Soups, baguette sandwiches. Lunch, dinner. Table service.
Boulangerie Pâtisserie – Pastries, quiches, coffee. Counter service.

INTERNATIONAL GATEWAY
Stroller & wheelchair rental, transportation to selected...

UNITED KINGDOM
Treasure – Traditional herb garden and maze.
Olde Globe Players – A troupe of comedy actors fracture Shakespeare and other playwrights with your help. ✸
Sue & Peter Barbour – Stiltdancing puppeteers. ✸

Restaurants, hosted by Bass Export Ltd.
🍴 **Rose & Crown Dining Room** – Excellent British fare, meat pies and afternoon tea, served inside or on the terrace. Lunch and dinner. Table service.
Rose & Crown Pub – Bass Export Ltd. and Guinness-Harp beers and ales and other spirits.

CANADA
O Canada! – CircleVision 360 showcases the nation's beauty.
Treasure – Victoria Gardens, designed after the famous Butchart Gardens in British Columbia.
Caledonia Bagpipes – Folk music, humor, and costume reflect Canada's British roots. ✸
Canadian Comedy Corps – Comedic antics and situations.

JOURNEY INTO IMAGINATION
Presented by Kodak
Discover how one little spark of imagination can trigger a world of innovation on this creative ride. ⚡
Magic Eye Theater – Absent-minded Professor Wayne Szalinski is at it again in "Honey, I Shrunk the Audience", and this time it's you that gets shrunk! ⚡
The Image Works – A creative playground.
Dreamfinder and Figment ✸

THE LAND
Presented by Nestlé
Harvest Theater – Dramatic film "Circle of Life: An Environmental Fable" Starring characters from The Lion King. ⚡
Food Rocks – A musical tribute to good nutrition. ⚡
Living with the Land – Take a boat ride through farming techniques of the past, present, and future, and the amazing agriculture technologies of the future. ⚡
Greenhouse Tour – 45-minute walking tours. Make reservations to the right of Soarin'. ✸

Restaurants
🍴 **The Garden Grill Restaurant** – Table revolves through scenes of The Land. Sandwiches, pasta. Lunch, dinner. ⚡
🍴 **Sunshine Season Food Fair** – Food and wine. Breakfast, lunch, and dinner.

INNOVENTIONS WEST
See, feel and touch the future at this showplace for the world's latest ideas and inventions.
Epcot Discovery Center – Educational products, resources for teachers. Your technical questions about Disney and Epcot are answered here.
Future Corps Band ✸

Restaurant
🍴 **Pasta Piazza Ristorante** – Omelettes and Danish for breakfast with a Disney Character ✸ Pizza, pasta, salads. Counter service. Hosted by Coca-Cola.
Fountain View Espresso and Bakery – Espresso, cappuccino, and fresh pastries served daily.

WORLD SHOWCASE LAGOON
IllumiNations – A rhapsody of lasers, lights, fountains, music, and fireworks encompasses World Showcase Lagoon. Presented by GE. ✸

FUTURE WORLD

Discovery Center

Guest Relations

UNIVERSE OF ENERGY
Presented by Exxon
Ride in cars powered by solar energy, and explore the forces that fuel our lives from the age of dinosaurs to energy alternatives for the future. Show lasts 45 minutes. ⚡

INNOVENTIONS EAST
An amazing exhibition of the newest products for home, work, and play, including the Magic House tour.
Future Corps Band ✸

Restaurants
🍴 **Electric Umbrella Restaurant** – Chicken sandwiches, burgers, salads. Lunch and dinner. Counter service. Hosted by Coca-Cola.
Desserts & Things – Snacks and beverages. Counter service. Seasonal. Hosted by Coca-Cola.

SPACESHIP EARTH
Presented by AT&T
Spiral 18 stories through a dramatic history of communications, climaxing with a "satellite's" view of our home planet, Earth. ⚡

THE LIVING SEAS
Presented by United Technologies
Descend fathoms into The Living Seas to an incredible manmade coral reef at Sea Base Alpha. View tropical fish, sharks and manatees, while exploring the secrets of a new frontier. ⚡

Restaurant
🍴 **Coral Reef** – Fresh seafood served with a superb underwater view of The Living Seas. The Coral Reef Breakfast under the sea. Lunch, dinner. Table service.

Epcot

LEGEND

♿	Rest Rooms
✚	First Aid
[✶	Touch 468 for toll-free Disney hotel reservations
△	WorldKey Information Service
🍴	Low-fat, low-cholesterol
✳	Consult Entertainment days and times
📷	Kodak "Photo Spot" for picture-taking location
📷	Two-hour Photo Express
👁	Viewing Area
💳	Automatic Teller Machine

Entertainment and information

Lost & Found and Package Pickup

Taxi pickup

Bus information

Bus parking

Stay in the Middle of the Magic! Disney Resort Hotel reservations can be made at Guest Relations, or at any WorldKey location, or call (407) W-DISNEY (934-7639)

Monorail Station

Disabled Guest Parking

Cards
The Official Card of Walt Disney World®

The most famous example of the loop pattern is the EPCOT park at Walt Disney World Resort. EPCOT is in fact composed out of a double loop, one of which is the Future World and the other is World Show-case, organized around a lagoon that forms the core of the plan and determines the pattern of walkways. Visitors enter through a circu-larly organized Future World and pass by Spaceship Earth, a geo-sphere with a diameter of 165 feet that acts as the symbol of EPCOT. Whereas geosphere's design was an interpretation of Buckminster Fuller's design for geodesic dome he invented in 1940s, its name is actually taken from the title of Fuller's 1969 book *Operating Manual for Spaceship Earth* (Fuller 1969). Eleven national pavilions are placed along the 1.3 mile-long loop. The central axis of the entire composition starts at the entrance, crosses the lagoon, and terminates at the North American pavilion called the American Adventure. The axis objectifies the entire configuration by assigning central symbolic role to the American pavilion that stands framed with a one-story building on each side.

Most theme parks based on the loop pattern have water at their geo-metric center, either a lagoon (such as in EPCOT), lake (Port Aventura), or a canal (Huis Ten Bosch). In most cases the loop pattern deter-mines one-directional procession and because there is no meander-ing of the pattern of movement, the footprint of the loop pattern has to be significantly larger than those of the other two internal patterns. For instance, the footprint of EPCOT's loop pattern is six times larger than that of Magic Kingdom. Within the loop pattern, the exchange program is both the point of entry and also where one leaves the park. This type of resolution in the loop pattern is challenged by the plan of Huis Ten Bosch where visitors enter through the one-directional Arrival Gate and leave through a one-directional shopping center. This type of resolution of the ending segment has become desirable because it optimizes the purchase-volume of the exchange program. Within the 11 national pavilions EPCOT designers have packed 56 shops featuring respective ethno-themed commodities. With nine shops

located in the Future World (exchange area), EPCOT offers a total of 65 retail venues. By its internal pattern and the underlying economic efficiency, EPCOT's loop pattern stands very close to the model of World Exhibitions. Other examples of the loop pattern, such are Huis Ten Bosch, Spain Mura or Port Aventura, have similar numbers of retail outlets on comparable footprint areas: for instance, Huis Ten Bosch has 63 retail outlets.

A variation on a loop pattern is the so-called 'Duell Loop', named after a theme park designer Randall Duell. Duell began his architectural career as a stage designer in Hollywood in 1940s and designed sets for MGM Studios's 1952 release Singing in the Rain as well as many other famed productions of the 1940s and 1950s. He began his prac-tice in late 1950s when commissioned by Texas billionaire Angus G. Wynne, Jr. to design his first theme park, Six Flags Over Texas, which opened in 1961. Since Wynne deliberately wanted to outrival Disney-land, Duell was asked to come up with the plan that would challenge Disneyland Park's internal pattern. Duell designed the now-famed loop that only allows visitors to choose a single direction of looping upon entering the park. Once the direction is chosen, one follows the loop until all attractions are exhausted. The economic efficiency of Duell loop is in its ability to link separate areas of the theme park into a sequential experience, and to lure visitors to each major attraction in an ordered and highly pre-programmed manner. Since loop pattern has no detours, it in fact represents the ideal utilization of time, a supreme internal pattern for the design of the path of optimum time. The other advantage of Duell's loop, and of the loop pattern in general, is that visitors have a desirable sense of orientation and grounding. The fact that once the direction is chosen there is no alternative to one-directional movement, and the ability of visitors to anticipate, and sometimes see, nearly all attractions along the loop, translates into the emotion of pleasure being directly stimulated. The feeling of comfort aroused by the simple fact that visitors can locate them-selves in space and time, and anticipate the time left until the end of the loop, translates into the emotion of dominance because visitors feel in charge of their own experiences. Finally, sometimes hidden environmental units along the loop, the syncopated surprises, can in this particular internal pattern induce arousal and excitement, which combined with the previous emotional clues, generates desirable emotional states in visitors and significantly reduces the load of the environment.

Services and Transportation in Relation to Internal Patterns
The internal pattern of theme parks is also determined by the type and volume of pedestrian circulation, disposition of service routes and spaces, available transportation means, and whether a theme park is of a destination type (caters to the tour market) or a part of an urban traffic network (caters to the one-day market). Huis Ten Bosch and WDW are destination theme parks of the resort type. Warner Bros.'s Movie World and Tokyo Disneyland Resort are parts of the regional traffic system and the interaction of visitors with the park's proper is immediate and more direct. Visitors get to Tokyo Disneyland Resort by taking a subway train and subsequently crossing a medium-sized pedestrian bridge that connects the subway station with the entrance gate. Getting to Walt Disney World Resort is a very different operation. John Hench tells a story about plans for moving guests from Orlando airport to the WDW by a wide-winged 'short-takeoff-and-landing' plane to fly guests directly to EPCOT. The landing strip was built, but plane was never developed (Hench 2003: 23). The Walt Disney Imagineering's concern was not only how to move guests from one place to another and not compromise identity of different 'lands', they also wanted main transportation devices to be attractions in their own right. Transportation as attraction thus became a motif for all Disney parks. Since transportation is both an attraction and a means of moving through the park, the routes designed for moving visitors around were never the shortest ones but the optimal ones. That meant that besides being visually attractive, the routes chosen also enticed either symbolic or actual consumption of the environment, by getting visitors to specific nodes from which they proceed further. Some devices, like in Disneyland Park and WDW, offer views across the park otherwise impossible because of a perpetual immersion. Such vistas can have a dramatic impact on overall experiential quality.

Internal means of transportation are among the most direct applications of controlling the experience of visitors that theme park operators could exercise. In WDW, parking lots are linked with the Ticket and Transportation Center (TTC) with trams that circulate parking lots. Once visitors reach TTC, they can proceed further either by ferryboat, monorail, or by double-decker bus. The ALTWEG monorail stops at EPCOT, Magic Kingdom, Disney's Contemporary Resort Hotel, Disney's Grand Floridian Beach Resort and Disney's Polynesian Resort. WDW transportation system handles over 5.5 million rides per week. Regardless of the type of transportation means, whether they are passenger conveyors, escalators, independent vehicles, monorails or railway, all of the means of transportation are designed to be an integral part of the internal pattern of the theme park. That implies that their visual appearance, sound and speed are adjusted to the environment within which they operate. The slow, turn-of-the-century-looking trams in Magic Kingdom are meant to move more than 20 000 visitors per hour (Wascoe 1991) circulating between the Town Square and the Central Square. The main attraction of EPCOT is the sophisticated, futuristic looking ALTWEG monorail system that moves at a speed of 45 miles per hour and is designed to move up to 10 000 people per hour (Wascoe 1991). Besides trams and monorails, theme parks also use boats (for water transport) and buses. Huis Ten Bosch and Spain Mura use specially designed taxi vehicles to move visitors from one part of the park to another. They are always designed in a way that optimizes visual sequences, enables a frictionless transition from one environmental segment to another, and either screens out or limits views outside the park.

ALTWEG Monorail stop in Magic Kingdom Park, Walt Disney World Resort, Florida. Used by permission from Disney Enterprises, Inc.

Services are usually grouped within each environmental unit. Restrooms, telephones, mail drops, and other services are often equally distributed through the theme park environment. Park information center and park headquarters are usually placed next to the entry area, as well as stroller and wheelchair rentals, customer service and first aid. Behind the scenes are commonly administrative and managerial staff, maintenance facilities, food outlets, storage facilities, machinery, workshops (painting, woodwork, metal shop), lockers, employee food facilities, security, and other amenities. Key elements of the internal pattern are service roads and corridors: restaurants, shops and attractions should be reached by the staff through perimeter service roads, behind the scenes corridors, and underground tunnels. As in theater design, theme park environments are commonly divided into the backstage and frontstage. The two are always strictly separated, culturally negotiated and physically regulated by walls, gates, doors and greenery. Backstage usually contains staff and service access, service areas and storage spaces, and those are usually kept strictly out of the visual field of visitors. In WDW, service spaces are hidden within the interior courtyards and connected by underground corridors. Access to underground corridors is camouflaged by artwork, gates, walls or foliage. Besides stratifying visitors from the staff, the theme park's design also reflects and reinforces the stratification of workers and the allocation of control over operations into different categories of employees. Johnson clarified the classification of theme park employees into four basic categories (Johnson 1981: 159): the first category are workers employed in transporting, cooking, cleaning and other services placed mostly underground or out of visitors's lines of sight; the second category are the guides who are commonly visible and representative of the company's values; the third category are technicians who operate the attractions and machinery, sometimes exposed to visitors; and the fourth category is all levels of management commonly hidden to the eyes of visitors. An exceptional example in that respect is the pseudourban environment of Huis Ten Bosch that necessarily renders service corridors, service vehicles and staff members visible and thus a part of the scenery. The effect of the service apparatus was designed to improve the image of efficiency by employing brand-new, well-designed, clearly marked low-noise vehicles that use non-polluting fuel. Workers participating in the performance (such are shopkeepers, ride operators, or tour guides) are always costumed in order not to contradict the narrative appeal. In Disney parks, they are called 'cast members' because they are not only staff members but also performers, as though they were actors in a film. Their costumes are carefully designed to authenticate the overall narrative (Hench 2003: 29).

A range of HTB service vehicles manufactured
by Nissan.

All supporting facilities (medical facilities, restrooms, rest areas) are designed and themed in a way that sustains the mood and atmosphere of the particular environmental unit. Their design has to sustain the suspension of disbelief. Restaurants and shops too are designed in the same manner, as furniture, wallpapers, graphics, signs, music, menu design, costumes and food (names of dishes) are all carefully themed. Besides sustaining environmental objectives, restaurants and shops also generate profit by enhancing the attraction's value through thematic connections to real artifacts that can be purchased, such are food or souvenirs. Connections between a ride and an adjacent shop can be sustained and intensified by the use of color, music, fragrances, scale and other means, such as the case of Pinocchio's Daring Journey in Disneyland Park that flows seamlessly into Gepetto's Toys and Gifts and the nearby Village Haus Restaurant (Hench 2003: 123). Food and retail opportunities maximize spending potential of theme park visitors. Around half of theme park's gross income is derived from food and retail. Some parks bring in outside

retailers under lease agreements. Walt Disney had lease agreements for Disneyland Park during the first 10 years of its operations. In theme parks like EPCOT, food is of crucial importance because it sustains the authenticity of national pavilions and sustains the overall 'cosmopolitan' atmosphere.

Individual food outlets are supplied from food distribution centers within and without the park through service routes. In Disneyland Resort, that is done through Utilidor, an underground service tunnel. Forgac reported that WDW has a 54 000 square feet Food Distribution Center that prepares and distributes food for the entire WDW (Forgac 1985). Its automated system produces 15 000 pizzas, seven tons of ground beef, 6000 pieces of bread and numerous other items every day. All of that is delivered during the night hours to points of purchase, food stores and restaurants throughout WDW. The calculations are commonly based on empirical findings. For instance, food concessions are commonly calculated based on the empirical observation

Medical Center, Huis Ten Bosch.

that 35 percent of the 'design day' in-park guests will eat during the peak meal periods, and they are called 'peak-time diners'. Based on the peak-time diners, four basic types of service are calculated in relation to the length of service per outlet type: beverage and snack to go, buffet, counter service or table service. Subsequently, the number of seats can be derived which would finally give volume (square footage) projections for both frontstage (dining) and the backstage (kitchen) areas.

Lines, Hench wrote, proved early on to be a major design problem in Disney parks (Hench 2003: 32). Walt Disney Imagineering invented the so-called 'switch-back lines' used today in all Disney theme parks to create an illusion of shorter waiting lines. Eventually they also added a story element to 'switch-back lines' and turned them into a 'preshow', aimed at introducing story elements, theme and mood together with a clear sense of progression. Preshows can both educate and entertain, and at the same time reinforce the ride experience

LIVING IN A HISTORIC MODE

Much before the establishment of theme parks, as we know them, people have had inhabited environments that bear many similarities with the subject matter of this discussion. Dreamland, a Coney Island amusement park, was probably one of the most extreme examples designed and developed in 1904 by Senator William H. Reynolds who initially divided it into some 15 attractions,[1] that all together shaped a horse-shoe plan (McCullough 1957). The most controversial of all was the attraction called Lilliputia. Senator Reynolds collected almost 300 Lilliputians previously dispersed around the United States as attractions at various freak shows, circuses and fairs (Wasserman 1978: 57). He placed them into a permanent residential community within his property, a community that had an essentially experimental character: on weekends, it had almost 250 000 visitors. The only condition that residents had to satisfy was to be there and perform simulated daily life routine for the viewing pleasure of the senator's customers. However bizarre this residential community was it worked, for the Lilliputians were already used to living in cages and the showing off to insatiable visitors of country fairs. Reynolds intended to organize Lilliputia in both architectural and institutional terms: he designed an axial plan in with the entrance-gate at one side of the central axis, and the parliament building on the other. Along the central axis, he placed a fire house, a church, different communal activities, and the beach, institutions to which Lilliputians have previously been denied admittance in the outside world. Lilliputia remained a part of Coney Island until destroyed by fire in 1911. Henry Ford's Greenfield Village and Rockefeller's Colonial Williamsburg bear some similarities with Lilliputia, and were both fabricated communities where people have inhabited an idealized, yet personal vision of the past. If the driving force behind Dreamland was pure financial profit, the *tour de force* behind Henry Ford's Greenfield Village and Rockefeller's Williamsburg was nostalgia.

Colonial Williamsburg in Virginia was conceived in the 1920s by John D. Rockefeller Jr. as a monument to colonial America and its values, and it opened its gates to public in 1932, complete with horse-cars, a traditional United States Post Office, Victorian costumes, slave quarters, neat gardens and comfortable front porches. Much of what has happened to

Williamsburg has marked its transformation into a living-history theme park. During the 1960s and 1970s, it was under the direct protectorate of the United States government and proclaimed a national monument. Robert Stern featured Colonial Williamsburg very prominently in his film series on American architecture titled *The Pride of Place* as a place that successfully reconstructs and preserves permanent values of the American society (Stern 1986). Such theme parks usually mark 'the restoration of harmony among private property, public interest and national imagination' (Cummings 1955: 12).

Henry Ford began the construction of his Greenfield Village in 1927,[2] and in 1929 the Village finally opened its gates to public (Upward 1979). It was situated within a landscape park that combined the influence of the English Landscape Park and the American Pleasure Park. Alarmed by the evident loss of traditional values and forms of life and stimulated by childhood memories (much like Disney and Hearst), Henry Ford had created an enormous collection of artifacts from pre-industrial times. In creating the setting for his collection, he clearly employed the principles of the early Great Exhibitions. Instead of constructing differences between contrasted cultures as Great Exhibitions had done, he constructed narratives that made 'the present' and 'the past' different conceptual and thematic regions. Instead of simulating travel to distant, exotic cultures he simulated travel to a distant as well as exotic national past. Like the Great Exhibitions and the period rooms, Ford's Village was not authentic, but rather it presented an idealized version

itself. Preshows are also utilized for the environmental cross-dissolve because indoor holding areas succeed the outside line, and are designed to appear as a part of the preshow narrative sequence. They are designed to accommodate one guest-load, sometimes only up to the seating capacity of the holding zone. They also reduce environmental load and control emotional states from frustrating experiences of waiting in lines. In 1964, at the occasion of New York's World Fair, Walt Disney invented the 'postshow' for It's a Small World ride in order to enhance the exit experience and provide a proper opportunity for the presence of the corporate sponsor (Hench 2003: 34). Even though the throughput and carrying capacity of each environmental unit is calculated much in advance in order to estimate the optimum volume, either through the industry standards described earlier or through a company-specific methodology (WDC uses the model called 'Dedicated Guest Capacity Model'), traffic congestions are usually created during peak hours (lunch time or during daily parades) and can hardly be fully anticipated. Analogically, even though a typical managerial strategy would lead towards totalization and hyper control of the theme park environment for the sake of predicting and influencing behavioral outcomes, the typical human response to such efforts is to turn all manipulation into advantage and every environmental 'pretext' into an 'opportunity' (Certeau 1984). Following de Certeau, one could claim that whereas corporate strategies for the creation and operation of the theme park can be analyzed and foreseen through the mechanisms of development, totalization, and control they inscribe into the total landscape, alternative and simultaneous spatial practices of the visitors are virtually unforeseen. To make visitors's movement more predictable and thus efficient, theme park operators have designed, and sometimes successfully applied, a variety of different methods. In 1999, WDC invented the concept of the 'timed ticket', used in order to enable visitors to 'plan' their procession through the environment. A Timed Ticket would specify the time of attendance for each major environmental module chosen by the visitor, and visitors would then need to attend it at the specified time. Universal Studios had used a Plan Your Day handout to inform visitors of the best times to visit an attraction until 2001, when they launched a computerized timed ticket system in their two Florida theme parks. In 2001, Six Flags introduced the 'fast lane' concept that lets visitors skip the line for a ride and board immediately if they show up at the exact time printed on the ticket. Visitors are offered up to four free Timed Tickets per day. Both Paramount and Busch Entertainment launched tests of similar systems in 2001. Such methods of control can boost the operational efficiency of the theme park for up to 25 percent (Sloan 2001). Before closing each environmental module at the end of the day, WDC uses 'stacking' technique in order to discourage visitors from getting on a ride that is soon to close. That is accomplished either by letting the current line wait longer to create an illusion of an unreasonably long waiting time, or by displaying a long wait period (50 minutes) in front of the ride.

The Harlequin Dress[20]

Comparisons between theme parks and theaters have often been made, some argued that 'total immersion' in the theme park environment makes parallels with experimental 'total theater' of the 1970s more than obvious (Aronson 1977). As Tuan wrote, the immersion in Disney parks is very theatrical, so intense that 'to be there is to have arrived: no need therefore to worry about being elsewhere' as visitors are enveloped into the introvert timelessness of the thematic milieu (Tuan 1997: 195). The harlequin dress of most theme parks is deliberately constructed as an elaborated stage-set: 'All of us came from motion pictures' said John Hench, 'that's the reason the park is the way it is, like stage design. You design the environment for activity, for actions' (Dunlop 1996: 29) and not in order to subjugate design to imaginary canons of any given disciplinary thought or practice. In that respect contemporary theme parks are a part of the tradition of country fairs that in the Eighteenth Century began featuring first organized theater performances called 'stage-plays'. The architecture of these installations consisted of relatively elaborated facades made

of the pre-industrial culture focused on traditional artisanship. The paradox being that Henry Ford himself was one of the major carriers of industrialization in the United States, the fact that made him build a quarter-scale replica of his original Ford Motor Company plant, in order to make it fit within the Greenfield Village-setting composed of craft shops, a local inn, the Town Hall (also reduced in size), a school, a Congress Hall and a full-scale replica of the Independence Hall. In 1934, the remains of the original Ford's family farm were brought to Greenfield Village and reassembled on-site. Like *fabriques* in the English Landscape and Picturesque Garden, the architectural elements of the restoration village cannot be authentic if an idealized mode of life is to be preserved. Within such a totalizing practice, architecture is necessarily reduced to an iconic function as an associative device that acts as a stage set for the domestic anthropology that generates the overall narrative. A community of 300 people had inhabited Greenfield Village, including Henry Ford, who spent significant periods of time residing in his old family-house. The same happened in Colonial Williamsburg, Virginia where people have inhabited an idealized yet personal vision of the past. What by all means was a museum collection housed in an open-air ethno village became a habitat for real life, an idealized real life decontextualized and displaced from both the past and the present.

1. There are different versions of the actual plan of Dreamland, since the original plan does not exists. For reference see Koolhaas 1978.

2. It was initially named the Early American Village.

of painted wood and plaster, supported on the back by triangular wooden struts. Buildings, represented by mock-facades, were complementary to an artificial arrangement and their function within the stage-set was that of associational device, reduced to two-dimensional, iconic representations. This format of attractions and the method of construction were utilized also at Vauxhall, Ranelagh, and other pleasure gardens during the Eighteenth and Nineteenth Centuries. The architecture of both the country fairs and pleasure gardens operated on an iconic level to complement the underlying novelty of theatrical performance. Richard Francaviglia noted that ever since there was a Main Street, there was also the separation of the front facade from the rest of the building, because Main Street too always had the character of theater stage (Francaviglia 1996). Early World Fairs and Great Exhibition adopted essentially the same format. At the Paris Great Exhibition of 1867, French architects designed various national pavilions, over-emphasizing the idiosyncratic elements of the vernacular architecture of national pavilions, and reducing them to the level of cultural icons. Harlequin dress conceived on this level has usually been referred to as 'entertainment architecture, or 'leisure architecture', as it has no objective other than to evoke associations with the realm of folk or popular culture, literary fiction, movies, exotic cultures and places, or history commonly through the process of caricaturization. Historical role of 'leisure architecture' as a social mechanism of control aimed at the 'imposition of order and civic behavior' was first institutionalized by Hittorff in 1833 in Paris, and later utilized by Baron Haussmann and the early Great Expositions during the late Nineteenth Century.

The specificity of the harlequin dress is that it affects visitors's experiences in all three realms of processing: visceral, behavioral and reflective processing of sensory clues. All artifice has the capacity to influence human behavior both as symbolic constructs and as material forms. As a material form, every environment favors certain types of spatial behavior and restricts others through the configurations of surfaces, enclosures, passages, objects and so on. As a symbolic construct, a material environment communicates a variety of associations, myths, metaphors as well as its function. Design of all theme parks is based on the fact that material forms first arouse emotional responses and affect visitors subliminally, and subsequently lend themselves to reflective processing. In that sense, aroused visitors's emotions are essential to the credibility of form. John Hench invented a principle called 'fitness to form' to indicate complex intersections of stimulus generators that occur when color, movement, and music are timed to complement the form, to enhance the experience, and provide visitors with appropriate sensory information that makes each story environment convincing (Hench 2003: 20). Material form does not exist in isolation and cannot be properly conceptualized unless design considerations take into account variables as diverse as the actions of service and operation staff, transportation, environmental activity, and so on. 'Fitness to form' principle thus confirms the link between material form and the dynamic environmental process.

Materials employed within the theater of operations are chosen in relation to the emotional affect they have on visitors and their simultaneous ability to sustain the overall narrative. Materials are meant to undermine visitors's understanding of 'reality' and displace it into the realm of the imaginary, but at the same time they also need to fulfill important requirements such are safety, affordability, or maintenance. Disneyland Park is the only Disney park where structures were made of the original materials: Victorian wooden structures along Main Street, U.S.A. were built out of real wood, as were the replicated period door-knobs. The reason was twofold: the sophisticated synthetic materials were not commercially available in early 1950s, but also the awareness of the capacity of materials to participate in the creation of narratives was not fully understood. The immense attention to detail in using both natural and artificial materials has been a signature of Disney theme parks because a 'single out-of-place element can shatter an artfully constructed story environment.' (Hench 2003: 78) Since story telling has always been about order and control, the most important perception that visitors must have at arrival is the perception of order (Marling 1997: 85), and material treatment has been key to that. As Umberto Eco noted during his visit to Disneyland Park:

> The Polynesian restaurant will have, in addition to a fairly authentic menu, Tahitian waitresses in costume, appropriate vegetation, rock walls with little cascades, and once you are inside nothing must lead you to suspect that outside there is anything but Polynesia […] In Disneyland, when rocks are involved, they are rock, and water is water, and a baobab a baobab. When there is a fake—hippopotamus, dinosaur, sea serpent— it is not so much because it would not be possible to have the real equiv- alent but because the public is meant to admire the perfection of the fake and its obedience to the program. In this sense Disneyland not only produces the illusion, but—in confessing it—stimulates the desire for it […] Disneyland tells us that technology can give us more reality than nature can. (Eco 1986: 44)

In the 1970s, Walt Disney Imagineering invented the so-called 'eight foot rule' which recommends that natural materials are used only for the parts that visitors can touch, otherwise for objects above the height of eight feet, plastic and synthetic materials are used, such are fiberglass, porcelain panels, alloys, or metals. Synthetic materials are cheaper, lighter, safer, easy to assemble, and easy to maintain. Similar rules apply in selecting vegetation and elements of landscape. Walt Disney Imagineering 'casts' vegetation for appropriate sections of Disney parks, so that plants and greenery sustain the illusion and the overall thematic framework (Marling 1997: 107), since all land- scaping is considered to be props in the show. Plants must be 'native' to the themed area sustaining both the geographic and historical coordinates. When located near the areas that visitors can touch and smell they are 'natural'; when used to 'fill the envelope' and sus- tain the illusion of volume, depth, or length, plastic or rubber are also used. Plants thus vary in terms of color, texture, material, and smell. Signage too must sustain the overall theme of every environmental

module, whether a ride, restaurant or retail outlet. Historic themes, such as Medieval or Western, would demand the use of wood or iron, whereas futuristic themes would require the use of alloys, plastic, or neon lights. As Jeffrey Miekle has argued, the technocratic mental- ity of efficiency always successfully instrumentalizes such artificial surfaces, colors, textures, materials and odors in the service of its normative goals (Miekle 1995).

In addition to the character, texture and tactility of materials used, color is another key element of harlequin dress design, because more than half of initial impressions are made by color: color initiates bot- tom-up processing, induces specific mood in visitors and affects them emotionally by augmenting the theme park environment with emo- tional attributes. The sensation of color is important in distinguishing the mood of each theatron and the characteristic atmosphere of each environmental unit. Mood, as mentioned above, is created by accu- mulated and carefully orchestrated stimuli of color, but also of sound, smell, form and movement. For instance, windows along Main Street, U.S.A. are full of bright displays, shelves are full of colorful goodies, colors are bright, and all communicate feeling of comfort and inti- macy through 'heightened key sensory details'. Whereas colors used on the Main Street, U.S.A. facades are pristine, in 'other' areas some- times ten layers of different paint can be detected in order to make buildings appear old and run down, such as in New Orleans Square or at Mombassa Marketplace in Disney's Animal Kingdom Park. The same rules apply in theme parks across the world, as color pro- vides an exceptional means for communicating ideas, directing and focusing visitors's attention, and affecting visitors's emotional states. Visitors evaluate and judge color initially through numerous associa- tions with color, some of which are individual and other are derived from shared cultural templates through 'pattern-matching'. Color is also used to convey specific meanings: Jungle Cruise in Disneyland Park has lush green landscaping that implies the tropical setting of the Indiana Jones Adventure, located between New Orleans Square

View of Huis Ten Bosch's fabricated pastoral
landscape, with the entry sequence at the top
left and Wassenaar Villas at the top right.
© Huis Ten Bosch Co.

and Pirates of the Caribbean. In there, color helped construct the flow of dramatic moods in the Indiana Jones narrative, set up and resolve key scenes and sequences, and build guests's experience (Hench 2003: 107, 112). Whereas in most theme parks elaborate uses of color are often prohibited by modest capital budgets, Walt Disney Imagineering's sophisticated and expensive use of color can be weaved into the narrative by relating it to all aspects of an environment, from facades, to interior design, signage and to food: Rancho del Zocalo restaurant in Disneyland Park serves both Mexican dishes and barbeque. The 'Mexican' area of the restaurant is painted in white and 'jalapeño-pepper-greens', while the BBQ area is treated with 'caramel' to complement the color of barbeque sauce (Hench 2003: 116).

Color is also instrumental in facilitating transitions between different theatra and environmental modules. Theatron is a cluster of environmental modules framed by an all-encompassing, generic conceptual framework that allows for the creation of a variety of hierarchically arranged themes. For instance, Adventureland in Disney theme parks creates a conceptual frame for a generation of themes such as the Pirates of the Caribbean. The physical, visual and emotional boundaries of theatra are preserved with utmost care, using a variety of methods. Huis Ten Bosch uses bricks of different size and color for buildings in each of its theatra, so the transition between them is announced also by the change of environmental color and scaling. As noted before, Disneyland Park had elaborated the 'enveloping by theme' strategy used to clearly organize the environment thematically and enable 'zones' for transitions. Many theme parks create the in-between, neutral buffer areas between different theatra: such buffers offer opportunities for food and retail outlets, as well as lavatories and places for rest. Buffers in WDW are enveloped in greenery or other 'natural' boundary and thematic characters of individual theatra are preserved indeed by the 'neutral' character of the circulation spaces in-between. If buffer areas are thematically treated, their themes are distinctly different from adjoining themes. Transitory areas are in

that sense carriers of potential contradictions. In Disney theme parks, such contradictions are resolved by the use of film technique called 'cross-dissolve'. The objective of cross-dissolve is to turn a rough-cut into a smooth-flowing 'film' by moving less abruptly between two clips or stills, or by introducing the illusion of movement. Cross-dissolve *de facto* indicates fading of one image into another. For a cross-dissolve to work, the environments between which designers want the transition to take place must overlap in the timeline: the longer the overlap, the slower the dissolve and the shorter the overlap, the more abrupt the dissolve. In order to facilitate the cross-dissolve, Walt Disney Imagineering always *a priori* establishes a set of rules for each theatron, called Rules of the Land, that detail background narratives, geographic determinators, or historical narratives appropriate for each 'land' (Hench 2003: 79), and then introduce subtle sensory clues that indicate transition. From Main Street, U.S.A. to Adventureland, walkway surfaces change from concrete to cut stone, handrails change from iron to bamboo, background music to animal growls, and the planked bridge indicates the final stages of transition. The transition from Adventureland to Frontierland is signified by the gradual change from red resilient asphalt to degrees of green pavement. An extreme case of control upon the integrity of narratives is the introduction of the underground utility tunnel in Magic Kingdom Park at the Walt Disney World Resort, used by employees on their way to and from attractions. This subterranean infrastructure was introduced to facilitate the flow of costumed employees out of the experiential field of visitors. As it is clearly explained by Disney management to prospective employees, if you are employed as a 'cowboy working in Frontierland, you cannot walk through Fantasyland on your way to lunch' (Alridge 1992). Procession from one theatron to another is strictly controlled by all environmental means through an accumulation of sensory clues that include color, tactility, motion, smell and form. Sometimes, theatra are located on physically separated modules, such as in Huis Ten Bosch, where bridges link different theatra.

It is thus the material character of the harlequin dress that at first subliminally affects visitors's experience, and coaxes visitors into assigning values to their experience. It is only later that visitors process its fictive and symbolic character reflectively and attempt to make sense of it and configure meanings. The fictive character of harlequin dress is an important vehicle for the communication of meaning. As semiotic studies of theme parks show (Eco 1986, Gottdiener 1997), theme parks operate as sign-vehicles within universes of meaning that convey messages on many social levels. As a sign-vehicle, harlequin dress connotes a range of meanings, whereas as a sign-function it denotes its function. The function of harlequin dress is processed at the behavioral level where visitors recognize the material aspects of harlequin dress in relation to the behaviors that it enables as well as those that it prohibits. At the level of reflective processing, caricaturization of architecture becomes instrumental for the fabrication of meaning: each harlequin dress stands at the intersection between a particular socio-cultural context, the corresponding connotative ideologies of social practice, and

the processes of its production (Gottdiener 1995: 26). All three are grounded in the fact that theme parks cater to tourist consumption and are a constitutive segment of the global mass-tourist industry. The production of tourist experience has to take into account that 'the tourist looks for caricature [and he] seldom likes the authentic product [...] he prefers his own provincial expectations' (Boorstin 1964: 106). The idea that theme park design is derived through the process of caricaturization is not an uncommon one (Schank-Smith 1992). Obviously, caricature requires a reference in order to ridicule, thus caricature rests upon the representation of an original. Gombrich and Kris argued that 'caricature, showing more of the essential, is truer than reality itself' (Gombrich and Kris 1938) because it takes important aspects of the character to the extreme so that a character's visual image is easily recognized. They also discovered 'that similarity is not essential to likeness' and that the deliberate distortions of selected features are not incompatible with a striking likeness of the whole: 'The real aim of the true caricaturist is to transform the whole [...] into a completely new and ridiculous figure which never-

City Hall in Magic Kingdom Park, Walt Disney
World Resort, Florida. Used by permission
from Disney Enterprises, Inc.

Gouda's City Hall and the caricaturized
geographical and symbolic associations in
Huis Ten Bosch.

153

theless resembles the original in a striking and surprising way.'
(Gombrich and Kris 1940: 12)

The principle of caricature has been clearly, although not always
deliberately, utilized by Walt Disney Imagineering in the design of
Disney theme parks by employing three elements crucial for caricature: transformation, ambiguity, and condensation (Schank-Smith
1990). In Disneyland Park, and particularly along Main Street, U.S.A.
and its environs, buildings are neither 'authentic' nor copies of existing buildings but 'archetypal truths'. As John Hench suggested: 'We
own Main Street because we expressed the archetypal truth about
Main Streets everywhere.' (Dunlop 1996: 129) This implies that Main
Street, U.S.A. is *de facto* an attempt to initiate a dialogue on Main
Street, to say something about the idea of Main Street everywhere.
Nevertheless, almost all of the buildings that constitute Main Street,
U.S.A. are based on originals from mid-West towns: as Francaviglia
shows, all of the institutional buildings that sustain the illusion of
being in a 'real' place, such are the Victorian Railroad Station, the
Bank, the City Hall, the fire station, the Emporium and the Sleeping
Beauty Castle are based on the existing buildings: the Railroad Station
and the Town Square are copies of the originals in Marceline,
Missouri, the City Hall is a copy of the courthouse in Fort Collins,
Colorado, as it is the Bank. Harper Goff had made it clear that many
other buildings along Main Street, U.S.A. were also based on famed
existing originals (Francaviglia 1996: 148). This is an essential regularity of caricaturization as 'nearly every type of comic picture derives
from a dignified ancestry' (Gombrich and Kris 1940: 327). Castles in
Disney theme parks are a montage of famous French and Bavarian
castles, such as Loire Valley Chateaux at Chenonceaux, Chambord
and Chaumont, and Bavarian castles from the Black Forest. By turning
the top of Neuschwanstein Castle, built originally by King Ludwig II
of Bavaria, Disney caricaturizes the original and moves it into the
symbolic territory of imagination and play. Such transformations
are often humorous.

Huis Ten Bosch consists of numerous copies of Dutch architectural
monuments. To assure the utmost precision, HTB designers obtained
original construction drawings, some made in the Sixteenth Century,
and literally copied entire buildings including all of the details. Even
though one could not claim that the buildings themselves are caricatures, through their disposition in the TOP and the way in which they
relate to each other in the new setting, one recognizes an exaggerated
transformation through forced juxtapositions and distorted original
distances. Gouda's City Hall is placed next to Utrecht's Dom Tower,
which is in turn located across the canal from Amsterdam's Hotel
de L'Europe. Thus, the caricaturization of geographical or symbolic
connections that assigns meanings to individual buildings ultimately
caricaturizes the buildings themselves, as well as of the entire cultural
milieu of origin. Such juxtapositions are fabricated by extensive use of
forced perspective. Perspective, as the spatial ordering apparatus, is
used in theme parks in the most undeviating ways in order to control
time-spans and to standardize the experience of theme park visitors.
Perspectival spatial syntax in theme parks favors axial procession,
visual anchoring and forced layering all aimed at constructing sensory
clues that shape the experience of visitors.

In that respect, caricature is an important vehicle for the communication of meaning because it transforms the physical properties of
the original in order to make the meaning obvious and transparent.
As it is obvious in the above examples, such a simplification is necessarily followed by the distortion of either context or scale (Schank-
Smith 1992). The internalized arrangement of scale and context
removes the material environment of theme park from its signifying
load and allows it to float in a 'semantic field' independent from
that of the original model: not only a caricature of the architectural
original would be devoid of the complex social and cultural meanings
that the original in its true context carries, but also that a caricature
would stand for a concept alien to the period in which the original was
established. The extreme polysemy of meaning is generated by the

displacement of the signifier into a new 'universe of meaning'. In the case of the Victorian facades along Main Street, U.S.A., an elaborated Victorian City Hall facade denotes (as a sign-function) a certain function so that visitors can easily distinguish between City Hall and the Emporium, and the functions to which they conventionally ascribe. This Victorian facade is thus employed as caricature on two levels: on the first level, it ridicules the original by dissociating its representative function from the building as a whole and by distorting its features (context and scale); on the second level, it ridicules a notion of the Nineteenth Century City Hall because it fabricates an obvious paradox on the connotative level. A Nineteenth Century City Hall connotes a variety of associations that may include civic pride, democracy and national idealism. Upon entering a City Hall in a theme park, one realizes that the space behind the archetypal facade is occupied either by retail shopping or customer-service operation. Therefore the caricature of architecture is in theme parks employed on an iconic level.[21] As Eco shows in his study of similarity derived from Pierce's definition of icon, an iconic sign may posses optic (visible), ontological (supposed), and conventionalized (depending on iconographic convention which codifies the original experience) properties of the object:

> Anything taken as iconic sign must be viewed as a visual text which is not further analyzable either into signs or into figurae [...] At a certain point the iconic representation, however stylized it may be, appears to be more true than the real experience, and people begin to look at things through the glasses of iconic convention. (Eco 1976: 37)

For Eco, an iconic text is an act of code-making insofar as it establishes the coded value of a sign,[22] which brings one to the notion that the newly constructed artifice—a caricature of the Nineteenth Century City Hall attached to retail shopping—operates as a sign-vehicle, a signifying artifice deliberately constructed to convey particular concepts, ideas, or ideologies (Gottdiener 1997). In that sense, nearly every theme park is a sign-vehicle of its owner's ideolological

framework. Thus, by establishing an 'iconic convention', or the new interpretative code for this 'universe of meaning', theme parks legitimize 'the norm of consumption' as well as normative expectations that establish the culture of consumption in the total landscape. Nevertheless, the aesthetic seduction of this decorum is also generated by nostalgia for a moment in past when the architectural typology and cultural codes harlequin dress refers to had historical authenticity. Nostalgia therefore is a powerful vehicle employed to naturalize the credibility of iconic referentiality of total landscape and the caricaturization as its aesthetic convention, and is capable of reassembling everything into 'a spectacle of availability'—history, future, distant cultures and places—only in order to present itself as a natural format for the representation of the present.

In order to facilitate the fabrication of homogeneous experiences and corresponding meanings across scales, the design of harlequin dress is seamlessly merged with other sensory stimuli in all aspects of the theme park experience. In that respect, each individual environmental module is a test of such homogeneity. For instance, Walt Disney Imagineering designs most rides as representations of Disney animated features, such as Peter Pan Flight ride that closely follows the story line of the film.[23] Peter Pan's 'flight' is symbolic of the adventure that underlies the main concept of Adventureland theatron, while guests's sensory experience of the ride parallels that of Peter Pan as they also 'fly' trough the attraction (Hench 2003: 38–39). The use of color, motion, light, costumes, caricatures of late Victorian architecture, music and other stimuli resembles and fortifies the experience of the motion picture; in that respect, theme park industry recognizes two main approaches to thematization: literal thematization and interpretive thematization. Literal thematization is close to what Reyner Banham called the 'deadly accuracy' (Banham 1983) of Disney's perfection in detailing that literally reproduces buildings and artifacts. Parque España, for instance, has a replica of Gaudi's Parc Guell, while HTB has one-to-one copies of Dutch cultural icons. Many theme parks are based on combinations of literal and interpretive thematization. Interpretive thematization capitalizes on the evocative power of color, material, texture or form to build experiential outcomes. Whereas literal thematization relies exclusively on accuracy and authenticity as sources of credibility, interpretive thematization can also work with authentic elements, but construct metaphoric links between them. Main Street, U.S.A. is a good example of such a practice: street lamps, door knobs and a myriad of details are truly authentic, but individual buildings and the theatron itself are not. Together, they symbolize the archetypal identity of Main Street. Intentionally loose conceptual frameworks, such as that of the Asia Park in Kyushu, Japan, are excellent spring boards for interpretive thematization. Literal thematization of a kind practiced by HTB is extremely time consuming and expensive. Interpretive is much more flexible, affordable and socio-culturally more acceptable.

Rent-an-Event

In terms of the daily routine, the function of the Program is to outline the set of orders to be followed, features to be presented and numbers of people involved in such operations. What *de facto* puts the entire theme park apparatus in motion on the daily basis are scores. Scores put the theme park assembly line in motion by connecting different constitutive elements of the environment into a coherent arrangement of forces in the theater of operations. Scores define who participates, in what capacity, where, and at what time. Although the score employed in performance art can be an end in itself, in military science the score is a vehicle to carry out the program and is thus result oriented. In that sense, scores must be as precise as possible in describing processes leading to the total performance outputs over a specific period of time. In theme park environments, the score defines the experience of visitors before they enter the theater of operations. Themeparking exposes visitors to elements of the master score through television, advertising, films, web sites and so on. Their experience of the master score has been scripted much before they enact with it: once visitors enter the theater of operations, they actually become a part of the master score, or the so-called 'daily schedule of events'. The score conventionally takes into account people, space, time and their mutual interrelations as key variables and, as Halprin maintained, establishes 'lines of action' that ultimately determine interaction of all constituents and their total performance.

> The essential quality of a score is that it is a system of symbols which can convey, guide or control [...] the interactions between elements such as space, time, rhythm and sequences, people and their activities, and the combinations which result from them. (Halprin 1969: 7)

From the Paris Great Exhibition of 1867, where movement was determined by circular avenues, to the Osaka Expo of 1970 where the continuity of movement was facilitated by Kenzo Tange's trunk facilities called 'environmental equipment', different methods have been applied in choreographing vast numbers of people in large exhibition spaces. Whereas an urban environment can possibly be programmed by suggesting opportunities through the circumscription of the grounds on which events may take place, themeing scripts the interaction of visitors and the environment by *a priori* determining direct cause-effect relationships between the exact character of environmental activity and cumulative behavioral outcomes. The program alone does not allow for the level of control necessary to assure commercial success of theme parks. Each interaction is timed by the master score. The paradox is that visitors have a complete freedom of choice in a totally controlled environment; there is a promise of a choice of routes and tours, yet at the same time the structure of the theme park and the score reduce all possibilities to a single, frictionless and predetermined experience. The scores work together with all other environmental clues: guide maps are particularly important because they visualize 'possibilities' for interaction. What scores determine with immense precision is the structure of environmental activity. Everyone's performance is regulated by the master score: unlike conventional ways of choreographing interaction of crowds, themeing uses scores deceptively in order to produce desirable experiential and behavioral outcomes. Scores define aspects of environmental activity in relation to both space and time. An essential instrument of scores is 'events', fabricated and heavily scripted performances that occur within pre-determined time-frames and pre-programmed 'scenes'. Such 'events' are combined with soundscapes, light effects, olfactory and other sensory stimuli to produce homogeneous experiences.

'Events' produced in the theater of operations are deceptively presented as 'attractions' designed to surprise, to arouse emotional states of visitors, and sustain the production capacity of the theater of operations. Daniel Boorstin noted that the first use of the word 'attraction' attached to a tourist destination was registered at the occasion of the Great Universal Exposition of 1862 (Boorstin 1964). Gregory Ulmer suggested that the first American tourist attractions were spas and Mount Rushmore, recognition that eventually led Ulmer to establish the notion of 'monumental tourism', an activity whose motivation is economic but whose effect is symbolic (Ulmer 1990). All tourist attractions that have no other reason to exist but to cater to the fabrication of tourist experience share a 'factitious, pseudo-eventful quality', argued Boorstin, and indeed are themselves pseudo-events. A pseudo-event is a simulation, a man made occurrence, a synthetic novelty, and is different from a spontaneous occurrence such as an earthquake or a 'God-made marvel'. Pseudo-events are designed for the convenience of reproduction, which makes them more reassuring and dramatic than spontaneous occurrences. As Deighton argued, such pseudo-events should be framed as performances (Deighton 1992): visitors can in such performances be active or passive, in both cases visitors participate in the construction of overall narrative that acts as the cognitive organizer for fragments of visitors's experience. A lucid performance, argued Deighton, is the one that visitors can fluently translate into a narrative, because after all people tend to organize experiential fragments into a narrative

form. As Deighton asserted, in marketing cycles of human skills and artifice, the goal is to avoid the perception that events are mere occurrences; someone must always get credit because virtually everything encountered in the theater of operations is a product of human minds and hands (Deighton 1992). In theme park environments, daily parades, such is Mickey's Parade in Disney parks, are examples of ritualized performances. Besides, another one of Boorstin's regularities is that pseudo-events generate other pseudo-events, or sub-events, with geometric progression. Namely, the overall thematic framework of the theme park is a conceptual umbrella that can generate endless variety of pseudo-events and sub-themes. Each theatron has its own ritualized performances that are organized around its concept. Walt Disney understood this very well since animation and amusement parks existed before him but stories were never told (Eisen 1975). Animation was not his invention, nor were amusement parks, thematization of both was. Disneyland Park was specifically designed through the construction of cinematic experiences that articulated both time and space in terms of trying to create an environmental narration that parallels the narration of the media itself. Cinema time cannot be but manipulated: one can take 100 years and collapse it into a two-hour movie, or make a two-hour movie from an event that had extended over five seconds of linear time. However, theme parks go beyond the cinematic experience: they offer an environmental, multi-dimensional experience that, besides visual stimuli, includes sound, smell, tactility and environmental activity.

The internal pattern of the theme park determines the spatial envelope of each theatron and each environmental module. These environs and environmental targets determine the lines and directions of movement. For example, Town Square in Disneyland Park greets visitors, upon passing through the arrival gate, by the City Hall, the Emporium, the Bank, the Fire Station and the Railroad Station. In the background of the Town Square theatron is the Sleeping Beauty Castle as the visual anchor that stimulates axial procession. Thus, by the strategy of framing an exotic theme immediately upon arrival, visitors are positioned within the fictional narrative of the TOP. Moreover, by being funneled to the Main Street, U.S.A. and led by the image of the Castle (constructed as desirable location or environmental target) visitors are stimulated to move through the internal pattern from one theatron to another. Each theatron stimulates a procession towards the adjoining one(s) by forming lines of action and direction of movement, but the speed of visitors's movement, or the time that visitors dispose in each theatron, is determined by the score. In fact, the speed of procession is determined by a series of pseudo-events whose precise locations are pre-determined by theme park's designers and organized into an arrangement of visual and other environmental stimuli by the score. The visitors's total environmental experience is thus engineered by the simultaneous arrangement of theatra and pseudo-events.

Pseudo-events are therefore a key instrument of scores in designing and controlling the spatio-temporal consumption of theme park environments. The score determines the character of pseudo-events, their environmental (spatial) disposition, the time of occurrence and duration, frequency, the way they interact with visitors, and so on. The score also determines and orchestrates the number of performers, the character of performance and its extension through time. Moreover, scores orchestrate the performance of visitors within the distribution of pseudo-events in both space and time, through the construction of environmental activity. In extreme cases visitors are 'spontaneously' invited to interact with performers and act for the pleasure of other visitors, or are sometimes exhibited in the performance of intimate rituals such are the wedding ceremonies in Huis Ten Bosch. Visitors tend to like such situations precisely because they are transparently constructed and reassuring. Reassurance translates directly into memorable environmental images and positive total experience. In sum, scores visualize the public that comes together in these constructed situations and in societies where physical inter-action of people in public spaces is exiguous, this is arguably one of the most important aspects of the consumption of theme park environments. As Baudrillard suggested, 'what draws the crowd [to Disneyland Park] is undoubtedly much more the social microcosm' whose contrast with the elements of the 'real' America is total (Baudrillard 1983).

Themeing achieves the precise temporal programming by a sophisticated layering of the three basic time-frames. Firstly, the basic time-frame is generated by the socio-culturally pre-determined time of theme park's opening and closing, and meal times (lunch and dinner), as well as the hours of operation of individual shops, bazaars, spas, and other amenities a theater of operations offers. Secondly, each environmental module within the theater of operations (rides, shows, movies) has a strictly determined timetable, which is a pre-determined time-cycle when a ride starts, ends and the time between the two cycles. Finally, the daily score instrumentalizes the weekly, seasonal and annual timetable of pseudo-events. The character of these pseudo-events depends on the geographic and cultural milieu, the capacity of the theater, operating budget, availability and so on. The basic, socio-culturally determined time-frame is one of the few truly culture-specific aspects of theme parks that could also vary in relation to the season: commonly accepted is the notion that theme parks stay open until 10 P.M. in the summertime, whereas in winter they close at 8 P.M. The time determined for meals is culturally determined, but also closely related to the schedule of local attractors and specifically to the timetable of the 'main parade'. For instance, Mickey Parade takes place in Walt Disney World Resort at 1 P.M. daily, while the Royal Horse Parade in Huis Ten Bosch takes place at 2 P.M. The function of such parades is multifold: they commonly announce lunch time and symbolically break the day in two, but most importantly they are a vehicle for connecting the design of the environment with the symbolic universe of the corporate theater. Each theme park has a main parade of a kind whose function is to sustain the illusion by

GREAT EXHIBITIONS

Le Première Exposition des Produits de l'Industrie Français of 1798 was held on Champ-de-Mars in Paris with only 110 national exhibitors. For the first time, the wonders of mechanical perfection and products of new industrial machines such as watches, hats, and various mechanical devices for everyday use, were exhibited with the national suffix and separated from mechanical wonders exhibited at freak shows at pleasure fairs. The separation of industrial products from mechanical wonders was caused by the expansion of the industry as well as by the *Proclamation de la Liberté du Travail* of 1791. The last in the series of national exhibitions held in 1849 inspired Prince Albert to outrival the French and organize an international exhibition to be held in Hyde Park in 1851.

After the Industrial Revolution, and by the mid-Nineteenth Century, iron became major structural material due to fire protection, speed of construction and durability. Early con-

Aerial view of the International Exhibition in Paris of 1867.

performance, costumes, vehicles, music and at the same time also to establish the identity and uniqueness of the environmental image. For instance, Disneyland Resort offers over 600 parades every year with live characters that sustain the suspension of disbelief, and also often includes popular entertainers from the world of pop music or film. The annual and seasonal pseudo-events are to some extent determined by geo-cultural specificity, but generally the rationale behind them is entirely fabricated. In that respect, narratives enveloping pseudo-events are not accounts of events that took place elsewhere but events themselves (Blanchot 1982: 62), neither accurate descriptions nor authentic narrative sequences but both, that is both representation and simulation. Seasonal events are designed to relate to different seasons: for instance, March is in Huis Ten Bosch marked by the so-called Spring Festival that includes a series of sub-events. One such sub-event is the Tulip Festival that occurs during the first week of April every year. Besides main parades, pseudo-events may include street musicians performing locally in assigned theatra, street painters, clowns and other 'attractions' directly related to the conceptual framework of the theater of operations. Large theme park operators, such is the WDC, have in-house departments that conceptualize, design and build pseudo-events from scratch: costumes, stage sets, vehicles, soundscapes, scripted performances, and so on. Others rent many or all of their pseudo-events. Today, rent-an-event companies specialize in designing total event environments for a variety of purposes, including theme parks. Theme park operators rent events just as they would rent equipment, with live actors, in advance scripted performances, and everything else needed for a successful pseudo-event. They can choose from a wide menu of options as rent-an-event companies cover a range of thematic needs, from medieval bands to Renaissance Flag Masters and to Rock'n'Roll Star Gallery. History is also, in that respect, a treasure box, a repository of endless novelty and surprise, and as exotic a theme as any other theme may ever be (Lowenthal 1996).

Huis Ten Bosch has rented events through Office Two-One Inc. and also through Total Space Productions: TAIYO Inc. whose headquarters in Tokyo's Roppongi district were designed in the early 1990s by famed Japanese architect Toyo Ito. Just as the Master Plan and the Program regulate the distribution of environmental clues in spatial terms, scores design time by filling up every minute of the environmental envelope by activity. In doing so, scores make theater of operations totally eventful, without gaps, without a possibility to reflect on experience and thus sustaining the bottom-up behavior throughout the temporal envelope. As Umberto Eco noted, 'there is always something to see, the great voids of modern architecture and city planning are unknown here' (Eco 1986). In many ways, pseudo-events close the symbolic circuit of themeing and put the final touch on the production of total landscape. Nothing escapes the total design, not even a single thought. The symbiosis of temporal and spatial dimensions of the consumption of theme parks environments, that is to say the symbiosis of the 'schedule of events' with the internal pattern, reveal the rationale behind the apparatus of theme park. Every single employee and every single activity throughout the day is always scripted in advance and assigned a specific spatial and temporal envelope in the environment by the daily score. Each pseudo-event attracts a critical mass of visitors and by its locale, in both place and time, determines their behavior and funnels them through the consumption routes within the internal pattern. This is done in such ways as to stimulate consumption locally or to determine the consequent direction of visitors's movements that ultimately lead to another pseudo-event or environmental module. As previously shown, such an engineered occupation implies an optimized consumption of the theme park environment and is directly related to the acceleration of the purchase-volume.

Conditioning Theme Park Environments
As Steve Koonin, General Manager of Turner Network Television once said, 'one billion people per year pay US$7 a pop to be taken on

structions such as Victor Louis's *Theatre Français* of 1786, or *Galerie d'Orleans* in Palais Royale in Paris of 1829, together with numerous bridges, mills, workshops, Grand Halles and department stores, gave way to a new building sensibility initially manifested at the Great Exhibitions (Giedion 1949: 178–211). Grand Halles, Crystal Palace, and the Eiffel Tower are all part of that tradition. If the early French Exhibitions came as a desire to control and take monopoly over the emerging national economy, the International Great Exhibitions came as a result of an ever-growing desire for free trade without economic, political and religious restrictions. As Giedion noted, industrial Exhibitions grew out of old pleasure-fairs and all of them, since the first one in Paris of 1798, retained a festive character. He saw Exhibitions as substitutes for the previously dominant forms of mass amusement, whereas Christine Boyer saw them as 'the epitome of "rational entertainment"—the visual mélange of the spectacular and scientific—[…] that turned the industrial world into one immense picture show.' (Boyer 1994: 257)

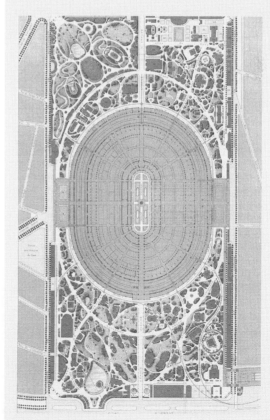

Plan of the International Exhibition in Paris of 1867.

Crystal Palace of 1851 basically applied the organizational format of French department stores, but it was not until 1867 and the Exhibition in Paris that the new organizational format was invented. The idea of representing the whole world in one building resulted in the elliptical structure as an allegory of the globe, designed by Gustave Eiffel.[1] Due to the growth of industry and number of exhibitors, the complexity of such a task gave a 1600 feet-long and 1245 feet-wide building organized as seven concentric galleries encircling an open-air Palm Garden at its core design by Jean Alphand. Machines were exhibited in the largest perimeter-gallery (Machinery Hall), whereas other galleries featured raw materials, fine arts, textile and clothing, furniture, and the History of Work in the first gallery that surrounded the Palm Garden. All circular galleries were connected to the core as well as to other galleries by transversal avenues. The innovation of the 1867 exhibition was the way that national and utility determinators were combined: if one walked radially through a gallery featuring clothing, one would walk through different national segments and get a cross-section of clothing production across the industrialized world (Giedion 1949: 181). If one stopped at the French clothing industry and continued to walk transversally towards the central garden, one would get to explore all other French industrial products. The labyrinthine web of walkways extended out of the building into an informal rectangular park based on the principles of the English landscape garden, where numerous national pavilions were placed including the Spanish, Dutch, British, Prussian, Russian, Moroccan, Tunisian, Egyptian, as well as the Austrian contribution in the form of an Austrian Village. These national pavilions presented national food, architecture, clothes, an early type of period-rooms, and real natives within their respective pavilions.[2] In this Vauxhall-type layout, the Paris Exhibition captured a true novelty: the simulation of the experience of world travel (Kaufman 1989: 22). If Vauxhall, Bartholomew's fair and the 1851 Exhibition had been credited for early simulations of travel, the Paris Exhibition marked a quantum leap in simulated travel-experience. Boyer notes that out of 33 major entertainments at the Paris 1900 Exhibition, 21 were simulated travelogues (Boyer 1994: 268).

Although the Paris Exhibition of 1867 anticipated the problem of complexity and congestion by organizing pavilion-

an emotional safari: to cry, laugh, scream and mourn' (Emmons 2002b). In many ways theme parks operate as environmental labs and the deliberate manipulation of environmental sensory clues in order to influence the behavioral responses of visitors is a common practice. The speculative employment of visual, tactile, aural and olfactory environmental stimuli is also aimed at fabricating a desirable environmental image in visitors. It affects visitors subliminally and is processed and judged on the visceral level much before it can be cognitively interpreted. Since visual behavioral stimuli such are form, color, material and texture have been discussed above, in what follows we will briefly look into the use of olfactory and aural behavioral stimuli.

Smell affects people subliminally and is also one of the most important associative vehicles. Researchers have known for long time that exposure to pleasant fragrances enhances task performance across the socio-economic and geo-cultural spectra (Baron 1998). Visitors's sense of smell is determined by two realms of recognition: firstly, recognizing if the smell is pleasant or not, and secondly memorizing it in terms of the type of experience it induces and in terms of the mental image that has been associated with it. Both realms are processed on the visceral level through 'pattern matching' and since theme park environments are deliberately designed to induce bottom-up behavior, they heavily capitalize on reducing the cognitive and on stimulating the emotional involvement. Certain universally recognized fragrances have the capability of inducing predictable responses (Weishar 1992): for instance, the smell of earth, or soil, would induce the concept of outdoors, pastoral setting, and the like; the smell of garlic induces the concept of ethnicity; the smell of coffee evokes the concept of home and domesticity. Large pharmaceutical and engineering companies utilize such empirical findings in the so-called 'affect infusion model', in order to manufacture mechanical equipment for interjecting fragrances into the air-conditioning and heating systems of various enclosed and semi-enclosed environments. A varia-

tion of the 'affect infusion model', often practiced in theme parks, is the use of mechanically engineered devices that redirect desirable fragrances (aromas of chocolate from the candy shop, fresh baked cinnamon roles, coffee) from backstage areas towards crowded areas on the frontstage. Such pleasant fragrances effectively induce shifts in affective states of visitors and play a significant role in stimulating their affiliative behavior (Baron and Thomley 1994). Besides, when visitors are exposed to fragrances they judge as pleasant, their task performance is significantly greater (Baron 1998). Cumulative olfactory stimuli in an environmental unit at any given time are a total combination of a variety of different sources of olfactory environmental factors that include both predictable (affect infusion, landscaping) and unpredictable stimulus generators (presence of others in the environment).

In theme park environments, sound patterns are designed to improve task performances in a variety of situations. Just as with all other types of stimulus generators, sound has the greatest effect on visitors's behavior when visitors are conditioned to have high affective and low cognitive involvement with the environment.

satellites around the central building, it is the Philadelphia Exhibition that stated this problem clearly: a single central structure could no longer sufficiently hold the world exhibits and the panoptical layout had to be decentralized. It was therefore not before the Philadelphia Exhibition of 1876 that the pavilion system was fully utilized. Here, national pavilions were designed as full scale mock-ups featuring artifacts of daily life and real natives now involved in the amusement of the crowds. The pavilion system was also used in the Chicago Exhibition of 1893 and the Paris Exhibition of 1889, and from then, it became a standard format for the arrangement of national exhibitors. Imported Venetian gondolas and gondoliers at the Chicago Exhibition of 1893 determined a new course of events: Great Exhibitions were no longer sites of scientific and architectural experiments as national pavilions became eclectic revivals of various historic 'styles', specifically in an attempt of newly formed nation states to identify recognizable national denominators. The main focus at the Paris Exhibition of 1878 was the central *Rues des Nations* where national pavilions were aligned to form a major procession runway.

At the Paris Exhibition of 1889, Charles Garnier designed one of the main attractions surrounding the Eiffel Tower: the History of Human Habitation. It consisted of 44 full-scale reproductions of traditional, national residential structures

The Ferris Wheel and the general view of the midway at the World's Columbian Exhibition of 1893.

Illinois Central Railway trains at the White City Station, World's Columbian Exhibition of 1893.

that featured more than 400 natives: Tahitians, Indochinese, Senegalese, and many others. Displaced from their original settings, these buildings worked on an iconic level sustaining and enhancing the 'international' narrative. Adjacent national restaurants and workshops were sites of both cultural and commodity consumption where cultural difference was a commodity to be tasted and consumed, and where visitors could consume both the process and the product of traditional skills (Kaufman 1989: 26).[3]

Each Exhibition had a central theme, a symbolic capital that drew in millions of visitors. Most of those symbolic themes captured by buildings and structures were kept as landmarks, such as the Eiffel Tower. One such symbolic feature was the first Otis elevator which was presented at New York's World Fair of 1853.[4] Earlier the same year, James Bogardus proposed a steam-powered elevator to play a major role in his design for the 300-foot Central Tower that would have played a central symbolic role at the same Exhibition (Giedion 1949: 208). As Giedion notes, at the Paris Exhibition of 1867, an elevator took visitors from the *Galerie des Machines* to the roof level, where they encountered a magnificent new experience: a view over the Exhibition building and the city of Paris. The next cabin elevator was installed in the Eiffel Tower, the central theme of Paris Exhibition of 1889. The elevator took visitors to the height of 980 feet, where, for the first time, visitors were able to observe the scenographic city space as the most refined spectacle of the fair, consumable scenery that could be revisited, and soon reproduced. This was a true paradigmatic shift in terms of visitors's understanding of the world and their ability to visualize it. In that respect, the experience was essentially analogous to the 20th July, 1969 telecast of the first human setting foot on the Moon, watched by over half a billion people around the world.

As Kaufman noted, three different themes emerge from looking at the Great Exhibitions and World Fairs as important factors in understanding contemporary theme parks (Kaufman 1989: 25–26): firstly, the fracturing of time and space that allows no coherent picture of the environment represented to emerge clearly; secondly, the mixing of heroic and quotidian elements in the representations; and thirdly, populating of such generalized images with ethnic figures, real natives, and adequate amusements.

As with olfactory stimuli, cumulative aural stimuli are also a total combination of both predictable and unpredictable stimulus generators. The predictable aural stimulus generators are foreground sounds (planned non-random music sequences), spontaneous sounds (planned non-random environmental activity such as street musicians) and background sounds (random environmental activity such as animal sounds). The unpredictable stimulus generators are those derived from unplanned environmental activities that come from presence of others in the environment or means that are beyond the control of theme park operators (such as an airplane flying or train passing nearby). All stimulus generators are intricately interwoven through the three main structural factors: time (tempo and

Street entertainer in Huis Ten Bosch.

rhythm), pitch, and texture (Bruner 1990). All three are capable of evoking non-random affective responses in visitors. Aural stimuli are most commonly employed in theme park environments either to direct the attention of visitors to proper targets within the field of vision, or to affect visitors's body initially through bio-physical processes, then create the 'mood,' and finally affect his motor system and his behavior (Schafer 1977). For example, individual retail outlets in theme parks are commonly defined by background music meant to create certain 'mood' in visitors; in retail outlets, volume level of background music has negative relationship with shopping time, but a positive one with the average sales-per-person ratio (Smith and Curnow 1966). When sound level is high visitors would spend less time in the environment, but sales per minute would be greater. General visitors's flow through the theme park environment is directly related to the music tempo: slower flow reflects slower music tempo whereas faster tempo is commonly followed by faster pedestrian flow (Milliman 1982). Music in peak hours is always faster and followed by intense environmental activity (parade, spontaneous environmental sounds) which results in faster and more efficient traffic flow. Nevertheless, behavioral responses to tempo are different. In the environmental modules where visitors are expected to shop, they are exposed to slower sound tempo, because sales volume has the reverse relationship to tempo. Faster tempo means fewer sales per minute, while slower tempo means significantly higher sales volume. In the environmental modules where efficiency is paramount, such are food outlets with seating capacities, visitors are exposed to faster tempo. Placing the influence of sound on human behavior within an ideological discourse, Hopkins argued that sound has the capacity to 'contextualize environments' by defining an autonomous 'acoustic space' (Hopkins 1994). He further argued that whoever controls the acoustic space controls the recipient of the sound and its total environmental experience. Since the experiential dimension of theme park environments goes beyond their geographic locale, soundscape too crosses the territorial confinements of the park as it melds with the

1. The idea of representing the whole world in one building was initially supposed to be allegorized by a circular building. Because of the lack of space at Champ-de-Mars, Gustave Eiffel finally designed an elliptical enclosure.

2. All of the national pavilions were designed by local, French architects. In that sense, the exhibition was more about the representation of otherness by French officials than about 'others' representing themselves within this totalizing setting. This specifically applies to participating countries form the middle-East and Africa.

3. As Kaufman reports, at the Royal Jubilee Exhibition in Manchester of 1887, an ideal version of Old-Manchester was designed and erected by Alfred Darbyshire and Frederick Bennett Smith (Kaufman 1989: 25), probably among the first historical theme villages ever designed on such a scale. It was organized much like a regular theme park today, with people wearing traditional costumes, an old post office, railway station, and other amenities (Tomlinson 1888). The Vienna Exhibition of 1873 featured a similar village composed of replicas of traditional rural houses form various parts of the ethnically diverse Austro-Hungarian provinces (Sonzogno 1874). Whereas Austrian version was to some extend homogenized, the Hungarian version exhibited at the Budapest Millennium Exhibition of 1896 was a realistic picture of the cultural and political situation: the Hungarian Street featured Hungarian rural houses, while the Nationalities Street featured rural houses of those under the Austro-Hungarian occupation (Balint 1897).

4. The first passenger elevator to be used in commercial buildings was installed in a department store in NYC, in 1857 (Giedion 1949: 208–211).

Garnier's History of Human Habitation pavilions at the Paris Exhibition of 1889.

media space of television, film and advertising. Larry Birman, ex-Disney Imagineer, designed music and soundscapes for Spain Mura in such a way that the same soundscape is used for its telephone answering system, television advertising campaigns, and to acoustically define the entrance to the park. The first experience upon entering Spain mura is that of *deja-vu*, but also of familiarity. The familiar sound reduces the unfamiliarity of the physical setting, and therefore it reduces environmental load, creates a 'pleasant' experience, and enforces emotions of pleasure and dominance. Well balanced and carefully designed spontaneous entertainments such are mobile vendors, news stands, food and beverage kiosks, clowns or street musicians significantly stimulate affiliative behavior in visitors and their desire to move and communicate with other people and the environment (Kaplan 1985). Thus, the presence of this type of pseudo eventful environmental activity that creates spontaneous sounds is an important aspect of environmental design and always stimulates people's affiliative behavior in theme parks. Thanks to digital technology, design of the physical properties of aural stimuli are nowadays limitless as the same digital algorithm used to simulate a growling lion can, with minor modification, also mimic a swimming dolphin, a singing bird, or sustain the environmental buzz (Krantz 1994).

Successful, cumulative layering of emotional and functional environmental clues facilitates the creation of desirable total experiences in visitors, and it directly translates into the creation of optimal environmental images, moods, and traits. These are in turn directly related to the dollar-volume of the environment and the total revenue that the theme park generates. Total landscape provides an underlying rationale for the conditioning of human environments in which the fabricated total experience outweighs all facts of life that do not clearly contribute to perpetuating its production capacity. The same 'formula' outlined in the last two chapters has been utilized for 'outdoor family recreation', for 'preaching the glories of the Lord', and for 'preserving regional cultural assets'. What actually brings all these

distinct types of operations under the same conceptual umbrella of total landscape is the economic framework together with normative technical procedures that utilize various types of 'symbolic capital' for the creation of real revenues. What matters the most on the level of Themeing is the efficiency and optimization of the theater of operations (which has been standardized over the years), but what obviously matters the least is the actual thematic framework, namely whether a theme park is promoting Mickey Mouse novelties or slot machines enveloped in a frontier narrative. Thematic novelties are thus subordinate to the production of capital, and in many ways irrelevant. Just as Vauxhall and Coney Island replaced once popular war narratives with urban-accident narratives, the economic framework devised for contemporary theme parks can easily accommodate any fashionable thematic proposal of the day and still maintain its production capacity at desirable levels.

NOTES

1. 'If I were now to rewrite the book', wrote Aldous Huxley in the preface of the 1946 edition of the *Brave New World*, 'I would offer the Savage a third alternative. Between the utopian and the primitive horns of his dilemma would lie the possibility of sanity.' At the time of writing this passage, Huxley was, upon the invitation of Walt Disney, employed at Walt Disney Studios in California working on the script for *Alice in Wonderland* (Dunaway 1989). In the same foreword Huxley writes: 'The theme of *Brave New World* is not the advancement of science as such [but] the advancement of science as it affects human individuals.'

2. Some of the important works includes Louis Kattsoff's *Design of Human Behavior* (Kattsoff 1947), Ernest McCormick's *Human Engineering* (McCormick 1957, 1964), Robert Woodworth's *Dynamics of Behavior* (Woodworth 1958), Robert Sommer's *Personal Space: The Behavioral Basis Of Design* (Sommer 1969), and the research field called the Environment-Behavior Studies initiated in 1969 together with the journal titled *Environment and Behavior*.

3. Online Etymology Dictionary: http://www.etymonline.com/ (Accessed on 1st May 2004).

4. Encyclopedia Britannica Online: http://www.britannica.com/ (Accessed on 1st May 2004).

5. In 1976, Kevin Lynch set out to create a normative theory of 'good city form' that was also supposed to deal with form and process simultaneously. His theory represented 'an understanding, an evaluation, a prediction, and a prescription, all in one.' (Lynch *1976*)

6. Not everyone in the theme park industry distinguishes between the initial phases of Conceptual Development and Schematic Design, some summarize everything under the umbrella of Conceptual Design, but such differences are rhetorical.

7. The modern word 'theatre' derives from the ancient Greek word *theatron* that comes from *theaomai*, meaning 'to behold' as a combination of words *thea* meaning 'a view,' *theates* meaning 'spectator' and *tron* as a suffix denoting place or location. Theatron signified an area where the spectators sat and observed the performance and as such it was often wrapped around a large portion of the orchestra. In its extended meaning it potentially signified an instrument for viewing, the viewing place, or the area from which to view. Some sources claim that by implication, the term could have signified a drama itself or the spectacle (Source: Etymological Dictionary Online. At: http://www.etymonline.com/ Accessed on 1st May 2004). In this book, I use the term to indicate a complex arrangement of individual environmental modules clustered around a clearly distinguishable concept.

8. Such conceptual clusters are distinguished on the basis of a unifying concept, thus visitors cognizant of such facts can make adequate choices. This particular sensory processing takes places at the reflective level and indicates a rare top-down behavioral situation to be found in theme parks.

9. In practice, Master Plan also specifies anticipated capital budget as well as a schedule for completing design and construction.

10. In practice, Design Development begins after the final Master Plan, Program, and Operating Plan are finalized and the capital budget is approved. Upon the completion and approval of Design Development, construction drawings are made and theme park is finally built. Whether this or similar procedure is followed through the entire process depends on a number of factors such are timetables, shifting budgets, scale of the theme park, geo-cultural milieu and so on.

11. Peak attendance is sometimes calculated as low as one percent of the projected annual attendance. Sometimes designers also work with the so-called 'peak in park' attendance which is commonly calculated as 65 percent of the peak attendance.

12. Such environmental units are in the theme park industry called 'anchor rides,' although major environmental units are not always necessarily rides, they may be shows or performances depending on the characteristics of the trade theater.

13. Physical size and properties, location, and market are what Randy White of White Hutchinson Leisure and Learning Group calls 'dimensions of mix.' He builds on the concept of 'focused assortment' that has been proven successful in retail, hospitality, and service industries. For a mix to work key criteria must be satisfied: critical mass of size and variety of the entertainment opportunities offered (anchored versus impulse attractions), repeat appeal, length of stay, value (perceived by customer in relation to the cost but also comfort, variety, service, convenience, cleanliness, emotion, souvenirs), storyline (memorable experience), and rhythm (pace, duration, cycles of play). White claims that successful mix creates a desirable variety and balance between the anchor rides and the so-called 'impulse objects' that generate revenue. As White points out, the aim is to keep per capita spending at desirable levels and at the same time stimulate repeat visits (White 1997).

14. Post Occupancy Evaluation (POE) is another commonly used model that empirically evaluates the environment in relation to a body of tasks, and subsequently enables customization to specific site and context conditions.

15. In shaping theme parks as commercial environments, visitors's behavior patterns have a direct relationship with the objective of the theme park environment: the dollar volume. Thus, theme parks are deliberately designed to stimulate consumer related behavior and constrain other types of behaviors. This book is not concerned with variables related to 'personality moderating' which stands for personal, internal responses to the theme park environment, and impressionistic accounts of theme park visits. For reference see Bitner 1993 and Sherry 1998.

16. Technicolor had originally developed the Technicolor White for the use in motion picture industry: the color photographs as pure white but in reality it is slightly yellowish white (Hench 2003: 135).

17. These five elements are derived from three different scholarly sources. Firstly, Kotler argued that tactical atmospherics has three basic functional layers: attention-creating (establishes the environment as unique), message-creating (establishes owners identity and communicates its intentions), and affect-creating (enhances desirable behavior through environmental stimuli) (Kotler 1973). Secondly, Rapoport argued that when an environment is designed, four basic elements are organized: space, time, meaning and communication (Rapoport 1982: 178). Meaning refers to interactions between people and the environment, whereas communication refers to interactions among people within an environment. Finally, Lynch argued that an environmental image can be deduced into three essential components: identity (what sets the image apart from other images), structure (spatial or pattern relations between observers and the environment) and meaning (that environment communicates to the observer) (Lynch 1960: 8).

18. The term 'internal pattern' is borrowed from Kevin Lynch who used it in his 1954 essay *The Form of Cities* (Lynch 1954).

19. Although symbolic roles were not very common, some had strong symbolic functions, particularly in the ritual of Initiation within the gardens of the Free Masonry.

20. In *Space, Time, and Architecture* of 1949, Giedion makes note of the term 'Harlequin Dress of Architecture' frequently used during the Nineteenth Century to mark a process initiated by the advent of cast-iron construction that 'reduced the revived forms of serious architecture to the status of false fronts.' Giedion employed it in reference to the separation of facade from the structural system of the building caused by the development and proliferation of the steel-frame structure, as it was obvious in Jules Saulnier's Chocolate Factory in Noisiel-sur-Marne of 1871 (Giedion 1949: 115). I am employing the term as related to the separation of the apparatus of representation from the realm of the building (structure, program, etc) obvious in ways in which denotation and connotation are inappropriately disconnected.

21. Icon is an object that exists on its own, but which resembles another object by the virtue of likeness and can therefore be used to represent that object (Broadbent 1978).

22. On the general (pragmatic) level, the key semiotic element is sign: sign is defined as everything that stands for something else, only if there exists a convention (semiotic code) that allows for the interpretation (Eco 1976: 16). Thus, semiotics studies the nature of representation and the object of its analysis could be everything that represents or can be represented. For Roland Barthes, the substance of the signifier is always material (Barthes 1968: 47), whereas Umberto Eco argued that although some environmental stimuli (such as olfactory stimuli) that affect people on subliminal level can 'in some respect or capacity act as signs to somebody', they cannot be regarded as signs (Eco 1976: 19–20). Music, for example, is a semiotic system without a semantic level (content plane). A semiotic study of the theme park would neces-sarily lead into an analysis of the ideological framework that generates the theme park's interpretative code.

23. As Hench wrote, Walt Disney Imagineering designs rides to communicate simultaneously at three different levels: symbolism, representation, and sensory information (Hench 2003: 38–39).

4

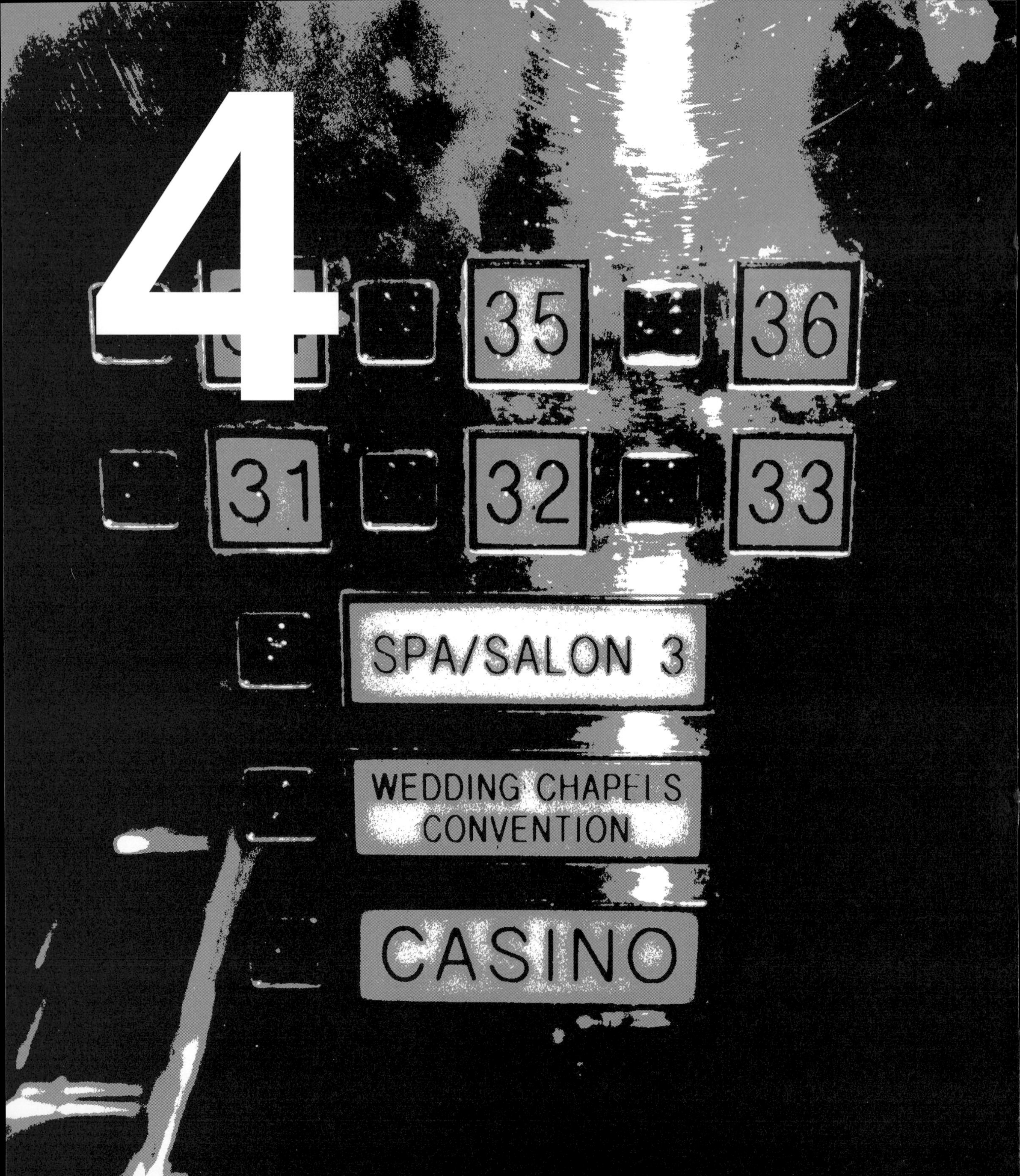

DEPARTING

How About Taking a 'World Tour?' You might not get to Italy or Egypt this year, but you can take the grand model tour of Westbrooke at Winston Trails. Nine fully-furnished models, situated within a beautiful park-like setting, are awaiting for your visit. With decor inspired by the countries their names represent, these homes will delight you. You'll experience the artistry of Africa, the classic designs from Ancient Greece, and the 'oo lá lá' elegance of France.

Begin your stroll with The Fairway Series of homes: The Cairo, The Copenhagen, and The Nairobi [...] Continue the tour with The Country Club Series. The Athens, The Sapporo, and The Antilles [...] The Master Series, featuring The Casablanca, The Venice, and The Paris, is 'top-of-the-line' with all the luxuries you've wished for—at no extra cost. Choose from three, four, or five-bedroom models. The Paris is especially spacious with 2,705 square feet of air-conditioned living area, an elegant loft, and huge master suite. Tiled foyers and dramatic entrances make these homes a pleasure to come home to.

Of course, Westbrooke homes are built to take advantage of the beautiful greens and fairway views of the Winston Trails Golf Course [...] West-brooke at Winston Trails is priced from the low $120s to the $160s and range in size from 1,649 to 2,705 square feet of air-conditioned living space. They offer a choice of three elevations, and now, homebuyers will be able to enjoy the recently completed swim and Racquet Club. Begin your tour of these wonderful residences today or call for more information.

WESTBROOKE COMMUNITIES, INC. (ADVERTISEMENT IN *ATLANTIC MONTHLY*, NOV. 1995)

Europa Boulevard in West Edmonton Mall,
Alberta, Canada.
© West Edmonton Mall Property Inc.

New York Hotel & Casino and MGM Grand Hotel
& Casino, Las Vegas.

One of the most fascinating facts about theme parks is the way in which they have been naturalized as the most effective method for the production of specific behavioral outcomes in large, superbly controlled and entertained crowds, and as such have departed from conventional theme park enclosures towards a diverse range of typological hybrids that predominantly emerged in the 1990s. Through this process, often deliberately and sometimes unintentionally, the condition of total landscape is effectively produced in the spaces of everyday life: shopping spaces, spaces of worship, museums, cultural centers or schools. The most popular and widely accepted departure from the theme park formula are Retail Entertainment Centers (REC), such are the Mall of America and West Edmonton Mall, where a combination of retail and themed entertainment has become the favorite formula for attracting customers in an increasingly experience-driven economy. On a larger scale, this chapter will discuss how, since early the 1990s, Las Vegas has placed incredible efforts into reframing itself as a giant, family-friendly REC. Another type of departure are theme parks that deliberately represent regionally bound cultural, historic, and geographically defined themes or particular religious world-views. I will discuss a few cases of religious theme parks across the world and how some of them have been reframed into living 'communities'. Theme parks that use regionally bound cultural, historic, and geographically defined themes are commonly framed as ethnographic and heritage centers and have been naturalized as the most effective method for preserving cultural values lost in the face of progress and modernization. The Polynesian Cultural Center and Shikoku Mura will be discussed in this chapter as typical examples of such tendencies. An intriguing variation on the heritage-center theme are what I will call 'living' theme parks, where a specific historical moment, a religious setting, or geo-cultural milieu has been carefully fabricated and detailed (sometimes preserved) for the enjoyment of visitors and permanent residents alike. Well-known historical examples of that tendency are Skansen, Colonial Williamsburg and the Greenfield Village. The most intriguing contemporary examples of the escalating process of fabricating desires for living and working within the strict boundaries of theme park territories are Huis Ten Bosch and Celebration. Celebration belongs to a tradition that has its origins in the eccentric relationship between Walt Disney and city-making, and even though it is very provoking and will be discussed in this chapter, most of the chapter will be dedicated to an in-depth analysis of Huis Ten Bosch for the two main reasons. Firstly, in order to bring the theme park discussion to a closure, in many ways because Huis Ten Bosch has been rightly named 'the theme park to end all theme parks'. Secondly, in order to open up the discussion towards another type of departure from the conventional theme park formula, namely towards what is usually referred to as the imposition of the 'theme park model' onto urban fabric in cities across the world. Chapter 5 will thus continue to discuss the process of expansion of the theme park apparatus beyond the strict boundaries of theme parks as a vehicle for the production of total landscape.

Retail Entertainment Centers

The most common departure from the conventional theme park formula is an indoor combination of entertainment, themeing, and retailing. This is also the fastest growing trend in industry as shopping centers, malls and other retail outlets are finding ways to stay competitive and attract shoppers in the increasingly experience-driven economy. The usual form is the Retail Entertainment Center (REC), a hybrid of retail complex and usually themed entertainment center that has been designed as the industry's answer to the emergent need to incorporate in its offers both active entertainment and unique experiences. A REC typically offers a mix of activities such as shopping, themed restaurants, rides, theaters, video arcades, sometimes bowling and pool, non-denominational chapels, child-care centers and other amenities. As Dorrett points out, the four key factors for the successful REC design are location, mix, environment and cost (Dorrett 1999). Simple examples of REC are traditional shopping center and malls that include low-cost additions to their mix such as

a carousel, a skating ring, a free children's play area or a live-music stage. In cases where the REC's primary trade theater is limited to a local community, a locally generated theme is often used for enveloping; in cases of a larger regional REC, a more complex cultural theme is sometimes employed. An early example of the REC formula was the West Edmonton Mall (WEM), developed by the Ghermezian family in 1985 and built in Alberta, Canada. WEM departed from both the indoor shopping mall formula and the theme park concept by mixing entertainment and shopping in the ratio of 40:60. Prior to WEM, no shopping mall ever had dedicated 40 percent of its available footage to pure entertainment purposes. WEM is also internationally known for the thematization of its retail spaces, its indoor amusement park and its Fantasyland Hotel with nearly 150 themed rooms, each promising 'to fulfill your quest for the ultimate travel adventure'. For instance, the African Room offers a luxurious dwelling complete with cheetah-designed carpeting, bamboo furniture, full-size Jacuzzi and a zebra-covered king-size bed: 'It's a theme room the whole family can enjoy!' Obviously, WEM targets both the local market and a destination-market, thus providing reasonable on-site hotel capacities for guests staying over night. In an obviously Disney-inspired move, WEM treats shopping, playing and vacation experiences as 'adventures' in this 'vacation paradise where adventure awaits around every corner'. The Mall of America in Minnesota is yet another example of this kind of departure from the standard theme park configuration. An REC commonly does not exceed 100 000 square feet in size and investment level of US$20 million. In that respect, it is similar to smaller regional theme parks in terms of scale and complexity. As an industry rule, not more than 40 percent of the total surface area is devoted to non-retail generating revenues such are rides, games, restaurants and cinemas. Variations on this model are Urban Entertainment Centers (UEC) and Location-Based Entertainment Centers (LBE), predominantly indoor facilities where ratio of retail to entertainment is inversed.

Although Las Vegas has historically been understood as an American Frontier paradigm where gambling played a major role in the development of the city, today the Las Vegas Strip is steadily approaching the characteristics of a massive REC that builds on the attraction of urban form, but simultaneously suppresses the condition of urbanity. Las Vegas's Caesar's Magical Empire, Omnimax theater, the Manhattan Zone, the MGM Grand, the Luxor Hotel-Casino, the Parisian, the Venetian, hundreds of themed restaurants, thousands of retail outlets and roller-coasters have transformed the gambling strip into a giant REC. Low costs of living and attractive wages attract thousands of new residents and tourists alike. In the early 1990s, 'gambling' was renamed into 'gaming' as Las Vegas made an aggressive shift towards family entertainment, a conceptual *salto mortale* yet a necessary precondition for its transformation. A Mercer study conducted annually as a comparative statistical analysis between Orlando (e.g. Walt Disney World Resort) and Las Vegas shows that 'in both places, there is intense competition by the leisure industry to increase market share and develop segments traditionally served by the competitor; however, the presence of theme park elements apparently has not convinced parents that Las Vegas is a good vacation destination for children'. (BW 1996) Only seven percent of Las Vegas visitors in 1996 cited theme parks and shopping as a strong influence in their decision to visit Las Vegas, whereas among the visitors to Orlando 89 percent reported they are 'very likely' to bring children under 18 years of age. In contrast, among the visitors to Las Vegas only 17 percent said they plan to bring children under 18 years of age, and over 60 percent of them thought gambling was a major influence in their decision to come to Las Vegas. Despite of all this, *Time Magazine* placed Las Vegas on its cover in 1994 as The New All-American City. Las Vegas as a family-friendly destination has also been featured in newspapers and magazines such are *USA Today, Forbes, U.S. News & World Report, Better Homes and Garden* as well as in tourist promotional materials. By the research done in Las Vegas by the Las Vegas Convention and Visitors Authority, seven percent of Las Vegas visitors surveyed in 1992 said they had someone younger than 21 in their group, the percentage then peaked around 12 percent in 1996, and fell again 10 percent respectively in 1999 and 2000 (Smith 2001). Only about 15 percent of the 36 million tourists that come to Las Vegas every year are local and regional tourists (Mihailovich 2004). Many of them are not actually tourists at all: businessmen attending conventions staged in Las Vegas hotels are significantly driving the hotel occupancy rates at very high level of almost 90 percent to a total of over three million overnight stays with an average per capita spending rate of US$92.13 per day. Statistics also show that the number of tourists attending secondary (non-gambling) attractions is steadily rising: Shark Reef at Mandalay Bay Resort & Casino in Las Vegas attracts more than one million visitors annually (O'Brien et al. 2002a). Since tourism is the largest industry in the State of Nevada, generating over US$35 billion in revenues every year by bringing in 48 million tourists, the state has also been attempting a departure from the conventional gambling image by turning its spectacular natural environment into a credible tourist offer, hoping to extend the length of stay in the area, diversify its revenue sources and change its public image. Under the 'family-adventure' theme, thus, a whole package including 'gaming' in Las Vegas also offers nearly 60 million acres of spectacular pristine landscape for recreational use such as camping, hiking, biking and eco-tourism (Mihailovich 2004). This totalizing operation will not only utilize anything available in the State of Nevada in order to perpetuate and enlarge its process of production, but it will also colonize and standardize the pristine landscape by emphasizing only those selected features that can support the process of production centered around concepts already established by Las Vegas as REC. Features of the landscape that are not needed in this process will simply be bypassed and represented as either 'distances' or 'times', or will be seen as either physical or psychological obstacles to the production process and, as such, will be neutralized.

Ethno Theme Parks and Heritage Centers

The construction of restoration villages, open-air architectural museums and living-history theme parks was arguably fostered by the Great Exhibitions of the late Nineteenth and early Twentieth Centuries. It was the Swedish philologist Arthur Hazelius who founded Skansen, the first permanent architectural open-air museum in 1891 (Conan 1996). On a 75-acre park in Stockholm, Hazelius attempted to preserve architecture, crafts, traditional costumes and lifestyles alike. Volunteers dressed in traditional clothes inhabited this themed village performing scenes from rural everyday life, songs and dances, old crafts and made traditional food. Real, unaltered rural houses were brought to this village and reassembled faithfully composing a stage-set for the preservation of native tradition. Inspired by Skansen, the trend of constructing ethnic villages spread all over Europe and the United States.

The Polynesian Cultural Center was founded by the Church of Jesus Christ of Latter-day Saints in 1963 to allow students at the Church College of Hawaii to keep alive and share their island heritage with visitors. Over 100 local people volunteered to help build the Polynesian Cultural Center on a 12-acre site. It opened its gates to the public on the 12th October 1963. In the early years of operation, villagers staged evening shows every night. Additions have been made in the 1980s, such as the 1850s Christian missionary compound, the Migrations Museum and the 1920s Yoshimura Store offering souvenirs. However, the 1990s have brought a brand new experience: in 1995, the center introduced a new show called Horizons! A Celebration of Polynesian Discovery, a new IMAX theater, The Living Sea and the Treasures of Polynesia, an all-new shopping plaza featuring a collection of authentic Island merchandise. The Polynesian Cultural Center is a typical example of heritage/ethno theme parks that, since the early 1980s, have become the most popular cultural and commercial strategy for preserving the cultural assets. In many countries they are also called open-air museums. The only thing the structures within the theme park have in common is the historical period within which they originated. In Taiwan, such theme parks have been constructed in the early 1990s as successful commercial enterprises: the Window on China features miniature replicas of famous Chinese cultural and architectural monuments, while the Taiwan Folk Village has rides and live performances featuring local dances and traditional songs. It is becoming increasingly difficult to draw a line of distinction between the ethno-theme parks, open-air museums and conventional theme parks. As Jeffrey Andrews noted, 'one could almost say that heritage areas are theme parks—except that the theme in each area is not imposed by a Disneyesque developer, but rather grows out of the unique geography, history, and living culture of the region.' (Andrews 1994)

That a fictive historic character can be framed as national treasure, turned into a symbolic capital, and subsequently used to generate significant revenues was clear to a board comprised of governmental officials and private investors that met in 2001 to discuss Dracula Land. The narrative structure of Dracula Land was to be based on the life of Prince Vlad Tepes who lived in the Fifteenth Century-Transylvania, now partly within the state of Romania. The myth of Count Dracula was launched in the 1897 novel Dracula by the Irish author Bram Stoker and has ever since been exploited both by the entertainment industry and by the entire sub-culture of Satanists and followers of Count Dracula. The novel was a fiction only partly based on the life of Prince Vlad Tepes, also called Vlad-the-Impaler. The us$60 million proposal was supposed to be located in the real home and the castle of Prince Tepes located in the town of Brasov, and was supposed to include a Dracula Institute, a conference center, a Dracula library and a museum (CNN 2002). The project was supposed to preserve the area and the castle itself, exhibit the cultural and ethnographic heritage, and to bring an anticipated 3000 jobs to the area, as well as potentially millions of foreign tourist to this very troubled post-Communist economy. Announcing the project,

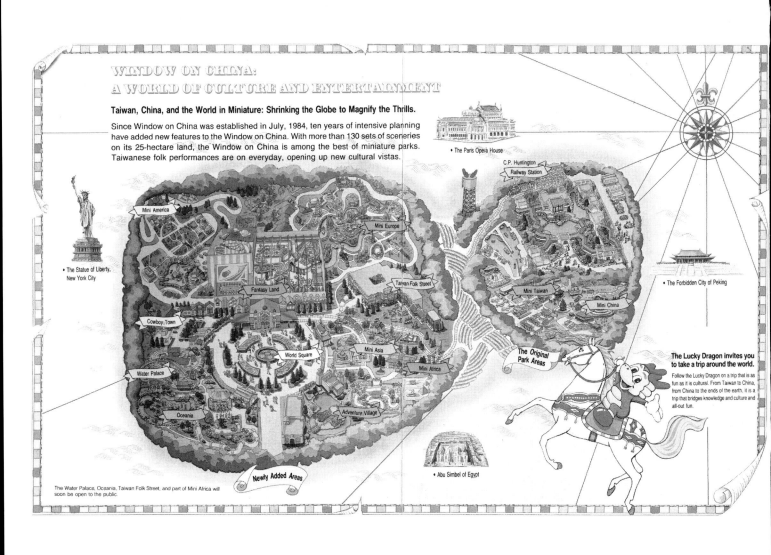

WINDOW ON CHINA:
A WORLD OF CULTURE AND ENTERTAINMENT

Taiwan, China, and the World in Miniature: Shrinking the Globe to Magnify the Thrills.

Since Window on China was established in July, 1984, ten years of intensive planning have added new features to the Window on China. With more than 130 sets of sceneries on its 25-hectare land, the Window on China is among the best of miniature parks. Taiwanese folk performances are on everyday, opening up new cultural vistas.

• The Paris Opera House

C.P. Huntington
Railway Station

Mini America

Mini Europe

• The Statue of Liberty,
New York City

Fantasy Land

Taiwan Folk Street

• The Forbidden City of Peking

Mini Taiwan

Mini China

Cowboy Town

World Square

Mini Asia

The Original
Park Areas

Water Palace

Mini Africa

Oceania

Adventure Village

**The Lucky Dragon invites you
to take a trip around the world.**

Follow the Lucky Dragon on a trip that is as fun as it is cultural. From Taiwan to China, from China to the ends of the earth, it is a trip that bridges knowledge and culture and all-out fun.

Newly Added Areas

• Abu Simbel of Egypt

The Water Palace, Oceania, Taiwan Folk Street, and part of Mini Africa will soon be open to the public.

Window on China theme park in Taiwan.
© Window on China.

Remains of F. L. Wright's Tokyo Imperial Hotel
preserved in Meiji Mura.

NEXT SPREAD

Map of Shikoku Mura. © Shikoku Mura.

the Romanian minister of tourism said the park would be a tribute
to Romanian history and to 'the image of a great Romanian hero'.
(BBC 2001) As the Romanian daily *Evenimentul Zilei* commented, since
Romanians 'cannot make Swiss watches, American films, Russian
bombers or German cars [...] we will build Dracula parks and export
Dracula dolls throughout the world'. (AP 2001) A global division of
labor *par excellence.* In July 2003, *Amusement Business* reported that
majority shareholders controlling nearly 90 percents of the shares in
a planned Dracula theme park withdrew their investments because
of potential environmental hazards, despite the fact that nearly US$3
million had been raised for the construction of the park (AB 2003).

In Japan, for instance, such ethno-theme parks are popular leisure
destinations, and in 1980s, a number of ethno-themed regional parks
were constructed in order to boost local economic milieus and protect
valuable cultural assets. These theme parks rely mostly on regional
railway networks and much less on the highway infrastructure as
opposed to American parks. Parking spaces in front of most of the
Japanese regional theme parks can accommodate up to 50 vehicles.
Never within urban concentrations, they are symbolically placed in
natural settings (parks or forests) and are significant attractions to
the urban populations. Usually located within 60 minutes from major
urban concentrations, they are easily reached by local trains. Places
like Meiji Mura and Edo Mura are composed of period buildings
brought from different parts of Japan and re-erected in the new settings. What unites structures in such a theme park into a common

thematic framework is a specific historical period. For instance,
besides other Meiji period buildings, Meiji Mura also contains the
salvaged remains of F. L. Wright's Tokyo Imperial Hotel. Shikoku
Mura is different in that it is composed of buildings from the Shikoku
region that are also brought to the site and assembled into an open-
air museum setting, but what unites them is not a specific historical
period but their geographic location.

Shikoku Mura

Shikoku Mura is a local theme park in the island of Shikoku promoted
as a part of the tourist offer of the regional capital Takamatsu. Due to
the punctuality of Japanese trains, visitors are informed that the trip
to Shikoku Mura will take 36 minutes by train, and an additional seven
minutes walking North-East from the station to the main gate of the
theme park. Shikoku Mura has also been called a folklore-village as
well as an open-air museum (*yagai hakubutsukan*), a fact that speaks
clearly about the confusion that everyone including theme park owners and operators still retains in relation to environments of this type.
This theme park opened in 1976 on the lower slopes of Yashima Hill
with the aim of 'preserving the folklore cultural assets and as a place
of social education'. It contains 23 structures brought from all over the
island of Shikoku and restored on the site. Most of the structures have
been designated as important national or prefectural cultural assets.
Many of the structures were reconstructed on-site by villagers from
the original areas. The only newly built structure is the Kazura-bashi
bridge built by villagers from Iya region who voluntarily came to build

源平ゆかりの地
屋島入口

四国村

重要文化財、旧下木家住宅・旧中石家住宅

市指定文化財
茶堂（遊庵）

こうぞ蒸し

猪垣

国指定文化財
砂糖しめ小屋、釜屋

国指定文化財
旧河野家住宅

県指定文化財
旧山下家住宅

市指定文化財
農村歌舞伎舞台

猪垣

前田家土蔵

県指定文化財
丸亀藩番所

石畳ながや

旧吉野家住宅
市指定文化財

かずら橋

異人館

出口

切符売場

入口

🦋 市指定文化財、小豆島の農村歌舞伎舞台

国指定文化財
　旧下木家住宅

添水唐臼小屋

猪垣

染が滝

三文化財
し亀藩御用蔵

久米通賢旧宅

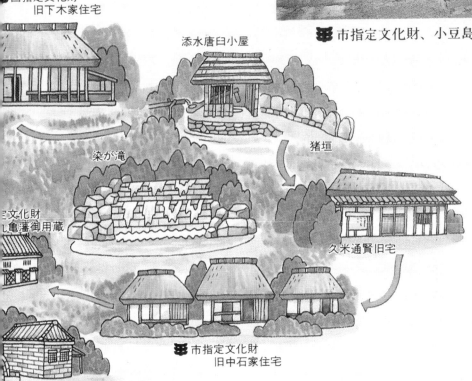

🦋 市指定文化財
　旧中石家住宅

石蔵とめがね橋

国指定文化財
　醤油蔵、麹室

🦋 重要文化財、旧河野家住宅

🦋 重要有形民俗文化財、砂糖しめ小屋

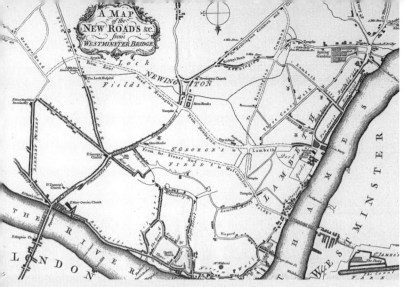

Map depicting road access to Vauxhall Gardens (top right) in relation to the city of London, c. 1752.

VAUXHALL PLEASURE GARDENS

Vauxhall Gardens opened in 1661 in a rather formal grid-like layout composed of three major avenues running parallel to each other—Grand Walk, South Walk and Lovers Walk—crossed by two perpendicular avenues and divided by rows of trees in between them. The fixed spatial reference inscribed through the basic grid of gravel walks combined with its ephemeral buildings was the reason for its phenomenal success (Chadwick 1966: 39). Its buildings were pavilions of lath-and-plaster and were easily transformed or replaced once the attraction became non-profitable. The speed of response to the market facilitated by the lightness of its symbolic load, together with the ephemerallity and exactitude of construction, became a standard operational frame for amusements parks. Vauxhall Gardens differed radically from other pleasure gardens that had adopted the metaphor of durability as their premise. Ironically, it was the desire for durability that determined the short life of popular pleasure gardens such are Ranelagh or Marylebone Gardens, as it was the notion of catering to the evolving taste of customers that kept Vauxhall opened for 200 years until 1859. Like most of the pleasure gardens of the time, it was an assemblage of popular-taste amusement (rides and visual attractions) with works of art (such as the sculptures of Apollo or that of Handel) and the simple pleasure of walking along the shady avenues. Pavilions were themed to fit the narrative of individual attractions: a Chinese Pagoda was made a part of the Chinese Landscape by locating the pavilion in front of a giant painting of a Chinese garden, and

a replica of the only remaining traditional suspension bridge made out of the woven vine trees. As one gets to the entrance of the Shikoku Mura, the Kazura-bashi (the Vine Bridge) spans over the Genpei Pond marking the entrance to the park:

> Kazura-bashi of Iya trembling though no wind blows... Take a walk back in time at Shikoku-mura. Set on the lower scenic slope of Yashima, you can examine the old building styles and household implements that were used for centuries in the Shikoku area. The adventurous will enjoy the suspension bridge woven of vines, which spans a pond near the entrance. The thick thatched roofs of the farm dwellings and the Noson Kabuki Stage complete with revolving center, highlighting the skill and ingenuity of the people of the time. (Takamatsu 1976: 9)

Besides private houses, the theme park also includes two bridges, a Kabuki theater, a tea-house, sheds for sugar pressing and paper mulberry steaming, a godown, a guard house and a restaurant. Most of them date from the early Edo period (1600–1868) to the mid-Meiji period (1868–1900). They are situated in a dense bamboo forest with more than 350 kinds of trees totalling over 30 000 on a sloped land of over one acre. The buildings are placed along the nearly mile-long pathway (promenade) designed by the sculptor and landscape architect Masayuki Nagare. Each structure is quite convincingly situated along the promenade following the novelty of its original location and use. For instance, before it was brought to Shikoku Mura, the house of Yamashita family had been situated on the top of a small hill in Northern Shikoku, enjoying a panoramic view of the town that surrounded the hill. Its position in Shikoku Mura reveals the same quality: the house is situated at the highest point of the theme park's site, allowing for a panoramic view on the Yashima town sitting peacefully at the bottom of the Yashima hill. In front of the house (as in front of every other house), there is a wooden panel with texts in both Japanese and English conveying the story of the Yashima family that donated the house, the history of the house, its original function, etc. Each house is equipped with a so called 'audio-guide speaker' conveying sounds that had been associated with the house in the time of its everyday use. For example, if the building was a residence, visitors would hear a baby crying in the background and former inhabitants chatting about daily problems, while the foreground voice belonging to the male head of the household would narrate the history of the family and the house. The water-powered rice-hulling mill would convey the rhythmic sound of rice hulling as well as the foreground voice narrating the story of predecessors and their resources through hundreds of years of hardship. Besides the general text about the history of both the family and the house, the last paragraph on the wooden panel would always bare the title 'Architectural Notes' and would give the precise measurements of the structure, the way it was constructed, names of the vernacular materials used and so on. Since each of the structures is also well equipped with traditional tools, clothes, furniture and decoration, each of them represents a precisely reconstructed anthropological and ethnographic situation. In order to attract repeat visitors, Shikoku Mura is also the site of various performances taking place throughout the year matching the season or a particular date. These performances are very popular among the visitors and local residents alike: traditional songs and dances related to the lives and customs of the old days are revived in each house by volunteers coming from the originating areas. The Noson-Kabuki theater-stage in Shikoku Mura was brought from the Shodo-shima Island still famous for its traditional Kabuki performed by farmers. Every year,

then placing the whole setting at the end of a walk so that the distance from which it was observed made it appear as if it was a part of the real landscape. The same strategy was used for other attractions: the Arcadian Landscape as a large scale painting placed behind simulated water springs (with real running water) and Poussinesque ruins. Other settings had historical and geographical denominators such was the Ruins of Palmyra. This one was framed with a series of Triumphal Arches made of canvas, wood and plaster and placed along the South Walk. This succession of frames in front of the distant setting was an attempt at achieving a dynamic, cinematic experience in moving through the park. Observed from a substantial distance these settings blurred the boundaries between the real and the imaginary, gradually displacing the subject into the realm of imaginary and introducing new and revolutionary entertainment novelty: travel. Just outside the busy and polluted city of London, one could travel to China, Italy, sites of famous battles, volcanic eruptions and a whole range of distinct imaginary places. As fashion changed, the Ruins of Palmyra and the Chinese Garden were replaced in early Eighteenth Century by Gothic temples, fountains and various other pavilions. The Orchestra was initially in 'Grecian style', but it also changed into the then fashionable 'Gothic style'. During the Seventeenth Century, weather conditions played an important role in the character of pleasure gardens and their operations, and many closed from September until early April. In the mid-Eighteenth Century, this limitation was overcome by new 'wet-weather attractions' for dancing, receptions, or performances (McKechnie 1969).

In the Nineteenth Century, Vauxhall's 'Gothic style' buildings were replaced by 'Gothic ruins' and this major change affected the character of attractions. Large, two-dimensional

Lithograph depicting a general view of Vauxhall Gardens, c. 1758.

paintings outlived their attractiveness as customers often demanded change. The new type of attraction was a 'three-dimensional painting' that was actually a large perspective painting depicting a rural scene: a water-mill was in the foreground with real water running out of it and a peasant house in the background. The re-articulated cinematic experience was facilitated by the use of forced perspective and scaling of 'buildings' so as to fit the scale of the overall setting. Hence, pavilions no longer had a distinct character of their own and there was virtually no building that would now escape the theme and scale of the overall thematic frame. Buildings became a part of the setting just like fireworks and paintings.

In 1817, all these elements were utilized in the new form of attraction: the 'live-show'. The most popular of Vauxhall's live shows was The Grand Spectacle: the Battle of Waterloo. Thousands of lamps, the sounds of canons firing followed by fireworks, huge paintings with soldiers and artillery, all made this a memorable experience. Another popular show was Naumachia that replaced the ground forces of Waterloo, a battle in which large warships moved back-and-forth while giant waves splashed sides of the attraction (South-worth 1941). Besides this type of entertainment, Vauxhall offered various events, such as rides, roundabouts or the circular Temple of Musicians surrounded by mobile seats where professional bands would perform on Sundays. Throughout its history, novelty and entertainment were the principal parts of this pleasure-garden.

In the early Nineteenth Century, the growth of cities into potential accident-machines made people permanently scared of London and its environs. Lack of immediate wars and an interest in war-based narratives, together with such fears created a series of entertainments based on large-scale urban accidents such as fire, earthquake or the eruption of a volcano. In the Great Fire of London the 'fireman' became a substitute for the 'soldier' providing the public with the desired pathos. The element of nostalgia evoked by travel into a foreign land or remote historical moment was replaced by the element of fear as visiting pleasure grounds became a travel into the alternative today. This brings one to the simulated fires of Coney Island in 1890s and a series of amusement parks in 1960s, such as Freedom-land, NY (1965) that had ironically disappeared in fires.

villagers from Shodo-shima perform at Shikoku Mura in order to preserve their rapidly changing cultural rituals.

As a theme park with a distinct character, Shikoku Mura is situated within its surroundings in an intriguing way: surrounding agricultural fields and the forest within which the village is situated are also a part of the environment of the theme park, including peasants that could be seen cultivating land on a few feet from the visitors. Many pathways extend into the fields and the theme park could be distinguished mostly by the density of its pathways and the intricacy of its landscaping. Visitors are encouraged to walk out of the boundary of the theme park and discover other places such are the graves of local Twelfth Century heroes who died in a decisive battle between the two ruling families, or places such as a popular on-site noodle restaurant.

> Our living standards have progressed greatly, and we are in the midst of a society filled with high-tech and information. But, we seek spirit more than material. And Shikoku-mura is just the right place to enjoy the origin of one's home. (Shikoku 1976: 4)

Religious Theme Parks

Since the mid-1980s, a number of religious theme parks has been proposed, designed, and some constructed, predominantly in the United States, but also in the developing theme park markets such as India and Brazil. Since a majority of such theme parks are founded as ministries, the major source of funding for these parks comes from followers's contributions. The large ones cannot commercially sustain the business by relying solely on donations, and must generate considerable revenues: the forerunner of large religious theme parks was Heritage U.S.A., founded by Jim Bakker as the Praise the Lord (PTL) ministry in Fort Mill, South Carolina in 1974. Heritage U.S.A. was a 2300 acre Christian theme park and also the home to its own cable television channel called the Inspirational Network. PTL also included a hotel (a new one was under construction when PTL fell into bankruptcy), a water park, a Barn Church and studio, a shopping center, a pyramidal office building, a replica of Billy Graham's childhood home, the Buffalo Park Amphitheater and it employed nearly 2000 people. PTL and Heritage U.S.A. fell into bankruptcy in 1988 and, the following year, Jim Bakker was convicted of defrauding the followers for US$158 million to build Heritage U.S.A. The amphitheater is still in use by the Narrow Way Productions ministry and large Christian productions are still occasionally held there, while a Christian-run condominium development and a PTA golf course (under the name of Regent Park development) have been added to the site. Large international ministries such as TBN, INSP or Opryland have followed the synergetic principles introduced by PTL: Trinity Broadcasting Network has a theme park called Trinity Music City U.S.A. in Hendersonville, Tennessee in addition to its home base complex in Santa Ana, California and a large complex in the Dallas-Fort Worth metroplex area. All of these facilities are capitalizing on the convergence of the television programming, themed retail and the commodification of spiritual experience in thematized environments.

On a more modest scale, Holy Land of the Americas, Inc. has been promoting its Bible World U.S.A. theme park since the early 1990s as the 'strongest Catholic experience ever'. It has been an ambitious theme park project still reportedly in the development phase: when completed, it will have 170 acres of attractions using Biblical stories as the rationale for its narrative structure. As the Bible is structured around a set of themes, these will be spatialized and visualized into life-size panoramas dramatizing the Bible, the Holy Land and its people. The setting is created as a replica of stories, people, customs, places, dress, wildlife, plant life, structure, food, bodies of water, mountains and other contents of the Bible World from Genesis through Revelation. The site for this theme park is strategically located at the intersection of the Interstate Highway IH-37, Loop 410 and Highway US181 in South-West San Antonio, Texas catering thus potentially to a day-drive radius within the so-called Bible Belt, but at the same time competing with giant secular attractions

If the physical formula of pleasure gardens was derived from public walks, and most directly from the Mall in St. James's Park that opened in 1660, the format of attractions was directly derived from the Picturesque Garden of the period, while the construction method came from the country fairs, such as Bartholomew's Fair. It was the time-span and therefore the commercial limitation of the country fair that pleasure gardens overcame, much as the theme park later overcame the commercial imperfections of World Fairs. Nevertheless, civil behavior and the elimination of trade made Vauxhall initially different from the contemporary country fair. When country fairs also eliminated trade, the major difference between the two was the civil order that pleasure gardens successfully maintained.

In the mid-1800s, pleasure gardens began appearing all over Europe, including Tivoli Gardens built in Copenhagen in 1843 and the Prater in Vienna built in 1850. The growth of London in the early 1800s made the land occupied by pleasure gardens too expensive to be kept for entertainment. Although financially successful enterprises, the profits derived from these commercial playgrounds were incomparable with the potentially unlimited profits in the ever-growing construction industry. By the 1850s, all of the pleasure gardens of London became building-sites for new Victorian structures (Ashworth 1954).

such are Six Flags Fiesta Texas and Sea World San Antonio. Placed 30 feet above the intersection will be the world's largest electronic picture Bible.

Zion's Hope, an evangelical ministry based in Orlando, Florida proposed a Christian theme park in the late 1990s to celebrate and promote Hebrew Christianity in the heart of a predominantly Jewish community of 25 000 people and about a 30-minute drive from Walt Disney World Resort. Despite strong protests from the Jewish community, it opened its gates to public in February 2001 as the Holy Land Experience, a US$16 million and a 15-acre theme park. As Mike Schneider of the Associated Press reported, at the opening day 'visitors were greeted by two actors dressed as Roman soldiers in armor, who talked about the history of Herod's Temple [...] On the steps of a re-creation of Herod's Temple, a half-dozen actors in biblical-period cloths sang songs about Christian persecution by the Romans and how Jesus would come back to save them' (Schneider 2001). Visitors's experience is supposed to represent that of walking through the ancient city of Jerusalem in B.C. 1450–A.D. 66 hence the park is also advertised as a 'living Biblical museum' (CNN 2001). In addition to live performances, the park also offers an interpretation of Jesus' tomb and the largest indoor-model of Jerusalem in the First Century A.D. including the plan of the city, the ancient Temple and scenes of everyday life. At the end of the tour, the theme park offers a gift shop with items characteristic of Hebrew Christianity.

Similar religious theme parks have been proposed in Nevada, in Columbus and Mesquite City (along IH-15), in Texas (Marianland along IH-6 South) and elsewhere in the United States. In Brazil, Magic Park in Aparecida is a Catholic theme park built on a 170-acre site located strategically in Vale do Paraíba on a day-drive radius from both São Paulo (110 miles) and Rio de Janeiro (160 miles). Besides its religious aspects, Magic Park is otherwise typical of the Brazilian theme parks that had emerged during the 1990s.

In the heart of Guruvayur region of India, a 2.5-acre site of the ISKCON's Krishna theme park is a fully equipped pilgrim center with facilities for mass-media communication 'to preach the glories of the Lord'. (ISKCON 1995) In March 2003, the International Society for Krishna Consciousness (ISKCON) and the Revival Movement (IRM) announced a purchase of a 20-acre site in Vrindavan, India. The land has been acquired to house the largest Krishna-Lila theme park in the world to be constructed by dioramas that will combine sound, light and movement using high-end digital robotics 'to produce what will truly be a spiritual Disneyland'. The first unsuccessful attempt to turn a predominantly rural Krishna community into 'a spiritual Disneyland' was launched by Kirtanananda, the guru for the Krishna commune in New Vrindavan, West Virginia in 1979 (Muster 1997: 54–60). The site for the latest theme park version is located on the major highway connecting Vrindavan with other regional and national urban concentrations and in close proximity to the Taj Mahal in Agra. This way, besides its potentially becoming a primary target for pilgrims and devotees, the Krishna-Lila theme park is also introduced as a secondary tourist target for millions of international tourists who visit the Taj Mahal. The theme park will also accommodate a newly designed township initially for 1000 residents who are anticipated to be devotees and who may wish to relocate their families to Vrindavan for the purpose of either retirement or to do service in the Holy Dhama' (IRM 2003).

Living in a Themed Mode
The nostalgia for East Germany, also known in Germany as *Ostalgie*, has spirited in the 1990s a couple of ideas for theme parks based on the ex-East Germany as a thematic framework. In 1994, in the ex East-German town of Prenden, located 20 miles north of Berlin, a board of local entrepreneurs had planned a theme park that would not only seal-off a number of Prenden residents from the rest of the world, but also facilitate their desires to continue living in a type of preservation (Kinzer 1994). The theme park was also supposed to facilitate

the desire of many others who never knew what life was like in the communist East Germany by coming to Prenden to experience it. Everyday items such are cars, clothes or food were to be limited to those previously used by people living under the Communist regime. In addition to conventional attractions like rides, a swimming pool and a zoo, there was also to be a museum of East Germany's social and political history and many other everyday things that characterized life in Eastern Germany. That such sentiments could be very profitable was clear after the film *Good Bye, Lenin* was seen by more than a million Germans. The film employed a similar narrative in which the main protagonist builds a themed stage-set in his apartment to protect his sick mother from the shock of German reunification (CNN 2003). Finally, in 2006, the idea might became reality: Massine Productions GmbH plans to recreate a 100 000 square-foot replica of East Germany in South Eastern Berlin district of Koepenick, in an abandoned industrial complex complete with border guards, rigorous customs inspections, authentic East German Deutche Mark banknotes, and restaurants with East German food (BBC 2003). The only major difference with the Prenden park, though, is that this theme park will have no residents. Another theme park in Germany that builds on the symbolic capital and the national nostalgia for a remote historical moment is Berlin's Babelsberg Studios, a theme park built on the grounds of the famous film studios where director Fritz Lang filmed his film *Metropolis* in 1926. *The Blue Angel* was also filmed there, as well as numerous Nazi propaganda films, some by Leni Riefenstahl.

Two contemporary examples clearly stand from a range of unsuccessful attempts to create such displaced living communities in a themed mode, but in radically different ways. Huis Ten Bosch, a Dutch town in Japan, fabricates a surreal living environment in Japan by instrumentalizing a foreign urban milieu as a metaphor for contemporary Japanese lifestyles. Celebration, Florida is a part of an historic attempt to conserve past cultural values and beliefs by creating an isolated ensemble self-metaphorized by its nostalgic employment of residential and civic architecture. Unlike Henry Ford's 1929 Greenfield Village and John D. Rockefeller Jr.'s 1932 Colonial Williamsburg in Virginia, Celebration was built from scratch.

Disney's Celebration

The emergence of Disney's town of Celebration in Walt Disney World Resort in 1995 has to be placed into a broader framework, not only with the fabricated contemporary desires of people to live and work within the theme park boundaries, but also in a peculiar relationship between Walt Disney and his version of city-making. As stated before, Disneyland Park was a nostalgic re-invention of an American mid-West town in which Walt Disney grew up. He was determined to re-create an idealized version of it, a clean, paved, disciplined and, above all, a predictable town. Foremost, it was conceived as an antidote to, and a rejection of the 'decadence' of the East-coast American industrial metropolis such as New York City; an attempt to create a place where people can walk safely, meet only the same type of people, and ecstatically consume, while learning about ever latent promises of the American free enterprise. This was clearly an antidote to the pedestrian in Manhattan who was, in Disney's view, afraid, alienated, and, foremost, unable to consume freely. Coney Island, Manhattan's paradise ground, was in Walt Disney's view a 'defective, poorly planned, conventional amusement park' (Findlay 1992: 63) that he inevitably intended to contrast. Since the latter had played a major role in the creation of metropolitan lifestyles, the metropolitan sensibility of Manhattan, it is not a coincidence that Walt Disney has constantly referred to this dialectical pair in order to make his point appealing: to Coney Island as an archaic type of amusement park, and to Manhattan as a 'malaise' he clearly wanted to contrast. Besides, Disneyland Park was not a replica of an existing urban model. The first theme-section in Disneyland to be based on an existing urban fabric was New Orleans Square, which opened in 1966. Here, a replica of New Orleans's French Quarter, more precisely a part of Bourbon Street, formed a themed island within the theatron of Magic Kingdom.

Therefore, despite of the fact that Disneyland Park was not conceived as a city, the rejection of the industrial metropolis model has been embedded in its creation (an attitude also obvious in HTB's relationship to the standardized model of provincial Japanese towns).

The ambition to make a city based on the experience of Disneyland came after accumulating the financial means, in the 1960s, when Walt Disney decided to build the Experimental Prototype Community of Tomorrow (EPCOT) in Florida. Initially, financial profit was not the only driving force behind Disney's plans for Disneyland as he understood it rather as a natural application of his public-service idealism and a sincere patriotic contribution: witness Disney's refusal to grant Russian President Nikita Khrushchev a permission to visit Disneyland Park during his visit to the United States in 1963.

> So that's what EPCOT is: an experimental prototype community that will always be in a state of becoming. (Walt Disney quoted in Prizer 1981: 36)

Until 1967, Disney acquired 27 000 acres of Florida's land with the firm intention to build this utopian city. Originally,[1] Epcot was designed as a radial city, heavily influenced by the planning methods of CIAM: as Walt Disney's early sketches show, the overall plan had a shape of dandelion. The circular core of the city was to be composed out of themed commercial facilities, restaurants, a city hall, numerous market stands, entertainment facilities and offices. Some early sketches show a large glass dome that spans the core of EPCOT, similar to that of Buckminster Fuller's geodesic dome designed to cover Manhattan. Later sketches show a glazed roof enclosing only commercial facilities. In any case, the dome was meant to assure perfect and stabile climate conditions within the leisure-oriented core of the city. Two, considerably tall[2] office towers formed the very center of the city and contained the majority of office spaces of EPCOT. Relatively high-rise apartment buildings[3] accommodating 20 000 residents enclosed the core of the city and were surrounded by a large

green belt. A series of roads developed radially from the core leading towards a low-density residential area accommodating nearly 50 000 residents and forming the outer edge of EPCOT. As Walt Disney put it:

> [EPCOT] will be a planned, controlled community; a showcase for American industry and research, schools, cultural and educational opportunities. In EPCOT there will be no slum areas because we won't let them develop. There will be no landowners and therefore no voting control. People will rent houses instead of buying them, and at modest rentals. There will be no retirees, because everyone will be employed according to their ability. (Walt Disney quoted in Mosley 1985: 287)

Walt Disney's effort to start the new tradition of inhabiting theme parks resulted in the town of Celebration, Florida, although significantly transformed and planned to 'house' up to 20 000 permanent residents. There is a rhetorical paradox here: in conventional architectural discourses, people 'inhabit' cities, here cities 'house' people. Celebration is a very peculiar theme park: it has no visitors, only permanent inhabitants. Besides the themeing of its environment, this town exercises most of the typical control mechanisms of theme parks. As in HTB, that means the total control over its theater of operations, facilitated by Disney's Government called Ready Creek Improvement District that has the right to control such public institutions as public schools, hospitals and public security. In conventional theme parks, admission fees figure as protection screens that keep unwanted visitors out of its gates. Likewise, property prices in Celebration effectively screen out unwanted potential neighbors based on the income-level criteria. Consensus entertainments at work. Besides the income requirements, potential inhabitants have to satisfy requirements imposed by the social and political agendas of this community: needless to say, Celebration is not a city based on any type of diversity, it is a conservative community based on unification, social segregation, exclusion, and the total control over the environment. The first glimpse of the plan and the entrance zone of Celebration reveals a very strong influence of Ebenezer Howard's garden-city concept and the first English towns he designed in the 1880s. A strong emphasis has been made on institutional 'anchors', in other words, on the traditional institutions which are heavily affected by, what Baudrillard has called 'the disappearance of the referential universe': post office, fire station, public square, bank, church, and school, the very same elements that formed the core of Lilliputia. These 300 000 square feet of 'high-architecture' institutional buildings were designed by a group of 'signature architects' including Aldo Rossi, Philip Johnson, Robert Stern, and Venturi Scott-Brown. The rest of the environment that creates a secondary appeal to the market segment targeted by Walt Disney Co. was designed internally by the Company. At the same time this is the only aspect of Celebration where an *a priori* resident participation and a relative diversity are allowed. 'We are not so rigid in our design as to not allow individualism', said Donald Killoren, Vice President of Celebration Company (Shanklin 1995) referring to the so-called 'Architectural Styles' designed to stimulates 'active relationship towards architecture'. In order to facilitate minimal customization, Celebration Company (a Walt Disney Company subsidiary) created a 'pattern book of architectural styles' supposed to guide both buyers and builders. There are six main 'styles' of harlequin dress linked to minor variations in internal patterns: Victorian (symmetrical in plan, with porches, verandas and steep sloped roofs), Classical (based on the old-south house, Greek revival with 'columned porches'), Colonial Revival (based on the 1920s–1940s house from the Tampa area, larger and symmetrical in plan), Coastal (also called French Colonial), French (based on 'French provincial architecture', with steep pitched roofs and stucco facades), and Mediterranean (stucco facades, red tile roofs, and arcades). Residents can combine the basic styles in a total of 15 variations, yet once the final configuration has been selected, no further customization is allowed to the principal look of the house, to colors, facades, roof tiles, window or door frames. The only area where individual owners are allowed to exercise their own 'style and taste' is on the 'sides, and rear entries of [their own] homes'.

As noted above, for both Celebration and HTB total control over environment means the control of all of the spaces, the organization and execution of pseudo-events, growth and development of towns to endless details, all public programs (which include schools, hospitals, post offices, fire stations, public security), TV broadcasting (CCTV), telecommunication lines, energy, heating, cooling, waste disposal, banking and all aspects of shopping. One recalls similar typologies, such as corporate towns, but residents of themed towns are not unified by a communal working environment. In both Celebration and HTB, a handful of residents work for the company. What brings these people together is a desire to live the difference, a predictable, ready-made, risk-free, consumable identity. The difference between Celebration and the rest of Florida's crime-watching neighborhoods and trailer-communities is significant. Likewise, the difference between HTB and the rest of Japanese provincial towns in which 24-hour convenience stores and vending machines grouped into 'Community Plazas' have replaced most of the communal functions is not to be underestimated. Identity acquired through clear marketing differentiation is the strongest marketing tool of both towns. Nostalgia for the moment in past when the architectural typologies they capitalize on had historical authenticity, goes hand-in-hand with the development of consumer capitalism and its need for clear market identity without which is difficult to commercialize any framework. Besides, both towns behave as laboratories possible only as isolated, precisely defined experiments that seem to appeal to an increasingly large numbers of people.

Huis Ten Bosch: 'A Town out of the Sea'[4]
In the period between 1983 and 1993, Japan experienced a 'theme park boom' as a direct consequence of an unprecedented economic growth and of the multiplication of Tokyo Disneyland Resort as a successful leisure-destination model (Yoshimoto 1994). Tokyo Disneyland Park opened in 1983 to immediate success: during its first year of operation more than 10 million visitors passed through its gates.

Quick and easy access from sea, land and air

■For more information, stop by the Huis ten Bosch Information Center at Hakata Station in Fukuoka. (tel.092-412-0080)

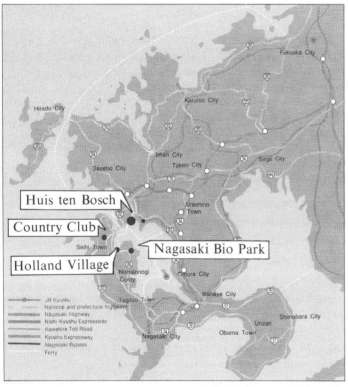

Access to Huis ten Bosch is available through JR Kyushu express train service, jetfoil service, and direct buses. A high-speed ferry links Huis ten Bosch to Nagasaki Airport for fast service for guests from Osaka or Tokyo.

To Huis ten Bosch on a leisurely, spacious bus : from Nagoya 1 hours and 10 minutes, from Osaka 10 hours and 10 minutes, from Kitakyushu 2 hours and 40 minutes, from Fukuoka 1 hour and 5 minutes, from Kumamoto 2 hours and 29 minutes, from Hirado 1 hour and 40 minutes, from Ureshino 46 minutes, from Nagasaki Shinchi 1 hour and 30 minutes, from Nagasaki Station 1 hour an 5 minutes and from Nagasaki Airport 51 minutes.

※Note that bus routes from Nagoya, Osaka and Kitakyushu are not direct route and that you will have to change buses midway.

Access to Holland Village

Holland Village is easy to reach by car or boat.
It is only 50 minutes by high-speed boat from Nagasaki Airport, 1 hour by car from Nagasaki City and 2 hours and 3 minutes by b from Hakata.

- by Amelia 40 minutes
- by Wapen van Hoorn 50 minutes
- by car 30 minutes

Let a personal guide take you around Huis ten Bosch!

While you are enjoying the sights and sounds of the park, our guest attendants will give you a full history of Huis ten Bosch, its concept and background.

TOUR	1-5 persons	6-10 persons	11-15 persons	16-20 persons
2 HOURS	¥10,000	¥12,000	¥14,000	¥16,000
3 HOURS	¥14,000	¥17,000	¥20,000	¥23,000

(Prices shown include consumption ta

Although Disney's attention to detail and the perfection of its systematic approach to design and management could have hardly been copied, Tokyo Disneyland Park was widely copied as an entertainment model by a series of small and mid-sized Japanese theme parks that targeted the day-market leisure seekers. As the statistics show, all of them were successful business ventures regardless of scale and size of their trade theater. Among them one can distinguish two basic types: the first represents different periods of Japanese culture and history, depicted as a set of ethnographic or anthropological situations (such are Nikko-Edo Mura in Tochigi Prefecture and Shikoku Mura in Kagawa Prefecture) and composed of buildings brought from different parts of Japan or from a particular prefecture. The second reinvents and represents the encounters of Japanese culture with foreign cultures (such as Huis Ten Bosch in Kyushu and Spain-Mura in Mie Prefecture) in which life-size simulations of foreign landscapes are carefully detailed (Yoshimoto 1994). The latter is the major Japanese type of theme parks and it is commonly called 'foreign village' (*gaikoku-mura*). Varying in scale and size, these theme parks represent countries as diverse as Turkey, New Zealand, Russia, Spain, U.S.A., Canada, China and others. Foreign villages have usually been criticized as an outcome of the 'traditional Japanese tendency to isolate and re-contextualize the foreign' (Robertson 1998). Such an attitude originated during the period of a rigorous self-imposed isolation (1639–1853, Edo Period) during which the Dutch had the privilege of being Japan's only trading partner.[5] The Dutch held a trading post on the remote southern island of Dejima near Nagasaki (Kyushu). Although their goods proliferated the territory of Edo Japan, Dutch traders were not permitted to leave the reclaimed island. The first Dutch ship, De Liefde, arrived at Dejima in 1600 bringing to the Japanese Western knowledge of astronomy, geometry, navigation, gunnery and shipbuilding. In 1820, a Dutch doctor Phillip Franz Von Siebold opened a private school (*Narutaki-juku*) in Dejima in order to disseminate the knowledge of Western medicine. It is thus through the Dutch that Western knowledge up until the Nineteenth Century was transferred

to Japan. Huis Ten Bosch (HTB) was built in 1992 near the old, Dutch port and it has been inaugurated as a continuation of 'the wide-ranging exchange through Nagasaki's long historical and cultural relationship with Holland' (HTB 1992).

Themeparking Huis Ten Bosch

By both the size of 60 acres and an investment budget of more than US$2 billion, HTB figures as one of the largest leisure facilities ever built in Japan. In order to justify its thematic proposal, HTB fabricates a mythological discourse within which it manipulates the actual historic facts and credits the Dutch for the development of modern Japanese science and culture. Japanese visitors are made to believe that they are not only re-examining the historically remote trading period with the Dutch, but also one of the most important parts of their own national history, and are simultaneously discovering the roots of modern Japanese culture. The Edo period is used as the mythological, historic repository that provides HTB with the important symbolic capital subsequently used to generate the enveloping narrative. The fact that HTB is built 'nearby the old trading post' is used to justify its ancestry character. Both HTB's location and its historic ties to Holland are manipulated to the extent that HTB presents itself as the natural and only possible format for the representation of that particular historic experience.

As its name instantly denotes, Huis Ten Bosch was conceptually modeled upon Holland. Moreover, both conceptually and visually, HTB is a Frankenstein-type bricolage made of various distinct parts of both the cultural and palpable landscapes of Holland. Themeing here is a manifold process as the historic ties and location form only one of the conceptual frames involved. The main theme is 'harmony between natural environment and living spaces' (HTB 1992), an acute theme for the contemporary Japanese society. Thus, the idea of employing Holland emerged from Japanese appreciation for the 'mastery that the Dutch achieved in balancing ecological concerns with progress'

(HTB 1992). This somewhat confusing conceptual layering generates the base for an intelligent marketing strategy: on each of the conceptual levels (ecological concerns, alternative living, Holland as tourist destination, national history and so on) HTB targets a specific segment of the Japanese tourist market. By combining the nostalgia for the glorious past inevitably lost by progress with an educational novelty of incorporating progress with ecological concerns, and with the desire to visit foreign places and cultures, HTB integrates apparently contradictory narratives. Nevertheless, as Jennifer Robertson noted, 'any given reinvented "traditional" village or "international" theme park constitutes an intersection and synthesis of apparently, and only apparently, contradictory trajectories [because they] erase as they reinvent the difference posed by places, artifacts, and peoples.' (Robertson 1998) As Sarah Chaplin pointed out, the consumption of foreign environments has a strong educational emphasis in Japan aimed towards developing Japan's 'cosmopolitan outlook as a nation' (Chaplin 1998). In order to make them even more foreign (*gaijin*) looking, names of these places are written in *katakana,* a script used to name cultural phenomena which are of essentially non-Japanese origin.

Nihon Sekkei designed and constructed HTB as a theme-park-town by parallel utilization of resort-town and theme park concepts beyond conventional definitions: they assumed that resort town conventionally implies both permanent residents and tourists while theme park implies enveloping of the visitors's environment by a homogeneous theme. Thus, the initial intentions accounted for 'full facilities of a resort-destination, [those] required for daily life in a city' (HTB 1992) as well as the standard theme park apparatus. The origin of HTB is in the early Holland Village (*Olanda Mura*) established in 1983 on the Western coastline of Omura Bay. Holland Village initially consisted of a fish restaurant called Bleomendam and a windmill. It was redesigned and enlarged several times under the supervision and management of a local businessman named Yoshikuni Kamichika and his Nagasaki Holland Village Co. Ltd. Holland Village had steadily expanded over the years and, by 1989, was able to attract over two million visitors a year. Since 1985, Holland Village began facing serious accessibility problems as a major obstacle to its growth: firstly, Holland Village's theater was located out of the reach of the major traffic infrastructure and far from the nearest railway line or airport. Its only supply artery was regional Road 206 that linked Holland Village with Sasebo and Nagasaki. This narrow, regional traffic corridor was too often jammed by visitors's cars and tour-buses.

Prior to the mid-1980s, the Japanese National government had the power to determine and control travel fares, to influence the fabrication and distribution of national tourist locations and to control the distribution of knowledge on these tourist sites through textbooks used in schools nationwide. After the economic boom of the early 1980s and the significant privatizations (the largest of which was that of the Japanese National Railways—JNR of 1987), the government was forced into partnerships with various private investors and venture capitalists in order to manage an unprecedented volume of passenger traffic related to increasingly complex tourist arrangements. These partnerships have been reflected in the highly sophisticated railway system of contemporary Japan. Within this system, the complex 'cluster-typologies' of post-war stations (Traganou 2003: 295) function as intersections of state and private investments. The railway system itself simultaneously facilitates the flows of patrons to specific destinations as it fabricates desires for them. This is of no surprise in the synergetic cycles of capital investments since the owners of the railroads also own real estate developments, amusement parks and department stores that are situated along the railway lines (Traganou 2003: 307). The Foucaultian system of 'openings and closings' that strictly determines both the time and ways of attendance to these heterotopian leisure territories (time factors and hauling factors mentioned above) is revealed also through the concept of 'play' (*asobi*). 'Play' is in Japan related to the category of 'spare-time' not entirely opposed to the continuum of 'work-time' and quite different

Aerial View of Huis Ten Bosch under construction in 1991. © Huis Ten Bosch Co.

from the Western 'free-time' (Huizinga 1949). Thus, in 'spare-time' that occurs on a couple of occasions annually, Japanese are engaged in a 'constructive pastime' that often takes a form of tourist travel. For instance, during the main national holidays such are *Obon* in the summer, the New Year (*Oshôgatsu*) and The Golden Week in May, millions of Japanese travel overseas or within the country. These occasions are reminiscent of military invasions as the entire national traffic network is organized to facilitate the movement of people from major urban concentrations to leisure locations. The so-called Bullet Train (*Shinkansen*) which moves at the speed of 160 miles pre hour leaves major train stations every three to five minutes and transports over half a million people a day. Major air-carriers increase the number of flights from urban concentrations to regional centers where leisure locations are distributed from one to four flights a day and can move more than 100 000 passengers a day. Within these entirely new economic conditions, Holland Village was unable to cope with the increasing tourist demand on one side and the old, regional (public) infrastructure on the other.

In 1985, Nagasaki Holland Village Co. made public its plans to massively expand its theme park and solve the traffic congestion problem. In September 1986, the Prefectural Government decided to assist

Nagasaki Holland Village Co. in the search for a new site by offering an abandoned industrial site in the region and by agreeing to finance and accelerate the construction of a new regional highway leading from Fukuoka to Sasebo (HTB). This highway would also link the new site with another major traffic node: Nagasaki International Airport. JR Kyushu (Japanese Railways, Kyushu Division) had agreed to construct the Huis Ten Bosch JR Station and had become one of the company's shareholders. All Nippon Airlines (ANA) also became a shareholder and built one of the major hotels on HTB's site. Over 120 leading Japanese companies invested into the HTB project, among them the Industrial Bank of Japan Group, Nippon Life Insurance, Nippon Yusen, NTT, Fujitsu, Matsushita Electrical Industrial Co., Mitsubishi Corporation, Mitsubishi Heavy Industries, JR Kyushu and ANA. Even Nagasaki Prefecture and the city of Sasebo became shareholders in Huis Ten Bosch Co. The new site was 60 acres of vacant, reclaimed land, originally designated for industrial development and within the reach of major national and regional traffic networks. In addition, its size was sufficient for future expansion plans. Subsequently, Nagasaki Holland Village Co. Ltd. changed its name to Huis Ten Bosch Co. Ltd. on the 1st October 1993.[6] An immense corporate interest and support for the project was embedded in the fact that HTB had been inaugurated as a tremendous experiment within which 'private enterprise will have

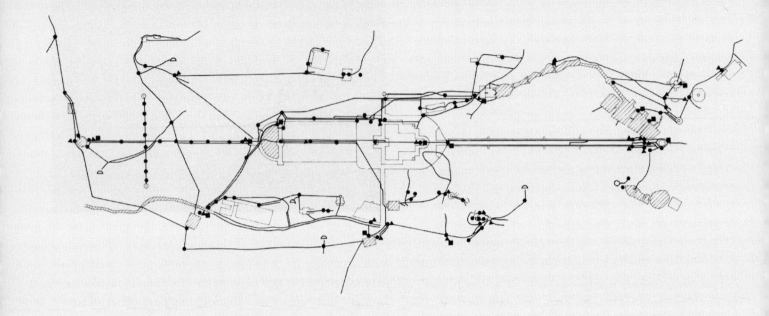

Map of Pratolino showing the sophisticated hydraulic system for the operation of the automata. Drawing by Luigi Zangheri, c. 1990. Used by permission from Mondadori Electa.

PRATOLINO—A THEATER OF AUTOMATA

Pratolino, a Xanadu of the Sixteenth-Century Florence, was owned and conceptualized by Francesco I de Medici, and designed by Bernardo Buontalenti, Tomaso Francini, Mastro Lazzaro delle Fontane and Bonaventura da Orvieto (1568–86). As a garden, Pratolino was an encyclopedic treasure-house of art, curiosities, marvels of natural world, mythical stories of the past, biblical narratives, and the technological wonders of the era (Zangheri 1987, 1991). The garden was divided into two distinct areas, the *Parco degli Antichi* (Park of the Ancients) on the north, and *Parco dei Moderni* (Contemporary Park) at the south side, with the Villa Medici located in the middle (Zangheri 1991a: 99). Its 'theater of automata' had a form of a labyrinthine open-air display with a series of scenes called 'theaters', most created as grottos depicting a particular historical or biblical scene (Ciuffoletti 1990). Gods like Apollo, Venus, Jupiter, as well as ordinary men, were represented with *automata*, hydraulic machines made of stone and powered by water (Jellicoe 1986: 454). These early animatronics were enacting scenes from daily life or particular biblical events. Each the-

the opportunity to manage a city' (Shigeyoshi 1994: 37). HTB's power to generate a wide palette of revenues was novel and included revenues ranging from the operation of the theme park (entrance fees, food concessions, souvenirs, etc.), to corporate sponsorships, corporate and individual membership fees, hotel operations, sales of real estate and to the daily purchases of HTB residents (merchandise, food and other necessities).

HTB's Socio-Economic Influence on the Region

Up until the mid-1980s, the Kyushu and Nagasaki Prefectures employed the majority of its work force in the ship industry and coal mines. Because of an enormous crisis in the ship industry, the policy of Kyushu government was to initiate a restructuring of the work force towards service industry, electronic industry and tourism. HTB is only one in a series of large-scale projects that changed the face of Kyushu in the 1980s and 1990s. With the support of the government and corporate shareholders, HTB initiated the restructuring of the regional work force and stimulated economic migrations on both the regional and national levels. In 1993, Sasebo city clearly registered a positive and desirable socio-economic climate for the first time since 1986 (HTB opened in 1992): almost 4000 new households started in its first year of operation had set a positive population trend. In 1993, HTB generated a turnover of US$924 million with all its adjacent services and suppliers. HTB alone made US$520 million, it employed nearly 4000 people on site and 13 000 people in the adjacent services. For instance, food suppliers alone employed nearly 200 people and generated a turnover of US$29 million; 500 people employed in agricultural services generated a turnover of US$11 million for 1993 alone. Of almost 60 food concessions in HTB, half are operated by the HTB Co. whereas the rest is operated by 50 small-size, regional companies. Sasebo city recorded an increase of over 10 percent in total tax revenues in comparison with 1992. All on-site employees were employed via Sasebo Work Service Co., a HTB Co. subsidiary. In 1993, nearly half of HTB's full-time employees and over three quarters of its part-time employees lived in Sasebo city, while the rest commuted from Nagasaki and other small towns in the region. Another significant fact is that HTB has changed the gender structure of regional work force by employing nearly 2000 women, nearly half of its entire on-site work force.

HTB was the first theme park in Japan to offer overnight accommodation. HTB's hotel facilities have been dispositioned on the site, keeping in mind the existence of the admission-fee zone and the admission-free zone. In 1993, there were five hotels built within the admission-fee zone with the capacity for 2000 guests. In 1996, two new hotels opened outside of the entrance-fee zone, close to the HTB's gate and the bus station, and within easy access to the park. In April 1996, HTB Co. and Nagasaki Jidosha, a regional automobile company, opened the Nikko Hotels International HTB. With nearly 400 rooms under its roof Nikko Hotels International HTB was the largest hotel in Nagasaki prefecture. During the first year of operation, it had

ater was composed of one or more *automata* placed in the foreground and the stage achieved by painted grotto walls that enhanced the illusion of *automata*'s act. Although the *automata* were able to repeat one or a few simple mechanical movements back and forth, water powered mechanisms imitating bird-songs or sounds of organs, together with other *giochi d'aqua,* completed the experience of this fairytale world (Mazzotta 1986).

Water for the *automata,* fishponds, lakes and plants was brought from distant springs several miles away through the hydraulic system designed by Bountalenti (Zangheri 1991: 59). Exotic plants, fish, birds and minerals, were exhibited as the wonders of natural world in this garden 'illuminated by knowledge'. Although wonders of the natural world provoked immense curiosity, technical inventions attracted most of the visitors's attention as they effectively popularized otherwise mythologized historical narratives. In doing so, Pratolino did not embed individual scenes into a coherent meta-narrative, but rendered each scene as a spatial and narrative fragment to be viewed and experienced separately, a practice enabled by the exclusionary character of the grottos. By juxtaposing the 'theater of automata' with exotic animals, plants and other wonders, Buontalenti blurred distinctions between the novelties of engineering, the wonders of natural world, and historical and biblical narratives: Pratolino also exhibited an encyclopedic paranoia Bountalenti called the 'world's wonders'. Technical perfection of the *automata* was the precondition for this project, because their perfection enhanced by background color and paintings, sound, and spatial exclusion formed a successful mechanism for an effective displacement of visitors into the

The Wonders of Mount Parnassus, Pratolino, Florence. Drawing by G. Guerra, c. 1580. Albertina, Wien.

field of imaginary. That is why Pratolino had a profound influence on European intellectual elite, and a series of garden-theaters based on the ideas first utilized in Pratolino emerged throughout Europe such as Fontainebleau, Hellbrunn, and Germain-en-Laye. Sadly, Pratolino was redesigned in 1819 by Joseph Fricks into a *giardino inglese* (Zangheri 1991a: 99).

an incredible 80 percent occupancy rate. In June 1996, HTB Co., JR Kyushu and ANA opened the ANA Huis Ten Bosch Hotel International, a 12-story building next to the JR HTB station at the entrance to the park. HTB's insurance company and one of the major shareholders, Dai Ichi Sei Mei, was also one of the owners of the new hotel. The ANA Huis Ten Bosch Hotel International was designed as a copy of the Amsterdam Railway Station although the scale of the building was 'adjusted to the available site'. Both hotels are chained with JR Kyushu, ANA and the Nikko Hotels International Corporation.

As is commonly the case in the theme park industry, 75 percent of HTB's overall profit is generated by its hotel business, especially from Hotel L'Europe with its 80 percent occupancy rate. By Japanese Tourism Biro (JTB) 1996 ratings, Hotel L'Europe was the most popular hotel in Japan, while HTB's Hotel Amsterdam ranked fourth. In 1995, HTB had the highest overall hotel occupancy in Japan with 96 percent: of over four million guests annually (until 2001), 500 000 stayed in hotels within HTB. Besides, the Average Guest Expenditure Rate (AGER) for Japan was US$40 500 per room in 1993; during the same period, HTB's Hotel Amsterdam had an AGER of US$80 800 per room annually.

The opening of HTB in 1992 boosted the regional hotel industry by the number of new hotels constructed in the area and by overall occupancy rates. Numerous new hotels and inns (*ryokan*) helped create nightlife in HTB and in turn increased the overall number of visitors to HTB and their length of stay. Since 15 percent of all HTB visitors stay overnight within HTB's proper and, given the average length of stay within HTB of five hours and 15 minutes a day, the remaining 85 percent of its visitors spend the rest of their time outside the park's gates. This has been clearly registered by occupancy rates of local inns (*ryokan*) and hotels outside HTB (in Sasebo city) as they doubled their occupancy rates and had recorded an overall occupancy rate of 65 percent during the first year of operations.

The most convenient way to register the impact of HTB on the region is to measure the increase in regional traffic flows: since September 1991, there was been an increase in highway traffic to and from HTB due to construction. In 1993, the closest highway interchange had a 30 percent average increase in vehicular traffic when compared to the 1991 figures. From 1992–97, slightly over 58 percent of all HTB visitors came by cars or buses, whereas 21 percent arrived by airplane. In 1993, Nagasaki Airport recorded the highest ever figures of 2.7 million passengers which meant an almost 12 percent increase since 1991. This groundbreaking figure was a direct consequence of increased number of flights to and from Nagasaki Airport introduced by major air carriers in 1992. JAS (Japan Air System) introduced a new Sapporo-Nagasaki route with three flights per week and Osaka-Nagasaki with one flight daily. JAL (Japanese Airlines) increased the number of flights on its Tokyo-Nagasaki route from one to two flights daily and ANA increased its Osaka-Nagasaki route from one to five flights per day. During the same period, almost 22 percent of HTB visitors arrived by train: JR Sasebo railway line also registered an increase of 22 percent, while other lines in Nagasaki Prefecture leading to competing tourist attractions (such as Nagasaki-Honsen) had a decrease

of 10 percent in the number of passengers. Since March 1992, the HTB Line between Hakata and HTB increased the number of trains from three to eight per day. Ship lines (Fujimaru, Aska and Oriento Binasu) also increased the frequency of their traffic from three to nine arrivals per day between HTB and the Sasebo Port. Over 90 percent of the visitors arriving by airplane to Nagasaki Airport choose to commute to HTB by ship; the remaining 10 percent uses bus services.

Constructing a Tourist Landscape

On the Prefectural scale, HTB has made a significant impact not only in terms of bringing new tourist flows to the region, but also by re-mapping the existing distribution of tourist targets and figures. When compared with the figures of 1991, 1993 figures registered an increase of 140 percent in the overall number of tourists to the Nagasaki Prefecture to almost 28.5 million. One-day tourists made the most significant increase of 24 percent, while tour-visitors had made only a two percent overall increase. However, main tourist targets prior to HTB (Nagasaki city and Kohama-cho) had registered a significant decrease in the number of visitors: four percent in one-day visitors and six percent in tour-visitors. At the same time, the Sasebo area had registered an increase of 10 percent in one-day visitors and five percent in tour-visitors. By April 1993, Sasebo city registered an increase of 115 percent when compared to 1991 figures. These figures are only

relatively high: the city of Kyoto, one of the nation's most visited tourist site, has nearly 60 million visitors per year with a permanent population of 1.5 million (Graburn 1983: 3).

Even though Japanese economy went into a severe recession in 1992 just before HTB opened, within the first year of operation, HTB recorded 3.75 million visitors. During the second year of operation (until April 1993), HTB registered a four percent increase in the number of visitors to 3.9 million despite the fact that one of the major trends in the theme park industry is the second-year decrease in the number of visitors. HTB avoided the customary decrease thanks to an aggressive marketing of its brand, new attractions added to the park and the new membership club called the Molen Club.

In terms of its trade theater, demographics, attendance figures and guest expenditure rates, a comparison between HTB and Tokyo Disneyland Resort (TD) is illustrative: unlike TD that covers one-day market HTB covers the tour market. This fact implies a few important differences. Firstly, the number of repeat-visitors in HTB is not significant (35 percent as opposed to 60 percent in TD) because the access time to HTB from major urban concentrations such are Tokyo and Osaka is up to five hours on average and it costs approximately US$500, while the average access time to TD is two hours and the cost is up to US$20.[7] Secondly, HTB's primary trade theater is populated by nine million people (the population of Kyushu), whereas TD's primary trade theater has a population of 30 million people (Tokyo Metropolitan Area). The attendance figures for 1996 show the difference: TD had 15 million visitors while HTB had 4.2 million visitors. Thirdly, even though HTB has fewer visitors due to their extended stay it also has a much higher expenditure rate: in 1996 HTB had the highest AGER (Average Guest Expenditure Rate) in the world at US$150 per day while TD had US$120 per day. HTB's AGER was composed of expenditures for admission (US$50), food (US$25), shopping (US$35), touring (US$10) and hotel (US$30). Although overnight stays in HTB averaged over US$100 per night, the fact that only 15 percent of guests stay in HTB's hotels lowers the average expenditure on overnight stay to US$30 per guest.

After the initial success and a drop in the attendance figures in 1994, HTB Co. realized that the only way to increase hotel occupancy, the length of stay and guest expenditure was to link HTB with other regional attractions and to advertise it as a part of the 'Kyushu tours'. The connection with other sightseeing spots in the area led to the project called HTB Sightseeing Cooperation. In April of 1997, HTB Co. founded a subsidiary HTB Sightseeing Co. after the market analysis suggested that the strength of HTB package-tour market lay in networking the sites of tourist interest in the region. The whole West side of Kyushu was turned into a resort area, thanks to the connection and network of tourist attractions within it. Some of them are also owned by HTB Co. such as Nagasaki Bio Park and Nagasaki Holland Village. HTB Sightseeing Co. was the 11th HTB subsidiary company with the business of expanding the interest into the region and therefore strengthening the position of HTB within it. The nature of the tour-market demanded such a move because three-night, four-day tours and four-night, five-day tours are the most common tour-types to Kyushu, for both Japanese and other Asian tourists. In the new arrangement, one out of three or two out of four nights in Kyushu

were spent in HTB hotels. Special events were designed for the tour guests: evening shows that started earlier in the winter, specialty shops that stayed open later in the summer, bars, night clubs and even gambling pubs. Special seasonal events were designed to further facilitate the making of package tours and also to increase the number of repeat visitors. They were specifically well suited to what is in Japan called the 'field-trip visitors': anniversary tours, graduation tours and honeymoon tours. In 1992, HTB was visited by 320 000 field-trip visitors, while in 1993, there were 420 000 such visitors. The Japanese commonly travel in groups varying from three to five people, to hundreds of people, depending on the nature of the tour. Group visitors and field-trip visitors constitute up to 60 percent of theme park visitors in Japan. There are two major group formations: one that has a tour format, a leader (or a tour guide) and is usually composed of peers from the same company, school children or college students; the second is a less hierarchical formation composed of friends and family members or honeymoon tourists.

One of the ways of increasing the number of regional tourists and the repeat visits was the invention of the Molen Club. The Molen Club is a membership system for Sasebo and Nagasaki area citizens with an annual fee of US$100. In 1997, Molen Club had 50 000 members who visited HTB restaurants after work and during holidays in order to enjoy the seasonal events, read a book or relax in its scenic environment. The membership status does not include entrance to the attractions, but allows one to visit HTB at any time (during its operating hours) and enjoys its scenery. The social practices of drinking coffee in an outdoor cafe, enjoying the movement of relaxed crowds, sitting on a bench and gazing at people passing by, let alone observing tulips and boats plying along the canals and facing a copy of Hotel L'Europe, are practices historically unknown to the Japanese. It is this element of social displacement, reinforced by the apparatus of the visual one, that places HTB within the realm of imaginary. Some of the members use HTB as their own garden, feed birds and enjoy what the

Private wedding ceremony in Huis Ten Bosch.

HTB Passport.

company calls the 'HTB original style'. The HTB Company, on the other hand, sees club members as future residents. With the member-card, visitors can also attend other attractions in the area owned by HTB Co.: Holland Village and Sasebo Bio Park. In order to enable the same movement to other tourists, HTB Co. has since March 1997 offered the so-called One Day Passport. Corporations are encouraged to pay the 'membership fee' and become members of HTB's Molen Club. Corporate membership provides a quota for a number of overnight stays in HTB's hotels for corporate employees. What that means practically is that where a regular tourist would have paid US$450 for an overnight stay in Forest Villas, a corporate employee pays only US$25 per person and the difference is covered by the corporate membership.

The demographics at play in HTB are typical for the Japanese tour market: 60 percent of all HTB visitors are women. Twenty five percent are women aged 25–30 years of age, and the rest are women between 30–35 years of age, or women over 50 years of age. They come in groups of two or three and normally on two nights, three days package tours. Because of their social status, women are the main target group for the tourist marketing in Japan. The nature of social demand on women turns them into shopper-travelers heavily manipulated by travel books. Within that context, both the social and cultural meaning of HTB are carefully negotiated public images created through the press, television, movies and movie trailers, Internet, advertising and most of all by books on travel. In Japan, travel books are brought to such a level of sophistication that each specific travel interests has a public discourse on its own that reaches far beyond the pragmatic meaning of travel literature itself. It affects and it is in turn affected by the life-styles of entire socio-economic groups (market segments). Thus, an intricate socio-cultural program is developed out of an interest in travel and its parameters are assigned by the fabrication of desires and expectations much before one visits the actual tourist site. The way one experiences HTB is largely predetermined and framed by these cultural artifacts. In that respect, Mark Gottdiener was right when he noted that 'the key economic relation of the consumer society is not the exchange of money for goods as it was in the Nineteenth Century, but the link between the promotion of desire in the mass media and advertising, and the commercial venues where goods and services can be purchased.' (Gottdiener 1997: 70) A typical travel book covering theme parks would always have a map that

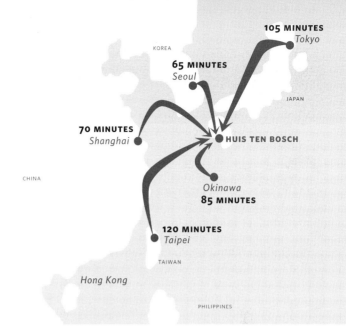

Map depicting distances between Huis Ten Bosch and major urban centers in the region.

105 MINUTES
Tokyo

KOREA

65 MINUTES
Seoul

JAPAN

70 MINUTES
Shanghai

● HUIS TEN BOSCH

CHINA

Okinawa
85 MINUTES

120 MINUTES
Taipei

TAIWAN

Hong Kong

PHILIPPINES

relates the desirable amusement destination to the traffic network, commonly railway. In HTB's case, the map locates HTB within complex railway, highways and air traffic networks and provides an estimate of commuting time and cost. Whether it is a holiday, a week or two week long tour, or a daily excursion, the travel book provides information on accommodation, sightseeing locations, attractions, seasonal events, shopping opportunities, regional food specialties and other travel information always through the universal, user-friendly templates.

One of the examples that describes the symbiosis of the world of media with the material world of HTB is the Noah Theater, designed and built in collaboration with the media giant NHK, a major National television station. The Noah Theater in HTB was built as a symbolic landmark that can be seen from the sea and, in contrast to the rest of HTB, buildings it was built out of white stone. The story of Noah is educational and it is related to the sea, harbors, tools and ships; educational films showing in this 360-degree theater are produced by the educational arm of NHK and framed by the major theme: 'Protection of the Environment'. The same films were aired to national audiences through a variety of NHK's educational programs. HTB Co. has been

planning other attractions in arrangements with the NHK aimed at further spanning the void between the world of television and the material aspects of themeparking.

The statistics show that, instead of reducing a desire to travel to Holland, HTB has actually increased the number of Japanese tourists to Holland to almost 140 000 in 1996.[8] Nevertheless, the number of Dutch and other non-Asian tourists is insignificant. Due to the geographic location of HTB's theater, HTB marketing has focused on developing trade areas primarily in the South-East Asia. The leisure and amusement activities in Japan at the time met almost 60 percent of overall demand for the entire South-East Asia, and was estimated at over US$60 billion (ICON 2002: 48). Nagasaki Airport is geographically located in the very center of Asia: from Tokyo to Nagasaki it takes one hour and 45 minutes, and from Shanghai to Nagasaki takes one hour and 10 minutes by air. HTB started in 1992 with less than 4000 Asian tourists, and only four years later, in 1996–97, it had registered an increase to 320 000 Asian tourists. The significant increase in the number of Asian visitors was a direct result of HTB's heavy marketing activities in Asia that began in 1993: initially the

KANKO MARU

This is a replica of the Kanko Maru, Japan's first steam/sailing ship, presented by King Willem III of The Netherlands to the Tokugawa Shogunate in the closing years of the Edo Period. This navy vessel became the training ship for the newly established Nagasaki Naval Institute, from which many influential leaders of that time graduated.

[Capacity] 300 passengers.
[Duration] 35 minutes.
[Departure]

1	12 : 00	During the months of
2	13 : 00	December, January and
3	14 : 00	February no cruises except
4	15 : 00	for public holidays and New
5	16 : 00	Year (Dec. 31 - Jan. 3)

● FARE

Adults	13 - 17 yr.	6-12 yr.	STARS
Yen 1,200	Yen 900	Yen 600	★★★★ ★★★★★

HARBOR CRUISER

Take a cruise in and around the harbor of Huis Ten Bosch on one of these colorfully designed small excursion boats. The beauty of Huis Ten Bosch's traditional Dutch scenery is even more striking when viewed from the sea.

[Operation hrs.] March - Nov: 09:30 - 17:40.
Dec. -Feb. : 09:30 - 16:40.

[Duration] 15 min.
[Capacity] :max. 12pers.

● FARE

Adults	13 -17yr.	6-12yr.	Stars.
Yen700	Yen500	Yen350	★★★★★

CRUISING THE CANALS AND BEAUTIFUL OMURA BAY.

CANAL CRUISER

Excursion boats designed in the classic image of 17th. century Dutch canal boats take you on a tour through the canals of Huis Ten Bosch in an atmosphere of tradition and gracefulness. Enjoy the beautiful view while sailing through the 6km. canals past the brick houses of the residential area Wassenaar, the terrasses of Utrecht and many more interesting places.

[Operation hrs.] Mar.-Nov.: 09:00 - 19:30.
Dec.-Feb. : 09:00 - 17:30.

[Duration one way] 13min.
[Capacity] 51 pers.
[Number of boats] 14.
[Route] Kinderdijk - Utrecht - Kinderdijk.

● FARE

ADULTS	CHILD (6~12yrs)	STARS
YEN800	YEN400	★★★★★★

PARTY CRUISER

These small party boats recall the private pleasure boats of the nobility. Charter one and create your own special memories while enjoying views of Huis Ten Bosch from the water.

[Operation hrs.] 09:00 - 20:00
[Capacity] Max. 12 pers.
[Number of boats] 5.
[Available cruises] :
S-course:30 min.max 12 pers, Yen 10,000.no food/drinks
A-course:60 min.,max 12 pers, Yen 20,000.no food/drinks
B-course: 60 min, 3 to 4 pers, Yen 30, 000.incl. hors d'oeuvres and drinks.
C-course: 60 min, 7 to 8 pers, Yen 40, 000.incl. hors d'oeuvres and drinks.
D-course: 60 min, 12 pers, Yen 50, 000.incl. hors d'oeuvres and drinks.
Reservation: tel. 0956-27-0011 or 0956-27-0526, at least 3 days in advance

Package-tour promotional material used by
Huis Ten Bosch Co. © Huis Ten Bosch Co.

Typical Huis Ten Bosch promotional material
used in theme park-related journals.

A typical lock-gate that connects Huis Ten Bosch canals with Omura Bay.

marketing campaign targeted Taiwan, Korea, Hong-Kong, Singapore, Malaysia and Indonesia. In October 1993, HTB had a promotional campaign for Taiwanese tourist agents in Taipei and offered the so-called Voucher Contract to tourist agencies in order to promote and facilitate the tourist flow. They created television commercials in all the major Asian languages and distributed them throughout Asia. Three quarters of all Asian tourist to HTB are Taiwanese tourists; moreover, in 1996, there was an 'HTB Boom' in Taiwan. HTB still figures as the most popular tourist destination for Taiwanese outside Taiwan. The number of Chinese tourists steadily increased since 1995, especially after Hong Kong's return to China in 1997. The ambition of HTB Co. has been to become 'The International Tourist Gateway to Asia' as Dejima was in the Sixteenth Century.

Although HTB had established a positive trend that culminated in 4.2 milion visitors in 1996–97, its attendance figures have steadily fallen due mostly to the large economic recession at work in Japan in the last years of the Twentieth and the first years of the Twenty-First Century. In 2003, HTB was visited by an all time low number of 2.3 million visitors. This trend, coupled with unsold housing capacities, an enormous debt (that came also as a result of serious undercapitalization), early unreasonably high investments into themeing, and a large pre-opening budget, have brought Huis Ten Bosch Co. to a debt

level of US$1.92 billion and a negative net worth of $31 million. Subsequently, Huis Ten Bosch Co. was forced into bankruptcy and HTB was placed in receivership (Zoltak 2003a). Given that the Nagasaki Prefecture and the city of Sasebo are shareholders in HTB Co., and that HTB has so systematically become the driving force of the regional economic growth, the Nagasaki Prefecture and the city of Sasebo have allocated US$3.6 million in financial assistance to HTB and have pledged a general public support for the theme park. The Kyushu Japan Railway Co. (JR Kyushu) has introduced discount travel fares in order to boost repeat attendance. As Zoltak reported, Ripplewood Holdings, an American investment fund, and Oriental Land Co., the owner of Tokyo Disneyland Resort, have expressed interest in purchasing or leasing HTB (Zoltak 2003a).

Themeing Huis Ten Bosch

HTB project began as a collaboration between Yoshikuni Kamichika and Takekuni Ikeda. Yoshikuni Kamichika, the President of Huis Ten Bosch Co., is a self-educated businessman and a native of Sasebo city. His ambitions with the HTB project were to improve his native region economically, make a living, and leave what he believed would be an important legacy. Takekuni Ikeda, the President of Nihon Sekkei, is a Tokyo University graduate holding a Ph.D. in Environmental Design. The reason for his involvement with the HTB project was his long-time ambition to build a sustainable urban environment, an ecologically visionary town that will 'last for centuries and grow old beautifully'. His insistence on the proper ecological attitude and the concern for environmental protection systems had increased the level of investment for over 50 percent to a total of us$2 billion. Therefore, as much as HTB was designed as a theme park, it was also designed as an environmental laboratory with the most sophisticated technology for environmental protection available at that time.

Most of the land covered with HTB's theater of operations was reclaimed during the Edo period (1600–1868). Reclamation was carried out a number of times and the present configuration of the site was achieved in 1977 for an unsuccessful purpose of establishing a major industrial complex. The project failed because of water shortage and the mid-1970s oil crisis. The site was 375 acres of vacant, reclaimed land with the entire basic infrastructure already built in. However, the concrete made quays and other alterations made during the reclamation caused an environmental disaster that began affecting the larger area of Sasebo. HTB designers initially attempted to return the site to its natural condition by bringing natural stone from the surrounding mountains and building old-fashioned wave breakers and 7.5 miles of seabanks in place of concrete quays. Besides, a fundamental alteration and renovation of plant and soil environment was undertaken and the ground was filled with 6.5 feet-deep landfill to enable settling. These early operations enabled the slow and incremental restoration of the natural ecosystem on the site. Nearly four mile-long canals were then built into the site connecting it directly with Omura Bay. Utmost attention was given to the quality of water in canals: the sea water was designed to change every four days by mechanical devices that induce the water flow through difference in sea level. As opposed to the Netherlands, where common vertical difference between the canal level and the pavement level is about three feet, in HTB the difference was designed to be eight feet because of the local site-requirements and safety reasons. The lock-gates that

connect HTB canals with the Omura Bay were constructed at two locations, and a traditional drawbridge was placed over each lock-gate. Canals were then spanned by bridges constructed at 25 locations. Additional facilities were constructed to handle the arrival and departure of cruise ships, high speed boats from Fukuoka, Sasebo, Nagasaki Airport, and the shuttle boats between HTB and Holland Village.

High ecological standards were also made possible by the rigorous organization of waste disposal: nearly 70 percent of solid waste is recycled on the site, and over 30 percent is burned. The main energy source for the entire theater of operations is natural gas from regional resources, as well as non-polluting fuels for service vehicles on site. There are three ways of waste disposal: recycling (for metal aluminum, cardboard and steal), burning (for light waste) and compost disposal for organic waste (still under development). Moreover, HTB's sewage treatment plant is the first private sewage treatment facility in Japan to receive state financing due to its positive impact on the region. The sewage treatment plant, energy plant, desalted water supply plant, main distribution center, and the man-power center are all located on the North-West perimeter line out of the reach and sight of visitors.

The HTB project established a new set of ecological standards for construction which have been used not only in the immediate region, but also nationally. Before HTB opened in 1992, the Biological Oxygen Demand of the sea level (BOD) in Omura Bay had a value of 2mgr/l, while Chemical Oxygen Demand (COD) level was 7.7mgr/l on the sea surface, and 7.1mgr/l at the sea bottom. Such levels were maintained through the construction process and later through regular use. Since the initial construction works began, the ecological conditions of the site (BOD, COD, gravity of sea water) were measured annually at nine different points in order to maintain a high level of ecological standards. The Japanese National Standard allows for the pollution level of sea water (PPM level) of 20, while HTB had established a new eco-logical standard by keeping PPM level at as low as two.

The next step in shaping the theater of operations was to record natural (environmental) sounds on the site and in the immediate vicinity over a 24-hour period, twice a year in spring and autumn. In parallel, by restoring the natural ecosystem, HTB designers also restored environmental sounds that had disappeared during the reclamation processes. The design team subsequently conducted an environmental impact study in order to anticipate peak levels of the design-day sound volume to be generated by future performances, machinery, and peak numbers of visitors. Based on those studies, the entertainment capacity of the park and the sound qualifying factors were taken into account and values of acceptable noise pollution were determined. In 1992, when HTB went into full operation new recordings were made and compared with the initial studies. Differences in levels were corrected then to make sure that noise pollution was reduced to a minimum. In order to maintain the level of noise pollution at acceptable levels, Nissan designed special HTB low-noise vehicles the speed of which is limited to nine miles per hour. All of the potentially noisy environmental modules (attractions and rides) were placed within building envelopes in order to reduce the emission of noise into the environment.

Before the buildings were erected, a two mile-long network of underground walk-in utility tunnels was built in order to facilitate maintenance of the infrastructure and other services needed for the operation of HTB. The tunnels are 20 feet wide and eight feet high, with main lateral entrances organized in the areas that are out of the reach of visitors, and secondary vertical entrances distributed around the park in order to enable daily maintenance. The tunnel is not used for food and other supply services, those are transported on the ground level and are visible to visitors. After the tunnel was completed, the grounds were covered by approximately 30 acres of pavement made of natural stone, and over 10 million bricks imported from the Netherlands. Just like in the Netherlands, bricks and stones are laid upon a layer of sand.

The entire planting and landscaping scheme was divided into three distinct areas. 'Urban zone' was planted with Formosa Gum, Chinese Elm, Horse Chestnut and Katsura trees. 'Forest zone' was planted with vegetation indigenous to the region such are Tabu, Camphor, Camellia and Japanese Laurel. Finally, the 'Green Belt' that mediates between 'Urban zone' and 'Forest zone' is planted with evergreen trees, deciduous trees and flowering trees.

In 1992, HTB won the '32nd Engineering House Prize' for the most superior environmental design in Japan. In 1993, Dr. Takekuni Ikeda created the Ikeda Institute, an environmental research institute that uses HTB as a permanent case study. In May of the same year, HTB introduced new attractions that promoted environmental protection as a viable theme. In parallel, they also created the backstage-tour featuring facilities and plants for environmental protection. By exposing the environmental philosophy underlying the HTB project as well as the infrastructure that puts it in motion, HTB Co. capitalizes on 'the new system of values that should serve as the model for the 21st-Century urban development in Japan', and presents itself as the naturalized leader of such efforts. The symbolic capital is then utilized as a theme for the consumption of the theme park environment.

In order to facilitate the flow of information and goods within the theater of operations, an advanced information integrated system was developed. There are three basic layers of the integrated communication cable network: BA LAN, DBA LAN and CATV. BA LAN (Environmental System Building Automation) is used for safety control (video surveillance), information on buildings, shops, hotels, electricity, air-conditioning, and so on. Building automation is divided into five zones: Service, Pastoral, Bay Town, Old Town, Amenities and Hotels Zone.

Resting points in the Port and in Binnenstad,
Huis Ten Bosch

Besides the central control monitoring device in the Energy Center that controls the five sub-monitoring stations, control has been decentralized so that each zone has its own automatic control point to handle daily maintenance problems. DBA LAN (Digital BA) is used for telephone lines and communications, both within and outside of the HTB network. CATV is an intelligent information network operating 24-hours a day and is used for emergency information and both visual and sound broadcasts. Its most elementary use is Voice Information, aimed at informing the visitors about pseudo-events, performances, weather conditions, and so on. On more advanced levels, CATV is used for FM broadcasting, TV broadcasting, and Video broadcasting. FM broadcasting defines the aural space by two external FM radio stations and 10 local music channels that provide the entire theater of operations with music and soundscape. The sound level and the choice of music are determined in the central control point and are synchronized with the daily score. Some shops in peripheral locations have tapes and CDs with Dutch music to choose from. TV broadcasting produces pseudo-events simultaneously on six local frequencies that feature 'information' on retail opportunities or previews of coming attractions. Satellite broadcasts are also available through CATV and there are several channels to choose from. Local TV broadcasts

of 'daily events' is probably the most didactic of the broadcasts aimed at broadcasting performances occurring in real time, as well as in evening and morning hours. Video broadcasting is facilitated by an automatic video library and the re-broadcasting production system. The video library is composed of video tapes made in the Netherlands and features filmic sequences of various parts of Dutch landscape, historic monuments, people and their customs, and festivals. It is meant to set the 'mood and atmosphere' for the consumption of HTB's totalizing narrative.

The total built floor surface of the theater of operations is over two million square feet in over 150 buildings. In terms of its size, HTB is nearly the same size as the small city-states of Europe such as Monaco and Luxembourg. As in Disney parks, HTB designers structured the environment using the 'enveloping by theme' strategy: since designers employed 'the rationale of Dutch city-making', theatra were formed by gimmicking actual principles of growth and development of Dutch cities. HTB designers studied the history of urban formations in the Netherlands and selected Amsterdam as a planning model because of its ur-quality, that is because its morphology immediately reveals its history. That morphological feature

was then employed as an ideal vehicle for visualizing the fictional growth of Huis Ten Bosch. The town was to be built and organized around a framework of canals, plazas and streets. The most important feature of this framework is certainly the canal because its form and layout determine the morphology of the town. Besides, the canal that physically divides the territory of the park also operates as a buffer area between the distinct theatra. The theater of operations was then divided into six principal areas: Old City District, New City District, Pastoral Zone, Port Area, Forest Zone and Residential Zone.[9]

The Old City District, also called Binnenstad, forms the core of the theme park environment and it was fictionally built in the period between the Twelfth and Fourteenth Centuries with narrow facades and smaller bricks used in construction. Prins Willem-Alexanderplein, as the central square is called, was modeled after the central square in Gouda, along with a copy of Gouda's Stadhuis as the visual anchor. As in Amsterdam, where canals separate different parts of the city that developed from its core, the canal separates the core from other theatra. Then came the imaginary development period between the Fourteenth and Seventeenth Centuries, and the town expanded forming the New City District, also called Nieuwstad, and also expanding towards the Port Zone and Paleis Huis Ten Bosch. This theatron has larger houses, wider facades, and larger bricks used in construction. Nevertheless, the town still remained within the medieval walls. In the imaginary Nineteenth and Twentieth Centuries, Huis Ten Bosch developed farther including now the residential area called Wassenaar, the HTB Railway Station, the Forest Zone, Breukelen and Kinderdijk. It goes without saying that this imaginary historical development has been squeezed into the five years that took to design and construct Huis Ten Bosch. This strategy thus allowed Huis Ten Bosch's designers to organize the theme park into semiologically and programmatically distinct environmental envelopes, theatra. As in the Netherlands, bridges span these 70 feet-wide canals and allow visitors to move between different theatra. It is precisely with the

ENGINEERING THE FIELD OF VISION

Versailles was a site of many peculiar events, one of which was the simulation of a medieval village designed by Hubert Robert and Rochard Mique for Marie Antoinette (Jellicoe 1986: 588) where members of the royal court acted as farmers at daily duties while Marie Antoinette performed as a milkmaid dressed in peasant clothes (Williams 1958: 20). In Baroque France, the royal château was replacing the previous model of the Italian villa, but it was still located on the site following the principles established in Italy during the Sixteenth Century: it was linked to the town on one side and the infinity of nature on the other, mediating between the two (Giedion 1949: 134–140). The Château of Versailles, designed for Louis XIV in 1680s, was 'U' shaped and contained the official residence of the King, together with various French ministries. A highway linked Versailles with the Champs-Élysées and the Louvre in Paris. In 1683, Louis XIV proclaimed Versailles his official residence, a move that caused strong opposition, much as Hadrian's decision to move his residence and the court to the site of Villa Adriana in the Second Century B.C. The complexity of buildings and the character of their juxtaposition with nature was quite novel at the time and as Giedion noted, this arrangement of buildings and gardens was directly confronted with nature, anticipating in many ways later planning principles of Haussmann (Giedion 1949: 72). The layout of the gardens was an application of the Italian Renaissance model displaced onto the flat lands of continental Europe, although monumental in scale. Nevertheless, the ambiguity conventionally associated with the symbolic role of the Renaissance *parterre* was broken in favor of an understanding of 'shapes' as 'indications of movement and rest' (Vérin 1991: 136). The separation of cosmic symbolism from the design of *parterres* was achieved by the end of the Seventeenth Century when the emphasis shifted towards visual laws of pattern-making and the application of various ready-made patterns such as Turkish embroideries or Italian tapestries (Vérin 1991: 142). The new visual *rigueur* emphasized the cumulative effect of the juxtaposition of different patterns. This was a direct consequence of the symbiosis of engineering and art through the strict application of military principles in garden design. Sight and movement had a crucial role in Baroque warfare: the economy of movement was an essential part of military theories, for warfare was based on the account of mechanical devices and troop movement. Optical techniques, the manipulation of scales, land-surveying methods and technology for altering huge masses of land were all developed and perfected for military purposes and then came to be known to the architects of this pre-*L'École des Ponts et Chaussées*[1] period. Visual imperfections, such as the notion that the line of sight is no longer straight beyond a certain distance, were utilized by Le Nôtre and he invented brilliant solutions to correct these anomalies (Vérin 1991: 140). Actual distances were optically manipulated to render objects closer by narrowing avenues in order to make them appear shorter: painted walls, diagonal interruptions, perspectival shortcomings, and the manipulation of scales were used to control the field of subject's vision.

Le Nôtre's design was based on two different types of subjects: the static and the moving subject. Louis XIV demanded that the entire magnificent scene be appreciated without leaving the palace, which required the masses to be strictly geometrical, instantly comprehensible and appreciated, and varied in texture and color. Thus, the focal point where all major visual axes were intersecting was Louis XIV's bedroom. From there, the line of sight led through the garden's *allées* dominating the countryside. The other requirement demanded that the entire landscape be comprehensive through movement at various speeds: walking and love-making demanded intimacy, sports and games demanded places specially designated to them, hunting required significant width of the avenues for riding and shooting, while festivals demanded places connected into a successive procession. However, one principle never undermined the effect of another in Le Nôtre's designs, it was rather a cumulative effect of the juxtaposition of different visual and spatial effects that formed a total environmental experience of all subjects involved.

Traditional medieval elements of garden design, such as hunting alleys, were redesigned by Le Nôtre and synthesized with new elements. He created a network of hunting rides, wide *avenues,* intersecting at a number of wide-opened nodes also used as picnic areas for observers. This device was named *patte d'oie* (goose foot), and was used to open the views from the garden into the park in various directions, much like the later network of Haussmann's squares in Paris. *Patte d'oie* gave not a mere succession of independent

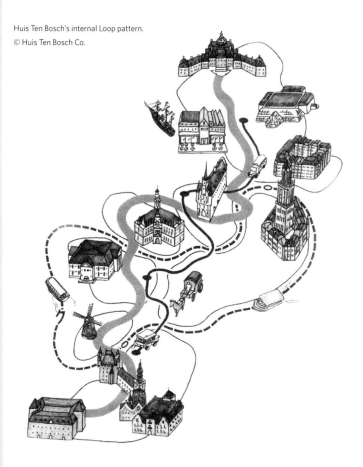

Huis Ten Bosch's internal Loop pattern.
© Huis Ten Bosch Co.

carefully designed network of bridges and streets that the procession of crowds is pre-programmed and controlled.

The Loop Pattern

HTB is an intriguing example of the loop-plan based on the idea of conveying narratives by forming a symbolic circuit where the beginning and the end are clearly marked. In this narrative format, the 'show buildings' are main carriers of meaning regardless of the character and the symbolic unfolding of narratives. In most cases, the loop-plan determines a one-directional procession where the point of entrance, the exchange program, is also the point where one leaves the park. This type of resolution of the loop-plan is challenged by the

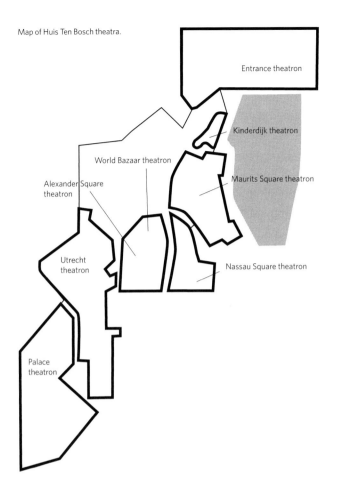

Map of Huis Ten Bosch theatra.

Entrance theatron

Kinderdijk theatron

World Bazaar theatron

Maurits Square theatron

Alexander Square
theatron

Nassau Square theatron

Utrecht
theatron

Palace
theatron

nodes but a succession of scenes forming a rhythmical progression through the environment (Adams 1979: 75–102). Used much later in both England and France, this method developed into the so-called 'landscape of radiating avenues'. The center would be a large circular terrace, metaphorically representing the absolute power of the monarch or the aristocracy, and there would be a number of wide avenues radiating outwards 'as far as the eye can see'. This panoptic apparatus also suggested the absolute control that one standing in the very center would have over the entire estate.[2] The use of water was magnificent in this, as Garrett Eckbo called it, 'plumbers' planning system' (Eckbo 1950). Here too, military technology was used in creating a vast water system to supply numerous fountains, water-sprays, plants and flower beds.

1. The School was officially founded in 1747.

2. This, however, was a variation on the previous model first introduced at Versailles as a scheme designed by Le Vau in 1662 for the Royal Menagerie (Mabille 1991). An octagonal observation-pavilion was placed in the center of the diagram, surrounded by the octagonal courtyard, and consequently by the eight walled courtyards containing exotic animals (Lablaude 1995: 69). An application of this scheme can also be found in the plan for Karlsruhe of 1715, where 32 avenues radiate from the octagonal core with the tower in the center. Another curious example is found in the plan for the Menagerie at the Gardens of Schönbrunn of 1750, in a form of an open-air panopticon with a fountain at its center, linked to the main entrance of the Palace by a diagonal avenue.

plan of Huis Ten Bosch, where one enters through the one-directional Arrival Gate, loops through the park, and exits through the one-directional exit-mall. This resolution of the ending segment optimizes the purchase-volume of the park, because it allows for additional retail opportunities exposed to leaving visitors. This ending segment works analogically to duty-free shops at international airport terminals and has been designed to facilitate a peculiar aspect of Japanese tourism called 'gift exchange'. When a group or an individual travels away from home or working place, it is a must that they are given either an amount of money to be spent during the trip or a small present related to their travel (*senbetsu*). It is also a must for people who travel to bring back presents (*omiyage*) as souvenirs related to the places visited on their travel (Graburn 1983). Amounts given as *sen-betsu* are very large and presents brought back have to amount to at least half of each *senbetsu* received, which often exceeds 20 to 30 percent of the total expenditures for the trip. Huis Ten Bosch, as all the other tourist facilities in Japan, is deliberately constructed to facilitate this cultural norm by offering a variety of items that could be presented as *omiyage*. The departure gate is a large one-way shopping mall designed specifically for the convenience of *omiyage* shopping. The exit-mall also contains fresh food products and ready-made lunch boxes (*bento*) conveniently packed for the visitors's travel back home, another cultural norm. The shopping mall itself is based on the conventional grid-layout with a one-way pathway that leads directly to the exit gate. The shopping mall is called Schiphol, named after the Amsterdam's Airport famous for one of the largest departure duty-free shopping malls in the world.

The core of shopping experience is The Passage, spread across eight buildings and designed by Italian designer Vittorio Garroni. HTB offers 22 000 different items for sale: from a US$10 key holder to US$100 000 for a piece of antique Dutch furniture. Although shops are dispersed through the theater of operations, most of the 61 shops and six corporate pavilions are concentrated in Binnenstad. There is basically no difference between shops and museums in attracting visitors's attention and determining the flow of movement. In fact, the only place with no shops is Museumstad, with 12 museums featuring Seventeenth Century Dutch and European art. All merchandise, food and materials used in the shops and restaurants are first received in the central distribution center, where everything is categorized and then sorted for distribution to various point of purchase within the theme park. HTB has 53 restaurants, varying from fast-food stands to luxurious five-star restaurants featuring both European and Japanese foods. In the Nieuwstad, six corporations run a restaurant mall with various themed restaurants: from Japanese, to Chinese, French, Italian and Korean. There are no franchised restaurants in HTB, a fact that makes

its theater of operations different from the surrounding landscape. A ship-restaurant was also made in the first stage of development and is usually seen cruising the Omura Bay.

As discussed in the previous chapter, on the level of arrangement of the copies of Dutch architectural monuments and the way in which they are related to each other in the theater of operations, Huis Ten Bosch is a clear example of the caricaturization of architecture as well as of Dutch culture. One easily recognizes the exaggerated transformation of the original landscape and the caricaturization of geographical and symbolic relations that give meaning to both individual buildings and the cultural landscape as a whole. Perspective is used here as an important vehicle for the caricaturization of meaning, because it transforms the physical properties of the original in order to make the meaning transparent. Transformations of scale, context and juxtaposition lead to a simplification of complex cultural and historic references, an operation that reduces environmental load and arouses emotions of pleasure and dominance in tourists. The internalized arrangement of both the scale and context removes the architecture of HTB from its signifying load and allows it to float in a semantic field independent from that of original Dutch models.

Huis Ten Bosch Theatra

The network of streets, accented by bridges, provides an onstage set of theatra to be framed and chronologically organized into a homogeneous chain of experiences. Divided by canals, each theatron is an island linked to the rest of the theme park only by bridges. Designers characterized each of the Huis Ten Bosch theatra by the so-called 'view', by the direction and speed of procession, and by the timetable of performances. 'Views' are 'scenes', they set the mood for a particular experience and indicate the general concept. The overall procession through the environment is defined through the ensemble of 'views': HTB designers distinguished among the 'welcome view', 'natural view', 'city view', 'harbor view', 'royal view', and the 'palace

The Schiphol shopping mall in Huis Ten Bosch.

view'. For example, the 'welcome view' greets visitors upon passing through the Arrival gate by a canal, a windmill and a tulip field: the iconography unmistakably associated with the Netherlands. In the background of the same frame is the 367 feet-tall Dom Tower as a clear environmental target that stimulates axial procession and enables easy navigation. Thus, by the strategy of framing an exotic theme by the force of an alien visual and spatial ordering system, immediately upon arrival visitors are displaced into the fictional narrative of this TOP.

The importance of 'views' was in HTB given major considerations. Designers have simulated the impact that visual imagery would have on visitors and how each would layer visual narratives into cumulative environmental image. The loop pattern facilitates such practices because it implies totally controlled, cinematic procession. Nihon Sekkei designers then designed the harlequin dress based on the evolutionary 'historical' placement of different elements, and had subsequently created a corresponding hierarchy of visual and other environmental stimulus generators. The construction of the harlequin dress received scientific attention: a committee composed of Japanese and Dutch experts selected a number of Dutch architectural monuments and approved their copying-and-pasting in the original scale and to unimaginable detail. Not all of the 150 buildings and

over 400 facades of HTB are replicas of Dutch counterparts. Many are based on the 'rationale of Dutch traditional architecture', in the same way in which contemporary Dutch architects operate when inserting new buildings into the sensitive tissue of historic cities. The knowledge on how to select and place buildings within the park was deduced from the research done in 18 cities in the Netherlands. Those that were supposed to have the strongest visual impact and to work as environmental anchors were subsequently constructed as a collection of 12 exact replicas constructed as free-standing buildings. Those include Paleis Huis Ten Bosch, Utrecht's Dom Tower and Nijenrode Castle, and Amsterdam's Hotel de L'Europe. Since Heineken was initially invited to take part in the project, its representatives proposed that HTB copies include copies of two of Heineken's most prominent Amsterdam properties: the old Amsterdam Brewery (now a museum) and Hotel de L'Europe. Sixteen buildings and a windmill were then copied with minor alterations. Hotel Den Haag in HTB was inspired by the Eighteenth-Century Scheepwart building in Amsterdam, today a ship museum. HTB also includes eight windmills, three out of which are operational and located in the Flower Garden, three inside the medieval walls for growing flowers, and the remaining two are Master Windmills in Kinderdijk powered by electric motors. One is open to public as a museum exhibit and is connected to the pond. A part of the HTB scenery are four wooden sailing ships made as replicas of Seventeenth-Century Dutch ships, two of which are serving as cruisers.

Besides individual buildings, entire environments were also copied: for instance, Prins Willem-Alexanderplein in HTB is a replica of Gouda's central square in 90 percent of the original scale. The Cheese Farm in the Flower Garden is based on the model of North-Holland farm, with the entire interior and furniture made in The Netherlands. Streets were modeled after the famous streets in Amsterdam, Leiden, Delft, Hoorn, Amersfoort and Spakenburg. The rows of buildings/ facades were arranged along the canal and then plazas were made as theatrical stage-sets. Twenty five bridges were placed according to their historical role and the original material: the oldest are the wooden bridges in the Binnenstad, the stone ones are in the Nieuws-tad, and steel bridges with the lock gates modeled after Lemmer and Alkmaar bridges divide HTB from the Omura bay. Original architec-tural plans were used to recreate buildings and environments that paradoxically no longer existed in the Netherlands: a special case is the Renaissance garden that was to be built behind the original Palais Huis Ten Bosch in the Netherlands in the Eighteenth Century. Original plans for the garden existed but the garden itself was never built. Nihon Sekkei designers found those plans and recreated the garden in 1992 to accompany HTB's replica of Palais Huis Ten Bosch. Each environmental module was designed in a way that would combine entertaining aspects of the experience with educational ones: many have strong educational impact and provide visitors with opportuni-ties to learn about the Netherlands, Japan as well as about environ-mental design. The only environmental module not placed within a building envelope is the old-fashioned roundabout in the World Bazaar. All the environmental modules, the harlequin skin and the environmental stimuli were then organized into a chain of theatra.

ENTRANCE THEATRON

The Entrance theatron sets the mood and creates the scenery that makes the first impression: Nijenrode Castle is in the foreground covering the visual field of visitors, lit with soft artificial lights. The Dom Tower is seen far behind, lit with bright artificial lights as a powerful visual anchor. On the left are the first rows of luxurious villas made of red brick and surrounded by canals: a glimpse on the pastoral landscape. It is a scene that simulates the environment of a living Dutch city. The one-way path eliminates competing meanings, and amplifies visual effects of the harlequin dress as well as of other environmental stimuli. It is a typical exchange-program theatron, where one first buys tickets and walks through the Entrance Gate where all the necessary information is displayed. The information displayed does not reveal the full range of surprises, but only the data necessary for the spatial and temporal navigation through this theme park environment. This significantly reduces the load of the environment and arouses the feeling of dominance. Visitors then follow the continuous path that leads to the Nijenrode Castle, made as a replica of the Eighteenth-Century Kasteel Nijenrode that works as a passage featuring the armor, swords and uniforms from medieval Holland. Although presented as authentically Dutch, they are made by a Spanish company as replicas of medieval trivia from various parts of Europe. A short description is assigned to each exhibit in a rather straight-forward manner. Dusty ceramic-tile floor, exhibits covered with spider web and the smell of humidity in this door-free castle are meant to create the atmospherics appropriate to the Seventeenth-Century Holland and set the tone for the next environmental experience.

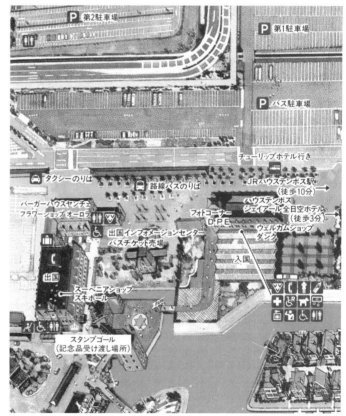

The gate to Huis Ten Bosch.

Ticket boots at the Entrance theatron,
Huis Ten Bosch.

Map of the Entrance theatron, Huis Ten Bosch.
© Huis Ten Bosch Co.

KINDERDIJK THEATRON

Upon passing through Castle Nijenrode and as they walk over a wooden bridge, visitors are greeted by a canal, windmills and a tulip field, symbols strongly identified with the Netherlands. The theme of this theatron is Dutch rural landscape and the canal leads the main 'vista' to the vacation-cottage quarter. On the other side, the view spreads over the city instantly creating the most powerful image of HTB: a town 'naturally placed' within greenery and water. Canals are lit with pole-lights, windmills are lit from the ground, and walkways are random lit with ground-lights. The loop further leads by the Boerenkaas pavilion, a one-story brick building made as a caricature of the typical Seventeenth-Century farmhouse. Besides the Eighteenth Century farmhouse-furniture brought from the Netherlands, it features a cheese making demonstration performed by Dutch agronomy and agriculture students wearing traditional dresses. Opposite the farm house is Museum Molen Dromer, a Seventeenth-Century wooden windmill turned into a museum exhibit. The predominant sound in this theatron comes from the wooden windmill, giving a moderate tempo to the environmental experience. The 'spontaneous sound' that complements the soundscape is composed of the sound of city bustle (which appears as a distant motif in the background of the acoustic space) and sounds created by pseudo-events. Colorful tulip fields structure the lower stimulus spectrum of this theatron, both as visual and olfactory stimuli. The smell of soil, tulips, and cheese together with a cacophony of aural stimuli complete the environmental experience.

View of the Kinderdijk theatron towards
ANA Hotel and Huis Ten Bosch station.

Cheese pavilion in the Kinderdijk theatron,
Huis Ten Bosch.

Map of the Kinderdijk theatron, Huis Ten Bosch.
© Huis Ten Bosch Co.

MAURITS SQUARE THEATRON

After passing over the Kinderdijk, visitors walk over a stone bridge and through the city-gate that frames the view of Nieuwstad (New City District), a Seventeenth-Century urban scenery. The city gate is a copy of the central Staadsport in Delft, which leads to the medieval part of the city. From here the vista spreads out on the Binnenstad (Old City District) surrounded by canals. The Dom Tower is seen behind lit with strong artificial lights as a powerful visual anchor that leads visitors forward. In the periphery of this oblique perspectival frame, on the left hand side, there is a dense forest that completes the scenery. Illuminated bridges reflected in the water, together with canals lit with pole-lights, compose dramatic scenery. Buildings are lit with soft artificial lights, whereas squares are lit with pole-lights. Numerous visitors simulate city bustle and, together with the scenery, complete the environmental experience of a busy Dutch town. Maurits Straat works as the funnel that leads visitors to the Maurits Square and is laterally extended into a south-bound street that flows back onto the Square. The street fronts are composed of Corporate Houses that feature corporate food products. Within their pavilions, corporate sponsors are autonomous: they can use their own colors, fragrances, interior design, although everything must be Holland-related. Moreover, corporate sponsors do not take part in the creation and execution of pseudo-events and have no right to control the soundscape that is at all times under the control of HTB Company. A large stone-fountain marks both the symbolic and geometric center of the square. The containment is absolute, an ideal theatron for the manipulation of the crowds. Besides the Royal Parade and other moving attractions, the schedule of Maurits Plein reveals that, almost without breaks, this place is the site of continuous pseudo-events taking place from 10 A.M. to 5 P.M. daily. The illusion of 'city sound' is total and it is composed of both the visitors that necessarily pass through on the way in and out, and by the 'spontaneous' sounds fabricated by musicians, clowns, jugglers, and other entertainers. The atmospherics is complemented by 'freelance' paint-

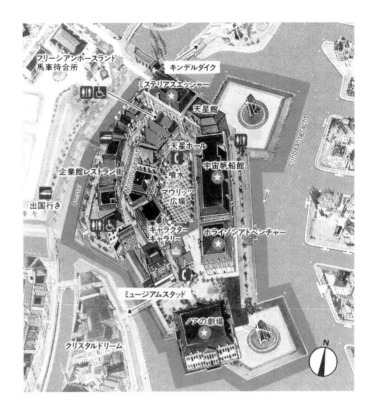

ers distributed carefully around the square. The east-side of the square is composed of structures that house large attractions, such as roller-coasters and movie-theaters, behind typically Dutch city-facades characteristic for institutional two- or three-story Eighteenth-Century buildings made of white stone. The West-side is composed of both outdoor and indoor restaurants and bars, and is visually formed by the red-brick facades of more modest, commercial posture. The olfactory stimuli that spread away from these buildings are dominant and bear strong associations to baked and fried foods.

Panorama of the Maurits Square theatron, Huis Ten Bosch.

Panorama of the Maurits Straat with Corporate Houses, Huis Ten Bosch.

View of the Maurits Square theatron with ANA Hotel to the left and condominium development to the right, Huis Ten Bosch.

NASSAU SQUARE THEATRON

There is only one way to move away from the Maurits Square, across the red-brick bridge to the Nassau Square, also called Museumstad. Museumstad theatron is composed of a series of museums and one multimedia café. The strong visual impact is made by the Musica Fantastica facade, turned diagonally North-East towards the incoming visitors. Its height and formal expression is the dominant visual feature of this theatron. The acoustic space is particularly interesting: due to its total acoustic and visual containment, the music coming from Musica Fantastica is echoed within the Nassau theatron. Musica Fantastica is a museum of sounds made by the self-playing pianos, street organs and music boxes made in Europe from the Seventeenth to the Twentieth Century. Above the entrance to the museum, there is a large self-playing music box that repeats short music sequences every few minutes. Opposed to it, there is Carillon Symphonica, a museum featuring carillons and bells from around the world. The sound of an out-facing carillon is also echoed into the acoustic space of the theatron. The combination of these gentle, slow-tempo sounds makes this theatron a buffer zone between the two busiest theatra in HTB. The Nassau Square theatron works as a conventional funnel, a narrow passage formed by the two-story, red-brick facades lit with soft artificial lights. The passage-like character of this theatron makes it an ideal site of up to 10 pseudo-events a day, each extending over a period of up to 15 minutes. They are mostly soundless clown performances that use the existing soundscape as the acoustic background.

ALEXANDER SQUARE THEATRON

Binnenstad is composed of two theatra: the Alexander Square theatron and the World Bazaar theatron. The Alexander Square theatron is the busiest theatron in HTB and forms the very core of this theme park. It was designed as a replica of Prins Willem-Alexanderplein in Gouda together with its Fifteenth-Century City Hall. The City Hall is turned into a glass museum, but it still acts as a symbolic center of the theatron and the theater of operations as a whole. The south side of the theatron is made of a single perimeter-block building divided into a series of fragmentary, yet texturally compact, narrow-faced Fourteenth-Century facades. The West side is made of four monumental, individual buildings employed as a post office, a fire station, a bank, and the central visitor information center. The other two sides are also composed of fragmentary Fourteenth- and Fifteenth-Century facades and feature mostly small scale shops offering a variety of commodities. All of these structures are three- or four-stories tall. Individual buildings are lit with soft artificial lights whereas the square is lit with pole-lights. The pavement is made exclusively of red bricks that fabricate the feeling of tremendous difference and change. Although physical boundaries of this theatron are clearly defined, the feeling of containment is not strong due to its volume. The schedule for Alexander Square reveals an uninterrupted flow of pseudo-events that begin at 10 A.M. and terminate at 5 P.M., in time for dinner. The sound of city bustle is overwhelming in this theatron. The environmental, spontaneous sounds of visitors are intermixed with sounds of various performances, as well as with the music that comes from the individual shops and small vendors. All of the music in this acoustic space is Dutch from different periods. The environmental stimulation of both the emotion of arousal and affiliative behavior is most obvious here. Constant movement and bustle make people move faster and expect even more environmental activity. This expectation is fulfilled by an ambitious score that incorporates an extensive shopping offer. At the North-West corner of this theatron, there is an interior shopping mall called The Passage. The Passage is a conventional two-story mall offering exclusive goods imported from Europe. Painted white and paved with white marble, it makes a strong contrast to the rest of the Alexander Square theatron. The North gate of the mall leads to the World Bazaar.

Panorama of the East façade of the Alexander Square theatron, Huis Ten Bosch.

View of the Alexander Square theatron, Huis Ten Bosch.

Panorama of the canal façade of Binnenstad, Huis Ten Bosch.

WORLD BAZAAR THEATRON

This theatron is divided into four units by a perimeter-block extending East-West which contains Mariscal's Acualinto water labyrinth, a large tent covering the World Bazaar, and an old-fashioned merry-go-round. Facades are two-stories tall, narrow and made of red brick, gimmicking archetypical Fourteenth-Century facades. The buildings contain small shops offering a variety of Dutch goods ranging from tobacco to freshly-made traditional Dutch bread and cookies. The North-East corner of the theatron is occupied by a traditional Dutch Bakery which generates olfactory stimuli that give a strong character to this theatron. As stated before, the bakery harvests the largest turn-over in the entire theater of operations. The acoustic space is defined by the continuous music coming from the merry-go-round that assigns a festive atmosphere to this theatron. The World Bazaar contains a covered stage where scheduled performances occur throughout the day. This theatron is also the site of many pseudo-events. Offered here are commodities from all over the world, side by side with Dutch artists and artisans making wooden clogs, drawings and jewelry. Rubens Straat is lit with pole-lights, while individual environmental modules are lit with soft artificial lights placed under the roof structure. Although this theatron has a well-balanced con-tainment and a moderately designed atmospherics, it is dominated by the presence of Alexander Square theatron adjacent to its West side. Moreover, the only way to get in and out of this theatron is from the Alexander Square theatron.

Panorama of the World Bazaar theatron,
Huis Ten Bosch.

UTRECHT THEATRON

Upon passing through the Old City District, visitors arrive to Oranje Square that opens towards the harbor. Hotel Amsterdam marks the East boundary of this frame, while the Seafood Market frames the harbor scene on the South side. The De Liefde ship is centrally located and makes a powerful image of the Seventeenth-Century Dutch original ship. The lighting design reinforces the dramatic visual impact of this theatron: Oranje Square is lit with pole-lights, buildings are lit from the ground, the De Liefde ship is lit with under-water lights, while the illuminated harbor is reflected in the Omura Bay. Both artificial and natural sea waves amplify the emotional impact of water and light. The North-East facade of Hotel Europe and the North-West facades of buildings along Utrecht Terrace form a powerfully forced perspective view of the Royal Guest House. The effect of the visual prism is farther emphasized by color: both sides are made of red bricks, up and down (sea and sky) is blue, whereas the Royal Guest House is made of white stone. The canal is lit with pole-lights, side buildings are lit with soft artificial light, and the Royal Guest House is lit with under-water lights that make striking effects on its relief façade; this visual stimulus is also complemented by the contour of the reflected in the canal. The Utrecht Terrace is the site of numerous indoor and outdoor restaurants and cafes, as well as the site of the cruise stop. They all generate a lot of environmental activity, a rich variety of environmental sounds, and at meal times, also the strong olfactory stimulation because they offer a variety of foods, both Japanese and European. Besides, this theatron is also the site for a continuous chain of pseudo-events, including clowns, jugglers, and street musicians: a five-member band performs at Oranje Square four times a day playing mostly Dutch music, together with some jazz sessions in evening hours. Rembrandt Street links Utrecht theatron to the Paleis Huis Ten Bosch.

View of Dom Tower and the Utrecht theatron, Huis Ten Bosch.

Royal Horse Parade passing through the Utrecht theatron, and the Royal Guest House in the background, Huis Ten Bosch.

View of De Liefde ship and the Port area of the lower Utrecht theatron, Huis Ten Bosch.

NEXT SPREAD

Map of the upper Utrecht theatron, Huis Ten Bosch. © Huis Ten Bosch Co.

Map of the lower Utrecht theatron (The Port), Huis Ten Bosch. © Huis Ten Bosch Co.

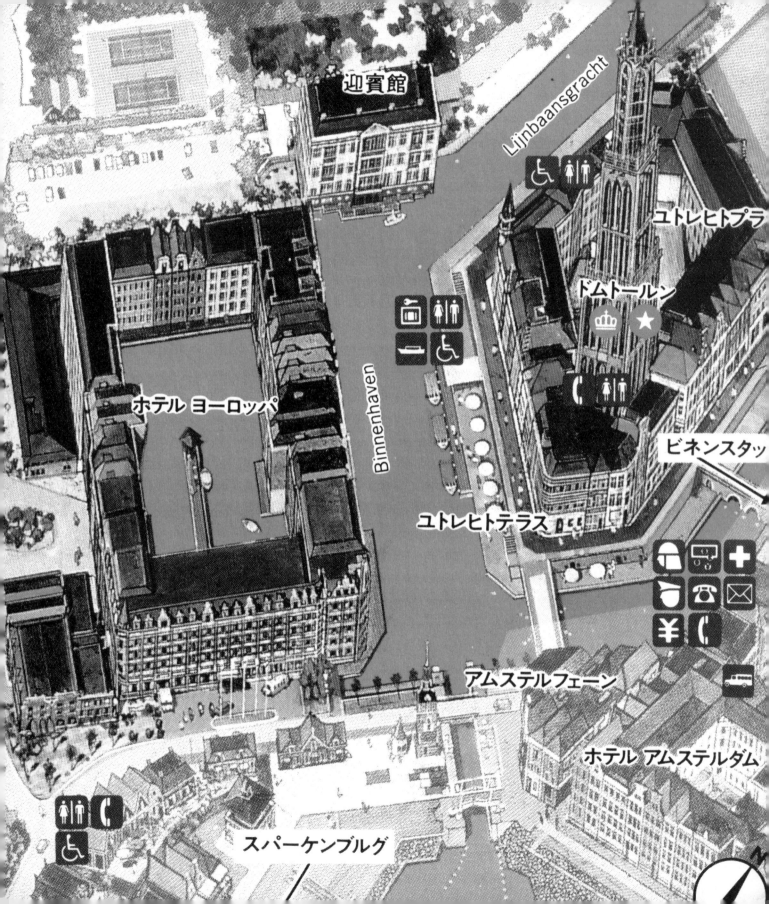

迎賓館

Lijnbaansgracht

ユトレヒトプラ

ドムトールン

ホテル ヨーロッパ

Binnenhaven

ビネンスタッ

ユトレヒトテラス

アムステルフェーン

ホテル アムステルダム

スパーケンブルグ

オレンジ広場

デ リーフデ

ハウステンボス マリーナ

オークション
ハウス

シーフード
マーケット

大航海体験館

ポルセレイン
ミュージアム

マリンターミナル
（海の入出国口）

定期高速船桟橋

帆船博物館

ベイクルーズ発券所

ロイヤル
クルーザー
「デ ハール」

ハーバークルーザー

オランダ村行き
シャトルクルーザー「アメリア」

ホテル デンハーグ

ハウステンボス ハーバー

観光丸

咸臨丸

Rembrandt st.

N

PALACE THEATRON

Rembrandt Street is the central walkway aligned with a platoon of trees that frame the view and lead to the main gate of the Paleis Huis Ten Bosch. Contours of the Formal Garden on both sides of the perspectival frame complete the scenery. The walkway itself is lit by pole-lights, while the Paleis is lit by soft ground lights that provide strong visual effects on its facade. The overall image is simple and pastoral, the scenery is serene, but produces striking visual effects and induces the emotion of pleasure. The Paleis Huis Ten Bosch is an exact copy of Queen Beatrice's residence in the Netherlands. The original Palais Huis Ten Bosch and the adjoining garden were designed by Pieter Post in 1645 in the typical late Renaissance style. In 1733, Daniel Marot undertook the reconstruction of both the palace and the garden, and designed a new garden which was never built in the original palace. Despite the fact that the original Paleis HTB in the Netherlands has no Seventeenth-Century garden, HTB designers received copies of original plans from Holland and decided to build that 'imaginary' garden behind the replica of the palace. All four sides of this theatron are formed by walls made of a variety of trees in different densities, textures and colors. The Palace theatron is the site of several sporadic pseudo-events and only one daily pseudo-event: the central Royal Horse Parade. The Parade arrives to this theatron at 2:15 P.M. daily, stops at the entrance to take the Royalty from the Palace, and then loops back towards the Utrecht theatron.

View of the Royal Palace, Huis Ten Bosch.

Map of the Palace theatron, Huis Ten Bosch.
© Huis Ten Bosch Co.

Temporal Arrangements: Scores and Pseudo-Events

HTB's pseudo-events are designed, organized and executed by the Event Division, composed of the Planning Section and Operating Section. The Planning Section employs 20 employees that make schedules and plan one year in advance. The Operating Section organizes and executes current events and employs 50 employees including performers. The number of employees varies depending on the time of year, the scale of the program, the character of seasonal scores, and so on. In HTB Co.'s parlance the Event Division is part of the so-called 'software group'. Most of the people employed in the Event Division are not HTB Co.'s employees, but are actually employed by companies that provide HTB with the 'software services'. Office Two-One Inc. is one such company with headquarters in Tokyo's Roppongi district. Office Two-One Inc. formed a Huis Ten Bosch Project team a part of which, including the Head of HTB project, live in HTB[10] as long as the company is in charge of HTB's Operation Section. Head of Operations coordinates various parts of the Operation Section making sure that both the daily and seasonal scores are correlated and executed with utmost precision. As well as the performances organized by the in-house Operations, HTB Co. also commissions companies to design performances for particular purposes or rents ready-made performances for a period of time. One such rent-an-event company is Total Space Productions: TAIYO Inc. and its Corporate Planning Department with headquarters in Tokyo's Meguro district.[11] This company specializes in designing corporate 'events' and has collaborated with several theme parks in Japan and abroad. They design performances for specific environments and purposes, conduct feasibility studies, determine choreography, number of performers, their movement through the theme park environment, and so on. They employ performers, train them, and send them to a theme park for a specific period of time. This type of total design is ideal for rent-an-event needs and HTB Co. utilizes such services regularly in order to complement its daily and seasonal scores with novel performances. Besides the rent-an-event practice

THE RENAISSANCE ENCYCLOPEDIC SYSTEM

The rediscovery and translation of Ancient treatises was the base of the Renaissance developments in science and technology; the awareness of the work done by the Greeks and the Romans in categorizing and describing the natural world helped to create a whole new idea of the garden as an enclosed encyclopedic system. The proliferation of new plants and animals helped to enrich knowledge of the natural world and Renaissance gardens became a way of summarizing and visualizing such knowledge: 'a walk round it is like turning over the pages of the book of the world' (Mosser 1991: 263). Exotic animals, real or carved in stone, became a regular feature of gardens: real tigers, lions, bears, or other wild animals were kept in some gardens, while others had collections of sculptured replicas of mythical creatures, dragons and centaurs. In both cases the encyclopedic system that formed the base of the garden had generated a great variety of organized display. Renaissance engineering was blossoming and was lavishly used in gardens (Lazzaro 1990). New fantasticly efficient machines for moving large tracts of earth, leveling terraces, hydraulics, pumps, or devices for raising water-level were used to alter land and create magnificent 'other nature'. Garden designers used water power to replace human power, pumps and hydraulic machines helped to incorporate water into garden design with revolutionary effects, unifying themes which, as Claudia Lazzaro noted 'allegorize the passage of water in nature': lakes, man-made rainstorms, fountains, and water-tricks. Engineering inventions were employed through the new novelty of surprise (as utilized early by Alberti or Rucellai) in order to create visual tricks, water sprays, fantastic sounds, magnificent fountains, and sculptures. Sculptures, composed of different mobile parts, operated now on water pressure that forced the air through the pipes so as to produce the effect of various parts moving at different intervals or making sounds. Artificial rainstorms, thunderstorms, the sound of artillery, surprising water-sprays, music-playing figures, singing birds, life-size statues with moving heads and eyes symbolized significant engineering achievements but also the new amusement and pleasure aspects of the Renaissance Princely Gardens. Shepherd and Jellicoe argued that it was Bernini who first expressed in his fountains the tremulous motion and shifting curves of water, nevertheless it was Bountalenti who achieved the highest level of perfection and sophistication in the garden of Pratolino (Shepherd and Jellicoe 1925). New knowledge in hydraulics had enabled the Renaissance engineer to bring water to the garden from very distant natural springs, without losing the pressure-power.

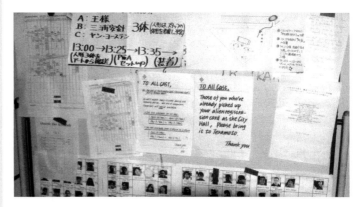

Daily score board at the Event Division offices, Huis Ten Bosch.

organized by the Planning Section, some in-house performances are highly customized and do not need such elaborated planning, such as 'spontaneous' street performances of jugglers, painters or street musicians, or the daily parade. Such events are planned and operated in-house by the Event Division. Most professional performers and artists hired for the in-house designed shows are foreigners. For instance, clowns are from the United States, painters, jugglers and acrobats are Chinese, whereas street musicians are European. The employment of performers and their placement within the theater of operations depends on the character of the theatron they perform in: Chinese painters are allowed to choose their own place in the park while those whose performance is strictly related to the score, such as Dutch street musicians or clowns, appear only on the places determined by the daily score.

Even though in-house performances, such as the daily parade, are organized internally, temporary external employees are needed in order to sustain the suspension of disbelief. Most of the employees that face visitors in make-believe settings cannot be anything else but Dutch. In order to facilitate the supply of Dutch employees to the park, HTB Co. established its subsidiary in the Netherlands called Japan-Europe Exchange Program. This Japanese agency in the Netherlands selects people for different operations within HTB, mostly amateur groups because they are less expensive, as well as high school and university students. A direct collaboration with Leiden

Clown in the Utrecht theatron, Huis Ten Bosch.

Dutch agriculture students performing in
the Kinderdijk theatron, Huis Ten Bosch.

Flag Masters group performing in the
Maurits Square theatron, Huis Ten Bosch.

University in Holland was also established and 15 students have
been sent each year for a year-long 'practical training' in HTB. Those
are commonly students of Japanese language and culture who, upon
arriving to Japan, live in HTB at the expense of HTB Co. and work in
the park for pocket-money. In order to enable the educational aspect
of their stay in HTB, the HTB Co. has turned some of the rooms in the
Paleis Huis Ten Bosch into classrooms and provided essential instruc-
tional facilities. Students are employed in the daily Royal Horse Parade
as Dutch Royalty and other places where presence of Dutch people
is necessary to sustain the illusion of visiting Holland. Employees
with useful practical skills, such are agronomy students making real
cheese in the Boerenkaas pavilion, are employed for adequate jobs.

Besides the planned performances that require hired performers,
HTB also enables visitors to perform, not in a fictitious show but in
'real' culturally determined rituals such as wedding ceremonies.
In 1994, there were 50 wedding ceremonies in HTB and by 1997, the
number increased to more than 200 annually. They are scheduled
months in advance. According to JNTB (Japan National Travel Burro),
90 percent of the honeymoon visitors to Kyushu in 1997 stayed at HTB.

Huis Ten Bosch has an elaborate timetable of annual, seasonal,
weekly and daily pseudo-events. Combined with other environmental
stimulus generators and assigned to specific theatra, they create a
chain of homogeneous experiences. Seasonal events are designed

in order to capitalize on seasonal changes and natural phenomena:
March is marked by the so-called Spring Festival, which includes
a series of sub-pseudo-events such as the Tulip Festival that takes
place during the first week of March every year. During this event,
'tulips' become the overall thematic framework of HTB and most of
the commodities available, as well as pseudo-events, are packed
into a tulip-related narrative. May is distinguished by the Windmill
Festival and June by the Hydrangea Festival. December is remembered by Christmas in the 1000-year-City Festival as well as by the
Countdown Show on 31st December. January begins with Happy
Year Dream Festival and February is specifically marked for Asian
visitors by the Chinese New Year Festival. The Chocolate-and-Cheese
Festival is a copy of the traditional Dutch festival which takes place
in Gouda at the same time of the year. These pseudo-events increase
the number of repeat visitors and also facilitate the creation of pack-
age-tours. Some of them are especially designed for anniversary tours,
graduation tours and the honeymoon tours.

The basic time-frame is spanned between HTB's opening-time at 10
A.M. and its closing-time at 9 P.M. These hours, however, determine
the hours of operation for the general public not residing within HTB's
proper. For HTB's residents and those who stay in one of the HTB's
hotels, bars, night clubs, and some restaurants stay open until the
early morning hours. The culturally pre-determined peak times for
meals are from 1 P.M. to 2 P.M. for lunch, and from 6 P.M. to 8 P.M. for

SCHEDULE OF DAILY EVENTS, HUIS TEN BOSCH (28-04-97)

OUTDOORS / INDOORS

Time	Nijenrode Castle	Kinderdijk	Maurits Square	Nassau Square	Bus Stop	PWA Square	Utrecht Terrace	Oranje Square	Seafood Market	Great Voyage Theater	Palace HTB	World Bazaar	WB Stage
9:00													
9:15													
9:30													
9:45													
10:00			Cast 2-1			Cast 14-1							
10:15			Cast 5-1	Cast 10-1	Cast 7-1	Cast 1-1							
10:30	Greeting	Musician	Juggler 1-1	Cast 12-1		Cast 9-1		Band		Clown 1-1		Cast 3-1	
10:45						Cast 4-1							
11:00	Flagmasters		Cast 8-1			Juggler 2-1	Acrobat 1-1		Rainbow			Cast 6-1	Shanghai
11:15									Show				Acrobats
11:30		Musician	Flagmasters		Cast 7-2	Cast 4-2		Band				Cast 11-1	
11:45			Juggler 1-2	Cast 10-2		Cast 9-2				Clown 1-2	Greeting		
12:00												Cast 3-2	
12:15			Cast 2-2	Cast 12-2		Cast 8-2							
12:30			Cast 14-3			Acrobat 1-2						Cast 6-2	
12:45			Cast 9-3			Cast 5-2							
13:00						Cast 1-2						Cast 11-2	
13:15													
13:30													
13:45			Preshow			Preshow		Preshow					
14:00	ROYAL HORSE PARADE										Flagmasters		
14:15						Flagmasters					ROYAL HORSE PARADE		
14:30													
14:45				Cast 10-3	Cast 7-3								
15:00			Cast 8-3			Cast 1-3			Rainbow				
15:15			Cast 4-3	Cast 12-3	Cast 2-3	Cast 14-3			Show	Acrobat 1-3			
15:30						Cast 5-3						Cast 3-3	Shanghai
15:45			Juggler 2-2			Cast 1-4	Clown 1-3						Acrobats
16:00	Greeting					Flagmasters						Cast 6-3	
16:15			Cast 14-4	Cast 10-4	Cast 7-4				Acrobat 1-4				
16:30			Cast 5-4				Musician	Band		Cast 9-4		Cast 11-3	
16:45			Cast 4-4	Cast 12-4	Cast 2-4	Juggler 1-3				Cast 8-4			
17:00													
17:15													
17:30													
17:45													
18:00													
18:15													
18:30													
18:45													
19:00													
19:15													
19:30													
19:45													
20:00								De Liefde Laser Show					
20:15													
20:30													
20:45								Sound Galaxy Show					
21:00													

dinner. Because the main evening shows occur within the Utrecht theatron, at Oranje Square and around De Liefde ship, all shops in Eastern theatra close at 6 P.M. Shops and bazaars in the Utrecht and Alexander Square theatra stay open until 8 P.M. After 5 P.M., all attention is coaxed towards the Utrecht theatron.

Each of the individual performances distributed over the territory of the HTB has its own strictly determined timetable with the time when a ride begins, when it ends, and the time-between the two cycles. Environmental modules in the Eastern theatra are first to open to incoming visitors at 10 A.M. Environmental modules in the Utrecht theatron open one hour later because it takes 30 minutes to walk straight from the Entrance theatron to the Utrecht theatron. Likewise, as the attention and environmental activity moves towards the Utrecht theatron in evening hours, attractions in the Maurits theatron close at 5 P.M.

The most important 'daily event' is the Royal Horse Parade, which takes place from 2:00 P.M. to 2:30 P.M., making a loop through the park. This is a counterpart of the famous Mickey Parade in Disney theme parks. It starts from Friesian Horse Land, and moves throughout the park to the Paleis Huis Ten Bosch, where it turns and moves back. It is composed of three traditional Seventeenth-Century Dutch carriages, a dozen Friesian horses imported from Holland, and a number of costumed Dutch performers. Other pseudo-events include street shows, such as Italian Flag Masters, Clown Shows, music concerts, and theater shows, as well as numerous 'street events' such as street musicians, painters, and jugglers that gather individuals or small groups of visitors. Each theatron and each environmental module have their own elaborated daily timetable that attracts a number of visitors at a time in accordance with individual throughput volumes. The entertainment capacity of this theme park environment is coordinated with the daily score in such a manner that it moves the crowd East-West, until it reaches the last pseudo-event in the Utrecht theatron at 8 P.M.

The schedule for Oranje Square reveals only two breaks during the day: the first one from 9 A.M. to 10 A.M., before the first visitors reach this theatron, and another one from 2:25 P.M. to 3 P.M., just after the Royal Parade passes through the square. This time is preprogrammed for commercial advantages by coaxing crowds into the nearby World Bazaar and other retail venues. The rest of its daily score is divided into 15-minute segments, during which smaller 'street-events' attract the attention of visitors, or larger 30-minute segments reserved for performances like the Italian Flag Masters. The important aspect is that different pseudo-events never overlap within the same theatron and their succession leaves no gaps larger than a minute or two.

The first evening show, Bon Voyage De Liefde, starts at 7:30 P.M. in the Utrecht theatron. This large-scale musical combines a laser show with music and dance in an attempt to allegorize the travel of the first Dutch ship that arrived to Japan, De Liefde, on its dramatic voyage across the Ocean. After a 15-minute break, the last show in the daily score, Sound Galaxy, starts at 8:30 P.M. and goes on until 8:50 P.M. Sound Galaxy combines a laser-beam show generated by a synthesized recorded orchestra sound meant to 'introduce a world of illusion through a fusion of nature and science'. The last train leaves HTB station at 9:40 P.M., leaving 50 minutes for crossing the park back towards Schiphol, shopping for omiyage and eventually bento, and walking to the HTB JR Station.

Environmental Stimuli

Although HTB Co. decided not to use artificial olfactory stimuli, 'natural' fragrances are emphasized at many locations in order to enforce experiential outcomes and, at some locations, stimulate consumer-related behavior. For instance, the traditional Dutch bakery owned and operated by the HTB Co. has the smell of baked goods distributed into air in order to target the busy Rubensstraat at the North-East corner of Binnenstad. In other theatra, the smell of soil and fertilizers are easily detected, particularly in Kinderdijk where visitors come

SCHEDULE OF ANNUAL AND SEASONAL EVENTS, HUIS TEN BOSCH (1997-98)

	MARCH '97	APRIL	MAY	JUNE	JULY	AUGUST	
SEASONAL EVENTS	Tulip Festival 3/1–4/20 51 days		Windmill Festival 4/26–5/25 30 days	Hydrangea Festival 6/1–7/13 43 days		Big Voyage Festival 7/19–8/31 44 days	
Flower Themes	**Tulip**		**Poppy**	**Hydrangea**		**Sunflower**	
SPONSORED EVENTS		De Liefde Carnival 3/1–5/25 Marching Band 3/20–4/6	Clown Fest 4/26–5/5 Italian Flag Masters 4/26–5/5	Flower Parade 6/1–7/13 Shanghai Magic Performance 4/27–7/18 Weddings 6/1–6/30 Bridal Competition 6/1 Windsurfing Championship 5/17–5/18		Stant Adventure 7/19–8/31 Twilight Fantasy 7/19–8/31 Summer Fest. 8/3 Dream in the Sky 8/14–8/16 Mid-Summer Festival 8/16 HTB Yacht Cup 8/24	
REGULAR EVENTS		Voyage De Liefde Show		Canal Fantasy Show Dream in the Sky (daily) Sound Galaxy (daily)			
EXHIBITIONS		Irene Meyer 4/12–6/1				Barbizon 7/19–9/29	
CEREMONIES	400 Years NL-JPN 3/1	HTB 5th Anniversary 3/24–3/25		Escher's 100 years 6/17			

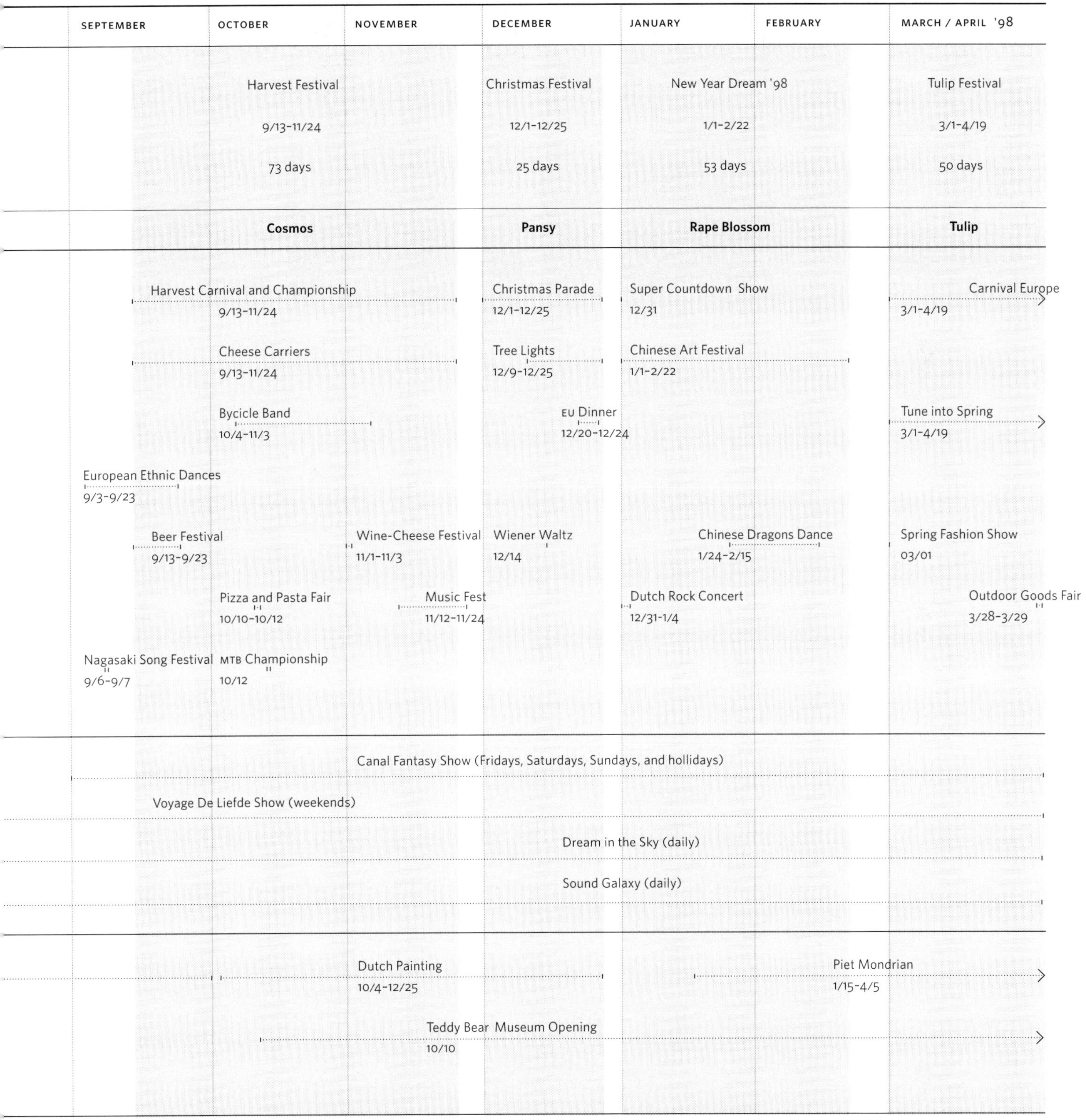

SEPTEMBER	OCTOBER	NOVEMBER	DECEMBER	JANUARY	FEBRUARY	MARCH / APRIL '98
	Harvest Festival		Christmas Festival	New Year Dream '98		Tulip Festival
	9/13-11/24		12/1-12/25	1/1-2/22		3/1-4/19
	73 days		25 days	53 days		50 days
	Cosmos		**Pansy**	**Rape Blossom**		**Tulip**

Harvest Carnival and Championship
9/13-11/24

Cheese Carriers
9/13-11/24

Bycicle Band
10/4-11/3

European Ethnic Dances
9/3-9/23

Beer Festival
9/13-9/23

Pizza and Pasta Fair
10/10-10/12

Nagasaki Song Festival   MTB Championship
9/6-9/7   10/12

Christmas Parade
12/1-12/25

Tree Lights
12/9-12/25

EU Dinner
12/20-12/24

Wine-Cheese Festival   Wiener Waltz
11/1-11/3   12/14

Music Fest
11/12-11/24

Super Countdown Show
12/31

Chinese Art Festival
1/1-2/22

Chinese Dragons Dance
1/24-2/15

Dutch Rock Concert
12/31-1/4

Carnival Europe
3/1-4/19

Tune into Spring
3/1-4/19

Spring Fashion Show
03/01

Outdoor Goods Fair
3/28-3/29

Canal Fantasy Show (Fridays, Saturdays, Sundays, and hollidays)

Voyage De Liefde Show (weekends)

Dream in the Sky (daily)

Sound Galaxy (daily)

Dutch Painting
10/4-12/25

Piet Mondrian
1/15-4/5

Teddy Bear Museum Opening
10/10

Wassenaar Villas with ANA Hotel in the background, Huis Ten Bosch.

Daily life in Huis Ten Bosch.

Bank in Huis Ten Bosch.

close to tulip fields and wind mills. The Kinderdijk theatron was designated by HTB designers as the one to set the mood for the whole park by introducing the most tangible elements of Dutch landscape: the rich visual imagery, the smell of tulip fields, and the sound of wind mills.

Light environment has been created so as to correspond to daily as well as to seasonal changes. There are three dominant themes in designing artificial lights for HTB's environment: light-ups made of halogen lamps spotting the buildings aligned along the canals, miniature yellow lights illuminating the bridges, and light-ups for the plants and trees. The intensity of these lights change depending on time of day and season and is adjusted to the daily schedule of events. The desire to direct and focus the vision of tourists by the use of bright light is clearly expressed in the following statement: 'At night, however, the illumination from light ups, lanterns and streets lights, present us the opportunity to show people what we wish them to see of the town, when we wish them to see it and how we wish them to see it.' (Nihon Sekkei 1994: 224) As Weishar's noted, 'if you can get your customer to see what you want them to see, they will probably buy what you want to sell.' (Weishar 1992)

HTB as a Residential Community

The initial idea behind the most careful planning and construction of HTB was to build a sustainable, ecologically visionary and technologically advanced town that would last for centuries. Early feasibility studies anticipated that, with an annual flow of four million visitors, HTB would be debt free by 2012. By that time, it would work as a theme-park-town, whereas after the year 2012 it would open its gates to the public without charging entrance fees. The rationale behind this calculation was that gates and entrance fees are the only matters that place HTB under the conceptual umbrella of theme parks. Total control over the environment, the crucial aspect of theme parks that goes far beyond gates and fees, has therefore been deliberately left under the conceptual, bureaucratic sovereignty of the future city-government of HTB. In 1993, the Prefectural Government designated HTB as Huis Ten Bosch-cho,[12] interpolating HTB, unlike other regional theme parks, into the regional geographic map as a real town. This bureaucratic apprehension is paradigmatic of a general conceptual ambiguity that exists between theme parks and cities.

Huis Ten Bosch was designed as an architectural stage-set, meant to inspire a 'relaxed, resort life-style' in a residential environment 'never before seen in Japan' (HTB 1992) including facilities such as the City

Hall, post office, police station, recreation center, shops, restaurants, the Omura Bay, canals, a marina, and a Jack Nicklaus golf course, to name but a few. Even though HTB has been deliberately designed as a theme-park-town, it was hard to imagine proximity of housing facilities and amusement grounds: within the amusement grounds there are only lodging accommodations for visitors, while the housing facilities are aligned along the site's perimeter. As a residential community, HTB was not designed for any type of social diversity whatsoever: although Japanese society has various deeply rooted and sophisticated mechanisms of social control, HTB applied a universal one by which prices were determined in such a way as to prevent all but wealthy to inhabit this town. The residential zone was initially composed of 120 villas and 130 condominiums intended to accommodate permanent residents. Villas have been designed as an interpretation of the Wassenaar canal-house typology: they are constructed out of red, Dutch bricks with pitched tile roofs and white door and window frames, and with a small garden in front of the main entrance and a larger, back-garden facing the canal. In the absence of permanent residents, most villas are utilized on special occasions as cottages rentable for various periods of time.

In August 1995, the first phase of condominium development called Huis Ten Bosch Hills, comprised of 85 apartments and some communal facilities, was completed and the entire complex was sold in one day. In April 1996, the following phases two and three (with a total of 130 apartments) were sold within two weeks. In August 1996, the first residents moved into the condominiums. The most popular condominium type was the three bedroom type priced at US$1.3 million. Prices for other condominium types went up to US$2 million. Eighty percent of condominium residents have been from Nagasaki Prefecture, whereas 60 percent are from the neighboring Sasebo city: they moved to HTB permanently, although a great majority has not been employed at the HTB Co. Phase four of HTB Hills began in March of 1997 and included nearly 280 apartments. The goal was to have 3500 apartments by 2012 with approximately 10 000 inhabitants that would form the core of the city of HTB. Inhabitants are free to move within HTB proper and pay no entrance fees for the amusement grounds. However, in order to facilitate unlimited access and free circulation of its residents and subscribers alike, HTB Co. introduced the so-called HTB Passport.[13] As with any conventional, national passport document, HTB Passport has a place designated for the photograph and signature of its owner on the second page, as well as the pages designated for the stamps of the respective administrative authority.

Although a community of 10 000 people was planned to develop by 2012, late 1990s brought a severe economic recession that left Huis Ten Bosch Co. with unsold villas, due largely to the inflation of prices to up to US$4 million. Despite the fact that condominiums are priced more reasonably, the orientation towards the top-end of the Japanese market was obvious. The statistics show that nearly half of HTB's visitors have been over 60 years of age, and the majority of potential residents, as well as overnight visitors, belong to this demographic group. Given the current state of economic recession, HTB is confronted with two possible trends. Firstly, there has been a tendency towards selling its housing stock to wealthy retirees that originally come from Nagasaki or Sasebo areas. After retiring in the Tokyo and Kansai regions, many wish to come back and live in the area. HTB ideally caters to such potential buyers. Such a development, though, would turn HTB into a retirement community, in which case HTB would be even less attractive to younger audiences. Secondly, current trends in regional capital restructuring are not optimistic and they are the major determining factor in both regional and national migrations. Thus, if both local and national economy does not 'boom' once again as in the early 1980s, HTB will remain a theme park, and the dream of developing a true living community will never come through. In that sense the developments of the day seem to be moving in the latter direction: today, only 500 households (about 750 people) inhabit Huis

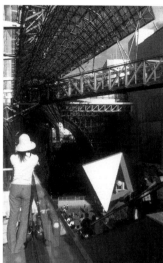

HADRIAN'S VILLA

In the Second Century A.D., many Roman officials built residences in areas surrounding Rome, such as Tibur, located 15 miles from Rome. The reason for such a practice was two-fold: firstly, Romans generally located their pleasure-parks out of the cities, in the countryside; and secondly, by Roman law, senators and state officials were obliged to live in the city of Rome or within a 22-mile radius. With splendid views, spring water and beautiful landscape, Tibur and the surrounding areas were ideal sites for residences and summer houses alike. Houses and adjacent gardens in Tibur picturesquely romanticized and elaborated both Greek and Islamic concepts of garden-making (Masson 1961). One of the most brilliant of Tiburian residencies was Villa Adriana (*Villa Tiburs*) at Tivoli, built in A.D. 117-133 by Emperor Hadrian. In A.D. 114, Hadrian began preparing plans for his residence in Tibur and soon after began altering the site for huge operation to come. A network of underground tunnels large enough to accommodate people and carts was built during the first stage (Ricotti 1973) prior to the beginning of ground works in A.D. 117.[1] This network of tunnels was closely articulated with plans of the buildings above ground and care-fully camouflaged. The buildings were then carefully removed from all major visual and processional axes, and no vista revealed the existence of these buildings.

Hadrian spent almost half of his rule on travels motivated by curiosity and by a desire to unify Rome and its provinces. From A.D. 118 until A.D. 134 he traveled through Gaul (France), Germany, Britain, Spain, Greece, Sicily, Asia, Syria, Arabia, Egypt, Judea, Crete, the Balkans and many other provinces. In-between his travels, he would come to Rome to unload his ships and rest. History has credited Hadrian as being a curious observer and passionate collector of art works and architectural imagery: from what has been found at the site, and from what has been written about him, it is clear that buildings of Villa Adriana were reminiscences of famous buildings and places visited during Hadrian's travels.[2] As Colin Rowe wrote, Hadrian's villa was 'an accumulation of disparate ideal fragments' orchestrated into a harmonious configuration covering nearly 300 acres (Rowe 1978: 86-94).

The fact that the villa was arranged into a series of self-contained and fragmented complexes is a result of the

Ten Bosch Hills. The building fund is owned by one of the stockholder companies, but it has been operated by HTB Technical Center.

HTB Co.'s concern with the political aspects of land ownership has been peculiar. Potential buyers of the Wassenaar villas were also offered the land on which the house stands, thus each purchase reduces the surface of land owned by HTB Co. This, however, does not mean that Huis Ten Bosch Co. loses control over the town because all of its 'public spaces' and both the social and physical infrastructure will stay under its control. For Huis Ten Bosch, total control over the environment means the control over the entirety of space with all its extensions, both corporate which the company calls 'public' and the so-called 'private', the organization and execution of the pseudo-events, the control over the town's growth (to infinite details such as balcony additions) and control over all the public programs which include schools, hospitals, post offices, fire stations and public security (private security forces). Besides, TV broadcasting, telecommunication lines, heating, cooling, banking, shopping, even wedding ceremonies are planned and controlled by HTB Co. Simply put, most of the aspects of one's life are potentially controlled by the company. Despite the catastrophic implications of all the above, one could argue that in the United States and Japan, there is an increasing, market-stimulated desire of people determined to live (and sometimes work) within the strict boundaries of theme park territories. HTB is far from being the only example.

HTB should also be placed in the context of the creation of large, privately owned public facilities during the 1990s that have caused a perplexity in the Japanese perception of urbanity. These new public facilities—particularly Tokyo International Forum (TIF), Kyoto Station (KS), and HTB—fabricate and promote a new type of urbanity, a new mode of being in public, and consequently of a new type of public space as a function of mobility, a publicly accessible yet privately owned, controlled and managed space. In many ways, these new projects have sharply contradicted a general tendency over the last 15 years for the preservation and reconstruction of traditional Japanese values that have supposedly been lost due to modernization, but also more importantly, they contradict a general drive towards encouraging citizen participation in public life. As Jinnai Hidenobu asserted, the European concept of urban public space was officially introduced in Japan in the 1910s during the Meiji Restoration (Jinnai 1995). After the 1923 Kanto earthquake, this process was seen as an important component of the national urban design policy for symbolic and practical reasons (such as fires and hygiene). The principles of European rationalism, although alien to the Japanese society in the early years of Meiji modernization, were imposed on the Japanese urban fabric. The principles obviously included symmetrical disposition, perspectival vision and a totalizing axial-ordering system within which larger traffic nodes were turned into public squares. Even though Japanese cities have thus been restructured partly through the alienation of the cognitive from the perceived and lived, the degree to which KS, HTB, and TIF create a spectacle out of such an alienation is groundbreaking. They visualize the proximity of large numbers of individuals neither necessarily by bringing them any closer, nor by reconstituting a public realm of any kind, but by

different stages in Hadrian's travels, as well as different periods in which they had been built. As Pinto and MacDonald suggest, each travel would inspire new construction cycle and a new aesthetic framework (MacDonald and Pinto 1995). There had been three major construction periods: the initial cycle started cca. A.D. 117 until A.D. 121, the following one began in A.D. 125 and went until A.D. 133, and the last from A.D. 133 to A.D. 135. During the first phase, most of the important buildings were erected such as the Great Court (*Peristilio di Palazzo*), the Throne Room (*Sala a Pilastri Dorici*), the Garden Stadium complex, and the Baths (*Terme Grandi*). This implies that even initially Villa Adriana was designed as an official residence. The second stage of construction reveals an emphasis on its leisure character: *Terme Piccole,* theaters, Accademia and other fragments were added to the complex. Although fragmentary, the Villa Adriana was unified by the set of six major axes that, together with formal symmetries, allowed for permanent expansions. The hybrid mix of architectural elements stood for the cultural and ethnic diversity that the empire represented. As Taliaferro Boatwright notes, 'the Egyptian statues stood with copies of Greek masterpieces, copies of Erechtheum Caryatids, and of Hellenistic sculptures, in places framed by a very Roman colonnade of alternating flat and curved lintels.' (Taliaferro Boatwright 1987: 149)

Whether Villa Adriana was an expression of Hadrian's criticism of Imperial Rome and, therefore, the proposal for an alternative city model, as Colin Rowe read it, remains a moot point. The fact that various parts of the complex are named and shaped after different parts of the Roman world, much as Walt Disney does in EPCOT, stands for an imperialist drive towards generalizing contradictions, homogenizing differences, and unifying all elements by a relatively flexible conceptual framework that can accommodate any strategic and tactical change. In this sense, Villa Adriana could be seen as direct, spatial inscription of Hadrian's cultural ideology and his political agenda. If Rome was to be the center of such an empire it would have to have been politically, culturally and spatially based on the model of Villa Adriana.

1. Various authors share doubts as to the beginning of the first stage of works, for discussion on this see Aurigemma 1962.

2. This practice existed before Hadrian, as in B.C. 800 Assyrians had a habit of bringing back exotic trees and fish from the countries they conquered. King Tiglath-Pileser I was an early ancestor of Hadrian, since he constructed special settings, parks, to shelter the fish he received as present from foreign monarchs, and plant the foreign trees he selected in his conquers. He and his successors constructed ponds and small hills on the top of which they would build pavilions and shrines, they built sophisticated water drainage systems, brought goats, elephants and foreign animals into the parks. After B.C. 700, parks for Persians became a customary additions to every palace, and they were mostly used for hunting, walking, and ceremonies or gatherings of various kinds. Persian parks remained walled off, closed for public and open only to the privileged (Source: Lasdun 1991: 1-21).

creating opportunities for spectacular vistas. Either this type of spectacular space is organized according to simple and transparent principles where social relations are spatialized, or the architecture itself is turned into powerful and seductive images. Just like the other two environments, HTB employs a ready-made, Western urban model to create a desirable type of urban experience, and like TIF, it employs architecture on an iconic level to materially produce the urban realm and fabricate an urban spectacle. The new type of public space, and the experience of urbanity that these three buildings fabricate and promote, is in clear contradiction to traditional Japanese public spaces that have been based on lateral movement and multi-sensory experience, but also in contradiction to a general need to 'return' to traditional values in urban planning, as they simply alienate potential sites of traditional public life. In all three cases, the processes of denotation and connotation are inappropriately disconnected, as the cultural milieu does not enable the average Japanese to decode the 'true meaning' of any of these environments, let alone to contemplate participation. The decontextualization of shared assumptions and interpretative conventions potentially creates the pretext for a new social doctrine that has been curiously spatialized in these environments. In that respect, the remapping of social relationships and urban practices promoted by these environments could indeed be compared to the manifestations of Meiji modernization. However, the change they promote is meaningless if the traditional Japanese way of urban life is to be preserved:

> It is urgent today to reconsider the logic of urban planning. A glance at the history of modern Japan makes it obvious that transplanting the European notions of artfully arranged squares and tree-lined streets directly onto Japanese soil has failed to create a space that is both interesting and full of energy. Rather, it is only in disorderly, thriving, and appropriately small spaces, where human feeling and not an expanding vista take charge, that one can find a properly Japanese urban life. The best way of making our cities attractive again, I think, is to restore such spaces—which have been either lost to modern urban reconstructions or gradually driven underground—to life on the surface. It is, after all, such humanly scaled spaces that make the city familiar and appealing for those who live in it. (Jinnai 1995: 83)

NOTES

1. There is a significant discrepancy between the two versions of Epcot: the one imagined by late Walt Disney in 1960s, which I discuss in this chapter, and the one built by Walt Disney Company in 1982.

2. Different sources indicate a variety of heights involved. Obviously, Walt Disney's ideas were constantly changing. The differences scholars indicate are between 20 and 50 stories.

3. As early sketches indicate, there are up to 12-stories high.

4. Unless otherwise noted, all facts used in this chapter are derived from the HTB 1992–97, Nihon Sekkei 1994, from the interviews with HTB Co.'s executives Matsuda Yuji, Henk Boer and Ben Steenkist, as well as from the interviews with Nihon Sekkei executives Ikeda Takekuni, Okamura Kazunori, Motokazu Tashiro, Minoru Tsuneoka and Shinzo Konomi, all conducted in April 1997. This chapter is original to this book, however some parts of this chapter, specifically on Huis Ten Bosch, were presented at scholarly conferences and published before. See Mitrašinović 1997a, 1998, 2002b, 2002c.

5. New discoveries that appeared in the 1990s challenge that fact and argue that Chinese traders also had the right to trade with the Japanese during the Edo period.

6. On 24th April 1993, Nagasaki Holland Village changed the name to Holland Village.

7. Both costs were recorded in 1996.

8. The statistics were received from the Press Office of the Netherlands Tourist Bureau in NYC and from Amsterdam's NIPO, a commercial institute for market research, both in May 1997.

9. Terminologies employed by HTB Co. and Nihon Sekkei (designers) vary, sometimes they are use the term 'zones', other times 'districts'. However, both terms refer to what is in this book called theatra.

10. The interview with Fujita Yoji, Office Two-One Inc. employee and Head of the Huis Ten Bosch Project, was conducted on HTB premises in April 1997.

11. The interview with Minagawa Takeo, Manager of the Corporate Planning Department at Total Space Productions TAIYO Inc., was conducted in May 1997 in his Tokyo office.

12. 'Cho' indicates that HTB is a real town with population under thirty thousand inhabitants.

13. The HTB Passport is also extended, in various capacities, to members of the Molen Club as well as to visitors that pay for the entire amusement package.

BECOMING

Theme parks provide not only social and psychological potential, but also hold much urban design possibilities. Here we have an efficient movement system in an atmosphere of optimum cleanliness and security that provides a pleasurable experience for varied socio-economic groups while making a profit without polluting the environment. All this within a well-ordered, completely planned framework that serves as an excellent urban planning model. While the architecture of the amusement park may not hold all the answers or all the problems, as Peter Blake, Charles Moore and Paul Goldberger have pointed out, it is time for architects to take a close, undespairing and professional look at this architecture of play and good nature and to start documenting how and why it works and how we as design individuals can implement it. **(WASSERMAN 1978)**

Since the Seventeenth-Century public walks that transgressed the boundaries of European medieval fortifications in search of amusement, Western, and to a certain extent also Asian amusement installations, have always maintained a dialectical relationship to the city center and urban traffic networks. Early amusement parks and contemporary theme parks were made possible by the development of modern traffic networks and the modern time-table that, together with the spatial zoning, have assigned programs to specific space-time locales. The first ones were placed at the end of tramlines in order to stimulate commuting on weekends and holidays. Analogically, within the early Twentieth Century metropolitan model of urban expansion, cities—as cultural, social and political centers—had always determined the peripheral character of amusement practices and amusement installations. Within the contemporary megalopolitan model in which the distribution of goods, people, energy, information and wealth recognizes no difference in topographic and cultural detail, amusement installations and historic city-centers are just nodes of different degrees of accumulation. In such a situation, we face a complex ensemble of relationships between the previously distinct entities of the urban center (historic city) and the theme park. It is an ironic notion that, after being institutionalized in 1950s by the establishment of Disneyland Park, mass amusement installations have today come to restructure the very center of what was previously the axis of centrifugal urbanization by virtue of which they were marginalized as social, cultural, and urban satellites. Walt Disney had *de facto* exchanged the idea of ephemerallity, which has dominated the development of leisure facilities, for the ideas of permanency and durability—ancient architectural metaphors—that have always been the premise of the construction of cities. Even more ironic is the fact that, while unavoidable historical processes are transforming urban public spaces and cities at large, authentic urban environments have been 'preserved' as stage set imagery for the simulation of generic urban experiences in the increasingly privatized cities. This fact, however, must be placed into a broader framework, not only within contemporary trends in urban entertainment and urban redevelopment, but also with the often underestimated tradition of spectacular self-representation and re-invention of cities that originated at the World Fairs and Great Exhibitions. As Christine Boyer has shown, it is since the second half of the Nineteenth Century that architecture and the production of scenographic city-space has offered the spectator a 'packagable and consumable manner of looking at cities' within a time-frame programmed and planned for commercial advantage (Boyer 1994: 301–302). In *The City of Collective Memory* Boyer brilliantly shows how such tableaus have historically evolved and have come to restructure contemporary urban environments. Besides, historically speaking the theme park is not the only entertainment apparatus that has been used as an organizing principle of the technology of power in urban milieu. Colin Rowe clearly showed in *Collage City* how Versailles was employed as the model for Haussmann's reconstruction of Paris, and how Hadrian's Villa was conceived as an allegory for the organization of Roman Empire. Rem Koolhaas demonstrated in *Delirious New York* how Coney Island was employed as a template for the transformation of Manhattan. In these and other examples, an idealized notion of 'garden' has been employed, both as a critique of the city and as a way of redefining the city as a symbolic reflection of the metaphysics of power. All of these models were initially presented as heterotopian collective fantasies of escape, yet intrinsic to the realm of ideology they naturally came to control, in one capacity or another, the respective social realms. Galen Cranz observed that each urban park has historically represented a strategy for moral and social reform that subjected each citizen to a layered and cumulative ensemble of moral lessons (Cranz 1982: 253). Cranz argued further that since the majority of urban parks in late Nineteenth and early Twentieth Centuries have come to existence through the philanthropic efforts of the rich and the powerful—that included sanitary and health concerns—the naturalized, proper role of the rich was considered to be taking care of the poor (Cranz 1982: 236). The disappearance of the philanthropic drive and the emergence of the drive for short-term profiteering, together with generally improved living conditions in urban areas (in terms of sanitary and health concerns) have caused different urban realities today. Nevertheless, historically speaking, cities have always embodied some sort of scholastic program, they have always assumed educational roles and performed some disciplining of bodies-and-minds aimed towards attaining the virtues of civility: more often than not such programs were instrumentalized through the apparatus of mass entertainment. The difference, however, between these historical examples and the 'theme park model', and for that matter also the total landscape, is in the degree to which present convergences of all media have moved scholastic and disciplinary programs institutionalized by the 'theme park model' far out of the realm of democratic choice. Furthermore, I will discuss in this chapter how the production of privatized urban public space disables critical engagement on the part of the citizens by mystifying the complex processes that bring it into being. In that respect, this chapter will discuss how the so-called 'theme park model' has been imposed onto urban public space, and analyze the production processes that bring theme park and the transformed urban public space together into a comparative framework.

The Theme Park Model [1]

As noted earlier, the first theme park, Disneyland, was conceived neither as a city, nor as a replica of an existing urban model, although it has been clearly conceived as an antidote to the metropolitan experience of urbanity and as such it had supported Disney's thesis on the destruction of cities by Modernism. This thesis, combined with the enthusiasm for a highly technologically advanced type of public facility, and a clear nostalgia for the pre-industrial age and pre-automobile world, was embedded in the very creation of EPCOT. Although EPCOT was never built as a city, this project symbolically marks the beginning of an era in which parallels between theme parks and cities will often be made. Early critical writings on Disneyland Park and its

lessons, such as those of Charles Moore (1965), Peter Blake (1972) and Paul Goldberger (1972), had indeed made the connection between theme parks and cities possible, although they had perceived neither Disneyland nor EPCOT as a new type of city. They referred instead to the lessons that architects and city planners could have learned from Disneyland, not in operational terms (as to 'how to' design a contemporary city) but in terms of understanding immense structural changes in the character of public spaces and public infrastructure. As Charles Moore wrote in 1965:

> By almost any conceivable method of evaluation that does not exclude the public, Disneyland must be regarded as the most important single piece of construction in the West, in the past several decades [...] Curiously, for a public space, Disneyland is not free. You buy tickets at the gate. But then, Versailles cost someone a great deal of money, too. Now, as then, you have to pay for the public life. [...] Even more basic than the absence of the viable architectural idiom for making public centers is the absence of any establishment ready to shoulder the responsibility for, to take a proprietary interest in, the public realm [...] There is no need and no time to wait for a not-yet-existent establishment to build us the traditional kind of monuments, or for a disaster gripping enough to wake the public conscience to the vanishing places of the public realm we got for free. Most effectively, we might, as architects, first seek to develop a vocabulary of forms responsive to a marvelously complex and varied functions of our society [...] Then we might start sorting out for our special attention those things for which the public has to pay, from which we might derive the public life. The existing prospects, not surprisingly, show up best at Disneyland. (Moore 1965)

Consequently, they opened up the field of comparison in two possible directions: firstly, in terms of the parallels made between the character of public space in Disneyland Park and that of the contemporary city; and secondly, in terms of the significance of a sophisticated infrastructure, particularly traffic, for the proper functioning of the contemporary city. Peter Blake called both Disneyland and Walt Disney World 'a lesson in pedestrianism' and an important accomplishment in terms of urban psychology and urban technology (Blake 1972). Nevertheless, one of the most obvious facts was that all the fascinating aspects mentioned by Blake, Moore and Goldberger would have probably happened in cities too if cities had the financial resources and a political consensus to do so. Lois Wasserman's proposal in late 1970s, with which this chapter opened, instrumentalizes theme parks as a method of urban revitalization for very much the same set of romantic reasons.

Many critics were right that Disneyland Park was designed as a complex movie set. It was designed by filmmakers, set designers, choreographers, animators, and also by architects, and therefore, as Umberto Eco noticed, 'every step was planned and every view framed [...] like the Hearst Castle, Disneyland also has no transitional spaces; there is always something to see, the great voids of modern architecture and city planning are unknown here.' (Eco 1986: 48) In terms of design, Disneyland Park introduced the symbiosis of the design of procession and performance with the design of the material environment, and an immaculate precision with which all could be programmed; the use of color, light, fragrances, pavement-material, background sound, foreground sound, the employment of behavioral sciences and environmental psychology, choreography and set-design that architects and planners of urban spaces had forgotten, have not had a chance to use, or simply refused to employ for ethical reasons. Besides, Walt Disney Imagineering used scores and scripts in order to program the environments. However, what was curiously missed by critics, and was also truly groundbreaking about Disneyland Park, was the fact that its design dissolved boundaries between itself and the world of media. As shown in Chapter 2, Walt Disney and the ABC television network introduced this paradigmatic move in 1953, when Roy and Walt Disney made an agreement with ABC to supply a weekly Disney show in return for a line of credit needed for the completion of Disneyland Park. Since Disney's ideas were born out of television, film, and animation, his interest was aimed at creating a complex dynamic environment where the narratives, images, desires and expectations previously fabricated by the media would

be supported by the experiences in the material world, creating in the process an unknown convergence of the previously largely separated domains of human experience. For such a convergence to take place, a homogeneous human experience was fabricated by creating layered narrative procession across a multitude of scales achieved by designing a smooth, frictionless procession from the realm of television and film to the realm of theme park and retail: a totalizing environmental experience. Disneyland proved that human experience is a mode of economic output and just like all other commodities it can also be designed, standardized, produced, consumed and reproduced. In terms of management, Disneyland had shown that private-sector management of spaces designated for public use could not be compared with the public sector one based in 'public-service idealism'. Since Disneyland Park was the largest privately owned public facility at that time, efficient security and management technologies were of crucial importance for its successful performance.

In early 1990s, the term 'theme park model' began appearing in the critical literature on theme parks, signifying a privately-owned and gated environment, organized around a set of specific themes and opened to restrictive and highly controlled public access. The design and planning aspects, combined with mechanisms of social control and entertainment are in this model based on Ritzer's four basic premises that put forth the principle of systematic totality: efficiency, calculability, predictability and control (Ritzer 1996). Edward Soja was concerned with the rise in the popularity of this model and argued that its dissemination signifies an aggressive expansion of the 'hyperreality principle' out of the 'localized enclosures and tightly bounded rationality of the theme parks.' (Soja 1992) Others have identified the 'theme park model' as a 'trope' for future urban planning (Findlay 1992) and the transposition of the control aspects of the 'theme park model' as potentially beneficial for the revival of the dying core of industrial metropolis (Gottdiener 1997), while simultaneously arguing that the type of spatial and social control that theme park implies is dangerous and threatening (Zukin 1995). In Zukin's view, the 'theme park model' is a part of the conceptual framework of 'symbolic economy'[2] that fundamentally restructures urban environments across the world. The mid-1990s also brought along a series of careful maneuverings in moving the theme park discourse from the margins of critical literature to the core of cultural interest and prominence. One of the critical events was the exhibition titled The Architecture of Reassurance: Designing Disney Theme Parks that opened at the Canadian Center for Architecture on the 17th June 1997, recognizing 'the theme park as a cultural phenomenon in the public domain.' (Marling 1997: 11) The exhibition was followed up by a publication of a sizable 200-page volume edited by the University of Minnesota Art History Professor Karal Ann Marling, who also curated the exhibition (Marling 1997). Besides, in the mid-1990s, the employment of the 'theme park model' in medical and therapeutic environments became a breakthrough as hospitals around the world began spending large resources on determining how to create the most desirable 'healing experience' possible in order to increase their market share, but also to ensure better experiential outcomes in patients (Flower 2000). In a strange twist of destiny, those who designed themed restaurants and theme parks found themselves employing themeing in designing thematic hospitals where interactive artwork, hallways and communal rooms, food and drinks, music and crafts, as well as signage associated with the overall theme were all subject to a systematic treatment analogical to the one applied in theme parks. Not surprisingly, the application of the 'theme park model' has renamed anesthetic treatment into 'behavior management' and sick patients needing medical help into 'valuable guests'. David Rockwell Group designed Children's Hospital at Montefiore in Bronx, NY in 2001, guided by the conceptual frame that immerses sick children in the center of the narrative through which they act as explorers on a journey to healing. Peter Betts, the ex-CEO of the East Jefferson Hospital in Metairie, Louisiana, was the first individual outside of Walt Disney Company ever to receive Walt Disney Co.'s

Mouscar Award in 1997. He and many of his managers studied principles and techniques of competitive hospitality at the Disney Institute's Healthcare Training Program in Orlando from 1992 through to 1997. As a result, the hospital is designed around Disney's four principles of guest relations—safety, courtesy, show, and efficiency—and divided into on-stage and off-stage areas with themed healing rooms and hallways with clear signage, a thematic dress code, murals whose colors correspond to the environmental tasks, flooring that distinguishes different areas, and many other cues taken from Disney theme parks, together with renaming 'patients' into 'guests' and 'employees' into 'team members' (Pine and Gilmore 1999: 54).

The reputation that the 'theme park model', and with it Walt Disney Co., were gaining in the business community motivated 42nd Street Redevelopment Agency to approach Walt Disney Co. regarding the Times Square project as a trusted and honorable partner that could bring prestige, the know-how embedded in the 'theme park model', and a sizable budget to the redevelopment of 42nd Street. Unlike competitive hospitality, where the notion of 'public' is limited by the very character and need for a specific type of interaction, where highly controlled accessibility is desirable, and where behaviors of all stakeholders are heavily scripted, competitive urbanity is based on a different set of premises altogether. One characteristic they do share, though, is the metaphor of 'healing', in the former as a vehicle of patient recovery, and in the latter a vehicle for 'revitalizing' urban public space.

The Therapeutic Discourse
In the initial definition of public space, I claimed that public spaces are commonly understood as traditional sites of public interaction where public comes together in face-to-face situations, and have preliminarily defined it as an environment designed to allow for [open and unrestricted] citizen communication and exchange [on equal footing] whose forms and practices have been defined by public law as well as

FABRIQUES

As William Wrighte noted in 1790, the Eighteenth Century faced an increased need for classifying the emerging typologies of park buildings, such as 'Chinese, Gothic and natural grottos, cascades, baths, mosques, Moresque pavilions, grotesque and rustic seats' (Wrighte quoted in Lasdun 1991: 110). Indeed, a new architectural typology was born with an inherent scale, aesthetics, and the mode of construction. Indian pavilions, brand new Gothic and Antique ruins, mosques and Chinese pagodas, were radically different from the eclectic architecture of the main house and the utilitarian buildings dispersed through the park. These were real buildings, as opposed to the plaster simulations of buildings used at the same time in Pleasure Gardens such as Vauxhall, and pleasure fairs such as Bartholomew's. *Fabriques* was the term used to signify show buildings in gardens that had mainly a cultural role, and less often also a symbolic one (Mosser 1991: 263).[1] Within the art of the garden, the art of *fabriques* was an entirely new discipline. Time and space were arranged through the sequence of fabriques as forming a set of scenes to partake in the fabrication of the desired narrative. Although landscape garden could have provided a narrative setting, the carriers of the meaning were buildings. One-way paths, often loops, were introduced in the reappearance of a kind of perambulation ritual where each *fabrique* was a scene along the path associated with a particular part of the narrative (historical event, place, time, or hero). Architecture conceived on this level was a key associational vehicle of the picturesque garden. Regardless of the character and symbolism, this was a new format of conveying narratives through the garden by forming a symbolic circuit where the beginning and the end are clearly marked. As Mosser notes, not all the fabriques were situated along a path: some of these eccentric buildings were scattered over the garden, such as The Indian House in the gardens of Augustusburg in Brühl of 1750, or the bizarre Mosque in the gardens of Schwetzingen of 1761. Nevertheless, all of them worked as surprises, syncopated fragments of novelty and surprise.

1. Most of these buildings possibly had also some symbolic functions, particularly in the ritual of Initiation within the gardens of the Freemasonry (Mosser 1991: 273).

by the cultural, political and socio-economic milieu. Direct application of the 'theme park model' would certainly change this definition to 'a highly controlled, privately-owned environment designed for restricted public interaction, a site of limited accessibility whose forms and practices are defined through a compromise between public law, cultural norms and belief systems on one hand, and its purpose, task, and the objective of its owner on the other'. Why the 'theme park model' is specifically interested in producing sites of public interaction is its need to instrumentalize public interaction as a means of mass-consumption, as well as its struggle to institutionalize the norm of consumption in urban environments across the world. As mentioned earlier, if one applies the point of view of total landscape to looking at public space, public space must be seen as complex, multi-dimensional dynamic system in action composed of material artifacts (buildings, greenery, benches, cell phones: 'from the spoon to the city'), immaterial stimuli (sound, smell, taste, light, color), constituents and stakeholders of all kinds (both as producers and consumers), and ensembles of social relationships (formed by public policy, cultural patterns, ideologies, consumption). Such systemic and complex definition allows for public space to be further defined in terms of ownership, modes and types of accessibility, degrees of enclosure, types and degrees of control, and its purpose. In a sharp contrast to such a systematic understanding, public agencies, elected public officials, and promoters of public space commonly see and present isolated sites and sporadic manifestations of public space, and provide simplistic schemes for their re-design commonly based on the largely unrealistic and misunderstood concept of 'place-making'. Even when public agencies understand public space somewhat holistically, they often come to predictable conclusions. In 1990, the Public Space for Public Life project was launched by the New York City Parks Council and the Central Park Conservancy Group (a public-private partnership) in order to bring attention to the need to understand the public space as a complex system whose appropriate treatment leads to economic revitalization, social improvement and community renewal. They argued that contemporary rationalized systems of maintenance and security have called into question the idea of 'public space as a public good' (Weiss 1993: 3) and have fragmented the system of public spaces into disparate modules. The comprehensive and holistic public space framework[3] they proposed was to be composed of sidewalks, greenways, beaches, parks, plazas, sanctuaries, green oasi, and other public amenities. In 1993, NYC had 26 369 acres of municipal parklands with 479 parks and a total of over 2 million trees, 15 miles of beaches, 890 playing fields, 862 playgrounds, 1885 handball courts, 2000 basketball courts, 511 tennis courts, 12 golf courts, 46 swimming pools, and 6 skating rinks. At the same time, NYC had 12 000 miles of sidewalks that no state and city agency was de facto in charge of, although numerous agencies balkanized its maintenance and operation into separate domains. As Agnotti reports, the Department of Transportation and Police Department are responsible for keeping sidewalks clear for pedestrian traffic: the Department of Transportation regulates the placement of newsstands, newspaper boxes, bus shelters, and bicycle racks. The Department of Sanitation is responsible for trash, whereas the Parks Department plants and maintains trees. The City Planning and Buildings Departments regulate size and characteristics of public spaces as mandated by the zoning code, while the Department of Consumer Affairs controls sidewalk cafes and small retail outlets (Agnotti 2003). Such heavily separated and unrelated these agencies are, that public space as a system is in fact no-one's explicit responsibility. The most controversial of all issues seems to be the one of management: in a bureaucratic twist typical for the total landscape, the Public Space for Public Life project recommends that such a systematically and holistically framed public resource be further compartmentalized, divided and offered to local management of public space based on public-private partnership, arguing that private management is the ultimate solution to the crisis of public management and control over public space, due to three central issues: accountability, effectiveness, and equity (Weiss 1993: 27). Such a view is fuelled in part by

the growing tension between elected public officials accountable to their constituents, and urban entrepreneurs most of whom, as Kayden brilliantly points out, live in the suburbs (Kayden 2000).

The focus of the debate on public space has been intentionally shifted from an essentially dysfunctional political and economic system unable to cope with its complexity, to the compartmentalization, individualization, and privatization of public space through the rhetoric of therapy.[4] Namely, those who promote such a view argue that the 'welfare ethos' that brings public space into being commonly implies crime, violence, and the 'homeless problem' caused by 'the breakdown of family structure, personal responsibility, and social order in too many areas'[5] of society. Individual public spaces that carry commercial potential (due to location, size, and symbolic relevance) are thus framed, demonized as 'dysfunctional', and privatized: subsequently, a locally-applied therapy in the form of 'placemaking' is proposed. Here we come to another incredibly hideous attribute of total landscape, namely its 'therapeutic ethos' (Cloud 1998: 68). As we have seen so far, total landscape demands that the solution to such a problem is privatization, and the economic rationale behind such decisions is naturalized to such a degree that, as Lawrence Lessig put it, for this question there is apparently no debate as 'the whole world is best managed when divided among private owners' (Lessig 2001). Most of the debate around public space and public resources in general has been focused on how best to divide up public resources. The assumption is that well divided resources will always work best. As Lessig argued, such a taken-for-granted, conservative view has been debated during the last hundred years and that debate has come to an end. Over the past century, the question exciting political philosophy has been which system of control works best and should resources be controlled by the state or by the free market, but as Lessig put it, the market is obviously a better tool for controlling resources than the state and 'between the two, there is no real debate.' Whether public space is thus privatized or privately managed through public-private partnership mechanisms, the basic assumption behind both public officials's and private interests's rationale is that private(ized) spaces that recognize basic public functions (such as seating and drinking fountains) will benefit the public at large as well as private owners and developers alike. Besides privatization, the therapeutic ethos also implies, as Cloud has forcefully argued, that therapeutic narratives replace potential political discourse with 'family responsibility' (Cloud 1998: 74), and consequently the responsibility of public agencies and the government.[6] It is, in that sense, that the process of totalization that brings theme parks and public space into the framework of total landscape is not obvious through formal similarities, but through systematic ones, through the system of (family) values, conditions and techniques that have been systematically extended upon the entire social realm. Theme parks and public spaces operate according to a shared ideological rationale that may or may not make them visually similar. 'Family values' are at the core of such a moralistic therapeutic discourse that produces a specific ensemble of social relationships, spatialized into its form of 'public space'. As indicated before, 'private' and 'public' are not properties of space, but of social relationships that are produced in a specific location. Public resources such as walkways and streets are not, by definition, public spaces, because public space is not as much a space as it is an experience, that is to say 'public' is not so much about the material characteristics of a public environment, its authenticity, whether its new or old, but about the degree to which an environment enables a type of human experience we call public today. A consensus on what type of experience we call 'public' today is pre-emptively grounded in pseudo-universal, conservative 'family values' spatialized as PROPASt and framed by the therapeutic narrative. In that sense, there is no competition between public and private capacities in terms of producing a desirable 'public' experience: just like Ford set the standards of assembly-line based industrial production, Walt Disney set standards for the production of 'public experience' enveloped in the therapeutic, family-value themed narratives.

PROPASt

The archetypal space of total landscape in the urban context is the privately-owned publicly-accessible space typically organized around a specific theme: PROPASt. Just like the theme park, PROPASt is a task-specific artifice, composed of material artifacts (built forms, landscape, topographic elements), visual, tactile, aural and olfactory environmental stimuli, and, most importantly, of the heavily scripted and controlled practices and relationships of its stakeholders and constituents (visitors, managers, employees, suppliers). As with the theme park, PROPASt is another powerful vehicle for the production of total landscape and it has been enabled by the convergence of governmental and corporate power in the second half of the Twentieth Century: namely, it appeared as a result of an economic, ideological and 'political struggle over the forms and powers of the bourgeois state and its relationship to civil society', between public institutions on one hand and the 'surplus capital seeking new areas of valorization' on the other.[7] As Zukin argued, since the second half of the Nineteenth Century, technological advances in transportation and telecommunication technology have helped create a hybrid urban culture, with respective public use of private spaces that, together with mass-consumption, led to what Henig called 'a shrinking of the realm of possible and a shrinking of the realm of public, simultaneously.' (Zukin 1991: 54) The enormous growth of corporate power in all spheres of life has propelled the effort to control large areas of public realm, particularly in the areas of transportation and communication (mass media and entertainment industry). Consequently, these events created a void between the space previously occupied and controlled by the power of state, and the emerging power of private capital and its need for establishing control over public realm. The symbiosis of governmental and commercial interests play a major role in producing PROPASt: for example, the infrastructure utilized for PROPASt is commonly constructed by state funds. The paradigmatic changes that occurred in the 1980s have created a new set of economic and political mechanisms that have allowed urban entertainment developers to design partnerships with city and state governments, based on mutual financing of the material infrastructure needed for PROPAST, in return for promised new jobs or expected tax revenues generated by its presence. In that respect, it is impossible to oversee how politics has been embedded in PROPAST's form. The same tripartite arrangement that brings the condition of total landscape into being—composed of a socio-economic system organized upon the idea of systematic totality, an infrastructural system that establishes its dominance 'on the ground', and a system designed and operated by the media industry that establishes its dominance in the collective consciousness and cultural imagination—powers the rationale of the production of PROPAST that can be analogically found in the tripartite structure that represents the above concerns: firstly, the production of PROPAST within the realm of media and entertainment industry, as well as by state laws and regulations (normative expectation, fabrication of desires, timetables, labor divisions, maps, marketing, branding, economic rationale, incentive zoning); secondly, the production of PROPAST by the establishment of new material infrastructure and also by the appropriation and use of the existing public infrastructure; and finally, the production of PROPAST by the establishment and production of locations, target destinations such are urban public resources previously controlled by the state, where one encounters total landscape 'in flesh'. And it is precisely out of a condition of such immense convergence of a variety of media, of individual and group experiences of history and future, of far and near, of general and particular, of material and immaterial, tangible and intangible, possible and impossible, abstract and concrete, as well as of the methods and techniques of production, that total landscape does not propose the reconfiguration of notions of individuality, particularity, public or private. What it proposes instead is the fundamental change of the principles of socio-economic mapping that render such categories relevant. In that sense, for a simulated experience of urbanity, of being in public space, categories such are 'private' or 'public' are rendered largely irrelevant precisely because the experience of either one is *de facto* privatized, individualized, and commodified as such.

In operational terms, PROPAST is a theater of operations typically produced through a mechanism that entertainment corporations and their planners call 'urban entertainment projects' (ULI 1996). The basic principle of that mechanism is what they call 'synergy', which to them means assembling a sufficient critical mass of different entertainment opportunities in one urban location (Adler 1995), or intensifying urban areas by entertainment opportunities. Such urban entertainment projects commonly show inclinations towards various forms of symbiosis with conventional urban (re)development projects, and have been naturalized as the way to revitalize (yet another therapeutic term) 'problematic' urban areas. In the mid-to-late 1980s, after corporations moved their operations to the suburbs in order to cut costs and improve efficiency, city centers remained virtually empty. In the face of such deindustrialization, in the late 1980s, city governments faced serious fiscal difficulties and offered tax-concessions, together with other incentives, in order to motivate the migration of industries back to the cities and revitalize the dying downtowns. The first to move back were entertainment corporations that by that time called themselves 'culture industry'. Much of the culture industry today colonizes urban spaces through public-private partnership schemes designed to divert funding from the reconstruction of inner-city slums to entertainment-based substitutions and theme-based reconstructions. As Hannigan reported (after a Harvard University Business School Report) key issues for such urban entertainment and revitalization projects are the following: establishment of a strong network between political, social and business constituents of the project; the organizing vehicle is a non-profit organization because corporations can only legally contribute to non-profit groups; positive media coverage that creates public interest; commissioning a major consulting firm that would give the project credibility; the project has to be linked to other revitalization projects in the area

Panorama of Bryant Park, New York City.

for legitimacy and symbolic reasons; lastly, the project is best off if building on a crisis situation where it can save an urban area or a building from immanent demolition (Hannigan 1998: 58–59).[8] Besides, it has been commonly perceived that a successful revitalization has to revolve around a flagship project such are waterfronts, sports arenas, museums or entertainment districts. Universal Studios's City Walk in Los Angeles and Disney Co.'s projects for the transformation of 42nd Street into an entertainment area with all the idiosyncratic features of PROPAST, are telling examples of such efforts.

PROPAST thus perpetuates the production of total landscape by intricately weaving an ensemble of techniques, methods and processes that include the following: interlocking and convergence of the domains of mass-media (television, advertising, film, Internet) with that of PROPAST environment; diversification of corporate portfolio through marketing synergy; production and standardization of the experience of 'public life' as a clear economic output, and the fabrication of public space as consumable good; reconstruction of the 'dysfunctional' urban areas into a desirable image of urban life and civility; denial and recontextualization of social conflict through private management and consensus entertainments; limited and tightly supervised accessibility; employment of sophisticated mechanisms of surveillance, control, and private security forces in the function of public safety; reliance on urban tourism; imageability; caricaturized thematic treatment of historic urban areas framed as historic preservation; public-private partnerships; and therapeutic ethos framed in 'family values'.

Public-Private Partnerships

Public-private partnerships were invented to bypass resistance to privatization and private management posed by public opinion advocates, community associations and neighborhood groups, but also to avoid conservative mortgage lenders, preservationist groups, and beautification committees (where they exist), as well as declining public subsidies for urban reconstructions. Since the 1950s, public-private partnerships in the United States were practiced in urban renewal projects as collaborations between semi-public redevelopment corporations and private developers, where conventional procedures for municipal policy-making had to be sidestepped (Pacione 2001: 316). Even though city governments assumed an entrepreneurial image through such efforts, their role in urban entertainment projects has been standardized and mostly reduced to facilitating land acquisition, infrastructure upgrades, tax benefits, and regulatory (legal) relief. At the same time, public agencies frame such projects as desirable due to promising tax revenues and new jobs generated in construction, service and entertainment industries. Besides, private management produces the type of 'order' over public spaces and the proper 'image of civility' (Zukin 1995, Hannigan 1998) that public agencies have failed to deliver. A typical example of public-private partnerships is the so-called Business Improvement Districts (BID). BIDS were created by the New York State Legislature in 1983 in order formally to allow business and property owners to take care of the local services that city government could no longer effectively provide. In many ways, BIDS are an elegant legal solution for colonizing public space by those who have an obvious stake in maintaining and developing it, and initially was meant to focus mostly on security and loitering.

BIDS are a continuation of the so-called public-private partnerships that were initially promoted in the 1970s, but also of a specific type of financing (tax increment financing: TIF) that was introduced in the 1970s as a mechanism that allowed redevelopment agencies to impose tax increases in order to finance the construction of flagship projects, such as convention centers and sport arenas. As a legal proposition, a BID is an autonomous entity (in fact a developer) that financially and politically lives off its right to impose additional taxation of property owners based on square footage. The taxes paid in addition to local and state taxes are collected by the city government and subsequently funneled to the BID in order to finance improvements in its area of jurisdiction. In many ways, a BID is a clear form of local government that largely excludes public influence. Bryant Park Restoration Corporation (BPRC), a subsidiary of the Bryant Park BID in NYC, is a typical example of BID's ability to successfully produce PROPAST. BPRC was established in 1980 by the Rockefeller Brothers Fund as a non-profit association composed of a group of citizens that represented businesses, property owners, and corporations surrounding Bryant Park (Zukin 1995: 6–7). The first directors of the BPRC were Andrew Heiskell, then Chairman of Time Inc. and the New York Public Library, and Daniel A. Biederman, a consultant on urban management issues who also founded the 34th Street Partnership and the Grand Central Partnership (the largest BID in the United States). BPRC was formed in order to restore historic Bryant Park, where New York's first World Fair, the Crystal Palace Exhibition, took place in 1853–54. Bryant Park is ideally located in Midtown Manhattan, on one side attached to New York City Library and on the other facing Sixth Avenue between 40th and 42nd Street. In its current footprint, it was origi-nally conceived in 1934 as a cover for the then new library stacks located beneath its grass lawn. Since the park suffered a severe decline during 1970s, the 1980 masterplan conceived by Heiskell and Biederman called for a redesign of the park in an attempt to bring the public back to it and in the process generate revenues. In 1981, William H. Whyte and Project for Public Spaces conducted an in-depth analysis of the park, sponsored by the Rockefeller Foundation and commissioned by the Bryant Park Restoration Corporation. Since 1982, a series of design projects were commissioned, and the final one heavily regulated the access to and circulation through the park by isolating entry points in order to enable effective control on the ground. The park finally reopened in April 1992 with a budget six times larger than that under prior public management (Lederman 2003). It has also been claimed that Bryant Park is the largest effort nation-wide to apply private management backed by private funding to a public park (NYCG 2004). Needless to say, crime has been reduced by 100 percent since the Corporation's founding. In 1996, Bryant Park won the Urban Land Institute Excellence Award for public projects. Its central position in the city, its size, and its critical mass of potential consumers that work in the surrounding blocks, makes Bryant Park a powerful PROPAST, whose theme is the commodified urban experience. The environment is scripted through a range of daily, seasonal, and annual pseudo-events such as the Mercedes Benz Fashion Show taking place in February, or summer film festivals sponsored by Citibank and HBO. City Library has organized an open-air 'reading room' that lends free materials and books to park visitors. New York Chess and Backgammon offers chessboards for US$6 per hour of use. And there is a an old-fashion merry-go-round on the

Entrance to Bryant Park from 6th Avenue and 42nd Street.

Public art at display in Bryant Park.

40th street-side of the park. The schedule of events and the list of public amenities can also be found at Bryant Park's website, together with the code of behavior, its history, and other useful information. BPRC hired private security forces and made an agreement with the New York City Police Department on the reciprocity of the security force so that each side provides four uniformed officers a day to guard the park (Zukin 1995: 30). In addition to that, the lease money from the two privately-owned restaurants and kiosks leased to Starbucks and Ben and Jerry is used to maintain the park, pay for security and pseudo-events. Public access is regulated by dress and behavior codes as well as by the operating times. After hours, no-one is allowed in the park. Such developments capitalize on the empty space left by the government's inability to find appropriate manage-ment solutions. As Julia Vitullo-Martin, a senior fellow at the Manhattan Institute, wrote: 'Bryant Park's successful privatization is a tribute to a selfless innovation by the public sector—permitting the private sector to step in with resources and operational skills to restore and manage a splendid public space. Most public officials wouldn't have had the courage to let the private sector take over.' (Vitullo-Martin 2004) In other words, as Vitullo-Martin wrongly argues, the public sector inno-vates when it leases public resources to private corporations. On the

other hand, Vitullo-Martin is right in arguing that public sector has indeed attained a considerable degree of selflessness. Needless to point out, area rents have increased by US$20–25 per square foot and property values have soared, whereas the park now nets more than US$1 million from operations and has a total annual operating budget of US$4 million (French 2005).

New York City's Privately Owned Public Spaces

Privately owned public space is, what Jerold Kayden called, 'law's oxymoronic invention', a part of the public-private partnership aimed at addressing pressing urban concerns in New York City. New York City's Privately Owned Public Space (POPS) was inaugurated in 1961 on the occasion of adopting a new zoning resolution that had replaced the city's first zoning resolution of 1916. The 1961 resolution, also called 'incentive zoning', has enabled the city to trade off with devel-opers by offering extra floor area bonuses to developers willing to construct open spaces for public use designed in accordance with the Zoning Resolution standards (Kayden 2000: 1). The surface covered by NYC's 503 POPS is more than 82 acres (3,58 million square feet, the size of nearly 30 average city blocks) and provoked Kayden to refer to it as 'the decentralized Central Park' (Kayden 2000). On the other

Chess boards for rent at Bryant Park.

The Reading Room at Bryant Park.

Private police force at work in Bryant Park.

hand, the developers of nearly 300 office, apartment and hotel towers have been allowed to build an extra 16 million square feet of floor area, about the equivalent of seven Empire State Buildings. The first generation of major POPS were plazas, arcades and atria. Over the years, other types were added to the resolution such as 'elevated plazas' and the 'through block arcades'. The 'through block' arcade has been defined as 'a continuous area within a building connecting one street with another street, plaza or arcade adjacent to the street'; building one would authorize a developer to a bonus of six square feet for every foot of it. A plaza was defined as an 'open area accessible to the public at all times [...] a continuous open area along a front lot line, not less than 10 feet deep (measured perpendicular to the front line), with an area of not less than 750 square feet [...] unobstructed from its lowest level to the sky' (Kayden 2000: 11). Due to numerous manipulations conducted by developers or their tenants, the City has changed zoning provisions numerous times: in 1975, it has replaced the term 'plaza' with 'urban plaza', 'sidewalk widening', and 'open air concourse', three new categories of POPS. Today, the City recognizes 12 distinct types of POPS, as well as numerous sub-categories that emerged out of mass customization of the provision: plazas, arcades, urban plazas, residential plazas, sidewalk widenings, open air con-

courses, covered pedestrian spaces, through block arcades, through block connections, through block galleries, elevated plazas, and sunken plazas (Kayden 2000: 25). Each of the types has a characteristic set of legal actions that govern its design and use, such are space requirements, footprint and volume, hours of public access, amenities required, and so on. Functional and visual amenities were also mandated by the new provision so that, for instance, for every 30 feet of urban plaza, one linear foot of seating was required (Kayden 2000: 17). Signs have been also required to be posted at visible locations, indicating the owner's name, list of amenities, operating times, and a note informing the public clearly that they are in a spatial envelope that allows open public access. Unlike public property owned by the city (such as Bryant park), or unlike private properties entirely devoted to public access and use (such are theme parks or department stores), POPS were legalized as a 'physical place located on private property to which the owner has granted legally binding rights of access and use to members of the public, most often in return for something of value from the City to the owner' (Kayden 2000: 21). As Kayden indicates, even though owners of POPS have legally ceded significant rights associated with their private property, including the right to exclude members of the public, in practice many failed

Panorama of the Park Avenue Plaza, New York City.

to comply with the law and have exercised the right to exclude the undesirables either by blocking access by material means, psychological means, or simply by building a department store in what was supposed to be an urban plaza. Kayden also identified three major categories of violation: lack of required public amenities, denial of or a reduced public access, and annexation by commercial tenants for private use.

As Kayden wrote, such a public-private partnership was driven principally by real estate economics and has been productive in locations that are attractive to developers (Kayden 45). Areas of the city that cannot attract such developments will not have an equal chance in producing such a form of public space. Thus, a critical mass of potential consumers should already be present at the targeted location, desirably in motion (not because of an existing program that will be eradicated) and the brand to be imposed should already have a resonance in the context (such as Starbucks, or Ben and Jerry). The major difference between private parties developing public spaces and communal, public organizations doing it is the leverage: Sony, Disney or Universal use PROPASt for the development and promotion of other products such as television shows, music productions, film productions, theme parks, or merchandize, so that losses from its production can be offset by other profitable products. Communal agencies have no way of leveraging losses by other products because, for them,

public space is both the product and a means of producing it. In that sense, one of the essential effects of total landscape is that there can never be a true competition between public and private aims in terms of producing public space. Despite the potential losses that corporate sponsors can absorb if necessary, they also often have a clear profit interest in it, and customarily count on an operating profit of 25 percent of gross revenues. Directly linked to that is the return rate on the capital investment which for urban entertainment projects is usually up to 20 percent. This level of return is conditioned upon many of the requirements that capital lenders extend to developers of urban entertainment projects. One of the requirements that is most obvious to common consumer is the one that demands more than half of the retail spaces should be pre-leased. Such a requirement results in predictable tenant-lists and their relationships in commercial environments, such as the link between Barnes and Noble with Starbucks.

Since there was never a systematic effort in designing public space in New York City, the 'scatter diagram of public space within the four principal clusters portrays an archipelago lacking any supervening organizational principle' (Kayden 2000: 45) with no spatial coherence, visual hierarchy, and any experiential logic at all. Some accidentally networked spaces extend through a couple of blocks as passageways and through block connections. Based on site visits in 1998 and 1999, the study concludes that nearly half of the POPs do not comply with

city rules and are of only marginal value even when they do meet the design requirements.[9] As Kayden wrote, 'harnessing the profit motive in ways that encourage enhanced stewardship by the private owner and a better public space experience for everyone, has been encouraged by the Zoning Resolution and its administration' (Kayden 2000: 57) but it had sadly fallen short of achieving the desired effect. Redefining terminology used to describe types and properties of public space did not preclude private developers from militarizing public space and remapping the rhetoric on the ground. In a similarly nostalgic attempt to introduce order and systematic logic, the Chinese Government issued in the 1990s, new codes for naming an ever increasing number of quasi-public spaces such as malls, large department stores, shopping arcades and commercial 'town squares', in order to protect its public spaces from polluting commodity rhetoric that began misleading the Chinese public. The adjective 'public' can, in mainland China, be attached only to spaces that possess 'real attributes' traditionally associated with public spaces. Thus, a 'public square' would have to be an openly accessible environment without controlled mechanisms and with the possibility for a diverse public to satisfy their public needs. On the other hand, a 'shopping arcade' would have to be predominantly reserved for shopping and would have to have arcades, as they are traditionally defined and conventionally understood.

Therapeutic Discourse in Action: Revitalization of Problematic Urban 'Zones'

One of the common treads that many PROPAST share is that they commonly come into being through the process of revitalization of 'problematic' urban areas. Through aggressive marketing and public relations campaigns before the reconstruction begins, PROPAST developers fabricate a large symbolic capital needed to convince the public in the inevitability of private management for public good. A number of such projects marked the 1990s, with a few exceptional examples built in Japan. The Universal CityWalk, Universal Studios's reconstruction of a problematic urban district in Osaka that opened in 2001, in many ways marks a quantum leap in scale and complexity of PROPAST. It combines theme parks, hotels, office spaces, conference centers, cinemas, theaters, retail shopping, restaurants, spas, and many other programs in a planned total surface area of two million square feet. The other two significant Japanese examples, both built in the mid-1990s, are Canal City in Fukuoka and Festival Gate in Osaka. Both of these projects mark attempts to solve deeply rooted economic and socio-political conflicts in 'problematic zones' of both cities by revitalizing them through the production of PROPAST. Osaka's Festival Gate is an open-air, themed shopping mall inserted into the existing, dense urban fabric. Accessibility and control issues are easily resolved here: gates are large and obvious, and they are guarded by a uniformed, private police force. Just like the Mall of America, West

View of the Festival Gate complex, Osaka.

Attractions at the Festival Gate complex, Osaka.

Edmonton Mall or any similar venture, Festival Gate is a hybrid of theme park, shopping mall, hotel, cinema, restaurant, wedding chapel, a gigantic Japanese spa, and numerous other amenities that turn this location into an urban resort. It is located in an area called Tennoji, historically a 'dangerous' area of Osaka, where unemployment ran unusually high for the Japanese standards, and where prostitution and street fights were the norm. The area was densely built out of cheap constructions and shanties, and mostly ruled by gangs (*buraku-min*). It still bears many traces to its past. The construction of Festival Gate, although meant to cover only a small portion of Tennoji, was seen as a way to impose order and the rule of law on the entire area. When reconstruction began, people whose property was demolished were given dissent accommodation, allowances, and promised jobs in construction and in new businesses. Once the construction was completed, many were employed throughout the Festival Gate as janitors, waiters, cooks, or maintenance personnel. It is easy to locate and identify them in this sanitized environment, because most of them have extensive tattoos and other symbols so different from those of the visitors. It is that very element of locality, of vernacular quality that is being used in Festival Gate as a symbolic capital in order to generate real revenues by attracting the crowds to this urban safari. One can still have a simulated feeling of danger in Festival gate

by being served by a true, tough-looking Tennoji man, while at the same time taking pleasure in shopping at GAP in an overall sanitized and safe environment. The environment of Festival Gate includes a hotel, a large spa resort facility, a roller coaster that runs through buildings and symbolically frames total experience, a variety of shopping experiences, rest areas beautified with life-size plastic palm trees, and much more. Uniforms of all employees are color coded to match the color of the area they are in: trash cans, pavement color, plastic trees, benches, facades, furniture, flowers, and uniforms are carefully orchestrated into a homogeneous and therapeutic environmental image.

Canal City in Fukuoka was born out of similar ideas of revitalizing a problematic urban area and turning it into a profitable image of urbanity. A US$1.4 billion urban entertainment project was designed by Jon Jerde Partnership in 1996 in Fukuoka, Japan. Unlike Festival Gate in Osaka, Canal City does not have the physical enclosure similar to a conventional theme park. The environment merges with the surrounding urban fabric in a relatively unassuming way, transforming it inconspicuously into a PROPASt based on the 'civic center' theme. Obviously, the commodified civic theme envelopes shopping and entertainment. Besides shops, wedding chapels, hotels, restaurants,

Views of Canal City, Fukuoka.

Fukuoka City Theater at Canal City, Fukuoka.

a river walk, an AMC multiplex cinema, and the Joypolis Sega game arcade, it also includes the City Hall and the 1200-seat City Theater. The environment is programmed and scripted in very elaborate ways that include a number of diverse pseudo-events such are 'street musicians', jugglers, food festivals, concerts, and so on. As Jon Jerde, the architect of the Canal City in Fukuoka and Universal's City Walk in Los Angeles wrote, his office is increasingly 'applying this approach to obsolete urban environments in need of regeneration, helping them to become animated and revitalized.' (Jerde 1998) In operational terms, both Canal City and Festival Gate are real theaters of operation with most of the characteristics discussed in Themeing.

The 'healing' of Time Square, or the so-called Time Square transformation project, started in the mid-1980s by the founding of a non-profit public-private partnership titled the 42nd Street Redevelopment Agency. As Hannigan reported, its task was initially to organize and publicly express disapproval of existing buildings, tenants and business (many of pornographic character), design the redevelopment scheme, secure the financing by identifying the future tenants and making them commit to the project, and among many other issues organize and launch an overwhelming public relations campaign (Hannigan 1998: 103). The partners initially identified were

Walt Disney Co., Tussaud, AMC and Livent as entertainment giants, Park Tower Realty, Tishman Urban Development and Forest City Ratner as developers, and Prudential as an insurance company of global magnitude. Contrary to popular belief, it was the 42nd Street Redevelopment Agency that initially had approached Walt Disney Co. regarding the Times Square project. Times Square was a new territory for Walt Disney Co. because it is a 'living' place, with hundreds of thousands of passers-by daily and over 20 million tourists annually. The immediate trade theater of Times Square is populated by over 20 million people. Also, Times Square is a place with a strong historical character and in this case, Walt Disney Co. is not capitalizing on its own symbolic depository only, it is also displacing and appropriating the symbolic capital of Manhattan. As in any other theater of operations, reconstructed Broadway theaters and individual environmental modules that make the actual strive towards maximum economic efficiency have been designed by corporations themselves, while the 42nd Street Redevelopment Agency assigned the Miami-based architectural firm Arquitectonica to design the new landmark-building, an environmental target. In 1995, the 42nd Street Redevelopment Agency held a design competition for the tower that marked the North-Western tip of the Times Square redevelopment project. Arquitectonica and the developer, Tishman Realty & Construction,

Disney's New Amsterdam Theater on 42nd Street at Times Square, New York City, 2005.

Street sign for New 42nd Street at Times Square, New York City, 2005.

Times Square BID security officer, New York City, 2005.

were selected to carry on the project. The Westin Hotel that occupies the tower stretches between 42nd Street and 43rd Street on Eighth Avenue, is a part of the redevelopment effort that also includes four office towers around Times Square, new movie theaters, retail destinations, residential projects, and the restored historic theatres along 42nd Street. As Paul Goldberger wrote, the tower 'is fascinating, if only because it makes Times Square vulgar in a whole new way' (Goldberger 2002). How the tower interfaces with 42nd Street is through the 17-story base programmed with entertainment and shopping content, adding thus to the reprogramming and scoring of the Time Square theater. This theatron contains a multiplex cinema, shoppertainment and eatertainment, and is cladded with neon advertising panels so characteristic of the 'old' Time Square. Once again, the result is a Broadway 'that never was and will always be', but on the actual site of the real Broadway. Besides Walt Disney Co., all major entertainment companies, such as Sony, Warner Bros. or Universal, have in-house departments whose task is to perpetually search and identify similar opportunities for new urban entertainment projects. In parallel, together with IMAX Corporation and Iwerks Entertainment, their research and development departments constantly work on developing miniaturized technology that allows urban entertainment developers to adjust theme park experiences to complex urban locations often limited in size, such as reconstructed theaters, music halls, semi-enclosed public spaces, and other similar venues. Despite immense technological advancements in developing urban entertainment projects, it is still unknown how can PROPASt be designed in order to assure the supreme economic efficiency that is otherwise easily achieved within the territorial confinements of traditional theme parks. According to Disney's chief-architect Robert Stern, Michael Eisner, the CEO of Walt Disney Co., advised the Times Square design team, when they arrived at the moot point, with the following words: 'Gate the whole street off and take it over!' (Adler 1995) Unexpectedly low revenues at the Universal Walk in Los Angeles alarmed Walt Disney Co. and other urban-entertainment developers because the pleasure of urban interactions is not necessarily attained through the act of monetary exchange and consumption. Since visitors to Universal Walk did not have to pay an entrance fee, they simply enjoyed this 'urbanoid' (Goldberger 1996) environment in a traditional and almost forgotten ways without spending a penny.

Marketing PROPASt

As the 'spending routes' extend far beyond the physical boundaries

of PROPASt, the profit achieved within it is only a part of the overall financial revenues. As discussed in Chapter 2, Universal Walk or Times Square are, for Universal and Disney, symbolic projects linked into an intricate web of cross-marketing schemes and, just as theme parks, they are not core-generating revenues; due to interlocking schemes they are simply utilized to diversify corporate portfolios. All giant theme park developers and operators use theme parks as vehicles for the promotion of other products. What more powerful a vehicle for promotion can one imagine than an active presence in the Times Square theater? For instance, as discussed before, for Vivendi Universal theme parks simply act as a node in the network of cross-promotional and interlocked marketing schemes by providing important revenue diversification in addition to its other business that include television and cable channels, film production, publishing, and retail. On a smaller scale, the developer and urban entrepreneur James Rouse was diversifying the offer of his Festival Marketplace theaters by subsidizing small theatra that catered to special consumer needs and desires, such as specialty wine and cheese markets or European deserts: he called such a subsidy system 'pre-servicing' and believed that both the community and the James Rouse Corporation would benefit from such a practice (Satterthwaite 2001).

The confluence and interdependence of PROPASt, the theme park industry, the airline industry, the cruise industry, the railway industry, the car rental business, the hotel industry and the tourist industry (the engineering of leisure), telephone and communication companies, the credit card industry, and other interests is increasing exponentially with the consolidation of the entertainment market. Based on the conclusions drawn from the marketing analysis typical of themeparking, where the boundaries of the trade theater and the specifics of the theater of operations are defined, an adequate concept and thematic framework of PROPASt is designed to target the specific audience(s). Given that its theme is always based in the concept of urbanity, marketing proceeds by establishing the 'value' of the PROPASt's offer or the estimate that customers make in relation to the ability of a PROPASt to satisfy their desires and expectations. Analogous to theme parks, boundaries of PROPASt environments are not defined only by their geographic locales, but also by their media presence, and desires and expectations are accordingly fabricated by the media where the PROPASt is used as a backdrop for a variety of television programs, movies, sports competitions, conventions and convention-related television broadcasting. Marketing synergy enables the PROPASt to promote movies, movies to promote merchandise and merchandise to promote theme parks, so that cycles of synergetic marketing expand endlessly into entertainment space. Companies like Walt Disney have a strong brand presence in the global market, represented by the confluence of the company name, logo, storyline, theme and characters with the media presence and the physical presence of Walt Disney theme parks, retail locations, urban entertainment centers (Times Square or DisneyQuest) and the themeing of each and every PROPAST (physical, visual and sensual environment). It is therefore easier for Walt Disney Co's to fabricate emotional bonding with its brand identity that connects the experience in each of Disney's PROPAST and facilities with its media presence. How Walt Disney Company's totalizing cross-promotional strategies and interlocking marketing schemes are related to PROPAST was successfully detailed in Janet Wasko's essay 'The Magical-Market World of Disney' of April 2001 (Wasko 2001) that discusses an aggressive array of promotional activities related to the release of Walt Disney Pictures' 35th animated film *Hercules* in North American theaters on the 27th June 1997.

The promotion of *Hercules* started with the initial announcement of the film in entertainment and trade magazines and in Disney-owned media during the pre-production and production process. As Wasko indicates, during the 1996 Christmas season trailers for *Hercules* were shown before each theatrical screening of *101 Dalmatians* and were included on copies of the *Toy Story* and *The Hunchback of Notre Dame* videocassettes. In February 1997, the Walt Disney Company started their third MegaMall Tour co-sponsored by GM, McDonald's and Chevrolet spanning five months in 20 North American cities, and featuring 11 different attractions, including *Hercules* promotional multimedia experiences, Hercules-themed game booths, introduction of the new *Hercules* games by Disney Interactive and many other attractions. In parallel, Walt Disney Company opened its *Hercules On Ice* show planned to play in 28 cities over a five-year tour. Accompanying each of 300 presentations were concession stands selling some

Hercules gifts out of a choice of nearly 7000 different products made by over 100 carefully selected manufacturers worldwide. These products, together with a range of promotional materials, have been featured by the tie-in partners including K-mart, McDonald's, Nestle, Quaker Oats, General Motors Corp., Mattel, Pyramid and others. As Wasko further indicates, the film's soundtrack was released by Columbia Records on the 20th May 1997, together with the interactive merchandise such as Walt Disney's Animated Storybook, *Hercules Disney's Print Studio,* Walt Disney's *Hercules* Action Game and others. At the same time, the Walt Disney Company launched the *Hercules* Internet site featuring details of its MegaMall tour, the *Hercules* story, a downloadable film's trailer, advanced ticket-purchasing, information about the characters of the animated film, film-inspired games and an ESPN-inspired OSPN: Olympus Sports Panhellenic Network. During the weekend of 13th–15th June 1997 Disney, featured *The Hercules World Premiere Weekend* in New York that included a variety of promotional events scattered around Manhattan and covered fully by the Disney-owned and other media outlets. This complex event featured live performances, jugglers, dancers and other street entertainers, interactive games, animation demonstrations, exhibits, sneak previews, sweepstakes tickets that appeared in New York-area newspapers and so on. On Saturday the 13th June, the Heroes from Around the World show was held in front of the Disney-owned New Amsterdam Theatre on 42nd Street, featuring Disney's CEO Michael Eisner, New York Mayor Rudolph W. Giuliani, Robin Roberts of ABC Sports and ESPN, and as Wasko reports, a group of 'world-class athletes known for their Herculean efforts'. The world premiere of the film was followed by the *Hercules Electrical Parade* that started on 42nd Street and continued up Fifth Avenue all the way to 66th Street. The parade was a redesign of the traditional Disneyland Park's *Main Street Electrical Parade* and was prepared for showing in Walt Disney theme parks worldwide. Disney management also arranged for the city and surrounding shop owners to turn off all lights (including all street lights) along the planned route so that its 500 000 light bulbs can create a precisely desired effect. Over one million people attended the parade. *The Hercules Summer Spectacular* at the New Amsterdam Theatre started on Sunday the 14th June as a 12-day exclusive New York preview before the official release of the film, including a live stage show, a full orchestra and a cast of Disney characters. The Walt Disney Company aired an ABC-special prime-time television program, introducing *Hercules* and two specials on the Disney Channel. One of them, the *Hercules Strikes Manhattan* show, was built on the move of the *Hercules Electrical Parade* through the streets of Manhattan. Disney-owned A&E cable channel featured *Hercules* on their Biography series. In parallel, the movie theater in Celebration, Florida was showing *Hercules,* and finally the *Hercules Victory Parade* opened at Walt Disney World Resort in Florida. Wasko provided plenty of examples of Walt Disney Company's intercorporate synergy including the following: shortly after the Disney-ABC merger, the *Roseanne* show featured several episodes about visits to Walt Disney World Resort, and several *Good Morning America* broadcasts were done directly from the same theme park. In 1997, ABC Sports coverage of the Tour de France bicycle race included a feature on Disneyland Paris Resort, and, finally, one of the events that took place at Walt Disney World Resort in November 1998 was ABC's *Super Soaps Weekend* show (Wasko 2001).

Scores, Pseudo Events, and Urban Tourism

What *de facto* puts the entire PROPASt apparatus in motion are precisely defined scores. Just like in the case of the theme park, scores put the PROPASt assembly line in motion by connecting different constitutive elements of the environment into a coherent arrangement of forces within the theater of operations. Scores define who participates, in what capacity, where, and at what time. An essential instrument of scores is pseudo-events: Hercules Parade is an obvious example of such a pseudo-event that had put in motion the entire Manhattan. Pseudo-events are a key instrument of scores in designing and controlling the spatio-temporal consumption of PROPASt

THE THIRD NATURE

Besides inheriting the symbolism and the sites of monastic gardens and classical villas, the microcosm of the Renaissance garden also reflected the macrocosm of the universe and the divine order on which it was based. The Renaissance had found the garden to be an ideal vehicle with which to represent the symbiotic relationship between art (culture) and nature. This symbiosis was hard to define, generally it was named 'the third nature,' or 'the other nature' (Puppi 1991: 56). This concept was one of the most important subjects of the Renaissance discourse and appeared regularly in discussions of art, medicine, alchemy and architecture.[1] Another strong concept underlying the symbolism of Renaissance thought was the relationship between the visible and the invisible: the general cosmic order was believed to embody both visible and invisible forces. The garden was meant to rationalize and visualize this concept by the use of scientific apparatus: mathematical perspective, proportional relationships, symmetry, strong geometric forms, and so on. Taking all this into account, Renaissance gardens cannot be read solely through abstraction of transcendental archetypes and through iconic and cosmological associations, since the divine order they represented was not only embodied in the garden itself but also in the intellectual and bodily experience of the human subject (Comito 1991). The bodily experience of the subject was made possible by a shift from medieval, two-dimensional arrangement of *parterre* to a multidimensional kinesthetic experience and the utilization of perspective as the main ordering device. When natural elements such as trees or bushes were shaped and arranged into these sophisticated architectural compositions, it was not to subordinate nature to geometry as it was to 'please the eye'. This subordination of nature to design principles was seen as 'artificial': in that sense artificiality had become an essential element of the 'symbolic iconography' of Renaissance gardens because the garden was essentially 'a piece of fiction, a work of the imagination' (Puppi 1984: 15–20). Forms, textures and colors of the plants used played important roles in architectural compositions: Renaissance architects have studied ancient ways of garden-making from the ruins of Hadrian's Villa and other important structures.

1. Palladio, for example, attempted to define architecture as 'other nature'.

environments. Score determines the character of pseudo-events, their environmental (spatial) disposition, the time of occurrence and duration, frequency, the way they interact with visitors, number of performers, and so on. In the case of PROPASt, scores also orchestrate the performance of tourists and passers by through the construction of environmental activity. Rent-an-event companies supply PROPASt operators with a range of pseudo-events from daily needs such as street bands, magicians, clowns, jugglers, and dance performances to more elaborated seasonal or annual needs, such as fashions shows, film or music festivals. Jon Jerde argued that his designs for PROPASt created a negotiated place of dialogue between performers and an ever-changing audience: since the audience also has a performative role in PROPASt, the success of such an environment lies in its capacity to visualize the audience in its internal and external interactions (Jerde 1998). Script, Jerde wrote, is a symbiosis of planning, programming, and architecture and in order to enable the participation of audience, 'script has to be flexible so as to encourage interaction':

> Districts are clustered around event spaces to reinforce a sense of place. These spaces are strung together like pearls on a necklace, providing an organic collection of variety, vitality and interaction. These types of experiential spaces invite an almost cinematic sequence of mystery, anticipation, unfolding and surprise. We attempt to create spaces of memorable sensory stimulation, sometimes subliminally by stretching or shrinking scale, or by abstracting the indigenous vernacular, often through layering of graphics, landscape and multimedia. (Jerde 1998: 69)

The consumption of such Jerdesque urban pseudo-photo-opportunity locations, and the experience of being in public that they successfully fabricate, is facilitated by the apparatus of urban tourism, which also plays a key role in the production of PROPASt. Urban tourism today facilitates the circulation of people to specific urban locations that are consumed as 'ludic spaces' (Lefebvre 1991) or 'tourist spaces' (Gottdiener 1998: 13) within the cycles of the production of entertainment space. Unlike in the early 1990s, when trade theaters located outside of major urban concentrations began acquiring resort-like

forms, in the early 2000s, trade theaters located within large urban concentrations which provide a steady influx of tourists are capitalizing on an increasingly prevalent idea of visitors to stay 'closer to home'. Together with the economic recession and the reduction of discretionary income, the 1990s have also brought about an attempt to rationalize leisure pursuits in terms of safety. In a strange way, the two have been woven together in the late 1990s. Many of the practices that city governments, in collaboration with the tourist industry and private operators, are involved in signify a move towards total landscape. For example, the problem of controlling escalating influx of tourists that goes beyond the carrying capacity of historic urban centers has in Europe been resolved in many cities by the so-called 'tourist card'. A tourist card is an incentive to tourists to plan their visit ahead and thereby enjoy many savings on food, shopping, transportation, and other services. There is only a limited number of such cards every day, and after they sell out, the city provides no such incentives until the next day. Through such a system of motivations, historic cities, such as Venice, not only struggle to regulate peak tourist traffic and allow residents to go about their daily lives, but also effectively remap the tourist experience. It goes without saying that those businesses and service providers that offer incentives listed on the tourist card will have a significant advantage and will be visited first. It seems that this is a desirable way to protect the historic city and allow tourists to experience it first hand in a 'civilized and organized manner' that would create financial and symbolic benefit to both the city government and the businesses promoted by the card. However, the conditions in many cities are worsening due to the growth of urban tourism, a development that prompted the city of Venice to draw up a 10-point 'code of conduct' printed on the back of the tourist card (Bush 2003). The code contains 10 suggestions that determine rules of behavior in the city, from dress code to advising tourists to 'always keep to the right when walking around the city', not to wash their feet in the water, to use maps in finding ways around the city, and not to stop when walking across bridges. The day when the historic city will close to those without a 'passport', such as the one HTB provides, is not far. At that point, the difference between the historic urban core and the theme park will be that of degree rather than of kind. The Italian Minister of Tourism told the BBC that Venetians are 'horrified at the possibility of becoming something like Disney World [...] We want to keep the town alive. We want people to come back to live in Venice.' (Bush 2003) Along the lines of this argument, Peter Hall also anticipated that the industrial city of the late Nineteenth and early Twentieth Centuries will rapidly become an artifact from the past, isolated from the continuum of dynamic urban systems in action, to be visited in the form of an open-air museum or theme park, just like New York's South Street Seaport (Hall and Brotchie 1991). Venice used to be a city of nearly 200 000 people, but as a result of tourist invasions, businesses and people that did not directly benefit from urban tourism evacuated from the city in search of more affordable places to live and more comfortable environments to do business in. Today, Venice has 60 000 residents, and the number of residents is steadily declining while the number of tourists is increasing soon to reach the level of 15 million a year. Many argue that traditional public spaces in cities across the world have been colonized by urban tourism and those are no longer the sites of public life. New public spaces are not emerging unless their privatized clones appear as a manifestation of mass-consumption practices, either a shopping mall, or a theme park, or perhaps an urban event: a type of PROPAst to be sure. Thus, the experience of public life has been diminished by urban tourism and urban entertainment. Where there are traces of such authentic experiences of public life left, those have also been increasingly turned into tourist attractions. For suburban tourists, the type of interaction that forms the core of urbanity, including crime and danger, are significant attractions when observed from a safe distance. Witness urban safaris, built to cater to such tourist desires, as they are becoming a world-wide phenomenon. The City Safari in Rotterdam features US$60 'explorations' of the areas of Rotterdam that neither residents nor tourists would otherwise dare visiting 'through doors that normally remain closed.' As such safaris are advertised, 'residents and entrepreneurs will welcome you into their homes or places of worship, stores or workshops, cafés or restaurants.'[10] As Tracy Metz points out, the tour includes homeless shelters, a center for Iraqi refugees seeking political asylum, artists's studios, 'underground' tattoo parlors, and many other venues that have traditionally been hidden from the tourist eye (Metz 2002: 101). Similarly, tour buses packed with Japanese and European tourists visit African American churches in Harlem on Sunday mornings in order to attend performances by gospel choirs (Hannigan 1998: 74). Thousands of small urban communities across the world, striving to find sources of economic revitalization, are competing in identifying what makes their five city blocks unique by trying to unearth cultural, historic, topological and other features and landmarks that could be turned into symbolic capital. As Dave Eagleson of Forrec advices such communities, after they identify promising 'opportunities' they should proceed to identify private developers with the means and experience to turn such opportunities into actual attractions, and then provide them with all the support possible to make it happen (Eagleson 2002), including infrastructure improvements, legislative support, and the rest. Subsequently, developers will pack all of the amenities in one distinctive, attractive, easily communicated concept that will bring tourists to their area and make them stay longer. Eagleson cites as a case study Montreal's 2002 sale of the financially-troubled La Ronde amusement park to the Six Flags Corporation, arguing that a leading theme park developer and operator such as Six Flags 'brings to the table a mastery of the tricky mechanics of attractions management the city itself could never hope to possess.' If and when cities depend on the 'tricky mechanics of attractions management', they have no choice but to do just that.

Economic impact of urban tourism and of urban entertainment projects usually suffers from profit-leakage and has a negative economic effect on the urban context. Even though, on a macro-economic scale, the production of PROPASt can be seen as successful and desirable, the micro-economic scale shows a very different picture as profits are drained from the area and directed to corporate headquarters, in every instance when a major multinational corporation develops an urban project. Empirical evidence shows that there are no examples where profit stayed in the immediate community. As shown in Chapter 2, direct external investments related to theme parks also suffer from the 'profit leakage' because profit never stays in the region where the actual operation takes place, but in the region of investment's origin. In that respect, BIDs may be an obvious exception because there is no significant profit leakage per se. However, not only that the urban region where the BID's theater of operation is located does not fully benefit from its economic performance, but the higher the economic multiplier becomes, the more damage is actually done to the local community. As the Bryant Park example shows, rents, insurance rates, prices of food and beverage prices, as well as many other indicators in the immediate vicinity have risen significantly, pushing those who cannot compete under such conditions out of its theater of operations. And those who cannot compete are usually those whose businesses are not of an entertaining nature, and do not support the overall objective of the theater of operations as defined by Bryant Park. Hundreds of such small business and individuals have been evacuating the area in search of a more affordable place to live and do business. As we have seen above, similar developments occurred in Venice where small souvenir shops, hotels and restaurants profit but all other business not related to tourism see little economic benefit and much cost inefficiency.

PROPASt and the Environmental Control

Design of every public environment affects human behavior patterns and enables certain practices while it disables others. It is a common notion that, just like the theme park, the PROPASt operates as a behavioral laboratory, given that corporate strategies are focused on the manipulation of human behavior in order to achieve desirable out-

comes out of the human-environment interaction. Since the PROPASt is an essentially commercial environment where the objective of profit-making (dollar volume) is clear, it exhibits a restrictive interest in human behavior and a restrictive menu of possibilities for human interaction. A deliberate manipulation of the behavior of entire social groups towards privately-centered, narrowly framed aims is repulsive, but the degree of control that a public environment exercises is always directly reciprocal to its objective. The PROPASt is a task-specific environment that largely represents public ethos formed by essentially conservative but also middle class, suburban values and beliefs. It is no coincidence that the PROPASt attracts an audience that shares such values; after all, one has to see the world in a certain way to be persuaded by a metaphor. Since the 1980s, theme parks have become prototypes for environmental control, especially in their ability to shape the 'user response'. Inducing positive affiliations in visitors and coaxing individuals inclinations to interact with the environment has, to a great extent, been a result of the PROPASt's ability to measure and manipulate environmental stimulus (load). That means that the PROPASt would follow design principles at work in theme parks and would speculatively employ visual, tactile, aural and olfactory environmental stimuli aimed at fabricating a desirable environmental image in visitors. Just as in theme parks, the PROPASt is deliberately designed to induce bottom-up behavior and stimulate emotional involvement. Sound patterns, colors, materials, and other environmental stimuli across the stimulus spectrum are designed to improve specific task performances in situations anticipated by the score. Carefully designed pseudo-eventful environmental activity such as mobile vendors, news stands, food and beverage kiosks, clowns, and street musicians significantly stimulate affiliative behavior in people and their desire to move and communicate with others. In the PROPASt, the creation of successful, cumulative layering of emotional and functional environmental clues is much more complex than in theme parks, due to a lack of absolute enclosure. Given that the PROPASt is not gated, complex variables must be brought into an ideal yet flexible balance that would facilitate the creation of desirable total experiences in visitors, and it directly translates into the creation of optimal environmental images, moods, and traits. The environment of PROPAST is thus an adaptive system, whose value emerges out of a constant interplay between 'state descriptions' and 'process descriptions', moreover its value mediates between its own form and the social processes it enables. As in theme parks, the more obvious the control is, the less value is produced. The more seamless the control mechanisms are, the higher the value of the environment. This equation, however, is also directly related to the dollar-volume of the environment and the total revenue that PROPAST generates: the lesser the environmental value, the lesser its revenue will be. That is why the image of choice is deliberately fabricated, while at the same time the tendency is to reduce choice-behaviors to a minimum, so that environmental fractures in terms of decision-making situations are minimized by design. Referents are emptied to the point that there is either nothing to say about such a public experience or what was experienced cannot be put in words, talked about. In that respect, the design of the PROPAST is directly linked to the ways in which human beings communicate in public spaces, and fabricates the illusion that public space is possible without points of contact, lines of communication, or realms of human exchange. Sadly, many believe that such a public realm is not only possible but also desirable.

Whereas a plurality of writings in social and political theory have been preoccupied with the term 'public' as it refers to the notion of physical access to privatized public spaces, the term's relation to ownership over the PROPAST has been mostly obscured. Physical accessibility, that is, the ability of human subject to physically access the PROPAST, is only one aspect of the degree to which the PROPAST is open to the public and to which it enables a 'public' experience. As Kayden shows, privately-owned public space in New York City has been obstructed precisely in the realm of physical accessibility by constructing walls, gates, and impenetrable physical barriers. However, accessibility can also be visual, social, and psychological. Visual accessibility relates to the proximity, transparency, and attributes of physical boundaries and other, immaterial boundaries, whereas social accessibility relates to the socio-economic, class or ethnic stratification of citizens, tourists, and employees, or ticket prices assigned to aspects of 'public' experience in the PROPAST. Psychological accessibility is related to a variety of psychological barriers that make an emotional impact on the 'public' experience in the PROPAST. It goes without saying that the nature of accessibility is a direct consequence of ownership and control over both space and time in the PROPAST. Analogous to themeparking, both physical and psychological variables have to be identified and calculated into the PROPAST equation by either removing them from the environment as clear obstructions, by neutralizing them by attention-diverging methods, or by turning them into a real or symbolic capital by acknowledging their existence and often by caricaturizing their presence. Environmental variables are treated in ways that would effectively enable optimal frictionless access to identified targets within the theater.

The control exercised in theme parks and PROPAST cannot be placed on entirely different grounds from the control exercised in the society as a whole. Compartmentalization of spaces, social practices and identities, and above all the division between the producer and consumer are reflected and condensed in these playgrounds. When layered, these varied aspects of accessibility give a more precise picture of the actual degree of exclusion that the PROPAST exercises through private control, surveillance or other means. Such varied policies of exclusion are bad news for a number of traditionally marginalized socio-economic groups that have historically found refuge in public spaces (Pfeffer Solomowitz 1997, Betsky 1997, Brent Ingram 1997). For most of them, the way the PROPAST instrumentalizes policy of exclusion is through consensus entertainments. Just like in the Reform Park, in theme parks, and in any other apparatus of control in urban areas seriously fragmented by economic class, race and ethnicity, the

Public art in the 590 Atrium at Madison Avenue and East 56th Street, New York City.

Takashi Murakami's Reversed Double Helix installation at Rockefeller Center, New York City.

PROPAST builds a meeting point around consensus entertainments as common denominators such are sports, popular properties, Hollywood, or public art. PROPAST are always accompanied with some sort of a public art project, supposed to enrich the experience of citizens in the PROPAST, and customarily it is paid for by corporate patrons. Public art occupies a peculiar place within the total landscape: the PROPAST has instrumentalized public art as a symbolic vehicle for expressing empathy with the aestheticized and purposefully idealized notion of 'public', while at the same time utilizing it as a way of colonizing time and controlling the PROPAST by imposing art works as physical barriers meant to regulate physical accessibility and determine desirable pedestrian flows. Often, such art is either didactic or decorative, abstracted in search of a common denominator, emptied of any significance, derived through direct corporate sponsorship and no public discourse or public appeal whatsoever. As Princenthal has forcefully argued, 'public art has become a specialized

professional technique, conservative in nature and necessary in function', used to reinforce the condition of late capitalist city into which it has been integrated (Princenthal 1996). The PROPAST's 'public art' is also linked into the cycles of production by working as a tourist attraction in the fabrication of pseudo 'photo opportunity' locations within any given urban context. In short, public art is instrumentalized as both psychological and physical opportunity that simultaneously controls access, while it adds to the PROPAST's market value.

If one assumes that public spaces, such as Times Square, figure as the principal part of the civic realm in the sense in which Hannah Arendt (Arendt 1958) would have perceived them, and therefore as a part of 'political arena' composed of 'equals who are different', then the PROPAST strongly refuses 'social conflict' and offers militant strategies for gentrification and class seclusion. As Mark Gottdiener noted, when high crime threatens enjoyment of urban public spaces, whoever their owner is, the PROPASt becomes a 'desirable substitute for urban experience' (Gottdiener 1997: 112). Another key aspect of themeparking, which the PROPASt parallels, is identifying and enclosing target markets, and at the same time, drawing clear symbolic and material boundaries that would exclude those whose presence in the PROPASt would negatively impact the experiential outcomes of desired 'guests'. This delicate process is conducted through a simultaneous working of the mass-media, as well the design of the actual PROPASt locations, in an attempt to avoid the extinction of public space successfully outlined in Mike Davis's book *City of Quartz* (Davis 1990). Davis documented the reconfiguration of Los Angeles's public spaces into battle zones with adequate security and surveillance procedures, technological apparatus, and design methods that followed, such as the extensive use of reflective glass or elevated streets (Davis 1990). The subsequent 'commodification of security' led to repression, surveillance, exclusion and the criminalization of the poor, and finally extinction of the democratic civic space. Video surveillance technologies created what Davis called 'scanscape', a 'space of protective visibility' linked with the realm of multi-dimensional security systems into 'a seamless continuity of surveillance over daily routine.' (Davis 1998: 366–367) Thus themeparking PROPASt is a delicate balancing act, positioned right in between the idealized notion of public space as 'political arena', and radical solutions that would possibly make all public space extinct in the name of safety. In that sense, the PROPASt offers a vision of civility bounded by consumption (Zukin 1995: 55), and protected by gates, entrance-fees and private security forces in an aggressive attempt at combining general access with social control.

The simplicity with which the proprietorship over the socio-economic production of the PROPASt has been addressed has narrowed the 'public space discourse' to the following question: 'Is it still public if we have to pay for it?' (Branch 1990). This, however, is not the right question. The real question is: 'Can civil rights and liberties, as a complex ensemble of social practices guaranteed by law, be exercised in a public environment totally controlled by private interest?' Proprietorship over spatial extensions of significant size that are intended for a controlled public access indeed implies a significant difference in the degree of control that may be exercised in such environments. While most critics would agree with Neil Postman that entertainment has become the natural format for the representation of all human experience, and with others who argued that popular entertainment has always been one of the basic dimensions of urbanity, total control over public space is still the *terra incognita* of contemporary liberal democracies. By the regulation of 1968, the Supreme Court of the United States of America extended the right of free speech to 'private property used as public space'. In 1975, this regulation was annulled at the national level, leaving the possibility to individual states to extend such rights. Only a few states in the United States currently still guarantee the right of free speech in PROPASt.[11] Examples of how this manifests itself in daily life are too numerous to list here, but one will suffice: Stephen Downs and his son Roger were stopped in March 2003 by Cross Gates Mall security guards in Guilderland, New York and asked to remove their shirts that read 'Peace on Earth' and 'Give Peace a Chance' or leave. Stephen Downs, a lawyer with the state Commission on Judicial Conduct, refused to take the T-shirt off and was arrested for trespassing. The mall management explained the move by indicating that Downs's behavior and the T-shirts 'were disruptive to other shoppers' (AP 2003), and could have affected other shoppers's emotional states in ways that would impact their purchasing behavior, obviously an undesirable effect. However, not only private owners of the PROPASt are to be blame for the changing nature of public space. Governments also play a role in these developments by passing laws and institutionalizing normative expectations that change the nature of interaction in public space, such is the 2004 French prohibition of religious symbols in public spaces that caused widespread protests by Muslim women. 'The concept where the state could control everything seemed to have suffered a resounding, definitive defeat, but no: defeated on the economic front, the enemies of liberty are looking for victories in other areas' said Italian Defense Minister Antonio Martino, according to Reuters, in the face of the 10th January 2005 smoking ban in Italy (DT 2005). The ban provoked wide-ranging protests, of which the most interesting was the comment by an Italian journalist, who claimed that 'repression has killed more people in human history than smoking'. Italy's Health Minister, Girolamo Sirchia, said that banning smoking in public places was 'only the beginning of the war' against the giant tobacco industry multinationals. An extreme example in that respect is the state of Florida's unprecedented policy of 1964, which granted Disney Co. (and its Reedy Creek Improvement District) the right to fully govern its 27 000 acres property in central Florida, as discussed in Chapter 2. Dress rules and regulations that have traditionally applied in suburban shopping malls are nowadays transferred to urban public spaces. Those who decide on the appropriateness of behavior and dressing in malls are the same people that today check dress codes on Times Square: private security forces.

Public Space, Private Control

As Zukin writes, in parallel with the erosion of public authority, employment in the security industry boomed in the 1980s and 1990s (Zukin 1995: 39–40), so that in many North American cities, there are four officers in the private security industry to each one in the public sector. Alison Wakefield has pictured a similar situation in the United Kingdom and argued that, in parallel with the governmental promotion of the virtues of privatization and individual responsibility since early 1980s, as well as its inability to effectively control the public realm, both the public and corporations are increasingly demanding greater security in urban public spaces (Wakefield 2003). Special cases are, of course, the privately owned facilities that cater to public use, such as shopping malls, or what is in Britain called 'mass private property'. As the public life of citizens increasingly unfolds in such spaces, it is also increasingly important that the methods of operation, core functions and most importantly the objectives of private security

forces will radically differ from that of state police. The private security force will naturally abandon public interest and work towards accomplishing the objectives of its private client. In recent years, partnerships between state policing and private security agencies have grown into a security industrial complex, a legal partnership between government and private industry operating in the name of public security (Jennings 2005) in almost every country that allows private security agencies by common law. The way in which such 'commodification of security' instrumentalizes space in total landscape (in the interest of profit making) is aimed at preserving specific social orders by establishing desirable configurations in space in terms of crowd control, purchasing behavior, and in terms of eliminating undesirable behaviors. Undesirable behavior can jeopardize the dollar volume, discourage purchasing behavior or generally affect people's emotional states in undesirable ways, and as such, have to be discouraged by all available means. Unlike the traditional police force whose aim is predominantly to bring offenders to justice after the fact, private security forces are mainly employed to proactively eliminate all potential offenders from the public space. The strategy of pre-emption has been facilitated by the development of sophisticated surveillance technology that ranges from the closed circuit television (CCTV) to the use of biometrics. Biometrics is a real-time digital verification of an individual's identity authenticated by one or more biological data traits that include fingerprints, hand geometry, earlobe geometry, voice verification, signature dynamics, blood vessel flow, retina and iris patterns, and body odors. The key to all types of biometrics is that the measured characteristic is distinct, unique, and unchangeable when repeated over time for the same individual. In 1995, Walt Disney Company contracted Swiss firm BioMet Partners to test a three-dimensional, two-finger geometry device (called Digi-2) at entrance turnstiles for holders of season passes to Walt Disney World Resort in Orlando, Florida (Davis 1997). In early 1996, Disney launched this new system to identify users of annual and seasonal passes. As of the 2nd January 2005, all current WDW admission media use the finger scans and all annual and seasonal pass holders, 10-day World Hoppers, as well as cast members who have been enrolled in the biometric finger geometry system. Finger readers are installed at all turnstiles in the park and individual visitors insert their finger into the reader for verification as they enter the park. Finger scans are not required for children under the age of 10, nor are they required for visitors with disabilities who cannot use finger scanners. One of the reasons why finger scans are not demanded from the above two demographic groups is that biometric readings cannot be successfully done for humans whose bio-geometry is damaged or unstable. In such cases, biometric readings have to rely on more tangible biometric properties, such as body odors. Body odors (identified and recognized through the chemical odor analysis) are unique to each human being and can be digitally recorded and used with biometric security devices. Together with complex software applications, biometric surveillance technology will enable every security officer, public or private, to have access to one's private data records in seconds as one passes a turnstile. Robert O'Harrow indicates that software applications such as MATRIX and NORA were originally invented for the commercial private sector (O'Harrow 2005). The original MATRIX was redesigned in 2001 to be used by the federal government and renamed into Multi-State Anti-Terrorism Information Exchange. NORA (Non-Obvious Relationship Awareness) was developed in Las Vegas for identifying non-obvious data traits between people potentially involved in casino fraud and is capable of instantly stripping away false identities. Both software applications are capable of searching billions of data records in minutes and finding the connections that took months and years to find with conventional security procedures. Data banks are provided by private corporations that specialize in digitizing public data such are citizens's addresses, phone numbers, social security numbers, and credit card numbers. Such private data is not considered private information protected under the fourth amendment, because people voluntarily disclose such information whenever they engage in commercial transaction of any kind, whether

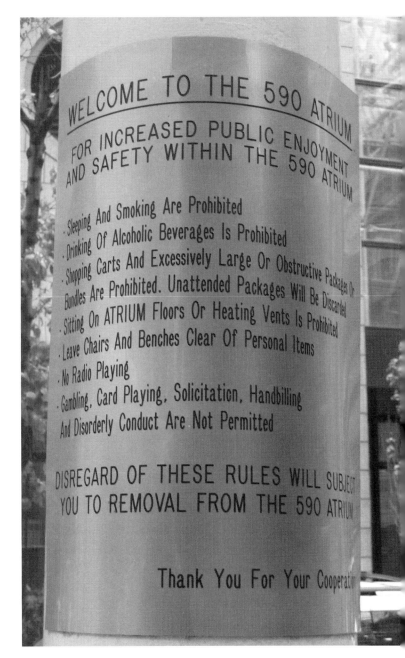

when booking a hotel, while Internet shopping, or enrolling in a fitness program. As O'Harrow points out, the convergence of surveillance technology, laws that enable fast data collection and analysis, and the dehumanization of data inevitably lead towards a 'total information convergence' in all aspects of contemporary life.

The privacy issue of biometric technology is questionable because the main reason biometrics works for identification is that an individual cannot control these unique aspects of their biology: a person cannot change their fingerprint or the identifying features of their iris (Oliver 1999). Many do not feel confident in the security of personal identity captured by biometric technology and feel strongly about the lack of a regulatory framework to govern the use of biometric data. Another realistic fear that Wakefield successfully charts is the one that comes out of the quality of personnel employed in the private security industry in the United Kingdom, United States and Canada (Wakefield 2003): namely, most security officers are badly-paid, generally uneducated, mostly white males of 40 years of age and above, often with military or some security background, and not rarely with a criminal record. Besides, most of them are not unionized, because non-unionized labor is more efficient and less costly than unionized public employees that used to guard and maintain public spaces (Zukin 1995: 29). Given that their authority over

public spaces and public life is growing, the above are terrifying developments. Private security forces, combined with sophisticated surveillance technology, and with subtle measures of control built into the design of PROPAST environments, compose an effective technological apparatus employed in maintaining public safety while inducing apparently consensual behavior patterns of visitors in building 'memorable experiences'.

Representation and the Experience of Civility

The thematic frameworks of PROPAST environments are often more closely related to the world of media and marketing than to the actual urban space they colonize. The fabrication of thematic frameworks relies on the synergy of cultural, political and socio-economic factors that are inseparable in the contemporary world of media and synergetic marketing. I argued in Themeparking that totalizing principles at work within the procedures of themeparking turn any given landscape into a meta-landscape by imposing a fictive, alien and irrelevant thematic content upon it. Simultaneously, they erase or neutralize all traces from such a meta-landscape except those that can support its production, and that can be manipulated as sources of revenue generation. With the PROPAST things are different, in that the theme of the PROPAST is commonly a caricaturized and idealized experience of urban public space. It is a form of supreme irony that the theme of

POPS transformed into the Retail Atrium at 575 Fifth Avenue, New York City.

Signs indicating the code of behavior at the Tilyou Playground, Coney Island, New York City.

Sign indicating code of behavior at the Sony Wonder Plaza, New York City.

Surveillance cameras at the 590 Atrium, New York City.

Bryant Park is an idealized public space of New York City, a simulation of urban experience in the heart of Manhattan. Besides such a generic thematic framework, each urban milieu contains a treasure box of symbolic values that can be used for the fabrication of a PRO-PAST's thematic envelope and storyline. The example of Bryant Park shows how symbolic values and cultural intangibles—such as the attachment to New York City Library or the utilization of the site of Crystal Palace Exhibition—can play a significant role in the cycles of themeparking. Analogous to theme parks, each theme identifies, isolates, manipulates and capitalizes on specific symbolic values that already exist within the chosen urban milieu by either exploiting them for the fabrication, enhancement or diversification of a PRO-PAST's brand, or employing it as a treasure box of ideas and concepts that marketing uses as symbolic capital.

As indicated earlier, for the total landscape to work, a homogeneous human experience across multiple scales has to be fabricated. Total environmental image is an accumulated, layered impression that combines influences generated by the media world with those related to a particular PROPAST, such as the internal pattern, the harlequin dress, sensory stimuli, and the pseudo-events organized by the score. Successfully designed interplay between layered clues facilitates the perception of a PROPAST as an interrelated, singular image. Ironically,

however, what a PROPAST proposes is the suburban image of 'desirable urbanity'—as initially materialized in Disneyland Park and proposed by Walt Disney 50 years ago—'good natured' urbanity as seen from suburbia: clean, predictable, safe. That particular image of urbanity has an aggressive agenda of its own, an agenda based in middle class, suburban values. Its agenda is, strictly speaking, political in nature. Seen from the suburban position, urbanity is indeed possible as a chain of private experiences, a succession of controlled private spaces, because public space has traditionally been excluded from the suburban domain. Seen from a truly civic position though, such urbanity, and such a vision of civility, are simply not possible, unless one either redefines the meaning of these terms, or etymologically and rhetorically anew defines the hybrid forms of development that occur when such an image of urbanity is imposed onto cities. As argued in the introductory chapter, total landscape works precisely by favoring essentially rural values (built into the suburban mentality) over urban ones. Herbert Muschamp recognized this process as an attempt to apply suburban, middle-class values to urban public space by fusing 'suburban security and standardization with urban congestion and pizzazz.' (Muschamp 1995) Goldberger noted that the resulting 'urbanoid' environments 'provide middle-class residents with a measure of urban experience in what is essentially a suburban context' (Goldberger 1996). Since most urban tourists are suburban families on urban safaris, a PROPAST to them has a reassuring, comforting and therapeutic role because it confirms that what they know resonates with what they perceive and experience in the material world. The fact that people search and make an effort to enjoy material environments that represent an extension of the commodified public realm of television, advertising, films, retail and mass-tourism is a confirmation of their struggle to maintain sanity. Following Hench's 'credibility of form principle', images and narratives fabricated by the world of mass media have to match corresponding image of urban public experience supported in part by adequate harlequin dress. The fictive, caricaturized character of harlequin dress is an important vehicle for the communication of meaning: how ideal then is the neo-classical building of the New York City Library as a backdrop for the simulated urban experience and the self-metaphorization of Bryant Park.

One wonders how it is possible that, despite an ever-increasing complexity of contemporary culture(s), despite the extreme miniaturization and proliferation of digital (information) technology which supposedly democratizes civic realm, urban architecture is simplified, dishonored, and reduced to decorum whose purpose is the simulation of civic, urban experience? We habitually assume that architecture was once in a position to represent society, its culture, its history, and to spatialize and manifest social relationships between its constituents. The relevance of contemporary critical theory to architecture has been clear in the context of the debate about the decline of public sphere in the era of mass media and entertainment: 'critical theorists have argued that present convergences of all media (that have created new technologies, discourses and methods of communication) have replaced architecture as the mode of representation that ultimately defines the dimensions of human experience in the world.'[12] If one steps away from the idea that architecture is the ultimate mode of representation of civility and urbanity, and looks carefully at the production of a PROPAST as a method of representation, one will

potentially recognize that a PROPAST does not propose the act of representation to be a reflective or mimetic practice of representing meaning 'which is already there' because, as Stuart Hall writes, no meaning exists unless represented (Hall 1997: 15). In other words, PROPAST does not only reflect selected, existing social values, but aggressively fabricates new ones. The process of representation has thus entered the creation of meaning, and it has become a constitutive part of the meaning itself. Therefore, the practice of representation has become the practice of the production of meaning (signifying practice) and, as such, it has entered the domain of the production of spatial manifestations of civility, as well as of urban public space itself. PROPAST thus represents civility as a mere commodity to be acquired by taking part in its version of the public realm, and fabricates redefined notions of civility by spatializing specific propositions for civic life and configuring them into a web of social relationships and shared cultural practices, which are then represented by the public art, mass media, education and other pseudo-processes that configure the cognitive, perceptual and lived aspects of urban life. A synergetic functioning of such representations across scales and domains can be identified in the ways in which a PROPAST, public art, museums, art galleries, sport halls and theaters are all linked in never-before experienced ways, in terms of the aestheticized experiences of being in public to the extend that being in public has become a matter of aesthetic appreciation. As Boyer noted, such noncritically positioned experiences 'foreground the pleasurable look of the city while obscuring the agents of re-presentation and those that compose consensus.' (Boyer 1994: 461) In an immensely ironic twist of fate, urban public space is PROPAST's chief mode of representation, namely the 'self-metaphorization' of the PROPAST represents a historical condition of a mode of human interaction that has no history and no future outside of the idea of urbanity. For it is operative urban interaction, not the picturesque public space, that forms the essence of urbanity and of city life. In sharp contrast to the audience of abstract modernism that rejected symbolic and narrative content,

the audience of PROPASt expects the restoration of the visual codes of recognizabillity, the reinstatement of figuration and narrative cohesion. Since the public experience of the PROPASt works through the caricaturization of urbanity and civility, the aesthetic 'seduction' of this decorum is also generated by nostalgia for a moment in past when architectural typologies and unified cultural codes that harlequin dress of the PROPASt refers to, had historical authenticity. As discussed earlier, nostalgia is a powerful vehicle, employed to naturalize the credibility of iconic referentiality of total landscape and caricaturization as its aesthetic convention, and is capable of reassembling everything into 'a spectacle of availability' in order to present itself as a natural format for the representation of the present. The paradox thus is that the PROPASt caters to nostalgia for the illusionary period when public life was dignified. In that sense, the current mandatory signs reading 'This is a Public Space' in New York City (supposed to regulate public accessibility) will appear to be a record of the historical period when the existence of public realm was not certain, and more importantly, when the concept of public space was in an obvious and agonizing transition. In a Gramscian sense, it is precisely within the fissure between the traditional forms of public life that are dying, and the new ones represented by the PROPASt, that 'a great variety of morbid symptoms appear' (Gramsci 1991).

Mandatory signs indicating the purpose and
content of public space at Sony Wonder Plaza,
New York City.

Speculations on Closings and Openings

> There can be no perfecting of the natural world, and the human being
> in particular is a dangerous imperfection. If the world is to be perfect, it
> will first have to be made. And if the human being wishes to attain this
> kind of immortality, he must produce himself as artifact also and expel
> himself from himself into an artificial orbit in which he will circle forever.
> (Baudrillard 1994)

In order to close this discussion I will, in what follows, reflect on some of the key points made in the book, clarify why I have exposed an immense amount of data, documented hundreds of human practices related to total landscape, and unearthed the theory of total landscape. Finally, I will open up the discourse in a few speculative directions. I began this book years ago, not because I was interested in theme parks, but because I was intrigued by a specific ensemble of conditions as much characteristic of late modernity as they were of the emerging postmodernity. I was puzzled by them, enthusiastic about some aspects of their promise, but also troubled by their totalizing effects. For the reasons laid out in the opening paragraphs of this book, I named it 'Total Landscape'. I believe, and I hope I have persuaded the reader also, I have been right in arguing that the theme park and the PROPAST are its archetypal specialized spaces, and that both are the ur-forms of total landscape. In that capacity, they successfully reveal both subjects and objects of contemporary human knowledge as well as their complex and intricate relationships. The form that such a knowledge increasingly takes has been dramatically departing from two humanistic beliefs: firstly, that the human being must be at its center, and secondly that such a knowledge must be grounded in specific places. Even though the second belief has been irreparably shattered by total landscape, the first one still holds true, but in radically different ways: the human being has been objectified, abstracted, rationalized and instrumentalized as a means to a normative end. In that respect, the theme park and the PROPAST are 'ideal symbols' of the Twentieth Century, precisely because the general conception of human being, as well as human knowledge of it, reveal themselves immediately in a particularly illuminating form. It is for such reasons, I have argued here, that the theme park and the PROPASt are the theory of total landscape. If I am right, one can, without doubt, see how the human being has been erased as the subject of human knowledge, 'like a face drawn in sand at the edge of the sea', under the effect of the emerging technocratic establishments and their instrumentalization of human knowledge towards totalizing aims.

Total landscape is enabled by an immense and never-before experienced complexity of the man made, artificial world, together with the unprecedented convergences of all media, and the degree to which they have blurred the boundaries between the cognitive, perceived and lived aspects of contemporary life. By mapping out a variety of examples as different means employed to the same end, I attempted to expose the innerworkings of a totalizing system of forces at work within an artificial universe that methodologically links every artifice into a universal, densely woven, complex system in action. The ability to reproduce standardized human experiences has enabled the cycles of systematic totality to treat the entire social realm as an object of systematization that has to be perfected in order to be complete, as such is the totalizing logic of total landscape. However, it is through the striving for technological optimization and perfection that any artifice achieves its best and, in fact, only possible condition, the condition of a totality of its existence; if an artifice is not totalizing, it is not good enough. It is, however, exactly at the point when an artifice is brought to the state of perfection—when one no longer understands how an artifice or an artificial system is structured, when its innerworkings are perfectly concealed within its total image—that one cannot be critical about it because one cannot critically engage in the processes of its production. Ironically, the image that perfectly optimized artifice conveys is one of simplicity. This is the paradox of total landscape: that is, there is no such thing as simplicity, if and when it appears, it is only a mask for complexity. As this book shows,

the image of simplicity is deliberately fabricated in both the theme park and in the PROPASt, and it is precisely through such a fabrication that total landscape disengages participation and disables an adequate understanding of how the world works. It is indeed only when the artificial realm opens up to a profound understanding that its constituents may be critically engaged within a trajectory that may potentially lead to critical action. There is no critical action, and no change in the world of total landscape, if there is no understanding of how that world works. If there is no opportunity for action, and no possibility for an artifice to evolve, adapt, change through use, and accept varied challenges that come its way, there is also no possibility to build a human culture that would represent more than the normative expectations built into its artefacture. Here lie the essential dilemmas of all artifice and therefore all designing. Firstly, how to design an artifice as a mechanism for constructing the condition in which the act of construction itself will represent the full complexity of the world without simplifying the intricacies of its production? Secondly, the dilemma of naturalization: namely, it is precisely when an artifice attains the desirable level of perfection that it becomes seamlessly naturalized into the social system it serves to the point where no critical reflection is possible, and even desirable. Central, thus, to the notion of total landscape, and for that matter, central to any discourse on contemporary world, is the notion of artifice. Central to the notion of artifice are the notions of totalization, naturalization, and complexity.[13] Central to these notions is the notion of representation. After all, the act of representation is *de facto* the act of (re)constructing the world. The question then becomes is it at all possible to conceive of a social system as separate from its artefacture, in other words as separate from the act of designing, and then how to design a social system that will deliberately step away from the strive for technical optimization, totalization and therefore perfection? Obviously, the point of such an effort would be to enable critical reflection, engagement, and after all, critical action, that is to say, to make the reflective action possible. In that respect, the significance of the theme park and the PROPAST for a critical understanding of the relationships between designing and the key socio-economic processes that characterize the late Twentieth and early Twenty-First Centuries is absolutely essential. This book was conceived as an infinitesimal contribution towards a systematic understanding of the set of conditions out of which total landscape arises, and the totalizing condition of convergence it strategically fabricates.

The introductory chapter states that the book attempts to construct a critical trajectory, not a position, in relation to its subject matter by exposing the production processes of the world it criticizes. Being critical today is about being able to design the theoretical gear for a dynamic mapping of the world in which one lives, and simultaneously to construct a way of critically engaging in its production. The world cannot be fixed, but is in perpetual motion, and being critical in relation to complex systems in action that make the world what it is, means being able to establish critical judgments on the move. In the words of Ignasi de Sola Morales, one needs 'to find simultaneously for each new step an object and a foundation.' (Sola Morales 1989) A move from the notion of critical position to the notion of critical trajectory is crucial in how one acquires the capability to be critically engaged. One must simultaneously recognize that the topography of total landscape is made of an infinite number of intricately woven human practices that may bring both economic and social well being, and some de facto can save important cultural artifacts from destruction. However, naïve and non-critical practices often also have a totalizing cumulative effect, and that is precisely why I believe the world of total landscape had to be unpacked by exposing a plethora of minute details, thousands of specific human practices, methods and procedures together with their effects, and their own logic of exposure. Unearthing the voice of each of the examples I discuss meant that many parts of the book were free from my immediate critical reflection. In that, I attempted to create a critical trajectory that will not be totalizing in its own right, because unpacking one totalizing narrative

with another does not make sense. In that respect, I attempted to enable each example to argue for itself and expose its own argumentation. I believe this is a critical stance, necessary in establishing an anticipatory, holistic and sustainable understanding of the world of total landscape. Finally, besides the fact that one cannot be critical before one understands how the world works, the point is not only to attain such an understanding in order to interpret the world, but more importantly to acquire the capability to ultimately change it.

A clear political agenda here is rather obvious: the sources of the implicit metaphorical thought that lies underneath both the PROPAST and the theme park, as well as total landscape as a whole, have to be traced back to conservative moral and political values combined with neo-liberal economic policies. There is no shadow of a doubt that the political agenda of total landscape is conservative in nature. That is not to say that total landscape is a conservative conspiracy, or that a specific socio-economic or political group deliberately manipulates the public at large into undesirable configurations. However, the fact is, most of the metaphors employed throughout total landscape are indeed grounded in conservative values: 'family values' discussed in the last chapter are only one such example. Why such an agenda is problematic is not only in the values themselves, but also in the fact that such moral values are presented both as a mask for the fake simplicity of the world, and also as a pretext for moral lessons and scholastic programs. Both the theme parks and the PROPAST are indeed designed as scholastic programs. Such a mythologizing of the world effectively disables critical engagement, as well as any dialogue that may potentially occur. This is not only a political or economic challenge, it is also a question of vision, responsibility, and resources that each individual and every community will have to commit in order to open up a discourse on these issues. However, creating a vibrant, colorful and textured dialogue is an almost impossible task, in part because the public has not only internalized commercially fabricated needs and desires, but has also naturalized them through the unsuspicious consumption of commodity forms—some of which, of course, are PROPAST and their vision of commodified urban experience—and also by embracing and uncritically taking part in the production of fictious and displaced lifestyles that such commodification suggests. Realistically speaking, a carefully balanced interplay between public choice and economic necessity would seem to be the right answer, at least to the question of balance between public needs and those of urban entrepreneurs. But this is not a trivial question, because it is precisely out of an inability of the public to recognize itself, to get to know itself as a social constituent, and to understand its potentially powerful role in these processes, that private capital has been able to take advantage of public resources. Needless to say, the project of commodification and privatization of public resources has a specific operative public agenda in mind, the one that objectifies public as a means to the normative end. As is clearly argued, both in this chapter and in the book as a whole, total landscape and the PROPAST teach us that the understanding of public space has to move beyond its simplistic definitions as sporadic sites of often demonized face-to-face contacts, to a systematic understanding of public space (and public resources) as a multi-dimensional social system in action. Only then, only when such a comprehensive understanding reaches the public mind, will it be possible for the public to capitalize on its own resources. This is also a potentially explosive political question: namely, this book opened by exposing the fact that one percent of all Americans possess more than 50 percent of the entire American non-residential real estate property. In some North-American states, more than 98 percent of land ownership is in private hands. In many other countries in Europe, particularly in the United Kingdom, as well as in Japan, the situation with land ownership has historically been analogous. Such statistics *de facto* show why planning has been an impossible profession to practice ethically in the parts of the world mentioned above. The ratio of private to public is intensifying by the day, less and less people own more and more resources, and that is why *Total Landscape* has to my mind been a critical topic to engage in.

In the last two chapters of the book, I attempted to map out some of the departures from the standard operational framework of Themeparking, and specifically of Themeing, outside of the conventional enclosures of theme parks. Even though, as I claimed in the first chapter, the purpose of this book was indeed not to search for a non-totalizing conception of the theme park, and therefore for an alternative to the condition of total landscape it produces, there are isolated instances where its effects are beneficial. I would argue that examples such as Meiji Mura, Shikoku Mura, or the Polynesian Cultural Center, and in many ways also HTB, brought both economic and social well-being to the adjacent communities. In the case of HTB, I have clearly attempted to both qualify and quantify such influences. Another departure that holds many promises, and was only partly touched upon in the book, is in the realm of 'edutainment'. There are many sides to this argument though, because one could argue that theme parks are a form of edutainment in that they already operate as deliberately designed scholastic programs. Edutainment, however, holds another promise as museums, cultural centers, pre-schools and schools, as well as universities worldwide attempt to incorporate new technologies and methods of learning based in entertainment. PowerPoint presentations and colorful digital images, thought by many to be the key to such educational practices, are now receding behind a new recognition that systematic attempts will be needed in the Twenty First Century in order to design sustainable educational experiences across the age spectra. Universities also recognize that a holistic approach to designing such experiences will have to move beyond the student-teacher relationship towards simultaneously incorporating strategic and tactical decision-making across all scales by bringing campus design, web design, on-line learning systems, television programs, landscape design, phone answering systems, university's logo and brand image, color palette, staff uniforms, vehicles, restaurants and coffee stands together with each academic program, its curriculum, every laboratory and lecture hall, and each individual syllabus into a harmonius total environmental image. Similar to competitive hospitality, both state and private universities will soon find themselves deliberately designing ways to improve their imageability in order to increase their market share, but also to improve learning and ensure better experiential outcomes in students. Moreover, just like in competitive hospitality, the notion of 'public' is, at universities, increasingly limited by the need for highly controlled accessibility, heavily scripted behaviors of all stakeholders, and types of human interaction of a very limited scope. Therefore, universities face a complex challenge in the Twenty First Century: how to incorporate new technologies, discourses and methods of education (based in entertainment, digital technology and mass media) into the learning process,[14] and simultaneously resist totalizing effects that necessarily appear when the convergences of media and scales are instrumentalized towards creating homogeneous, and not rarely hegemonic, educational experiences. The fact that identifying 'educational experience' as a new normative outcome of the process of education implies turning the existing educational practices upside-down and inside-out has not yet been fully comprehended. Placing 'experience' at the very center of the discourses on education is a shortcut to an ethical *salto mortale,* because if uncritically and hastily executed, it will effectively produce the condition of total landscape in every campus and every classroom. The differences between theme parks and universities will then be those of degree and no longer of kind.

One example of the use of themeing has been of particular interest to me and has *de facto* been instrumental in leading me, like a light at the end of a dark tunnel, through the writing of this book. Namely, in the 1990s, the employment of themeing in designing medical and therapeutic environments became a breakthrough in treating Alzheimer's disease. The strict systematic and thematic treatment of environmental design has proven to stimulate the mnemonic apparatus in Alzheimer's patients and provide cues that help initiate focused conversations or 'purposeful wanderings'. Similar results are appearing in treating other neurological conditions such as Parkinson's disease. In many ways, the damaged cognition, memory loss, and language deterioration are improved by carefully orchestrating environmental clues so that all senses are simultaneously stimulated and engaged in a strictly defined thematic envelope that places patients in familiar, historically grounded settings. In that sense, the traces of operational theory of total landscape I have attempted to sketch in this book can potentially become instrumental in adequately designing environments that effectively treat specific neurological or psychological conditions and liberate such patients from the hygiene, sanitation, terror and violence of the conventional medical environments that came into being through modern technical and pseudo-scientific optimization. The results of the pioneering work in this area of design are immensely encouraging.

Many of the questions that this book poses will certainly remain unanswered, many of the predictions and insinuations, especially in relation to the privatization of public space, may become true. But who is to know, for who knows if anyone listens. After all, as military strategist general Liddell Hart suggested, 'the only confident thing is that nothing will happen as suggested, but there is a possibility that it might.' (Hart 1954: 139)

NOTES

1. This chapter, as a whole, is original to this book. However, parts of this chapter were presented at scholarly conferences and published before. See: Mitrašinović 1997b, 2002a, 2004.

2. Zukin defines symbolic economy as a new economic order based on entertainment, tourism and media industry (Zukin 1995).

3. The first comprehensive program for the construction of public space was built into the plan of Manhattan in 1811.

4. I am applying here an analogical model that Dana Cloud developed in order to map out similar totalizing principles at work between family therapies and a dysfunctional economic system at large: the conservative political rhetoric has been intentionally shifted, Cloud argues, from an essentially dysfunctional political and economic system towards identifying and labeling dysfunctional families, treating them by adequate therapeutic means, and arguing that 'some areas of society' have ethical, moral, genetic, psychological and other problems that have to be resolved not through 'welfare ethos', but through giving everyone a chance to work (Cloud 1998).

5. Dan Quayle quoted in Cloud 1998: 61.

6. In this particularly conservative view, nations are indeed identified as large families, governments as parents, and disobedient individuals (or in this case the space they produce) may be identified as deviant children to be punished or in other ways disciplined. An illuminating discussion on this subject was provided by a cognitive linguist, George Lakoff, who attempted to delineate the use of metaphors and intangibles in political rhetoric of both conservatives and liberals, and how both are based in a specific view of family values. In that respect, he distinguishes between two basic models of the family and two basic metaphors employed: 'the strict father metaphor', characteristic for conservative world-view, and 'the nurturing parent metaphor', characteristic for the liberal world-view (Lakoff 2002).

7. In 1988, writing about the balance of forces between commercial and public, non-commercial broadcasting in Western Europe, Nicholas Garnham wrote: 'The current struggle is an ideological struggle [...] a political struggle over the forms and powers of the bourgeois state and its relationship to civil society [...] and an economic struggle by surplus capital seeking new areas of valorization.' (Garnham 1988: 132)

8. Hackett identified the following six major sources of private funding for urban entertainment projects: venture capital, hedge and leveraged buy-outs, strategic investors, initial public offerings, specified purpose acquisition companies, and real estate investors (Hackett 1995: 27). In addition to that, there are five major constituents involved in each urban entertainment project: corporate lenders, real estate developers, entertainment companies, retail operators, and public agencies (most of which are public-private partnerships) (Hannigan 1998: 105).

9. After observing the 503 POPS, Kayden identified five major types of POPS in relation to how they are used: destination space (high-quality public space that attracts employees, residents, and visitors from outside to socialize, eat, shop, view art, or attend a programmed event), neighborhood space (high-quality public space that draws residents and employees from the immediate neighborhood, including the host building and surrounding buildings within a three-block radius to socialize or take care of children), hiatus space (public space that accommodates the passing user for a brief stop), circulation space (public space that materially improves the pedestrian's experience of moving through the city with the principal purpose to enable pedestrians to move faster from point A to point B), and marginal space (public space that, lacking satisfactory levels of design, amenities, or aesthetic appeal deters members of the public from using the space for any purpose) (Kayden 2000: 45).

10. The quote is taken from the Rotterdam Tourism site that advertises the Rotterdam Safari Tour as well as other tourist attractions. At: http://www.vvv.rotterdam.nl/uk/themapagina/topattracties/ (Accessed on 1st May 2004).

11. Mitchell indicates that United States Supreme Court made, in that respect, important distinctions between 'pure speech', 'expressive conduct' and behavior. Such distinctions are meant to limit rather than open up what can be practiced in public spaces (Mitchell 2003: 7).

12. Gregory L. Ulmer, personal notes to the author, April 1996.

13. In that respect, I rely on Herbert Simon's groundbreaking work on the 'sciences of the artificial' in which he claimed that central to the notion of artifice is the notion of complexity, and central to the notion of complexity is the notion of representation (Simon 1969). For an illuminating discussion on related issues see Margolin 2002.

14. In that respect, the work of Gregory Ulmer (and Florida Research Ensemble) and his notion of Electracy, which is to digital media what literacy is to print, will be instrumental (Ulmer 2003).

Bibliography

AB (2000) 'Chase Bank Arranging Hong Kong Disney Financing'. *Amusement Business,* 37 (112), 11th September: 55.

AB (2001) 'Pricing Deals in 2001: Family Price Index for U.S. Amusement Parks'. *Amusement Business,* 24 (113), 18th June: 19.

AB (2002) 'Top 10 Amusement/Theme Park Chains Worldwide'. *Amusement Business,* 51 (114), 23rd December: 16.

AB (2003) *Amusement Business,* 27 (115), 7th July: 1.

AB (2003a) 'Walt Disney World: Deal Offering Free Admission'. *Amusement Business,* 42 (115), 20th October: 6.

AB (2003b) *Amusement Business,* 43 (115), 27th October: 5.

Adams, W. H. (1979) *The French Garden: 1500-1800.* New York: George Braziller.

Addison, J. (1712) *The Spectator,* 414, 25th June.

Adler J. (1995) 'Theme Cities'. *Newsweek,* 11th September: 68-72.

Agnotti, T (2003) 'The Sidewalks of New York'. *Gotham Gazette,* December. At: http://www.gothamgazette.com/article/landuse/20031216/12/806 (Accessed on 1st May 2004).

Alexander, C. (1964) *Notes on the Synthesis of Form.* Cambridge: Harvard University Press.

Alexander, C. (1977) *The Pattern Language.* New York: Oxford University Press.

Alridge, J. (1992) 'Disney Casts Recruits for European Venture'. *The Independent,* 7, January: 3.

Anderson, E. W., Fornell, C., Lehmann, D.R. (1993) *Economic Consequences of Providing Quality and Customer Satisfaction.* Cambridge: Marketing Science Institute.

Andrews J. (1994) 'New Preservation Approach Aims to Save Cultural Landscape'. *The Christian Science Monitor,* 5th December: 9.

AP (2001) 'Politicians Fight Over Dracula Theme Park'. *Associated Press:* 14th November.

AP (2003) 'Mall Wants to Drop Peace T-Shirt Charges'. *Associated Press:* 6th March. At: http://www.nytimes.com/aponline/national/AP-Mall-Activists.html (Accessed on 1st May 2004).

Arendt H. (1958) *The Human Condition.* Chicago: University of Chicago Press.

Aronson, A. (1977) 'The Total Theatrical Environment: Impression Management in the Parks'. *Theater Crafts:* 35-76.

Ashworth, W. (1954) *The Genesis of Modern British Town Planning.* London: Routledge & Kegan Paul.

Augé, M. (1995) *Non-Places: Introduction to an Anthropology of Supermodernity.* New York: Verso.

Auricoste, I. (1991) 'Leisure Parks in Europe: Entertainment and Escapism'. In: Teyssot, G. and Mosser, M. (Ed.) (1991) *The Architecture of Western Gardens: A Design History from the Renaissance to the Present Day.* Cambridge, Mass.: MIT Press: 483-494.

Aurigemma, S. (1962) *Villa Adriana.* Rome: Istituto Poligrafico dello Stato.

Ayto, J. (1990) *Dictionary of Word Origins.* London: Bloomsbury Publishing Ltd.

Baer, D. M. (1997) 'Some Meanings of Antecedent and Environmental Control'. In: Baer, D. M. (Ed.) (1997) *Environment and Behavior.* New York: Westview Press: 17-23.

Balancia, D. (2003) 'Visitors to EPCOT Have Voted: The Wonders of Life Pavilion Will be Going on Vacation'. *Florida Today,* 14th December. At: http://www.floridatoday.com/NEWSROOM/moneystoryB1215EPCOT.htm (Accessed on 1st May 2004).

Balint, Z. (1897) *Die Architektur des Milleniums-Ausstellung.* Vienna. As quoted in: Kaufman, E. (1989) 'The Architectural Museum From World's Fair to Restoration Village'. *Assemblage,* 9, June: 21-39.

Ball, E. (1993) 'To Theme or Not to Theme: Disneyfication Without Guilt'. In: Karasov, D. and Waryan, S. (Ed.) *The Once and Future Park.* New York: Princeton Architectural Press Inc.: 31-39.

Bale, P. (1995) 'Romanians Flock to Dallas and Kitsch Castle'. *Reuters:* Slobozia, Romania, 12th November.

Banham, R. (1961) 'Design by Choice'. In: Banham, R. (1981) *Design by Choice.* New York: Rizzoli International Publications, Inc.: 97-107 [Originally published in *Architectural Review,* July 1961].

Banham, R. (1983) 'Insider's Eye in Florida'. *New Society,* 65 (1078): 60-61.

Baron, R. (1998) 'The Sweet Smell of...Helping: The Effects of Pleasant Ambient Fragrance on Prosocial Behavior in Shopping Malls'. *Personality and Social Psychology Bulletin.* 1 (24): 26-34.

Baron, R. and Thomley, J. (1994) 'A Whiff of Reality: Positive Affect as a Potential Mediator of the Effects of Pleasant Fragrances on Task Performance and Helping'. *Environment and Behavior,* 6 (26), November. New York: Sage Publications Inc.: 766-784.

Barsky, J. D. (1995) *World-Class Customer Satisfaction.* Burr Ridge, Ill.: Irwin Professional Publications.

Barthes, R. (1968) *Elements of Semiology.* New York: Hill and Wang.

Baudrillard, J. (1975) *The Mirror of Production.* St. Louis: Telos Press.

Baudrillard, J. (1983) *Simulations.* New York: Semiotext(e).

Baudrillard, J. (1994) *The Art of Disappearance.* Brisbane: Institute of Modern Art.

BBC (1998) 'Clinton Bids Africa Farewell'. *BBC News Online Network,* 3rd April. At: http://news.bbc.co.uk/1/hi/special_report/1998/03/98/africa/73107.stm (Accessed on 1 May 2004).

BBC (2001) 'Romania builds Dracula Land'. *BBC News Online,* 22nd March. At: http://news.bbc.co.uk/1/hi/world/europe/1234648.stm (Accessed on 1st May 2004).

BBC (2003) 'Mini East Germany Planned'. *BBC News Online,* World Edition, 28th February.

Betsky, A. (1997) 'From Cruising to Community'. In: Betsky, A. (1997) *Queer Space: Architecture and Same-Sex Desire.* New York: William Morrow and Co.: 140-177.

Benz, M. (2002) 'Anheuser-Busch, Viacom Happy With Park Ties'. *Amusement Business,* 14 (114), 8th April: 3.

Benz, M. (2003) 'Parks Face Financial Challenges in 2003'. *Amusement Business,* 24 (115), 16th June: 8.

Benz, M. (2003a) 'Opinions Mixed on Global Parks Market's True Forecast'. *Amusement Business,* 27 (115), 7th July: 3.

Bitner, M. J. (1993) 'Servicescapes: The Effects of Physical Surrounding on Customers and Employees'. *The Journal of Marketing,* 2 (56): 57-71.

Blackerby, C. (2003) 'Doom and Gloom' at Disney Parks?' *The Palm Beach Post,* 4th December: Section: Travel.

Blake, P. (1972) 'Walt Disney World'. *The Architectural Forum,* June: 24-40.

Blanchot, M. (1982) 'The Siren's Song'. In: Rabinovitch, S. (Ed. and Transl.) (1982) *The Siren's Song: Selected Essays of Maurice Blanchot.* Bloomington: Indiana University Press.

Bobić, M. (1990) *The Role of Time Function in City Spatial Structures: Past and Present.* Aldershot, Hants: Avebury Press.

Boorstin, D. J. (1962) *The Image or What Happened to the American Dream.* New York: Harper & Row.

Boorstin, D. J. (1964) *The Image: A Guide to Pseudo-Events in America.* New York: Harper & Row.

Bourdieu, P. (1977) *Outline of a Theory of Practice.* Cambridge: Cambridge University Press.

Bourne, L. S. and Simmons, J. W. (1978) 'The Nature of Urban Systems'. In: Bourne. L. S. and Simmons, J. W. (Ed.) *Systems of Cities.* New York: Oxford University Press: 3-15.

Boyer, C. M. (1994) *The City of Collective Memory: The Historical Imagery and Architectural Entertainments.* Cambridge, MA: MIT Press.

Braithwaite, D. (1968) *Fairground Architecture.* London: Hugh Evelyn Ltd.

Branch, M. A. (1990) 'Why (and How) Does Disney Do It?' *Progressive Architecture,* October: 78-82.

Branom, M. (2003) 'Fabulous! Disney Prepares for 13th Annual Gay Days'. *Associated Press Newswires,* 31st May: 07:06 P.M.

Branom, M. (2005) 'Playboy Founder Visits Disney World'. *Associated Press,* 4th February. At: http://www.miami.com/mld/miamiherald/living/people/10810463.htm (Accessed on 5th March 2005).

Braun, R. (1998) *Theme Park Development Case Study: Fiesta Texas.* At: http://www.hotel-online.com/Trends/ERA/ERAStudyFiesta.html (Accessed on 1st May 2004).

Brent Ingram, G. (1997) '"Open" Space as Strategic Queer Sites'. In: Brent Ingram, G. et al. (Eds.) (1997) *Queers in Space: Communities, Public Places, Sites of Resistance.* Seattle, WA: Bay Press: 95-126.

Bryman, A. (1999) 'Theme Parks and McDonaldization'. In: Smart, B. (Ed.) (1999) *Resisting McDonaldization.* London: Sage: 101-115.

Broadbent, G. (1978) 'A Plain Man's Guide to the Theory of Signs in Architecture'. *Architectural Design,* 7-8th July/August (47): 474-482.

Brown, J. R. and Fern, E. F. (1981) 'Goods vs. Service Marketing: A Divergent Perspective'. In: Donnelly, J. H. and George, W. R. (Ed.) (1981) *Marketing of Services.* Chicago: America Marketing Association.

Bruner, G. C. (1990) 'Music, Mood, and Marketing'. *Journal of Marketing,* October: 94-105.

Bryman, A. (1995) *Disney and His Worlds.* New York: Routledge.

Bryman, A. (1999) 'Theme Parks and McDonaldization'. In: Smart, B. (Ed.) (1999) *Resisting McDonaldization.* New York: Sage Press.

Buck-Morss, S. (1991) *The Dialectics of Seeing: Walter Benjamin and the Arcades Project.* Cambridge, Mass.: MIT Press.

Burke, E. (1756) *Philosophical Inquiry into the Origin of Our Ideas of the Sublime and the Beautiful.* Philadelphia: Printed for D. Johnson, Portland, by J. Watts [First American edition 1806].

Burke, K. E. (2003) 'Six Flags Reports Third Quarter and Nine Month Results: Official Earning Report by Six Flags Inc'. 12th November, Press release. At: http://www.kcsa.com (Accessed on 1st May 2004).

Burt, A. (1982) 'Al Burt's Florida'. *Miami Herald,* 1st August: 36.

Bush, S. (2003) 'Venice Lays Down the Law'. *BBC News,* 1st August. At: http://news.bbc.co.uk/1/hi/world/europe/3111187.stm (Accessed on 1st May 2004).

BW (1984) 'Problems in Walt Disney's Magic Kingdom'. *Business Week,* 12th March.

BW (1994) 'The Entertainment Economy'. *Business Week,* 14th March: 58-66.

BW (1996) 'Mercer Study Finds that Las Vegas and Orlando Rely on Unique Strengths to Attract Vacationers'. *Business Wire,* 1st May.

CABE (2002) 'Supplementary Memorandum by Commission for Architecture and the Built Environment (CABE) (PPG 26a): The Definition of Public and Open Space'. At: http://www.parliament.the-stationery-office.co.uk/pa/cm200102/cmselect/cmtlgr/238/238ap10.htm (Accessed on 1st May 2004).

Cain, S. (2001) 'Following the Mouse'. *Orange County Business Journal,* 20 (24), 14th May: 22.

Calcagni, T. and Checke, J. (2001) 'Travel Opportunities Abound to Meet Individual Traveler Needs'. *AAA Newsroom:* 1st October. At: http://www.aaanewsroom.net/Articles.asp?ArticleID=6&SectionID=&CategoryID=8&SectionID=4& (Accessed on 1st May 2004.)

Carbone, L. (2004) *Clued In: How to Keep Customers Coming Back Again and Again.* Upper Saddle River, NJ: FT Prentice Hall.

Carey A. (1996) *Taking the Risk out of Democracy.* Sydney: The University of New South Wales Press.

Carr, S., Francis, M., Rivlin, L. and Stone, A. (1992) *Public Space.* Cambridge: Cambridge University Press.

Cereghini, E. (1991) 'The Italian Origins of Rousham'. In: Teyssot, G. and Mosser, M. (Ed.) (1991) *The Architecture of Western Gardens: A Design History from the Renaissance to the Present Day.* Cambridge, Mass.: MIT Press: 320-322.

Certeau, M. de. (1984) *The Practice of Everyday Life.* Berkeley: University of California Press.

Certeau, M. de. (1986) *Heterologies: Discourse on the Other.* Minneapolis: University of Minnesota Press.

Chadwick, G. F. (1961) *The Works of Sir Joseph Paxton: 1803-1865.* London: The Architectural Press.

Chadwick, G. F. (1966) *The Park and the Town: Public Landscape in the 19th and 20th Centuries.* London: The Architectural Press.

Chaplin, S. (1998) 'Authenticity and Otherness'. *AD-Consuming Architecture,* 1-2 (68), January/February.

Cheske, J. (2002) 'Disney and AAA Renew Alliance through 2007'. *AAA Newsroom:* 11th February. At: http://www.aaanewsroom.net/Articles.asp?ArticleID=99&SectionID=&CategoryID=8&SectionID=4& (Accessed on 1st May 2004)

Cheske, J. (2002a) 'AAA's 100th Year Prompts Hundreds of Deals for Club's 45 Million Members'. *AAA Newsroom*: 28th February. At: http://www.aaanewsroom.net/Articles.asp?ArticleID= 101&SectionID=&CategoryID=8&SectionID=4& (Accessed on 1st May 2004).

Checke, J. (2002b) 'Preferred Partners of the Year Winners Announced by AAA Travel'. *AAA Newsroom*: 12th March. At: http://www.aaanewsroom.net/Articles.asp?ArticleID=107&SectionID =&CategoryID=8&SectionID=4& (Accessed on 1st May 2004.)

Choay, F. (1986) 'Urbanism in Question'. In: Lagopoulos, H. and Gottdiener, M. (Ed.) (1986) *The City and the Sign*. New York: Columbia University Press: 241-258.

Christaller, W. (1966) *Central Places in Southern Germany*. Englewood Cliffs, NJ: Prentice-Hall [originally published in 1933 as *Die Zentralen Orte in Suddeutchland*].

Cloud, D. (1997) *Control and Consolation in American Culture and Politics: Rhetoric of Therapy*. London: Sage.

Ciuffoletti, Z. (1990) *Pratolino, Villa Demidoff: Storia Arte Natura*. Firenze: Alinari.

Clayton, G. (1851) *Sermons on the Great Exhibition*. London: Benjamin L. Green.

CNN (2001) 'Christian Theme Park Under Fire in Florida'. *CNN Morning News*, 5th February.

CNN (2002) 'Dracula Theme Park Town Bites Back'. *CNN Online World News*, 30th September. At: http://www.cnn.com/2002/WORLD/europe/09/30/romania.Dracula (Accessed on 1st May 2004).

CNN (2003) 'East Germany Theme Park Planned'. *CNN News*, aired on 2nd March.

Comito, T. (1991) 'The Humanist Garden'. In: Teyssot, G. and Mosser, M. (Ed.) (1991) *The Architecture of Western Gardens: A Design History from the Renaissance to the Present Day*. Cambridge, Mass.: MIT Press: 37-46.

Conan, M. (1996) 'The Fiddler's Indecorous Nostalgia'. Unpublished paper presented at *The Landscape of Theme Parks and Their Antecedents* symposium, Dumbarton Oaks 17-18th May.

Cranz, G. (1982) *The Politics of Park Design: A History of Urban Parks in America*. Cambridge, Mass.: MIT Press.

Crary, J. (1992) *Techniques of the Observer*. Cambridge: MIT Press.

Csikszentmihalyi, M. (1990) *Flow: The Psychology of Optimal Experience*. New York: Harper & Row.

Cummings, A. L. (1955) 'Restoration Villages'. *Art in America*, May: 12.

Davis, A. (1997) 'The Body as Password'. *Wired*, 5.07, July. At: http://www.wired.com/wired/ archive/5.07/biometrics_pr.html (Accessed on 1st May 2004).

Davis, M (1990) *City of Quartz: Excavating the Future in Los Angeles*. New York: Verso.

Davis, M. (1998) *Ecology of Fear: Los Angeles and the Imagination of Disaster*. New York: Metropolitan Books.

DC (1999) *Procedures for Renting Public Space for an Unenclosed Sidewalk Café*. Washington D.C.: Government of the District of Columbia, Department of Consumer and Regulatory Affairs, Building and Land Regulation Administration, the Permit Center.

Debord, G. (1983) *Society of the Spectacle*. Detroit: Black & Red.

Deleuze, G. (1988) *Foucault*. Minneapolis: The University of Minnesota Press.

Deighton, J. (1992) 'The Consumption of Performance'. *Journal of Consumer Research*, December (19): 362-372.

Della Porta, G. B. (1658) *Natural Magick*. London: Young & Speed.

De Sola Morales, I. (1989) 'Weak Architecture'. *Ottagono*, 92: 87-129.

Diller + Scofidio. (1994) *Back To The Front: Tourisms of War*. F.R.A.C. Basse-Normandie.

Drew, B. (1998) *Crossing the Expandable Landscape*. St. Paul, Minnesota: Graywolf Press.

DOD (2004) United States Department of Defense Dictionary of Military Terms. At: http://www. dtic.mil/doctrine/jel/doddict/ (Accessed on 22nd May 2004).

Donovan, R. and Rossiter, J. (1982) 'Store Atmosphere: An Environmental Psychology Approach'. *Journal of Retailing*, 1 (58), Spring: 34-57.

Dorling, D. and Fairbairn, D. (1997) *Mapping: Ways of Representing the World*. Harlow: Longman.

Dorrett, G. (1999) 'Doing the Right Thing: Four Principles of Successful REC Design'. *Entertainment Management*, November. At: http://www.forrec.com/announc_articles.htm (Accessed on 1st May 2004).

Dunaway, D. K. (1989) *Huxley in Hollywood*. New York: Harper & Row Publishers.

Dunlop, B. (1996) *Building a Dream*. New York: Harry Abrams Inc.

DT (2005) 'Italy Bans Smoking in Public Places'. *Daily Times*, 13th February 2005. At: http://www. dailytimes.com.pk/default.asp?page=story_23-12-2002_pg9_3; (Accessed on 15th February 2005).

Eco, U. (1976) *A Theory of Semiotics*. Bloomington: Indiana University Press.

Eco, U. (1986) *Travels into Hyperreality*. New York: Harcourt Brace & Comp.

Eagleson, D. (2002) 'Recreo-Tourism is Hot: Here's How To Keep From Getting Burned'. *Municipal World*, April. At: http://www.forrec.com/news_art/art_recreotourism.html (Accessed on 1st May 2004).

Eckbo, G. (1950) *Landscape for Living*. New York: Architectural Record with Duell, Sloan, & Pearce.

Eisen, A. (1975) 'Two Disney Artists'. *Crimmer's: The Harvard Journal of Pictorial Fiction*, Winter: 35-44.

Ellul, J. (1967) *The Technological Society*. New York: Random House.

Emmons, N. (2001) 'Universal Studios Hollywood Adds TV-Branded Attractions for 2001'. *Amusement Business*, 9 (113), 5th March: 27.

Emmons, N. (2002) 'East Coasters: Movie-Themed Parks in Asia Continue to Draw Record Crowds'. *Hollywood Reporter*, 28 (372), 12th March: 19.

Emmons, N. (2002a) 'Weekdays Prove Strong for Tokyo DisneySea Six Months Into Operation'. *Amusement Business*, 14 (114), 8th April: 6.

Emmons, N. (2002b) 'Emotions Vital Part of Attraction Success: Panel'. *Amusement Business*, 49 (114), 9th December: 5.

Emmons, N., O'Brien, T. and Koranteng, J. (2002c) 'New Overseas Parks Push Gate Numbers Up'. *Amusement Business*, 51 (114), 23rd December: 8.

Evans, C. L. (1981) *The Impact of Motor Fuel Prices and Availability on Theme Park Attendance.* Unpublished Ph.D. Dissertation, United States International University.

Excelsior. (1851) *The Dial of the World, 1851.* London: Ward and Co.

Feifer, M. (1985) *Going Places.* London: Macmillan.

Findlay, J. M. (1992) *Magic Lands: Western Cityscapes and American Culture After 1940.* Berkeley: University of California Press.

Fjellman, S. (1992) *Vinyl Leaves: Walt Disney World and America.* Boulder: Westview Press Inc.

Flower, J. (2000) 'What Experience Are You Selling?' *Health Forum Journal,* 1st January.

Frampton, K. (1974) 'On Reading Heidegger'. *Oppositions,* 4, October.

Frampton, K. (1980) *Modern Architecture: A Critical History.* New York: Oxford University Press.

Frampton, K. (1988) 'Place-Form and Cultural Identity'. In: Thackara, J. (Ed.) (1988) *Design After Modernism: Beyond the Object.* New York: Thames and Hudson: 51–66.

Frampton, K. (1995) *Studies in Tectonic Culture.* Cambridge: MIT Press.

Francaviglia, R. V. (1981) 'Main Street USA: A Comparison/Contrast of Streetscapes in Disneyland and Walt Disney World.' *Journal of Popular Culture,* 15, Summer: 141–156.

Francaviglia, R. V. (1996) *Main Street Revisited.* Iowa: University of Iowa Press.

French, D. (2005) 'Community Builders Profile: Daniel Biederman'. *Urban Land,* January. At: http://www.uli.org/ (Accessed on 1st February 2005).

Friedmann, J. (1978) 'The Spatial Organization of Power in the Development of Urban Systems.' In: Bourne. L.S. and Simmons, J.W. (Ed.) (1978) *Systems of Cities.* New York: Oxford University Press: 328–340.

Freeman, M. (2001) 'Locals Welcome: Theme Parks Find Long-Distance Dollars Dwindle in U.S. Slowdown'. *The Associated Press Wire/The San Diego Union-Tribune,* 21st July.

Forgac, J. (1985) 'Walt Disney World's Food Distribution Center'. *Restaurant Hospitality,* May: 117–122.

Foucault, M. (1972) *The Archaeology of Knowledge.* New York: Pantheon Books.

Foucault, M. (1977) *Discipline and Punishment: The Birth of the Prison.* London: Penguin Books Ltd.

Foucault, M. (1985) 'Of Other Spaces: Utopias and Heterotopias'. *Lotus International,* 48/49: 9–17.

Fuller, B. (1969) *Operating Manual for Spaceship Earth.* Carbondale: Southern Illinois University Press.

Gallen, C. (2003) 'New U.S. Security Measures Driving Away Foreign Tourists, Industry Warns'. *Agence France Presse* wire, 17th August.

Garnham, N. et al. (1988) *The Economics of Television: The U.K. Case.* London: Sage Publications.

Giedion, S. (1949) *Space, Time, and Architecture.* Cambridge: Harvard University Press.

Gilles, I. (1953) 'Formulary for a New Urbanism'. In: Ockman, J. (Ed.) (1993) *Architecture Culture 1943–1968: A Documentary Anthology.* New York: Rizzoli: 168–171.

Glenn, S. S. (1997) 'Understanding Human Behavior: A Key to Solving Social Problems.' In: Baer, D. M. (Ed.) (1997) *Environment and Behavior.* New York: WestviewPress: 11–17.

Goffman, E. (1963) *Behavior in Public Places: Notes on the Social Organization of Gatherings.* New York: Free Press of Glencoe.

Goldberger, P. (1972) 'Mickey Mouse Teaches the Architects'. *The New York Times Magazine,* 22nd October: 28

Goldberger, P. (1996) 'The Rise of the Private City'. In: Vitullo-Martin, J. (Ed.) (1996) *Breaking Away: The Future of Cities.* New York: Twentieth Century Fund.

Goldberger, P. (2002) 'Miami Vice: Is This the Ugliest Building in New York?' 7th October. At: http://www.newyorker.com/critics/skyline/?021007crsk_skyline (Accessed on 1st May 2004).

Golledge, R. G. and Stimson, R. J. (1997). *Spatial Behavior: A Geographic Perspective.* New York: The Guilford Press.

Gombrich, E. and Kris, E. (1938) 'The Principles of Caricature'. *The British Journal of Medical Psychology,* 17: 321.

Gombrich, E. and Kris, E. (1940) *Caricature.* London: King Penguin Books.

Goodsell, C. (1988) *The Social Meaning of Civic Space.* Lawrence, Kansas: Kansas University Press.

Gottdiener, M. (1995) *Postmodern Semiotics.* Cambridge: Blackwell.

Gottdiener M. (1997) *The Theming of America.* Boulder: Westview Press Inc.

Gottdiener, M. (1998) 'Consumption of Space and Spaces of Consumption'. *AD-Consuming Architecture,* 1–2 (68), January/February.

Gottman, J. (1961) *Megalopolis: The Urbanized Northeastern Seaboard of the United States.* New York: Twentieth Century Fund.

Graburn, N. (1983) *To Pray, Play, and Pay: The Cultural Structure of Japanese Domestic Tourism.* Aix En Provence: Centre Des Hautes Etudes Touristiques, 26 (B).

Graburn, N. (1989) 'Tourism: The Sacred Journey'. In: Smith, V. L. (Ed.) *Host And Guests: The Anthropology Of Tourism.* Philadelphia: University of Pennsylvania Press.

Gramsci, A. (1991) *Prison Notebooks.* New York: Columbia University Press.

Greenhouse S. (1991) 'Playing Disney in the Parisian Fields'. *New York Times,* 17th February (3): 1–6.

Habermas, J. (1989) *The Structural Transformation of the Public Sphere: An Inquiry into a Category of Bourgeois Society.* Cambridge, Mass.: MIT Press.

Habermas, J. (1989) 'The Public Sphere'. In: Seidman, S. (Ed.) *Jürgen Habermas on Society and Politics: A Reader.* Boston: Beacon Press.

HABITAT (1996) *An Urbanizing World: Global Report on Human Settlements 1996.* New York: United Nations Centre for Human Settlements (HABITAT), and Oxford: Oxford University Press.

HABITAT (2001) *Cities in a Globalizing World: Global Report on Human Settlements 2001.* United Nations Centre for Human Settlements (HABITAT), and London: Earthscan Publications.

Hackett, V. (1995) 'Financing Urban Entertainment Destination Projects'. *Urban Land* (Supplement), August: 25–28. As quoted in: Hannigan, J. (1998) *Fantasy City: Pleasure and Profit in the Postmodern Metropolis.* New York: Routledge.

Hall, P. and Brotchie, J. (Ed.) (1991) *Cities of the 21st Century: New Technologies and Spatial Systems.* New York: Halsted Press.

Hall, S. (1997) *Representation: Cultural Representations and Signifying Practices.* London: Thousand Oaks.

Halprin, L. (1969) *The RSVP Cycles: Creative Processes in the Human Environment.* New York: George Braziller Inc.

Hannigan, J. (1998) *Fantasy City: Pleasure and Profit in the Postmodern Metropolis.* New York: Routledge.

Harris, N. (1978) 'Museums, Merchandising, and Popular Taste: The Struggle for Influence.' In: Quimby, I. M. G. (Ed.) *Material Culture and the Study of American Life.* New York: Norton Ltd.: 139-175.

Hart, L. B. (1954) *Strategy.* New York: Praeger.

Harvey, D. H. (1985) *Consciousness and the Urban Experience: Studies in the History and Theory of Capitalist Urbanization.* Baltimore, Md.: John Hopkins University Press.

Harvey, D. H. (1989) *The Urban Experience.* Oxford: Basil Blackwell.

Harvey, D. H. (1989a) *The Condition of Postmodernity: An Enquiry Into the Origins of Cultural Change.* Oxford: Blackwell

Heidegger, M. (1958) *The Question of Being.* New York: Twayne Publishers.

Hempel, D. J. and Rosenberg, L. J. (1976) 'Consumer Satisfaction: A Neglected Link?' In: Anderson, B. B. (Ed.) *Advances in Consumer Research (3).* Cincinnati, OH: Association for Consumer Research.

Hench, J., Lefkon, W. and Van Pelt, P. (2003) *Designing Disney: Imagineering and the Art of the Show.* Anaheim, CA: Disney Editions.

Hendry, J. (2000) *The Orient Strikes Back: The Global View of Cultural Display.* Oxford: Berg.

Herubin, D. (2001) 'New Park Not Exactly Soaring' Culture: By Most Key Measures, Disneyland's Companion Has Missed Its Marks'. *The Orange County Register,* 5th August.

Henig, J. R. (1986) 'Collective Responses to the Urban Crisis: Ideology and Mobilization'. In: Gottdiener, M. (Ed). (1986) 'Cities in Stress: A New Look at the Urban Crisis'. *Urban Affairs Annual Reviews,* 30: 243. Beverly Hills, California: Sage Publications. As quoted in: Zukin, S. (1991) *Landscapes of Power: From Detroit to Disney World.* Berkeley: University of California Press: 54

Hine, T. (1986) *Populuxe.* New York: Alfred A. Knopf, Inc.

Hjelmslev, L. (1969) *Prolegomena to a Theory of Language.* Madison: University of Wisconsin Press.

Hopkins, B. (2002) 'Riding the Economy: Visitors Decrease at Area Theme Parks in Wake of Attacks'. *Los Angeles Daily News,* 2nd January.

Hopkins, J. (1994) 'Orchestrating an Indoor City: Ambient Noise Inside a Mega-Mall'. *Environment and Behavior,* 6 (26), November: 785-812.

Huff, D. L. (1962) *Determination of Intra-Urban Retail Trade Areas.* Real Estate Research Program, University of California Los Angeles.

Huff, D. L. (1964) 'Defining and Estimating a Trade Area'. *Journal of Marketing,* 28: 34-38.

Huizinga, J. (1949) *Homo Ludens: A Study of The Play-Element In Culture.* Routledge & Kegan Paul Ltd.

Hunt, J. D. (1991) '"Ut Pictura Poesis:" The Garden and the Picturesque in England (1710-1750)'. In: Teyssot, G. and Mosser, M. (Ed.) (1991) *The Architecture of Western Gardens: A Design History from the Renaissance to the Present Day.* Cambridge, Mass.: MIT Press: 231-241.

Huxley, A. (1932) *Brave New World.* New York: Harper & Row Publishers Inc.

HTB (1992) *The Town Born out Of Sea.* Advertising brochure. Sasebo: Huis Ten Bosch Co.

HTB (1993) *Huis Ten Bosch, Economic Aspects: 1992-93.* Sasebo: Shinwa Bank Report. Internally Published Document.

HTB (1994) *Huis Ten Bosch, Economic Aspects: 1993-94.* Sasebo: Shinwa Bank Report. Internally Published Document.

HTB (1996) *HTB Current Situation and Future Plans.* Sasebo: HTB Company. Internally Published Document, April.

HTB (1997) *HTB Current Situation and Future Plans: The 5th Year of Operation.* Sasebo: HTB Company. Internally Published Document, April.

ICON (2002) *Asia—Amusement and Recreation Services—Market Potential for Amusement and Recreation Services in Japan.* Chapter 3: 48. At: http://www.icongroupedition.com (Accessed on 1st May 2004).

Illiewich, S. (1998) 'Deconstructing Destination-Image'. In: *Travel Research Roundup: Branding the Travel Market.* Proceedings of the 29th TTRA Annual Conference in Ft. Worth, Texas, 7-10th June 1998: 50-57.

IRM (2003) 'IRM Plans to Build a Spiritual Disneyland at Vrindavana'. IRM Press Release, Prabhupada Hare Krishna News Network, 3rd August. At: http://temples.krishna.org/Articles/2003/03/013.html (Accessed on 1st May 2004).

Ishimori, S. (1995) 'Tourism and Religion: From the Perspective of Comparative Civilization'. *Senri Ethnological Studies,* 38: 11-23.

ISKCON (1995) 'Kerala's Minister Consecrates Theme Park Property'. *ISKCON World Review,* 1 (14), May/June.

Jacobs, J. (1961) *The Death and Life of Great American Cities.* New York: Vintage Books.

Jackson, J. B. (1980) *The Necessity for Ruins and Other Essays.* Amherst, Mass.: University of Massachusetts Press.

Jackson, J. W. (2003) 'NASA Sees Disney Space Attraction as Way to Spark Children's Interest'. *The Orlando Sentinel,* 5th October: 1.

Jameson, F. (1991) *Postmodernism, or, the Cultural Logic of Late Capitalism.* Durham: Duke University Press.

Jellicoe, G. (1986) *The Oxford Companion to Gardens.* Oxford: Oxford University Press.

Jencks, C. (1971) *Architecture 2000: Predictions and Methods.* New York: Praeger Publishers.

Jennings, P. (2005) 'No Place to Hide'. *ABC Primetime,* 20th January [produced by Peter Bull for P. J. Productions].

Jerde, J. (1998) 'Capturing the Leisure Zeitgeist: Creating Places To Be'. AD-Consuming Architecture, 1–2 (68), January/February: 69.

Jinnai, H. (1995) Tokyo: A Spatial Anthropology. Berkeley: University of California Press.

Jones, J. C. (1970) Design Methods: Seeds of Human Futures. New York: John Wiley and Sons.

Jones, C. L. and Robinett, J. (1999) The Future of Theme Parks in International Tourism. At: http://www.hotel-online.com/Trends/ERA/ERARoleThemeParks.html (Accessed on 1st May 2004).

Johnson, D. M. (1981) 'Disney World as Structure and Symbol: Re-Creation of the American Experience'. Journal of Popular Culture, 15, Summer.

Johnson, R. and Pack, T. (2002) 'Travelocity.com to Offer Disney Hotel Reservations, Park Tickets'. The Orlando Sentinel, 2nd February.

Kaplan, H. (1985) 'Celebrating Urban Gathering Places'. Urban Land, 44, May: 10–14.

Karasov, D. and Waryan, S. (Ed.) (1993) The Once and Future Park. New York: Princeton Architectural Press Inc.

Kattsoff, L. (1947) The Design of Human Behavior. St. Louis: Educational Publishers.

Kayden, J. (2000) Privately Owned Public Space: The New York City Experience. New York: John Wiley & Sons, Inc.

Kaufman, E. (1989) 'The Architectural Museum From World's Fair to Restoration Village'. Assemblage, 9, June: 21–39.

King, M. J. (1981) 'The New American Muse: Notes on the Amusement/Theme Park'. Journal of Popular Culture, 15, Summer: 57.

Kinzer, S. (1994) 'Down Memory Lane with Stalinism'. New York Times, 8th November.

Knowlton C. (1989) 'How Disney Keeps the Magic Going'. Fortune, 4th December.

Krantz, M. (1994) 'Dollar a Minute: Realies, the Rise of the Experience Industry, and the Birth of the Urban Theme Park'. WIRED Magazine, 2.05, May. At: http://www.wired.com/wired/archive/2.05/ (Accessed on 1st May 2004).

Koolhaas, R. (1978) Delirious New York: A Retroactive Manifesto for Manhattan. New York: Oxford University Press.

Koranteng, J. (2001) 'European Parks Don't Slow Down'. Amusement Business, 47 (113), 26th November: 19.

Kosberg, R. and Eichler, M. (1991) How to Sell Your Idea to Hollywood. New York: Harper Perennial.

Kotler, P. (1973–74) 'Atmospherics as a Marketing Tool'. Journal of Retailing, 4 (49), Winter: 48–64.

Kotler, P. (1994) Marketing Management—Analysis, Planning, Implementation and Control. New Jersey: Prentice Hall.

Lablaude, J. P. (1995) The Gardens of Versailles. London: Zwemmer.

Lakoff, G. (2002) Moral Politics: How Liberals and Conservatives Think. Chicago: University of Chicago Press.

Lang, J. (1974) 'Theories of Perception and Formal Design'. In: Lang, J. (Ed.) (1974) Designing For Human Behavior: Architecture and the Behavioral Sciences. Stroudsburg: Dowden, Hutchinson & Ross, Inc.: 101.

Lasdun, S. (1991) The English Park: Royal, Private, Public. London: Andre Deutsch Ltd.

Lazzaro, C. (1990) The Italian Renaissance Garden. New Haven: Yale University Press.

Lederman, R. (2003) 'Privatizing NYC Parks: Bryant Park Fashion Show'. 11th February. At: http://lederman.911review.org/2-10-03-privatizing-nyc-parks.html (Accessed on 1st May 2004).

Lefebvre, H. (1976) The Survival of Capitalism. New York: St. Martin's Press.

Lefebvre, H. (1991) The Production of Space. Oxford: Blackwell.

Lessig, L. (2001) 'The Architecture of Innovation'. Paper originally presented as a Frey Lecture, Duke Law School, and later at the Duke Conference on the Public Domain, 9–11th November 2001. At: http://www.law.duke.edu/pd/papers/lessig.pdf (Accessed on 1st May 2004). [See also: Lessig, L. (2005) Free Culture: The Nature and Future of Creativity. London: Penguin].

Levinson, D., Ponzetti, J. and Jorgensen P. F. (Eds.) (1999) Encyclopedia of Human Emotions. New York: Macmillan Reference U.S.A.

Lofland, L. (1998) The Public Realm: Exploring the City's Quintessential Social Territory. Hawthorne, New York: Aldine de Gruyter.

Lowenthal, D. (1996) 'History is a Foreign Country'. Unpublished paper presented at The Landscape of Theme Parks and Their Antecedents symposium, Dumbarton Oaks 17–18th May.

Luckermann, F. (1961) 'The Concept of Location in Classical Geography'. Annals of The Association of American Geographers, 51: 194–210.

Lynch, K. (1954) 'The Form of Cities'. In: Banerjee, T. and Southworth, M. (Eds.) (1990) City Sense and City Design: Writings and Projects of Kevin Lynch. Cambridge, MA: MIT Press.

Lynch, K. (1960) The Image of the City. Cambridge: MIT Press.

Lynch, K. (1972) What Time is This Place? Cambridge: MIT Press.

Lynch, K. (1976) Good City Form. Cambridge: MIT Press.

Mabille, G. (1991) 'The Menagerie at Versailles'. In: Teyssot, G. and Mosser, M. (Ed.) (1991) The Architecture of Western Gardens: A Design History from the Renaissance to the Present Day. Cambridge, Mass.: MIT Press: 172–174.

MacCannell, D. (1976) The Tourist: A New Theory of the Leisure Class. New York: Schocken Books.

MacCannell, D. (1992) Empty Meeting Grounds. New York: Routledge.

MacDonald, W. L. and Pinto, J. A. (1995) Hadrian's Villa and its Legacy. New Haven: Yale University Press.

Maldonado, T. (1972) Design, Nature, and Revolution: Towards a Critical Ecology. New York: Harper & Row Publishers.

Margolin, V. (2002) The Politics of the Artificial: Essays on Design and Design Studies. Chicago: University of Chicago Press.

Marin, L. (1977) 'Disneyland: A Degenerate Utopia'. Glyph-John Hopkins Textual Studies, 1: 50–66.

Marling, K. A. (1997) The Architecture of Reassurance: Designing Disney Theme Parks. Montreal: Canadian Center for Architecture, and New York: Flamarion.

Marlowe, D. (1972) 'Area Indicators Chart Upward Economic Course'. *Orlando Sentinel*, 3rd September. Cited in: Fjellman, S. (1992) *Vinyl Leaves: Walt Disney World and America*. Boulder: Westview Press Inc.: 131.

Marshall, J. U. (1989) *The Structure of Urban Systems*. Toronto: University of Toronto Press.

Masson, G. (1961) *Italian Gardens*. London: Thames and Hudson.

Mazzotta (1986) *Il Giardino d'Europa: Pratolino Come Modello Nella Cultura Europea*. Exhibition catalogue. Milano: Mazzotta.

McCormick, E. J. (1957) *Human Engineering*. New York: McGraw-Hill.

McCormick, E. J. (1964) *Human Factors Engineering*. New York: McGraw-Hill.

McCullough, E. (1957) *Good Old Coney Island*. New York: Charles Scribner & Sons.

McDowell, E. (2001) 'Attendance is Lagging at "Destination" Theme Parks'. *New York Times Service*, 9th September. Published in: *The Charleston Gazette*, 9th September.

McKechnie, S. (1969) *Popular Entertainments Through the Ages*. New York: Benjamin Blom Inc.

McLuhan, M. and Powers, B. R. (1989) *The Global Village: Transformations in World Life and Media in the 21st Century*. New York: Oxford University Press

McNair, J. (2000) 'Get With the Program: Before You Build it, You Have to Know They Will Come'. *Park World*, May: 19-21.

McNair, J. (2001) 'How Old is Our Future?' *InterPark*, February.

Mehrabian, A. (1976) *Public Places and Private Spaces*. New York: Basic Books Inc.

Mervine, B. (2003) 'Splendid China Closing'. *Orlando Business Journal*, 30 December. At: http://orlando.bizjournals.com/orlando/stories/2003/12/29/daily9.html (Accessed on 1st May 2004).

Metz, T. et al. (2002) *Fun! Leisure and the Landscape*. Rotterdam, NL: NAI Publishers.

Meikle, J. (1995) *American Plastic: A Cultural History*. New Brunswick, N.J.: Rutgers University Press.

Mihailovich, S. (2004) 'Tourism Commission is Heading for the Open Spaces'. *Las Vegas Business Press*, 19th April. At: http://www.lvbusinesspress.com/articles/2004/04/19/columnists/col01gaming.txt (Accessed on 1st May 2004).

Milliman, R. E. (1982) 'Using Background Music to Affect the Behavior of Supermarket Shoppers'. *Journal of Marketing*, (46), Summer: 86-91.

Mills, S. (1990) 'Disney and the Promotions of Synthetic Worlds'. *American Studies International*, October: 66-79.

Miossec, J. M. (1976) 'Elements Pour une Theorie de l'Espace Touristique'. In: *Les Cahiers du Tourisme*, c-36. Aix-en-Provence: C.H.E.T.

Mitchell, D. (2003) *The Right to the City: Social Justice and the Fight for Public Space*. New York: Guilford Press.

Mitrašinović, M. (1997a) 'Wilkommen to Japan'. *Metropolis*, July/August.

Mitrašinović, M. (1997b) 'Living in a Themed Mode: Cities as Theme Parks, Theme Parks as Cities'. Unpublished paper, presented at the Annual Symposium of the American Association of Anthropologists, Washington D.C., November 19th.

Mitrašinović, M. (1998) 'Huis Ten Bosch-cho: A Town in a Themed Mode'. *Gomorra*, 1, January.

Mitrašinović, M. (2002a) 'The Theme Park Model and the American Urban Landscape: A Provisional Polemic'. AB—*Architect's Bulletin*, 155-156, June.

Mitrašinović, M. (2002b) 'Huis Ten Bosch: Hollande Miniature Pour Retraites Japonais'. *L'Architecture d'Aujourd'hui*, 341, July-August.

Mitrašinović, M. (2002c) 'Searching for a New Type of Public Space in Japan'. *Journal of Architecture and Building Science* [Journal of the Architectural Institute of Japan-AIJ], February.

Mitrašinović, M. (2004) 'The Harlequin Dress of Architecture'. In: *Architecture in Communication: Challenge and Opportunity in Building the Information Age*. Washington, DC: Association of the Collegiate Schools of Architecture (ACSA): 23-27. Proceedings of the 90th ACSA Annual Meeting in New Orleans, Louisiana, April 11-14th, 2002.

Mooradian, D. and Benz, M. (2002) 'What's Next for Parks? Amusement Business Examines the Ups and Downs of the Past Century in the Search for Answers'. *Amusement Business*, 45 (114), 11th November: 5.

Moore, A. (1980) 'Walt Disney World: Bounded Ritual Space and the Playful Pilgrimage Center'. *Anthropological Quarterly*, 53: 207-218.

Moore, C. (1965) 'You Have to Pay For the Public Life'. *Perspecta*, 9/10: 64-69.

Morell, J. (2000) 'Universal Partners With Animal Planet'. *Amusement Business*, 32 (112), 7th August: 14.

Morley, H. (1869) *Memoirs of Bartholomew Fair*. London: Frederick Warne and Co.

Morrison, A. M. (1997) *Hospitality and Travel Marketing*. New York: Delmar Publishers.

Mosley L. (1985) *Disney's World*. New York: Stein and Day.

Mosser, M. (1991) 'Paradox in the Garden: A Brief Account of Fabriques'. In: Teyssot, G. and Mosser, M. (Ed.) (1991) *The Architecture of Western Gardens: A Design History from the Renaissance to the Present Day*. Cambridge, Mass.: MIT Press: 263-280.

Mumford, L. (1942) *The Culture of Cities*. New York: Harcourt Brace.

Mumford, L. (1961) *The City in History: its Origins, its Transformations, and its Prospects*. New York: Harcourt Brace & World.

Muschamp, H. (1995) 'Remodeling New York for the Bourgeoisie'. *New York Times*, 24th September: 2-1, 38.

Muster, N. J. (1997) *Betrayal of the Spirit: My Life Behind the Headlines of the Hare Krishna Movement*. Chicago: University of Illinois Press.

Nakajima S. et. al. (1994) *Eiga Roman Kiko: Kyoto, the Cine-City*. Kyoto: Jinbun Shoin, 1994: 13-19. [This book is published bilingually in English and Japanese.]

NHV (1997) *Report: NHV—Nagasaki Holland Village Hotels International*. Internally Published Document.

Newman, O. (1961) *New Frontiers in Architecture: CIAM 1959 in Otterlo*. New York: Universe Books.

Nieuwenhuys, C. (1959) 'The Great Game to Come'. In: Ockman, J. (Ed.) (1993) *Architecture Culture 1943-1968: A Documentary Anthology*. New York: Rizzoli: 315.

Nihon Sekkei (1994) *Huis Ten Bosch: Design Concepts and its Development.* Tokyo: Nihon Sekkei and Kodansha.

Norberg-Schultz, C. (1971) *Existence, Space, and Architecture.* New York: Praeger.

Noritake, K. (1995) 'A Comparative Analysis of Tourist Industry'. *Senri Ethnological Studies,* 38: 51-63.

Norman, D. (2004) *Emotional Design: Why We Love (or Hate) Everyday Things.* New York: Basic Books.

Novak-Branch F. (1983) 'The Disney World Effect'. Published by the author. As cited in: Fjellman, S. (1993) *Vinyl Leaves: Walt Disney World and America.* Boulder: Westview Press Inc.: 140.

NYCG (2004). 'DOT Announces New Mid-Block Crossing on 42nd Street Between 5th and 6th Avenues'. 18th November. At: http://www.nyc.gov/html/dot/html/about/pr2004/pr04_136.html (Accessed on 1st May 2004).

OBJ (1998) 'Disney World Opens Animal Kingdom'. *Orlando Business Journal,* 22nd April. At: http://www.bizjournals.com/orlando/stories/1998/04/20/daily8.html (Accessed on 1st May 2004).

O'Brien, T. (2001) 'Discounts Take Edge Off Parks' Admission Fees'. *Amusement Business,* 15 (113), 16th April: 3.

O'Brien, T. (2001a) '173,978,900 Attend Top 50: North American Parks Finish 2001 On Par With Last Year'. *Amusement Business,* 51 (113), 24th December: 8.

O'Brien, T. (2002) 'Industry Has Taught Military How to Move for More Than a Century'. *Amusement Business,* 9 (114), 4th March: 13.

O'Brien, T., Burnside, M. W. and Emmons, N. (2002a) 'Aquarium Lures 1 Million'. *Amusement Business,* 33 (114), 19th August: 8.

O'Brien, T., Emmons, N. and Koranteng, J. (2002b) 'New Overseas Parks Push Gate Numbers Up: Worldwide Record in 2002'. *Amusement Business,* 51 (114), 23rd December: 8.

O'Harrow, R. (2005) *No Place to Hide: Behind the Scenes of our Emerging Surveillance Society.* New York: Free Press.

Okumu , F. W. (1998) *Reflecting on Clinton's African Safari.* At: http://www.theperspective.org/clinton_safari.html (Accessed on 1st May 2004).

Oliver, G. (1999) *A Study of the Use of Biometrics as it Relates to Personal Privacy Concerns.* At: http://faculty.ed.umuc.edu/~meinkej/inss690/oliver/Oliver-690.htm (Accessed on 1st May 2004).

O'Sullivan, P. and Miller, J. W. .Jr. (1983) *The Geography of Warfare.* New York: St. Martin's Press.

Pacione, M. (2001) *Urban Geography: A Global Perspective.* London: Routledge.

PBS (1998) 'African Odyssey: What Role Should the U.S. Take in Africa?' *PBS Newshour,* 2nd April. At: http://www.pbs.org/newshour/forum/april98/africa_4-2.html (Accessed on 1st May 2004).

Pearce, D. (1987) *Tourism Today: A Geographical Analysis.* New York: John Wiley & Sons, Inc. and London: Longman.

Peltier, L. C. (1966) *Military Geography.* Princeton: Van Nostrand.

Pfeffer Solomowitz, R. (1997) 'Voices of Homeless Girls in San Francisco: A Geography of Risk'. In: Drucker, S. J. and Gumpert, G. (Eds.) (1997) *Voices in the Street: Explorations in Gender, Media, and Public Space.* Cresskill, N.J.: Hampton Press: 185-200.

Pine, J. B. and Gilmore, J. H. (1999) *The Experience Economy: Work is Theatre & Every Business a Stage.* Boston: Harvard Business School Press.

Postman, N. (1985) *Amusing Ourselves to Death: Public Discourse in The Age of Show Business.* New York: Viking.

Postman, N. (1992) *Technopoly: The Surrender of Culture to Technology.* New York: Knopf.

Princenthal, N. (2003) 'In Praise of Anachronism: On Public Art and its Critics'. *ArtUS,* November-December: 24-28. Los Angeles: Foundation for International Art Criticism.

Prizer E. L. (1981) 'The Disney Decade'. *Orlando Magazine,* October: 36. As quoted in: Fjellman, S. (1992) *Vinyl Leaves: Walt Disney World and America.* Boulder: Westview Press Inc.: 114.

Puppi, L. (1984) 'Il Giardino Come Labirinto della Storia'. In: *Il Giardino Come Labirinto.* Palermo, Exhibition Catalogue: 15-20.

Puppi, L. (1991) Nature and Artifice in the Sixteen-Century Italian Garden'. In: Teyssot, G. and Mosser, M. (Ed.) (1991) *The Architecture of Western Gardens: A Design History from the Renaissance to the Present Day.* Cambridge, Mass.: MIT Press: 47-58.

Rabreau, D. (1991) 'Urban Walks in France in the Seventeen and Eighteen Centuries'. In: Teyssot, G. and Mosser, M. (Ed.) (1991) *The Architecture of Western Gardens: A Design History from the Renaissance to the Present Day.* Cambridge, Mass.: MIT Press: 305-316.

Rapoport, A. (1980) 'Cross-Cultural Aspects of Environmental Design'. In: Rapoport, A., Altman, I. and Wohlwill, J. F. (Ed.) (1980) *Human Behavior and Environment: Environment and Culture.* New York: Plenum Press.

Rapoport, A. (1982) *The Meaning of the Built Environment.* Beverly Hills: Sage Publications.

Rasmusson, E. (2001) 'Brand New World: How Walt Disney World Updated its Venerable Brand'. *Sales & Marketing Management,* 12 (153), 1st December: 56.

Reilly, W. J. (1931) *The Law of Retail Gravitation.* New York: G. P. Putnam Press.

Relph, E. (1976) *Place and Placelessness.* London: Pion Limited.

Reuters (1997) 'Attendance Figures for Disneyland Paris'. In: *The Japan Times,* Saturday, 12th April 1997: 10.

Reuters (2003) 'Weather, Travel Fears Slowed '03 Theme Park Visits'. *Reuters News Wire,* 19th December, 7:22 P.M.

Rice, J. (2003) 'Universal Lets Visitors Print Own Park Tickets'. *Los Angeles Daily News,* 30th August: U10.

Rice, J. (2003a) 'Wishing Upon a Star (or 2) to Promote Fall TV, Disney Turns Theme Park Into a Celebrity Stomping Ground'. *Los Angeles Daily News,* 5th September 5: U29.

Rice, K. (2002) 'Traveling Theme: How to Get Bargains on Theme Park Admission and Lodging'. *ABCNEWS.com,* 14th June. At: http://abcnews.go.com/sections/travel/FamilyAdventure/themeparks020614_rice.html (Accessed on 1st May 2004).

Ricotti, E. S. P. (1973) 'Criptoportici e Gallerie Sotterranee di Villa Adriana Nella Loro Tipologia e Nelle Loro Funzioni'. *Les Crypto-portiques dans l'Architecture Romaine.* Rome: 219-260.

Riley, R. B. (1988) 'From Sacred Grove to Disney World: The Search for Garden Meaning'. *Landscape Journal*, 2, (7), Fall: 136–147.

Rinne K. W. (1992) 'Give Them More Than They Can See and They'll Keep Coming Back'. *Architectural Education: Where We Are,* Proceedings of the 80th Annual Meeting of the Association of Collegiate Schools of Architecture held in Walt Disney World, Florida: 13.

Ritzer, G. (1996) *The McDonaldization of Society.* Thousand Oaks: Pine Forge Press.

Ritzer, G. (1998) *The McDonaldization Thesis.* New York: Sage Press.

Robertson, J. (1998) 'It takes a Village: Internalization and Nostalgia in Postwar Japan'. In: Vlastos, S. (Ed.) *Mirrors of Modernity: Invented Traditions in Modern Japan.* Berkeley: University of California Press.

Robinett, J. and Braun, R. (1999) *A Bumpy Road: Building the European Theme Park Industry.* At: http://www.hotel-online.com/Trends/ERA/ERAEuropeanThemeParks (Accessed on 1st May 2004).

Rojek, C. (1993) *Ways of Escape: Modern Transformations in Leisure and Travel.* London: MacMillan Press Ltd.

Rowe, C. and Koetter, F. (1978) *Collage City.* Cambridge: MIT Press.

Sadler, S. (1998) *The Situationist City.* Cambridge: The MIT Press.

Salen, K. and Zimmerman, E. (2004) *Rules of Play: Game Design Fundamentals.* Cambridge: MIT Press.

Satterthwaite, A. (2001) *Going Shopping: Consumer Choices and Community Consequences.* New Haven: Yale University Press.

Shigeyoshi, S. (1994) 'Profile of the Huis Ten Bosch Project'. In: *Huis Ten Bosch: Design Concepts and Its Development.* Tokyo: Nihon Sekkei and Kodansha: 37–40.

Schafer, R. M. (1977) *The Tuning of the World.* New York: Alfred A. Knopf.

Schank-Smith, K. (1990) 'Architectural Sketches and the Power of Caricature'. *Journal of Architectural Education,* November: 49–58.

Schank-Smith, K. (1992) 'The Caricature of Disney World'. In: *Architectural Education: Where We Are.* Washington, D.C.: Association of Collegiate Schools of Architecture (ACSA). Proceedings of the 80th Annual Meeting of the ACSA, Walt Disney World, Florida.

Shanklin, M. (1995) 'A Time for Celebration'. *The Orlando Sentinel,* 13th August 1995: J1.

Schmidt, S. (2001) 'California's Theme at New Disney Creation: US$1.4 Billion Park Anchors Anaheim Makeover'. *The San Diego Union-Tribune,* 4th February.

Schmitt, B. H. (1999) *Experiential Marketing.* New York: The Free Press.

Schneider, M. (2001) 'Christian Theme Park Opens in Florida Amidst Protests'. *Associated Press,* 6th February. In: *The Oak Ridger,* 6th February.

Schneider, M. (2001a) 'U.S. Theme Parks Expanding Overseas'. *Associated Press Online,* 28th December.

Schneider, M. (2001b) 'Hong Kong Park to be Small World of Harmony'. *Tulsa World,* 29th December: 16.

Schneider, M. (2002) 'North American Theme Park Attendance Takes a Plunge in 2002'. *The Milwaukee Journal Sentinel,* 26th December: 8.

Schneider, M. (2003) 'Theme Park Consultants: Disney Must Act With Sensitivity in Marketing New Space Ride'. *Associated Press Newswire,* 7th February.

Schneider, M. (2003a) 'Attendance at Amusement Parks Falls'. *Associated Press Newswire,* 19th December.

Sennett, R. (1977) *The Fall of Public Man.* New York: Knopf.

Sennett, R. (1994) *Flesh and Stone: The Body and the City in Western Civilization.* New York: W. W. Norton.

Sert, J. L. (1942) *Can Our Cities Survive? An ABC of Urban Problems, Their Analysis, Their Solutions; Based on the Proposals Formulated by the C.I.A.M., International Congresses For Modern Architecture, Congres Internationaux d'Architecture Moderne.* Cambridge: Harvard University Press.

Shanklin, M. (1995) 'A Time for Celebration'. *The Orlando Sentinel,* 13th August (J1).

Shepherd J. C. and Jellicoe, G. A. (1925) *Italian gardens of the Renaissance.* New York: Scribner's.

Sherry, J. F. (Ed.) (1998) *Servicescapes: The Concept of Place in Contemporary Markets.* Lincolnwood, IL: NTC Business Books.

Shikoku (1976) *Shikoku Mura—Heart of One's Home: An Outline of Shikoku Museum of Private Houses.* Shikoku Mura Museum Catalogue.

Shirahata, Y. (1995) 'Information Studies of Tourist Resources'. *Senri Ethnological Studies,* 38: 51–63.

Simon, H. (1969) *The Sciences of the Artificial.* Cambridge, Mass.: MIT Press.

Sitte, C. (1945) *The Art of Building Cities: City Building According to its Artistic Fundamentals.* New York: Reinhold Publishing Corporation [Originally published as Sitte, C. (1889) *Der Stadte-Bau Nach Seinen Kunstlerischen Grundsatzen.* Wien: Graeser & Co].

Sklar, M. (1997) 'The Artist as Imagineer'. In: Marling, K. A. (1997) *The Architecture of Reassurance: Designing Disney Theme Parks.* Montreal: Canadian Center for Architecture with New York: Flamarion: 13–17.

Sloan, G. (2001) 'Life in the Fast Lane'. *USA Today,* 13th July.

Smart, B. (Ed.) (1999) *Resisting McDonaldization.* New York: Sage Press.

Smith, H. (2001) 'Marketing Las Vegas: Child's Play'. *The Las Vegas Review-Journal,* 22nd April: 1F.

Smith, P. and Curnow, R. (1966) '"Arousal Hypothesis" and the Effects of Music on Purchasing Behavior'. *Journal of Applied Psychology,* 50, June: 255–256.

Snyder, M. (2001) 'Disney Dreaming'. *Tampa Tribune,* 25th February.

Soja, E. (1992) 'Inside Exopolis: Scenes from Orange County'. In: Sorkin, M. (Ed.) *Variations on a Theme Park: The New American City and the End of Public Space.* New York: Hill and Wang: 94–123.

Sommer, R. (1969) *Personal Space: The Behavioral Basis of Design.* Englewood Cliffs, NJ: Prentice-Hall.

Sonzogno, E. (1874) *L'Esposizione Universale di Vienna del' 1873 Illustrata.* Milan. As quoted in: Kaufman, E. (1989) 'The Architectural Museum From World's Fair to Restoration Village'. *Assemblage,* 9, June: 21–39.

Sorkin, M. (Ed) (1992) *Variations on a Theme Park: The New American City and the End of Public Space.* New York: Hill and Wang.

Southworth, J. G. (1941) *Vauxhall Gardens.* London: Country Life.

Spradley, J. (1980) *Participant Observation.* New York: Holt, Rinehart, and Winston.

Stern, R. (1986) *Pride of Place: Building the American Dream.* Grigor, M. (Dir.) Malone Gill Productions [VHS]. Part 1: 'The Search for a Usable Past'.

Stokols, D. (1977) 'Origins and Directions of Environment-Behavioral Research' in: Stokols, D. (Ed.) (1977) *Perspectives on Environment and Behavior.* New York: Plenum Press.

Sudjic, D. (1992) 'The Airport as City Square'. In: Sudjic, D. *The 100 Mile City.* London: Andre Deutsch Ltd.: 143–163.

Swarbrooke, J. (1995) *The Development and Management of Visitor Attractions.* Oxford: Butterworth-Heinmann.

Sweeney, L. (1989) 'A Mecca for Movie Buffs Opens at Disney World: Theme Park Takes Tourists Behind the Scenes'. *The Christian Science Monitor,* 1st May: 10.

Takamatsu (1996) *A Comprehensive Guide to Marine City Takamatsu.* Takamatsu City, Promotional material.

Taliaferro Boatwright, M. (1987) *Hadrian and the City of Rome.* Princeton: Princeton University Press.

Teyssot, G. (1991) 'The Eclectic Garden and the Imitation of Nature'. In: Teyssot, G. and Mosser, M. (Ed.) (1991) *The Architecture of Western Gardens: A Design History from the Renaissance to the Present Day.* Cambridge, Mass.: MIT Press: 359–372.

Teyssot, G. and Mosser, M. (Ed.) (1991) *The Architecture of Western Gardens: A Design History from the Renaissance to the Present Day.* Cambridge, Mass.: MIT Press.

Toffler, A. (1970) *Future Shock.* New York: Random House.

Tomlinson, W. (1888) *The Pictorial Record of the Royal Jubilee Exhibition,* Manchester 1887. Manchester: J. E. Cornish.

Traganou, J. (2003) 'The Transit Destinations of Japanese Public Space: The Case of Nagoya Station'. In: Dival, C. and Bond, W. (Eds.) *Suburbanizing the Masses: Public Transport and Urban Development in Historical Perspective.* Aldershot: Ashgate: 287–314.

Traganou, J. (2004) *The Tokaido Road: Traveling and Representation in Edo and Meiji Japan.* London: Routledge/Curzon.

Tuan, Y. F. (1974) *Topophilia: A Study of Environmental Perception, Attitudes, and Values.* Englewood Cliffs, NJ: Prentice-Hall, Inc.

Tuan, Y. F. (1997) *Disneyland: Its Place in World Culture.* In: Marling, K. A. (1997) *The Architecture of Reassurance: Designing Disney Theme Parks.* Montreal: Canadian Center for Architecture, and New York: Flamarion: 191–199.

Turner, V. (1969) *The Ritual Process: Structure and Anti-Structure.* Chicago: Aldine Publishing Comp.

Turner, V. (1974) *Dramas, Fields, and Metaphors: Symbolic Action in Human Society.* Ithaca: Cornell University Press.

Turner, V. (1978) *Image and Pilgrimage in Christian Culture.* Oxford: Blackwell.

Tyrwhitt, J., Sert, J. L. and Rogers, E. N. (Ed.) (1952) *The Heart of the City: Towards the Humanisation of Urban Life.* New York: Pellegrini and Cudahy.

ULI (1996) *Urban Entertainment: Lights, Camera, and Now What?* Urban Land Institute Seminar Proceedings, New York, 3–4th June 1996. Washington, D.C.: Urban Land Institute.

ULI (1997) *ULI Development Handbook Series: Resort Development Handbook.* Washington, D.C.: Urban Land Institute.

Ulmer, G. L. (1990) *Metaphoric Rocks.* Exhibition Catalog.

Ulmer, G. L. (2003) *Internet Invention: From Literacy to Electracy.* New York: Longman Publishers.

Upward, G. C. (1979) *A Home for our Heritage: The Building and Growth of Greenfield Village and Henry Ford Museum, 1929–1979.* Dearborn, Michigan: Henry Ford Museum Press.

Urry, J. (1990) *The Tourist Gaze: Leisure and Travel in Contemporary Societies.* London: Sage.

Vaporis, C. N. (1995) 'The Early Modern Origins of Japanese Tourism'. *Senri Ethnological Studies,* 38: 51–63.

Van Den Abbeele, G. (1994) 'Sites Blindes/Armored Sights'. In: Diller + Scofidio (1994) *Back to the Front: Tourisms of War.* F.R.A.C. Basse-Normandie.

Van Gennep, A. (1960) *The Rites of Passage.* London: Routledge and Kegan Paul.

Venturi, R. et al. (1972) *Learning from Las Vegas.* Cambridge: MIT Press.

Vérin, H. (1991) 'Technology in the Park: Engineers and Gardeners in Seventeenth-Century France'. In: Teyssot, G. and Mosser, M. (Ed.) (1991) *The Architecture of Western Gardens: A Design History from the Renaissance to the Present Day.* Cambridge, Mass.: MIT Press: 135–145.

Vickerman R. (1993) 'Tourist Implications of New Transport Opportunities: The Channel Tunnel'. In: Glyptis S. (Ed.) (1993) *Leisure and the Environment.* London: Belhaven Press: 210–221.

Virilio, P. (1989) *War and Cinema: The Logistics of Perception.* New York: Verso.

Virilio, P. (1994) *Bunker Archeology.* New York: Princeton Architectural Press.

Vining, R. (1954) 'A Description of Certain Spatial Aspects of an Economic System'. *Economic Development and Cultural Change,* 2 (3): 147–195.

Vitullo-Martin, J. (2004) 'The Fall and Rise of Bryant Park'. *The New York Sun,* 21st January.

Vogel, H. L. (1986) *Entertainment Industry Economics: A Guide for Financial Analysis.* Cambridge: Cambridge University Press.

Von Bertalanffy, L. (1968) *General Systems Theory: Foundations, Development, Applications.* New York: George Braziller.

Von Joest, T. (1991) 'Haussmann's Paris: A Green Metropolis?' In: Teyssot, G. and Mosser, M. (Ed.) (1991) *The Architecture of Western Gardens: A Design History from the Renaissance to the Present Day.* Cambridge, Mass.: MIT Press: 387–398.

Wakefield, A. (2003) *Selling Security: The Private Policing of Public Space.* Devon, U.K.: Willan Publishing.

Walker, R. (1996) 'Bugs Ist Ein Berliner in New Theme Park'. *The Christian Science Monitor,* 14th May.

Ward, D. (2002) 'Thrill Industry Bathes in the Heat of Media Spotlight'. *PR Week U.S.,* 10th June: Section: Media—Theme Parks—Media Roundup.

Warner, S. B. Jr. (1993) 'Public Park Inventions: Past and Future'. In: Karasov, D. and Waryan, S. (Ed.) (1993) *The Once and Future Park*. New York: Princeton Architectural Press Inc.: 17–23.

Wasko, J. (2001) 'The Magical-Market World of Disney'. *Monthly Review*, 11 (52), 1st April: 56–71.

Wascoe, D. (1983) 'Moving People from Fantasy to Reality'. *Mass Transit*, 8, August: 10–15.

Wasserman, L. (1978) *Merchandising Architecture: Architectural Implications & Applications of Amusement Themeparks*. Self-published by the author.

Webber, M. (1964) 'The Urban Place and the Nonplace Urban Realm'. In: Webber, M. et al. (1964) *Explorations into Urban Structure*. Philadelphia: University of Pennsylvania Press.

Weishar, J. (1992) *Designing for Effective Selling Space*. New York: McGraw-Hill Inc.

Weiss, M. et al. (1993) *Public Space for Public Life: A Plan for the Twenty-First Century*. New York: Parks Council and Central Park Conservancy.

Weiss, P. and Hartshone, C. (Ed.) (1931) *Charles S. Peirce: Collected Papers*. Cambridge: Harvard University Press.

Wharton, A. J. (2001) *Building the Cold War: Hilton International Hotels and Modern Architecture*. Chicago: University of Chicago.

Whately, T. (1770) *Observations on Modern Gardening*. Dublin: John Exshaw.

White, R. (1993) 'Customer-izing for Success'. *Family Entertainment Center Magazine*, 1st Quarter: 37–40.

White, R. (1995) 'Plan Before Your Leap: An Entrepreneur's Guide to the Feasibility Study'. *Family Entertainment Center Magazine*, November/December. At: http://www.whitehutchinson.com/leisure/articles/74.shtml (Accessed on 1st May 2004).

White, R. (1997) 'Building the Right Mix for Your Market.' *Roller Skating Business*, May/June: 55–58.

White, R. (1999) 'Niche Marketing: The Difference Between Hitting and Missing Your Target Market.' *FunWorld*, October. At: http://www.whitehutchinson.com/leisure/articles/99.shtml (Accessed on 1st May 2004).

Whyte, W.H. (1988) *City: Rediscovering the Center*. New York: Doubleday.

Wrighte, W. (1790) *Grotesque Architecture, or Rural Amusement*. London: I. Taylor.

Williams, J. E. D. (1994) *From Sales to Satellites*. Oxford: Oxford University Press.

Williams, W. R. (1958) *Recreation Places*. New York: Reinhold Publishing Co.

Willis, D. K. (1982) 'Renovating Cities of the Old World With New World Ideas: The New World is Helping the Old'. *Christian Science Monitor*, 9th August: 12.

Wood, S. (2003) 'Texas Six Flags Theme Park Moves Up a Notch in Ranking Despite Attendance Drop'. *Fort Worth Star-Telegram*, 20th December: 1.

Woodbridge, K. (1991) 'The Architectural Adornment of Cardinal Richelieu's Garden at Rueil'. In: Teyssot, G. and Mosser, M. (Ed.) (1991) *The Architecture of Western Gardens: A Design History from the Renaissance to the Present Day*. Cambridge, Mass.: MIT Press: 169–171.

Woodward, L. N. (1978) 'Modern Shopping Center Design: Psychology Made Concrete'. *Real Estate Review*, 2 (8), Summer: 52–55.

Woodworth, R. (1958) *Dynamics of Behavior*. New York: Holt.

Yoshimoto, M. (1994) 'Images of Empire: Tokyo Disneyland and Japanese Cultural Imperialism'. In: Smoodin, E. (Ed.) (1994) *Disney Discourse: Producing the Magic Kingdom*. New York: Routledge.

Zangheri, L. (1987) *Pratolino: Il Giardino delle Meraviglie*. Firenze: Edizioni Gonnelli.

Zangheri, L. (1991) 'Curiosities and Marvels of the Sixteenth-Century Garden'. In: Teyssot, G. and Mosser, M. (Ed.) (1991) *The Architecture of Western Gardens: A Design History from the Renaissance to the Present Day*. Cambridge, Mass.: MIT Press: 59–67

Zangheri, L. (1991a) 'The Gardens of Buontalenti'. In: Teyssot, G. and Mosser, M. (Ed.) (1991) *The Architecture of Western Gardens: A Design History from the Renaissance to the Present Day*. Cambridge, Mass.: MIT Press: 96–99.

Zoltak, J. (2003) '"Priceless" Campaign Heating Up'. *Amusement Business*, 13 (115), 7th April: 1.

Zoltak, J. (2003a) 'Huis Ten Bosch Park Placed in Receivership'. *Amusement Business*, 16 (115), 21st April: 5.

Zoltak, J. (2003b) 'Asia: Spurred By China's Vast Potential, Region Retains its Heat'. *Amusement Business*, 27 (115), 7th July: 8.

Zukin, S. (1991) *Landscapes of Power: From Detroit to Disney World*. Berkeley: University of California Press.

Zukin, S. (1995) *The Cultures of Cities*. Cambridge: Blackwell Publishers Ltd.

Zwicky, P. (1969) *Discovery, Invention, Research through the Morphological Approach*. New York: Macmillan.

Index

Photo Credits

Alphand, J. C. A. (1867–73) *Les Promenades des Paris*. Paris: J. Rothschild: 59, 159.

Anaheim History Room of the Anaheim Public Library: 51.

AsiaPark: 85.

Bud's Kitchen [Gloria Lee], diagrams: 96, 97 [both], 101, 106 [both], 197, 207, 228.

Burn, J. H. (1874) *A Collection of Tickets, Bills of Performances, Pamphlets, Ms. Notes, Engravings, and Extracts and Cuttings From Books and Periodicals Relating To Vauxhall Gardens*. London: 178 [left image], 179.

Diderot, D. and d'Alembert, J. L. R. (1751–72). *L'Encyclopédie ou Dictionnaire Raisonné des Sciences, des Arts et des Métiers*. Paris. V.1, PL. IV, P. 147: 116 [both images].

Disney Enterprises, Inc.: 70, 105, 129, 134, 140.

Dodds, K.: 236, 255 [right image].

Dumas, F. G. and De Fourcauld, L. (1889) *Revue de L'Exposition Universelle de 1889*. Paris: Librairie des Imprimeries Réunies: 133 [top image], 163.

Galerie Alain Gutharc, Paris: Cover page, *Barrier Bench (Banc de Jardin)*, 2002. Philippe Million.

Guerra, G. (c. 1580), drawing used with the permission from Albertina, Wien: 190

Hogarth, W. (c. 1707), lithograph: 73.

Huis Ten Bosch Company: 66, 150, 186, 189, 193, 196 [right image], 198, 204, 206, 211 [bottom image], 212 [bottom image], 213, 216 [upper image], 217, 222, 223, 224 [bottom image].

JR East: 82.

Kotler, P. (1994) *Marketing Management - Analysis, Planning, Implementation and Control*. New Jersey: Prentice Hall: 69.

London as it is To-Day: Where to Go, and What to See, During the Great Exhibition [With a map ... engravings, etc.] London: H. G. Clarke & Co., 1851: 48.

Miossec, J. M. (1976) 'Elements Pour une Theorie de l'Espace Touristique'. In: *Les Cahiers du Tourisme*, c-36. Aix-en-Provence: C.H.E.T.: 56.

Mitrasinovic, M.: 28, 86, 108, 127, 133 [bottom image], 135 [both images], 138 [left image], 139, 143, 144 [all images], 145, 152 [right image], 162, 171 [right image], 175, 178 [right image], 194 [both images], 196 [left image], 200, 203 [both images], 209, 211 [upper images], 212 [upper images], 214–215 [all images], 216 [bottom image], 218–219 [all images], 220, 221 [all images], 224 [upper image], 226, 227 [all images], 230 [all images], 232 [all images], 246–247, 248 [all images], 249 [all images], 250–251, 252 [all images], 253 [all images], 254 [all images], 255 [all images], 262 [all images], 265, 266 [all images], 267 [all images], 269 [all images], 270.

Motte, C. (c. 1800), lithograph used with the permission from Musée Carnavalet, Paris: 58.

Paxton, J. (1854), lithograph, used with the permission from The Victoria and Albert Museum, London: 88.

Pearce, D. (1987) *Tourism Today: A Geographical Analysis*. New York: John Wiley & Sons, Inc.

and London: Longman: 56.

Phillips, S. (1854) *Guide to the Crystal Palace and Park*. London: Bradbury and Evans. Tav. 1.: 93 [right image].

Rimmel, E. (1867) *Recollections of the Paris Exhibition of 1867*. London: Chapman and Hall: 158.

Shikoku Mura: 176–177.

Shima Spain Village Co., Ltd.: 89, 90–91, 93 [left image].

Swarbrooke, J. (1995) *The Development and Management of Visitor Attractions*. Oxford: Butterworth-Heinmann: 69.

The Crystal Palace Sydenham, Auction Catalogue. London: Hudson & Kearns, 1911: 92.

The Collections of the Henry Ford: 146.

The World's Columbian Exposition Reproduced. Chicago: Rand, McNally & Company, 1894: 161 [both images].

Toei Movie World: 138 [right image].

Traganou, G.: 152 [left image].

Warner Bros. Movie World Germany: 137.

Webber, M. et al. (1964) *Explorations into Urban Structure*. Philadelphia: University of Pennsylvania Press.: 53 [both diagrams].

West Edmonton Mall Property Inc.: 171 [left image].

Window on China: 174.

Zangheri, L. (1991) 'The Gardens of Buontalenti'. In: Teyssot, G. and Mosser, M. (Ed.) (1991) *The Architecture of Western Gardens: A Design History from the Renaissance to the Present Day*. Cambridge, Mass.: MIT Press: 96–99. Drawing used by permission from Mondadori Electa: 190.